HENRY
AND THE
TUDOR
PRETENDERS

HENRY VII
AND THE
TUDOR
PRETENDERS

SIMNEL, WARBECK
AND WARWICK

NATHEN AMIN

AMBERLEY

This edition published 2022

Amberley Publishing
The Hill, Stroud
Gloucestershire, GL5 4EP

www.amberley-books.com

British Library Cataloguing in Publication Data.
A catalogue record for this book is available from the British Library.

ISBN 978 1 3981 1246 9 (paperback)
ISBN 978 1 4456 7509 1 (ebook)

Typesetting by Aura Technology and Software Services, India.
Printed in India.

In memory of my wife, Katherine.
For my parents, Michelle and Mohammed.

Contents

Dramatis Personae

As to be expected from a book that covers several conspiracies that played out across a continental, rather than national, stage, *Henry VII and the Tudor Pretenders* features an array of principal figures who each played their part. Listed alphabetically, here is a brief biographical sketch of some of those figures. I have not included Perkin Warbeck and Lambert Simnel as their identities are disputed and explored within the book.

Arthur, Prince of Wales (1486–1502)

The first-born child of Henry VII and Elizabeth of York, Arthur embodied the union of the Houses of Lancaster and York. It was hoped his future reign would herald a second Arthurian golden age, aided by his marriage to Katherine of Aragon. Arthur would die aged just 15 in April 1502, and never became king of England.

Beaufort, Margaret, Countess of Richmond and Derby (1443–1509)

Mother of Henry VII, Margaret was the great-great-granddaughter of Edward III, and by the mid-fifteenth century one of the richest heiresses in the land. She was married four times, and in 1483 was actively conspiring against the new king Richard III in favour of her exiled son Henry. Once he was king, Margaret remained close to Henry, and was widely acknowledged for her influence over her son throughout his reign.

De la Pole, John, 1st Earl of Lincoln (1460–1487)

Nephew of Edward IV and Richard III through his mother, Elizabeth of York (Duchess of Suffolk and not Henry VII's queen), Lincoln was a leading figure in the reign of Richard III and may have been his prospective heir. Although initially reconciled to Henry VII after Bosworth, Lincoln rebelled to lead the Lambert Simnel conspiracy but was killed at the Battle of Stoke Field. It is disputed whether he was plotting for the crown himself.

De Vere, John, 13th Earl of Oxford (1442–1513)

Oxford was a noted Lancastrian military commander instrumental in helping Henry Tudor win the throne at Bosworth, and thereafter retain it at the battles of Stoke Field and Blackheath. He rose to become one of the greatest figures during the reign of the first Tudor king, and served as Lord High Chamberlain and Lord High Steward. It is debatable whether the Tudor army could have survived without his martial input.

Edward, 17th Earl of Warwick (1475–1499)

The son of George, Duke of Clarence, and nephew of Edward IV and Richard III, Edward of Warwick was overlooked for the crown in 1483 and 1485 due to his father's attainder for treason. Despite his young age, Warwick's royal blood and active support from rebels ensured he was kept under close observation in the Tower of London by Henry VII, until continuous plots in his name seized his fate. Often considered the last male-line Plantagenet prince.

Edward IV (1442–1483), King of England

The first Yorkist king of England, Edward IV won his crown on the battlefield at just eighteen years old. Apart from the brief readeption in 1470 under Henry VI, he reigned for twenty-two years and left behind two male heirs, Edward V and Richard of York, the Princes in the Tower. He was also father of Elizabeth of York and elder brother of Richard III.

Edward V (1470–1483?) & Richard, Duke of York (1473–1483?)

The sons of Edward IV and brothers of Elizabeth of York, the royal boys are collectively remembered as the Princes in the Tower. Edward V succeeded his father as king at just twelve years old, but his claim was declared illegitimate by his uncle, who instead ascended the throne as Richard III. Both boys were placed into the Tower of London and disappeared from public view. Perkin Warbeck would later claim to be the younger of the two, Richard.

Elizabeth of York (1466–1503), Queen of England

The daughter of Edward IV and Elizabeth Wydeville, Elizabeth of York was wed to Henry VII in 1486, becoming the first queen consort of the Tudor dynasty. She gave birth to seven children, including the future Henry VIII, and enjoyed what appears to have been a happy marriage. She was also sister to the Princes in the Tower. Elizabeth died in 1503 giving birth to Princess Katherine, and was heavily mourned by her husband.

Ferdinand II, King of Aragon (1452–1516) & Isabella I, Queen of Castile (1451–1504)

Known as the Catholic Monarchs for their fervent defence of their realm against Muslims and Jews, the marriage in 1469 between Ferdinand, King of Aragon, and Isabella, Queen of Castile, effectively transformed the two kingdoms into a united continental powerhouse. Both were consistent allies of Henry VII, arranging the marriage of their daughter Katherine of Aragon to the Tudor heir, Prince Arthur, and refusing to recognise Perkin Warbeck's claim. They are perhaps best remembered for sponsoring the successful voyage of Christopher Columbus to the New World.

FitzGerald, Gerald, 8th Earl of Kildare (1456–1513)

Known as 'The Great Earl', Kildare was one of the most powerful figures in fifteenth-century Ireland, serving as Lord Deputy under Yorkist and Tudor kings between 1477 and 1494, and again from 1496 until his death in 1513. He has been remembered as 'the Uncrowned King of Ireland' and played significant roles in the Lambert Simnel and Perkin Warbeck conspiracies, both for and against Henry VII.

Gordon, Katherine (1474–1537)

A distant cousin by marriage of James IV, the Scotswoman Katherine was married to Perkin Warbeck in 1497 to seal the Scottish alliance. Katherine left Scotland with Warbeck later that year, and was captured by Henry VII's men around the same time as her husband. She was afforded a role in Elizabeth of York's royal household and went on to marry three more times during the reign of Henry VIII. There are no known children from any of these unions.

Henry VII (1457–1509), King of England

Born Earl of Richmond in Pembroke, West Wales, in 1457, through his mother Margaret Beaufort Henry was descended from Edward III. As a potential Lancastrian pretender during the Wars of the Roses, Henry spent fourteen years in exile between the ages of fourteen and twenty-eight before invading England with a French-backed army in

August 1485. His forces defeated and killed Richard III at Bosworth Field, and he reigned for twenty-four years until his death aged 52 in 1509. Through his union with Elizbeth of York he was co-founder of the Tudor dynasty.

Henry, Prince of Wales (1491–1547)

The only son of Henry VII and Elizabeth of York to survive both parents, the young prince succeeded his father as Henry VIII in 1509. He would famously wed six times and oversee the English Church's tumultuous break with Rome, which brought with it the Dissolution of the Monasteries.

James IV, King of Scotland (1473–1513)

James IV became King of Scotland at just 16 after defeating his father James III in battle in 1488. Eager to make his name in war, James was an early rival of Henry VII, providing refuge to Perkin Warbeck in 1496 and invading England. He thereafter sought peace, and married Margaret Tudor, the eldest daughter of Henry VII. Despite this marital connection, James IV died in battle against the English army of his brother-in-law, Henry VIII, at Flodden in 1513. He is the last king from modern-day Great Britain to die on the battlefield.

Margaret of York, Duchess of Burgundy (1446–1503)

Sister of Edward IV and Richard III, and aunt of the Princes in the Tower and Edward of Warwick, Margaret had been duchess of Burgundy through her marriage to Charles the Bold in 1477. After the advent of the Tudor reign in 1485, she dedicated the remainder of her life to conspiring against Henry VII, offering support to both the Simnel and Warbeck campaigns and providing a base to Yorkist dissidents in the Low Countries.

Maximilian I, King of the Romans (1459–1519)

Maximilian I ruled a vast dominion during the late fifteenth century that encompassed much of central Europe, as well as being able to exert his influence on the lands of his young son, Philip, Duke of Burgundy. Using his German support as a base, Maximilian established the Habsburg dynasty as one of Europe's foremost, and emerged as a prolonged rival of Henry VII's, providing ample support to both the Simnel and Warbeck conspiracies to unsettle the English king to his own advantage.

Philip IV, Duke of Burgundy (1478–1506)
Son of Maximilian I, King of the Romans, and Mary, Duchess of Burgundy, Philip succeeded his mother as Duke of Burgundy at just three years old. He reached his majority in 1496 and although briefly opposed to Henry VII, unlike his father sought peace for economic reasons, rebuffing Perkin Warbeck against his step-grandmother Margaret of York's wishes. Philip married Joanna of Castile, daughter of Ferdinand and Isabella, and through her became King of Castile in 1504. He died just two years later aged 28.

Richard III (1452–1485), King of England
The last Yorkist king of England, Richard III was the younger brother of Edward IV and uncle of Edward V and Prince Richard, the so-called Princes in the Tower. After the death of Edward IV in 1483, Richard took the princes into his custody and assumed control of the kingdom, having declared the boys to be illegitimate. His reign proved controversial on account of the disappearance of the princes, prompting opponents to flee overseas to join Henry Tudor's court-in-exile. Richard III was killed at Bosworth Field in August 1485, the last English king to die in battle.

Stanley, William (1435–1495)
Though an avowed Yorkist for much of his life, Stanley was instrumental in the Tudor victory over Richard III at Bosworth in 1485. A step-uncle to Henry VII through his brother Thomas Stanley, Earl of Derby, the husband of Margaret Beaufort, William was well rewarded in the new reign, becoming Chamberlain of the Royal Household and recognised as the richest commoner in the land. Dissatisfaction with the lack of a noble title perhaps turned his head, and in 1495 Stanley was executed for colluding with rebels aligned with Perkin Warbeck.

Taylor, John
A native of Exeter and a former merchant during the reign of Edward IV, Taylor was an ardent Yorkist who refused to yield to Henry VII. He surfaced around 1490 in France, suggesting a new plot was imminent, and appeared the following year in Ireland alongside Perkin Warbeck. Using his French contacts, he was possibly the mastermind behind the Warbeck conspiracy.

Introduction

Pretender (/prɪˈten.dər/) *noun*
One who puts forth a claim, or aspires to or aims at something; a claimant, candidate, or aspirant.

Five hundred years since they walked and talked upon this earth, the Tudor dynasty remains a profitable and captivating industry steeped in our nation's collective consciousness, with little equal. For better or worse, the five monarchs that ruled between 1485 and 1603 are simply ubiquitous in the study of English and Welsh history.

It could have been a very different matter. The reign of the first Tudor, Henry VII, started in dramatic circumstances with the overthrow of Richard III at Bosworth Field, but his position thereafter was not as stable as many sixteenth-century scribes would have us believe. The traditional narrative, emanating from within the early Tudor administration itself, has been that at a stroke Henry VII ended the Wars of the Roses on the battlefield and brought peace to England, lowering the curtain on the medieval period and ushering in the Renaissance in which his descendants blossomed.

The enduring if historically flawed influence of William Shakespeare, who theatrically embellished the work of earlier chroniclers like Edward Hall, Robert Fabyan and Polydore Vergil, certainly played its role in promoting this myth that all was peaceful after the Tudor accession, when he wrote in *The Tragedy of King Richard the Third*:

O, now, let Richmond and Elizabeth,
The true succeeders of each royal house,
By God's fair ordinance conjoin together!

And let their heirs, God, if thy will be so.
Enrich the time to come with smooth-faced peace,
With smiling plenty and fair prosperous days!

Henry VII's reign, however, was in truth one replete with drama, intrigue and conspiracy that threatened to drive him from his hard-won throne before he could make his mark, which if successful would have reduced the Tudors to little more than a footnote in the vast annals of English history. Despite positioning himself as the great unifier between the warring Houses of York and Lancaster, Henry enjoyed anything but universal support.

Barely a year after his coronation, the new king was confronted by an international conspiracy nominally led by a child pretender who was put forward as an alternative option to the man who had usurped the crown from the White Rose of York. This child, it was claimed, was one of the Princes in the Tower who had survived the reign of Richard III. A rival coronation, invasion and battle would follow, a tense period that featured betrayal and defection from within the heart of the royal court. With the defeat of one pretender, however, another soon followed. Were these challengers truly the Yorkist princes they claimed to be, or rather imposters put up to the task by a handful of calculating and ambitious dissenters?

The civil wars which Henry VII claimed to have ended had witnessed four kings deposed, and though we have the benefit of hindsight, at no stage during the early part of his reign was it inevitable that this Tudor king would survive these threats. He himself, after all, had been an unlikely pretender-turned-king, perhaps the unlikeliest to ever climb the throne. It was understood more than ever in English history that by the 1480s kings could, and did, fall.

This book aims, for the first time ever in one account, to recount the struggles Henry VII experienced with all three of the pretenders he was forced to contend with during his tumultuous reign – Lambert Simnel, Perkin Warbeck, and Edward of Warwick. It is a period confused by contradictory sources, an absence of information, and natural scepticism over the various stories spun by both king and pretender. The eminent historian G. M. Trevelyan, however, once wrote that 'history, in fact, is a matter of rough guessing from all the available facts', and there still exists a wealth of material from which we can craft some degree of understanding about events that occurred some five hundred years ago. It makes for an enthralling journey through a series of clandestine plots and royal paranoia that engulfed England for over a decade.

The Tudor dynasty began in dramatic circumstances on 22 August 1485, but Henry VII's fight for survival proved just as fierce in the days, months and years that followed. At the heart of the story was the question of whether the Princes in the Tower had ever actually been killed as popularly believed, or if the third Yorkist prince to be lodged in the Tower, Edward of Warwick, was in fact an imposter who had been earlier switched with the real earl, spirited abroad to one day return. These doubts played on the minds of all involved, and the uncertainty only fuelled the shadowy conspiracies that dominated the final decades of the fifteenth century. Though he was writing about other matters at the time, it was the judgement of the contemporary Italian political theorist Niccolò Machiavelli just a handful of years after Henry's death, that:

Men are so simple and so ready to obey present necessities, that one who deceives will always find those who allow themselves to be deceived.

When it comes to the explosive reign of Henry VII and the various pretenders that plagued the first Tudor king, the question that must be asked is – who was deceiving whom?

Nathen Amin
York, 2020

Author's Note
For purposes of clarity, I shall refer to two of the pretenders using the names they have become popularly known by (Lambert Simnel and Perkin Warbeck), so as not to disrupt the narrative for the reader. As will be shown, there is much debate surrounding the names both used or were known by, but it is hoped that by adopting consistency in naming any confusion will be avoided.

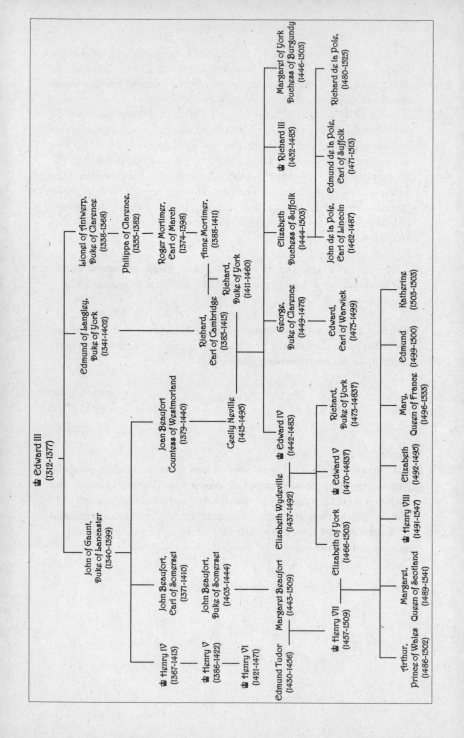

1

The Year of Three Kings

The Christmas festivities of 1482 promised to be a period of munificent celebration at the English royal court, presided over by the larger-than-life figure, literally and figuratively, of Edward IV. Clad 'in a great variety of most costly garments', each lined with pricey furs with hanging sleeves that resembled the frocks favoured by monks, the charismatic Yorkist king cut a 'most elegant appearance' according to the anonymous author of the *Croyland Chronicle*, who may have been present for the revelries.

King Edward had much reason to rejoice; over a twenty-two-year reign, split only by the brief Lancastrian readeption in 1470, he had vanquished all credible challenges to his supremacy, and now, cheerfully surrounded by much of his extensive family at Westminster Palace, feasted in splendour, secure in his position. Life was good, and the king was determined to enjoy every moment.

With two male heirs, Edward and Richard, and five daughters, there was little reason to suggest the House of York's tenure upon the English throne would not endure for many generations to come. The Wars of the Roses, as the conflict from which the king had emerged victorious later became known, was effectively over, secured in a devastating manner on the fields around Tewkesbury a dozen years earlier. Yet, by the following spring, much of Edward IV's admirable exertions and success in establishing his royal dynasty was undone in remarkable fashion, starting with his death on 9 April 1483.[1]

Within the space of just over twenty-eight months, Edward IV's namesake heir had been proclaimed king, disappeared in unclear circumstances, replaced on the throne by his uncle Richard, Duke of Gloucester, who in turn was brutally deposed by the invading Henry Tudor, who in due course established the mighty dynasty Edward IV had intended for himself. Further plots, rebellions and battles would follow, however, and England would not shake off the shackles of dynastic conflict for many generations to come. How had the situation deteriorated to such an extent so soon after the joyous merriment of Christmas 1482?

Edward IV's defeat of any serious rival to his crown allowed for him to become complacent in caring for his physical health in later years and by 1483, despite being only forty years old, the once fit king had grown corpulent. The handsome conquering warrior who cut his way through battle after battle was barely recognisable in the bloated face that greeted those who entered his presence towards the end of his life. His death, after a brief illness during the Easter period, proved disastrous for England, for his namesake heir was only twelve and, though raised to one day be king, was simply not ready to assume any form of personal rule. The prince was still a child.

Edward IV had been a steadying influence as sovereign, and since reclaiming the throne in 1471 had returned authoritative rule to the realm, restoring respectability to the office of king by rehabilitating the royal treasury and ensuring law and order was commonplace. His penchant for overindulging in food, drink and women in later years[2] failed to obscure the fact that Edward had been an ideal successor to the chaotic reign of the weak and malleable Henry VI. A strong, autocratic monarch, Edward's death evoked memories of Henry V, another dominant but popular king who left his crown to a child heir. The political fallout of that succession had arguably been one of the root causes that later led to the Wars of the Roses, as factions competed for royal control of an underage king, which created a legacy of division that would turn to violence in future generations. Religious scholars were only too aware of *Ecclesiastes 10:16*, which warned ominously, 'Woe to thee, O land, when thy king is a child.'

The death of Edward IV and the accession of a child did indeed renew factional discord unseen in England for a dozen years, though such issues weren't initially apparent on 14 April 1483 when news reached the Prince of Wales' household at Ludlow Castle. Young Edward had been sent to the Shropshire town in 1473 at just three years old to serve as nominal head of the Council of Wales and the

Marches, his upbringing entrusted to the prince's maternal uncle Anthony Wydeville, 2nd Earl Rivers, a 'kind, serious, and just man' considered a suitable choice to oversee the rearing and education of a future king.[3]

A decade under Rivers' tutelage had created a close bond between uncle and nephew, one which promised to endure beyond the youngster's inheritance of the crown. Another member of the Wydeville affinity based at Ludlow was Sir Richard Grey, young Edward's half-brother from Queen Elizabeth's first marriage. Over ten years the new king's senior, it would hardly be surprising if Grey was able to exert some degree of influence on his impressionable sibling, royal or not.

As a consequence of Edward IV's death, therefore, the future appeared propitious for Rivers, who by virtue of having in his possession a young king who was expected to rule for many years to come stood to wield considerable influence on behalf of the Wydevilles. It was an enviable position. Unfortunately for Rivers, Edward V, and in time the House of York itself, one man did covet that very position, justified or otherwise, and that was the boy's other uncle, Richard, Duke of Gloucester.

As Edward IV's youngest brother, Richard of Gloucester had proven unflinchingly loyal to his king, 'at home and abroad, in peace and war',[4] a clear contrast to the erratic, often selfish behaviour of the pair's other brother, George, Duke of Clarence, executed for his transgressions in 1478. Unlike Clarence, there is no evidence Richard ever considered betraying his brother, an admirable record of fidelity that probably compelled Edward to appoint the duke Lord Protector on his deathbed.[5]

Richard, however, had spent a considerable amount of time in the north towards the end of his brother's reign, whether serving as president of the Council of the North, attending to his Yorkshire estates, or personally overseeing the war with Scotland. In his absence the Wydeville faction, headed by the queen, her brother Rivers, and her two sons from her first marriage, Thomas and Richard Grey, were actively preparing themselves for a period of complete autonomy during the kingship of the new Wydeville-blooded sovereign. Such mobilisation, however, was not without opposition.

In contrast to the popularity of Edward IV, the Wydevilles had a reputation for rapacity and had never enjoyed wide support amongst the commons or nobility. Some members of the council even voiced their opinion that the guardianship of Edward V, 'so youthful a person', should be 'utterly forbidden to his uncles and brothers by the mother's side'. However, it was conceded that this would not be easily accomplished, for those relations already occupied 'the chief places about the prince'.[6]

The man some turned to for deliverance from a Wydeville-dominated regency was Richard of Gloucester, with William Hastings, 1st Baron Hastings, in particular, dispatching messengers to the north requesting the duke's urgent presence in London.[7] It was inevitable both sides would be pitted against one another to determine who would guide England until the king came of age, a situation not unlike the power struggle that engulfed the kingdom in the 1420s between a previous duke of Gloucester, Humphrey, and the Beauforts during the minority of Henry VI. Somebody, of course, had to govern on the king's behalf when he was too young to rule for himself. The events which followed next rank amongst the most controversial, and frustratingly confused, few months in English history.

One of Gloucester's first actions after learning of his brother's death from Hastings' message was to write his own 'soothing' letter to his bereaved sister-in-law Queen Elizabeth, one which assured her of his continuing fealty. According to the account in the *Croyland Chronicle*, the duke then organised a funeral service for the deceased king in York Minster, which featured 'plenteous tears' before oaths were sworn to the new king, with Gloucester himself the first to step forward.[8]

Polydore Vergil, who arrived in England during the later reign of Henry VII and was somewhat hostile to his master's predecessor, suggested it was around this point Gloucester begun to be 'kyndlyd with an ardent desire of soveraigntie', adding cuttingly that it was the duke who was 'the fyrst to vyolate' the oath he had been first to swear in York.[9] The consistent record of loyalty from Gloucester to this moment, however, strongly suggests any thoughts of usurping the sovereignty had not yet formed in his mind. His primary objective at this juncture was clear; to march south and assume the reins of government during his nephew's minority, in accordance with the apparent wishes of the deceased king.

Whilst Gloucester made his final arrangements, similar preparation was taking place in Ludlow. On 24 April, young Edward left behind his life as Prince of Wales and, at the head of a considerable retinue numbering around 2,000 men, started the 150-mile march for the capital. At his side, as ever, was his maternal uncle, teacher, and mentor, Earl Rivers. The Wydeville plan was for Edward to be crowned as soon as 4 May, an act which would abolish any requirement for Gloucester to undertake the office of Protector and clear the path for the family to personally guide the child king without unsolicited interference. Any plot to blindside the wary Gloucester, however, failed.

On 29 April, the duke reached Northampton where, according to the *Croyland Chronicle*, Rivers and his nephew Richard Grey were in the vicinity, for they 'came thither for the purpose of paying their respects to him'. The young king, Edward V as he was now regarded, was not present it seems, having been placed about fifteen miles south in Stony Stratford under the care of Thomas Vaughan, the elderly chamberlain of his household back in Ludlow. If there was any underlying tension between the two uncles of the king in Northampton, it wasn't initially apparent; Rivers even dined with Gloucester at the latter's invitation, who exhibited an 'especially cheerful and joyous countenance' before everyone present retired to their respective lodgings after an evening of 'very pleasant conversation'.

When Rivers rose the following morning, however, the situation had changed. Since joined by Henry Stafford, Duke of Buckingham, all the lords travelled together towards Stony Stratford to present themselves before their king, but just as they neared their destination, the bewildered Rivers was seized at Gloucester's command, along with Grey, Vaughan, and those in their retinue. There is no evidence of resistance on the part of those detained, which suggests they had been caught oblivious of any plot against them, and all were dispatched to Pontefract Castle in the north until further notice.

Gloucester and Buckingham, meanwhile, pressed on into the town for their summit with the king. The *Croyland Chronicle* is clear that the dukes paid Edward 'every mark of respect' he was due, such as uncovering their heads and bending the knee, but Gloucester did announce he was dismissing the king's attendants for his own protection and that he would now accompany Edward to London, rather than the boy's more familiar maternal relations.[10] According to the account of Dominic Mancini, meanwhile, an Italian visitor to England that summer who reflected some of the gossip prevalent at the time, the two dukes justified their actions to the quizzical young king by arguing that the country was 'so great a realm' that it should not be ruled by 'puny men', a reference no doubt to the Wydeville clan.[11] It is difficult to believe that Edward did not openly question the arrests of those he had been close to for most of his life, but he was surely wise enough to acknowledge he had little say in the matter.

News of Rivers' arrest reached London ahead of the royal procession, where Mancini noted that the 'unexpectedness of the event horrified everyone', although he did add that those same citizens came to reason that 'it was more just and profitable that the youthful sovereign should be with his paternal uncle than with his maternal uncles and uterine brothers'.[12] Realising that she lacked the popular support to muster any reasonable resistance, the panicked dowager queen scooped up her youngest son Richard and his five sisters and fled into sanctuary at Westminster Abbey. The City of London, meanwhile, was controlled by Lord Hastings, who awaited Gloucester's arrival to surrender his authority. England was descending into factional division once more, with control of the young king at the heart of the matter.

When Richard did arrive in the capital on 4 May, attired 'in blak cloth, like a mourner' according to a local chronicler, he placed the young king in the bishop's palace near St Paul's before compelling all the lords of the realm, spiritual and temporal, to swear another oath of fealty to the twelve-year-old sovereign. It was a request duly given, says the Croyland Chronicler, 'with the greatest pleasure and delight'.[13]

A subsequent meeting of the king's council debated relocating Edward to somewhere with 'fewer restrictions', and it was Buckingham who suggested the Tower of London, a proposal which was accepted by his peers after lengthy debate. Gloucester, meanwhile, was formally created Protector on 27 May, with 'the consent and good-will of all the lords', and empowered to act 'just like another king'. The coronation was also postponed until 24 June. Thus far, nothing appeared untoward, with Lord Hastings even voicing his opinion that governance of the realm had been rightly transferred 'from two of the queen's blood to two more powerful persons of the king's'. He may have been hasty, however, to his eternal regret, of boasting this had been accomplished 'without any slaughter'.[14]

On 13 June, two separate council meetings were scheduled by Gloucester, one at Westminster and another at the Tower of London, the latter being personally presided over by the Protector. The proceedings had barely commenced when, after a thunderous cry of treason, Gloucester's men rushed into the chamber and filled the room. In the ensuing commotion, Hastings was seized by the soldiers and unceremoniously dragged outside where he was summarily beheaded on the Tower Green. In Mancini's judgement, this respected Chamberlain and loyal servant of the House of York was slain 'not by those enemies he had always feared, but by a friend whom he had never doubted'.[15]

Other attendees at the Tower meeting, including most notably Thomas Rotherham, Archbishop of York, and John Morton, Bishop of Ely, were also detained, but spared execution on account of their holy orders and instead imprisoned in Wales. Later traditions suggest Thomas Stanley, 2nd Baron Stanley, was also injured in the process, though his presence is not mentioned by either Mancini or Croyland. The shocking events of that June morning would prove to be not just a turning point in the lives of the principal figures present, but also in wider English history.

When considering just why Gloucester acted as brazenly as he did in suddenly eliminating those he perceived as a threat during June 1483, often overlooked is the effect of the untimely death of George Neville, 1st Duke of Bedford, in shaping the Protector's mind during these tense days. Bedford was the only son and heir of John Neville, 1st Marquess of Montagu and younger brother of Richard Neville, 16th Earl of Warwick, whom history has remembered as *the Kingmaker*. With both elder Nevilles deceased by 1471, the colossal family hegemony in the north in theory passed into the possession of young George, around ten years old at the time of his father's death.

Gloucester owed much of his standing as a northern magnate to a grant he received in the 1475 parliament that handed him control of Bedford's lands for as long as a male Neville heir lived. The act, passed at the 'humble request and prayer' of Gloucester and approved in recognition of the 'great and laudable service' he had provided his brother Edward IV, handed the duke the Neville honours, castles, lordships and manors of Middleham and Sheriff Hutton, along with over forty smaller manors in the north, which would provide the core of his powerbase for the last decade of his life.[16]

On 4 May, however, less than a week after Gloucester had taken personal command of Edward V and ordered the arrest of Earl Rivers, Bedford passed away childless, and as per the terms of the parliamentary grant, the estates the royal duke held were now only in his control until his own death, whenever that should be. The significance of this would have been immediately known to Gloucester – after his demise, the vast Neville inheritance and the influence and riches associated with it would revert to crown hands rather than to his own son, Edward of Middleham, born and raised in the North.

Gloucester, therefore, had effectively entered a conflict with the Wydeville faction at the very moment his dynastic prospects had been severely weakened, and, facing ruin at the hands of an implacable adversary he could not be sure of overcoming, it is likely his initial objective to fulfil the office of Protector was compromised by thoughts of his own vulnerability. Without a northern powerbase, what did the future hold for his son?

It has never been satisfactorily determined whether Gloucester was justified in believing his life was in danger and therefore launched a pre-emptive strike against Hastings, who, he alleged, had turned his coat. Though the author of the *Croyland Chronicle* did point out that the duke, aided by Buckingham, had removed the strongest supporters of the young king 'without judgement or justice', enabling them to thereafter act 'just as they pleased', this fails to take into account that as Protector and Constable Gloucester had not necessarily acted outside his legal remit.[17] It cannot be denied, however, that the removal of Hastings, unquestionably devoted to the children of his longstanding friend Edward IV, to whom he owed his wealth and status, certainly aided subsequent events.

The following day, 14 June, perhaps acknowledging that his actions would create a degree of upheaval in the capital, Gloucester scribed an appeal to city of York requesting his allies in the north raise troops 'to aid and assist us against the queen, her blood, adherents and affinity, which have intended and daily doth intend to murder and utterly destroy us'.[18] This letter came only a few days after a similar missive was dispatched to Lord Neville of Raby in which the duke requested his presence in London, 'defensably arrayed', adding ominously, 'Do me nowe gode servyce, as ye have always befor don, and I trust nowe so to remember you as shalbe the makyng of you and yours.'[19]

Such desperate pleas for martial aid against the Wydevilles at this particular juncture do seem unwarranted; Rivers and Richard Grey were in captivity, Edward Wydeville had fled the kingdom, and the queen Elizabeth Wydeville was in sanctuary with her eldest son Thomas Grey, Marquis of Dorset. Perhaps based on the knowledge of what he was to do next, Gloucester, however, was evidently taking no chances with his safety.

On 16 June, two days after writing to the city of York, the dukes of Gloucester and Buckingham travelled to Westminster by water, 'armed with swords and staves' according to the *Croyland Chronicle*. Once outside, they compelled Thomas Bourchier, the elderly Archbishop of Canterbury, to enter the abbey complex and 'appeal to the good feelings' of the dowager queen to release her youngest son Richard of Shrewsbury, the nine-year-old duke of York and Norfolk, to the Protector. With little choice but to acquiesce to a demand that had been ominously reinforced with armed troops in the streets of Westminster, Elizabeth handed over the boy with the assurance he would be sent into the Tower to 'comfort the king his brother'.[20]

Further insight to this dramatic moment can be found in the private testimony of Simon Stallworthe, who wrote to Sir William Stoner from the capital on 21 June that the Protector received his namesake nephew at the door of Westminster Palace's Star Chamber, greeting him 'with many lovynge wordys'.[21] It also marked the final time Elizabeth Wydeville, who remained behind in the abbey with her daughters, would see either of the two royal sons again.

It isn't precisely clear when Gloucester first had designs on the throne, but by 22 June there can be little doubt a move was being made for the crown. It is reasonable to suggest that the duke may have gradually recognised that if his protectorship was to be terminated upon the young king's impending coronation, not only would he face removal from power as a result, but Edward V would almost certainly seek the restoration of his maternal relations to their former positions of prominence. Each of those Wydevilles and their associated supporters would surely seek to revenge wrongs done to them by Gloucester. The prospect of losing his grip on his northern estates must also have weighed on his mind.

Richard of Gloucester had, therefore, backed himself into a corner, and his sole way out was to establish a permanent ascendancy over his simmering rivals. The only rank that would give him the means to do so was king. It could be said he acted with far greater decisiveness than his father Richard, 3rd Duke of York, who a generation earlier had taken the best part of a decade to reach the same conclusion. Since the Duke of York's head ended up spiked on Micklegate Bar in York, the son had evidently learnt from the father's mistakes.

On that very day, several public sermons were given throughout London, the most prominent being that by Dr Ralph Shaa who openly declared that Edward IV's children were illegitimate on the ground that information had come to light that the deceased king had been married prior to his union with Elizabeth Wydeville, which as a result was rendered invalid. Considering the clandestine nature of Edward's marriage to Elizabeth, the notion that he had used this tactic before is not necessarily inconceivable. The timing of the discovery, however, is certainly suspect.

The consequences of such startling news, Shaa stressed to the crowds assembled before him, was that Edward IV therefore had left no legitimate heir, whilst Clarence's own surviving male heir, the eight-year-old Edward, Earl of Warwick, was barred from the line of succession on account of his father's attainder five years earlier in 1478. It was clear to Shaa, then, that 'no certain and uncorrupted lineal blood could be found of Richard, duke of York, except in the person of the said Richard, duke of Gloucester'.[22]

Gloucester, for his part, didn't seem to disagree. The messages he had earlier dispatched to the north had started to bear fruit, and a substantial force, 'in fearful and unheard-of numbers',[23] was in the process of marching south under the command of Sir Richard Ratcliffe. On the way, Rivers, Grey and Vaughan were executed outside Pontefract Castle, 'more of wyll thanne of justyce' according to one chronicler[24] and 'sodeynly withoute judgement' in the opinion of another.[25] Any opposition to the Protector was being systematically eliminated, and in a brutal, no-holds-barred manner.

Buckingham, meanwhile, who had emerged as a leading co-conspirator, even went to Guildhall to petition the mayor, aldermen, and assembled citizens to accept Gloucester's claim. Finally, on 26 June 1483, just four days after Shaa's sermon, the council, mayor and a great company of lords and gentlemen approached Gloucester and offered him the crown, a proposition which he accepted. The controversial reign of Richard III had started.

As for the fate of his two nephews, the *Great Chronicle* noted that during the term of the present mayor, that is some point before early November 1483 when the office changed hands, the boys were seen 'shotyng and playyng in the Gardyn of the Towyr'.[26] The *Croyland Chronicle* meanwhile mentioned how they remained 'in the custody of certain persons' throughout that summer, prompting some in the west and south of the kingdom to 'murmur greatly, and to form meetings and confederacies'. Soon, however, the same author wrote that a rumour was spreading throughout the realm that the two princes 'had died a violent death, but it was uncertain how',[27] whilst Robert Ricart, a town clerk of Bristol, believed they had been 'put to seylence in the Towre of London'.[28]

Dominic Mancini, who produced his work during those same summer months rather than after the Tudor ascendancy like most other sources, also reported on similar rumours in his account, noting how the children had been 'withdrawn into the inner apartments of the Tower proper, and day by day began to be seen more rarely behind the bars and windows, until at length they ceased to appear together'. The Italian further notes the reactions of the Londoners, observing how 'many men burst forth into tears and lamentations' when mention was made of Edward V, and how 'there was a suspicion that he had been done away with'. He was careful to add, however, that whether 'he has been done away with, and by what manner of death, so far I have not at all discovered'.[29]

Edward Brampton, a Portuguese Jew who had been in the service of both Edward IV and Richard III, would later refer to the princes' disappearance as 'the worst evil in the world' and write that they had, to his knowledge, been done away with,[30] whilst the anonymous author of the *Great Chronicle* could only surmise that by the end of Richard III's reign, 'Certayne It was' that they were 'departid from this world'.[31]

There is little doubt the real victims of 1483 were the two young sons of Edward IV, doomed by circumstance and destroyed by internal strife in the House of York that wasn't of their making. History had shown the fate of deposed kings of England was hardly auspicious; Edward II, Richard II and Henry VI were three examples of monarchs quietly dispatched after losing their crowns, feared by their successors as a focal point for counter-insurgency.

The last recorded public sighting of the brothers occurred in the autumn of that year, and their fading from view coincided with the collapse of a revolt led by the duke of Buckingham, who had deserted Richard III's side only a few months into the reign of a king he had been instrumental in establishing. Uncertainty over the fate of the children would cause considerable strife over the next two decades, as rebellions and persistent rumours of their survival abounded. Their bodies, after all, were never found.

By the winter of 1483, and certainly by 3 November when he was first proclaimed king in Cornwall,[32] a new candidate for the English throne had surfaced in response to rumours the princes were dead:

…word sprang quykly of a Gentylman beyng In the partyes of Bretayn [Brittany] namyd henry and sone unto therle of Rychmund

28

that made spedy provicion for to cumme Into England to clayme
the Croune as his Rygth, Concideryng the deth of kyng Edwardys
chyldyr, Of whom as then men fferid not opynly to saye that they
were Rydd owth of this world.[33]

This man was Henry Tudor, a descendant of Edward III through
his maternal Beaufort line, and with little obvious claim to the
throne. The age of the pretender had dawned, and its roots lay in the
catastrophic fallout from the untimely death of Edward IV.

2

The Triumphing General

After several hours of strenuous hand-to-hand combat in the sweltering heat of mid-summer 1485, the cacophony of clashing steel often obscured by the anguished screams of dying men gradually ground to a halt. After what must surely have felt like a hellish eternity to those who yet lived, the battle which had been fought with 'great severity' had finally reached its conclusion.[1] Scattered across the Leicestershire fields on 22 August lay thousands of lifeless soldiers of varying nationalities, amongst whom lay one bloodied corpse considerably more noteworthy than the rest.

That body, brutally shattered by halberds and speared indiscriminately with daggers, belonged to King Richard III, hacked down in his prime at just thirty-two years old. Far from an inglorious death, Richard had fallen in the field 'like a brave and most valiant prince' in the words of the Croyland Chronicler, with even the later hostile testimony of the Italian scholar Polydore Vergil conceding that the doomed king had resisted 'manfully in the thikkest presse of his enemyes'.[2]

Richard it would seem had summoned all his courage to fight to the very end, rather than flee the carnage when offered the opportunity, but such valour had been to no avail. At some point in the battle, he spotted his foe in the distance and launched a mounted cavalry charge towards his target, who had become isolated from his main host with only a small band of bodyguards around him. The king crashed through the towering figure of John Cheney with astonishing strength and killed the opposition standard bearer, William Brandon.

Before he could complete his task, however, Richard was set upon by the substantial retinue of William Stanley, who had waited until this vital moment to enter the fray. Stanley had been observing matters on the periphery of the battlefield, and until his men launched into Richard's, it had been uncertain for which side he would declare. The king was quickly overwhelmed by the extra numbers, and soon dragged from his horse. His helmet was ripped from his head, and amongst the panic and confusion he was 'pierced with numerous deadly wounds',[3] the most brutal of which were caused to the back of the head with a halberd. In a matter of moments and despite his noble effort, Richard III had lost his crown, and with it his life.

In his place stood a new king, a man 'without power, without money, without right to the crown of England, and without any reputation but what his person and deportment obtained for him'.[4] That man's name was Henry Tudor, forthwith regarded as King Henry VII, 'an angel sent down from heaven' in the words of Croyland, ready to deliver his people 'from the evils which it had hitherto, beyond measure, been afflicted'.[5]

It was a remarkable moment, and one can only speculate as to the bewilderment that must have run through Henry's mind as he grasped the enormity of what he had achieved. This was the first time since the Norman Conquest that a reigning English king had been slaughtered on the battlefield. According to Vergil, who would produce a history of England at the behest of the new conqueror, once Henry caught his breath, the new king was 'replenysshyd with joy incredible', and reverently gave thanks to God for his victory. He then removed himself to a hill near to the village of Stoke to personally commend his soldiers for their laudable efforts before dispensing orders to bury the dead, a grisly task made worse when the bodies were stripped of anything valuable before they were cast into the ground.

During Richard's final moments, the golden crown he had been wearing as the battle reached its climax had been knocked from his head, only to be found 'among the spoyle in the feilde'. Vergil stated that this crown found its way into the hands of Sir Thomas Stanley, 2nd Baron Stanley and the new king's stepfather, who stepped forward to place it upon Henry's head. Another chronicler, though, believed it was Stanley's younger brother William, the knight who had swung the battle in Tudor's favour, who did the deed, boldly stating, 'Sir here I make yow kyng of England.' Whichever brother was involved, it was fitting a Stanley symbolically crowned the new king considering their part in the victory. Henry's supporters responded favourably to the sight which greeted them, crying out, 'God save king Henry, God save king Henry!'[6]

With the day won and his men sufficiently refreshed, Henry ordered all baggage to be packed and riding at the head of his victorious army he departed the field of battle for the nearest town of note, which happened to be Leicester about fifteen miles to the east. The mutilated body of Richard III, which had been stripped of its armour and clothing, exposing the scoliosis he suffered in private to the world for the first time, had been slung over the back a horse and brought with them. As his limbs hung limply over the sides, further post-mortem wounds had been inflicted on Richard's body as it made its way through Henry's ranks, 'not exactly in accordance with the laws of humanity' in the view of the Croyland Chronicler. It was a degrading return to Leicester for a man who had started the day as king of England.[7]

Upon reaching the city, Richard's naked body was taken straight to St Mary's Church near the castle where for two days it was placed on public display. Henry's rationale for this macabre spectacle was clear; his predecessor was dead, and here was his punctured corpse to prove it, should anyone later choose to contest what had taken place earlier that day. Unlike the two Princes in the Tower, who disappeared amidst such mysterious circumstances, there would be no lingering uncertainty regarding the fate of Richard III.[8]

Perhaps pointedly, St Mary's Church was closely associated with the Lancastrian dynasty, and the dead king's body lay encircled by the tombs of figures such as Henry, 3rd Earl of Lancaster, his son Henry, 1st Duke of Lancaster, and Mary de Bohun, the mother of Henry V and grandmother of Henry VI. After two days had elapsed and word had spread widely that Richard was dead, his body was wrapped and 'with lytel reverence'[9] removed to the nearby Greyfriars to be interred 'without any pompe' in a hastily dug grave.[10]

For Henry, thoughts naturally turned to establishing his position and restoring order to the kingdom before Richard's lingering support could rally and revenge their master. This included ordering the execution of William Catesby, the dead king's loyal chancellor, and imprisoning the earls of Surrey and Northumberland, who had both been present at Bosworth on Richard's side. He also issued his first proclamation as king, which opened:

Henry, by the grace of God, king of England and of France, Prince of Wales, and Lord of Ireland, strictly chargeth and commandeth, upon pain of death, that no manner of man rob or spoil no manner of commons coming from the field; but suffer them to pass home to their countries and dwelling-places, with their horses and harness. And, moreover, that no manner of man take upon him to go to no gentleman's place, neither in the country, nor within cities nor boroughs, nor pick no quarrels for old or for new matters; but keep the king's peace, upon pain of hanging.[11]

Henry was keen from the outset to portray himself as a unifying force, and did not want to witness a series of revenge killings by the victorious side as had occurred after the battles of Towton and Tewkesbury. He knew that leading a slaughter of Richard's forces would have tarnished his reputation in a country to which he was a stranger. The battle was over; it was time to move forward together.

A knight named Robert Willoughby, meanwhile, was dispatched to Sheriff Hutton in the northern parts of Yorkshire to retrieve Richard's nephew, Edward, 17th Earl of Warwick, and safely oversee his transfer to the Tower of London where the prospective Yorkist heir could be kept under strict observation. Elizabeth of York, whom Henry had sworn an oath to marry twenty months earlier in Brittany, was also removed from Sheriff Hutton, but rather than the Tower was instead placed in the care of the new king's mother Margaret Beaufort at Coldharbour House, on the banks of the Thames.[12] It was a solid start.

After two days in Leicester, amidst much unconstrained merriment one imagines, King Henry led his troops out of the town gates, 'graced with the crown he had so gloriously won'[13] in battle according to the *Croyland Chronicle*. He passed through Coventry, Northampton and St Albans on the way to London, visiting each location for the first time in his life and appearing every inch 'like a triumphing general'. Promisingly for Henry, in each place Vergil claimed he was 'greeted with the greatest joy by all', with scores of his new subjects curiously lining the roadsides to catch a brief glimpse of their mysterious new king. His men, meanwhile, were equally thrilled no doubt to be met with 'laden tables and overflowing goblets' at every stop on their journey.[14] With each mile completed, it is not difficult to visualise Henry growing in stature, his heart swelling with pride for all he had accomplished against what may have seemed at times insurmountable odds. It truly was a rags-to-royal-riches tale, with little equal in English history.

By 3 September 1485, the royal procession reached Hornsey Park to the north of London where the king was met 'in good araye' by the city's mayor and his aldermen, each clad in their best scarlet-coloured finery. They had also been joined by another large gathering of inquisitive citizens eager to witness the arrival of a conquering king of whom they had little personal knowledge.[15]

Once all the customary civic duties were completed and the official welcome extended, the city elders escorted Henry into London and towards St Paul's Cathedral, where in similar circumstances to Edward IV in 1471, the king reverently offered all three of his battle standards at the altar. Thereafter, he took up residence in the bishop of London's palace for the next fortnight where his extraordinary victory continued to be celebrated amongst his closest supporters, including his mother Margaret, with whom he was reunited after fourteen years.

Henry had been a penniless exile with no experience of supervising an estate of even mediocre proportions, let alone a kingdom as complex and large as England. With little preparation, he not only faced learning on the job – hardly an ideal scenario at any time – but was also confronted with the mammoth task of reuniting a realm fractured by factional discord across the previous three decades. Establishing his own authority was imperative, particularly as an unknown quantity to those he now sought to rule, and wisely the king gave notice his coronation would take place on 30 October in Westminster Abbey. It was a week before the first parliament of the reign was due to assemble, and Henry followed established precedent by attending the first sitting already crowned. To be religiously recognised by the leading clergy of the land, anointed even as God's rightful ruler on Earth, would mean political leverage if his authority was challenged in any manner.

On the afternoon before his coronation[16] the bareheaded king departed his chamber at the Tower of London in his finest attire, including a doublet fashioned from green cloth of gold covered with a long purple velvet gown lined with ermine. He rode under a canopy also made from cloth of gold that was borne at all times by four knights, with a changeover of personnel at various points along the route to distribute the honour. Henry was also attended upon by the foremost lords of his kingdom, both temporal and spiritual, a visible and vivid sign to the people that the kingdom's elite stood side-by-side, literally, with their new monarch.

Riding before the king was his stepfather Thomas Stanley, recently elevated to the earldom of Derby, who proudly bore a sword of state, whilst to the right was the formidable John de Vere, Earl of Oxford, the skilled commander who had proven integral to the victory at Bosworth. Following Henry was the mayor of London holding aloft a ceremonial mace, and thereafter the dukes of Suffolk and Bedford. Behind were the recently made Knights of the Bath and the other members of the nobility, the various earls, barons and knights along with one hundred esquires attired in the king's green and white livery. It was an extensive convoy of figures from diverse backgrounds and often divergent loyalties whom Henry would now rely upon to keep his throne.

Together, the royal procession marched out from the Tower of London, through the crowded streets around Chepe and Fleet Street towards Westminster Palace, the royal presence broadcast every step of the way by scores of exuberant trumpeters buoyed by hundreds of heralds, squires and attendants, each taking great care not to deviate from strict protocol. After taking food in his chamber followed by a bath, the king retired for the night in preparation for the coronation.

In the morning, the king was dressed with assistance from chamberlain Giles Daubeney. He put on first two layers, one of fine lawn cloth and another of crimson Irish cloth. On top he wore a coat of crimson satin, with a further surcoat garnished with a ryband of gold. On his legs he had hose that had been made from crimson sarcenet, a soft, silky material. Over all of this, Henry donned a large furred mantle that had also been fashioned from crimson satin, and a little cap from the same material.

Entering the abbey's glorious nave through the famed west door, Henry was led through the choir to a throne covered in cloth of gold, from where he was presented to the assembled guests by Cardinal Thomas Bourchier, Archbishop of Canterbury, a clergyman of impeccable pedigree and experience. Bourchier was over eighty years old and had witnessed the turmoil and tragedy of the previous forty years at close quarters, emerging from the Wars as one of the only members of the aristocracy relatively unscathed by the bitter internecine conflict. Bourchier now announced to the expectant faces staring back at him:

Sirs, here is present Henry, rightfull and indoubted enherito by the Lawes of god and man to the Crowne and royall dignitie of Englande with all thinges thereunto annexid and apperteigning elect chosen and required by all three estates of this same Lande to take upon him this said crown and royall dignitie.

The aged cardinal then sought the consent of those present to proceed with the coronation, to which he was greeted with cries of 'yea, yea, yea' followed by 'King Henry, King Henry, King Henry'. Satisfied with the response, a vocal demonstration of the will of the people, Henry was solemnly led to the high altar where he dropped to his knees, protected only from the cold tiles by an opulent padded cushion, and assumed a countenance of pious humility as the archbishop continued with the service. Even kings, before they could ascend the throne, must be seen to submit before God.

A lengthy sermon followed by the bishop of Lincoln, John Russell, before Henry was questioned by Archbishop Bourchier, who sought to know if the king planned to grant and keep the laws and customs of England, to which he responded, 'I graunt and promit.' The king was further requested to protect the interests of the Church, to be just and merciful in all his judgements, and to keep his people in 'hoole peace and godlie concorde'. With 'good will and devowt sowle', he consented.

After yet more grovelling before the altar, Henry was summoned by the archbishop to be partially disrobed by chamberlain Daubeney and anointed with holy oil in the middle of his back, on both his shoulders, over his elbows and with the sign of the cross on his head. After the oil was dried with a linen cloth, the king was dressed in a white tabard with a white coif on the head. A long coat that fell to his heels was fastened around his shoulders, upon which were embroidered images in gold.

Henry was girded with a ceremonial sword, whilst an armil, a silk vestment woven with gold and set with precious stones, was placed around the neck. Throughout the ceremony, St Edward's Crown had been placed upon the altar, and at this point the archbishop stepped forward to bless it with holy water. The king approached to offer his sword before taking it back, a public recognition that his strength and power came from God and the Church. Permitted to take his seat upon the throne, Henry was handed a golden sceptre topped with a dove, which he accepted with his right hand. In his left hand, he received a golden rod. Finally, Archbishop Bourchier lowered the gleaming and blessed crown onto Henry's head, symbolically bestowing kingship upon his third English sovereign after Edward IV in 1461 and Richard III in 1483. The name of Henry Tudor was now added to that prestigious list, not to mention all of those who had reigned before them, though it does lead one to wonder if the aged cardinal, who had performed the same ceremony for Richard III just two years earlier, believed this latest king would keep his crown for long.

The main deed of the day done, all the bishops and peers of the realm deferentially approached their crowned king to pay homage and swear fealty. In turn, each pledged to forthwith be his 'Liegeman of Lief and Lymme, and of earthelie woshipp, and faith and trowth', and to reiterate their loyalty they further offered to 'susteine, defende, and support the king, and his crown'. As Henry sat there, looking out from his throne, it must have been a remarkable moment for him. At twenty-eight years old, only recently he had nothing he could call his own; now, in this very moment, he had everything.

The ceremony was a resounding success by any measure, and no expense had been spared to mark the religious recognition of the first Tudor king. The pomp, the pageantry, the cheers, the sermons, the smells, and the symbolism would stay with Henry for the remainder of his life. His court historian Bernard André would later report that his patron had enjoyed a 'most excellent coronation', and this seems a fair assessment even from the most partial of sources.[17] There was, of course, considered rationale behind such exuberant outlay, Henry was keen to portray his seizure of the crown to be just, a necessary act from which all Englishmen were freed from the supposed tyranny of previous years so that they could prosper under the peace of his reign. From the very outset, the Tudors understood the need to put on majestic displays to conceal any dynastic vulnerability.

Apart from the king, Henry's coronation represented the triumph of several other individuals from amongst his affinity, whom the appreciative sovereign honoured with estates, titles and offices. His devoted and remarkably resilient uncle, Jasper Tudor, was one such figure, rewarded for rescuing his nephew from the Yorkists at the age of fourteen and fleeing for Brittany and then France, where the pair remained until only three weeks before Bosworth. Elevated to the dukedom of Bedford and restored to his earldom of Pembroke, it was Jasper who was fittingly handed the honour of bearing his nephew's crown through the abbey during the coronation. Others given prominent roles at the coronation included Thomas Stanley, the new earl of Derby, who bore the king's sword, and John de Vere, recently restored to his ancestral earldom of Oxford and now entrusted with holding the king's train.

Throughout the ceremony, however, the loud lamentations of Lady Margaret Beaufort, the king's mother, widow of his father Edmund

Tudor, Earl of Richmond, but since remarried to Stanley, threatened to disrupt the proceedings. The Countess of Richmond and Derby, as she was now regarded, had become stricken with fear for her only child just months after his return from a difficult exile, apparently anticipating a series of viable threats to his person, despite his now being the man who occupied the throne, and so, in theory, the most powerful in the land.

During the funeral sermon given by Bishop John Fisher after Margaret's death twenty-four years later, in 1509, her behaviour during the coronation was recalled, with Fisher remarking how the countess would often 'dredde the adversyte', and that when 'the Kynge her Son was Crowned, in all that grete tryumphe and glory, she wept mervaylously' with trepidation.[18] Margaret's reaction appears extraordinary when one considers the momentous occasion at which she was present, particularly as her son's accession would bring her unparalleled influence, wealth and political leverage. As subsequent events would show, however, the countess's concerns were nothing less than justified.

Henry's first parliament opened one week later in Westminster Palace on 7 November, with the king authoritatively observing proceedings from his throne. It did not take long for his right to that throne to be raised, when Chancellor John Alcock, Bishop of Worcester and soon to be of Ely, announced that Henry's title had swiftly received the assent of the Lords Temporal and Spiritual, having been raised at the apparent request of the Commons:

> To the singuler Comfort of all the Kings Subjects of the same, and in avoiding of all Ambiguities and Questions, be it Ordeined, established and enacted, by auctoritee of thys present Parliament, that the Inheretance of the Crounes of the Roialmes of England and of Fraunce, with all the preheminence and dignitie Royall to the same pertaineing, and all other Seignaries to the King belonging beyond the See, with th'appurtenaunces thereto in any wise due or perteineing, be, rest, remaine, and abide in the most Royall person of our now Sovereigne Lord King Harry the VIIth, and in the heires of hys body lawfully comen, perpetuelly with the grace of God so to endure, and in noon other.[19]

The phraseology of the bill was a stroke of genius on the part of the clerk who devised the text, with the concluding line making it abundantly clear that the crown now rested solely in the bloodline of Henry VII, and no one, regardless of any supposed superior royal ancestry, could legally claim otherwise. As the bill had been put forward by the Commons, the chosen representatives of their constituents drawn from throughout the realm, the inference needed little clarification – Henry had in effect been invited to rule by the will of the people, and his right to govern England was not a matter considered open to debate.

Any attainders passed against Henry's supporters, whether dead or alive, during the reigns of Edward IV and Richard III were reversed meanwhile, and all castles, lordships, manors and other possessions of the duchies of Lancaster and Cornwall, and those of the honour of Richmond, were confirmed in the king's hands. As expected, new acts were passed against the key figures in the ousted regime, with Richard III, regarded as 'late in dede and not in right King of England' who had resorted to 'callinge and nameinge hymself, by usurpacion' king, posthumously attainted alongside twenty-eight other individuals.

The person chosen as Speaker of the Commons at the start of the parliament was the Norfolk esquire Thomas Lovell, and on 10 December it was Lovell who was tasked by his fellow Members of Parliament with publicly appealing to the king to take Elizabeth of York as his wife, particularly as her bastardy had been reversed earlier in proceedings. It may seem unusual at first that Henry had yet to honour his oath to marry the princess more than four months into his reign, but he had good reason for deferring the marriage until the parliament had concluded, and not just because he wisely desired to establish his kingship independent of any Yorkist spouse.

For a Lancaster–York union to succeed, it had to be considered valid in the eyes of the Church for any subsequent children to inherit the crown without challenge, and in this particular instance the prospective bride and groom were within the prohibited degrees of kinship, sharing a common ancestor in John of Gaunt. Henry did, however, agree with the supplication of his parliament, and papal dispensation for the marriage to go ahead was therefore sought.

On 14 January 1486, within one of the many chambers deep in Westminster Palace, the king and his intended bride formally appointed several proctors to represent them in discussions with the visiting bishop of Imola, the Apostolic legate to England and Scotland. The petition, drawn up by several of the king's most trusted clerks and witnessed by some of his most loyal nobles, appealed:

on behalf of his most serene prince and lord, the lord Henry, by the grace of God king of England and France and lord of

Ireland, of the one part, and of the most illustrious lady, the lady Elizabeth, eldest legitimate and natural daughter of the late Edward, sometime king of England and France and lord of Ireland of the other part, setting forth that whereas the said king Henry has by God's providence won his realm of England, and is in peaceful possession thereof, and has been asked by all the lords of his realm, both spiritual and temporal, and also by the general council of the said realm, called Parliament, to take the said lady Elizabeth to wife, he, wishing to accede to the just petitions of his subjects, desires to take the said lady to wife, but cannot do so without dispensation, inasmuch as they are related in the fourth and fourth degrees of kindred, wherefore petition is made on their behalf to the said legate to grant them dispensation by his apostolic authority to contract marriage and remain therein, notwithstanding the said impediment of kindred, and to decree the offspring to be born thereof legitimate.[20]

After two days examining the case, the bishop of Imola was satisfied with what he had been shown and assented to the union, having been granted power by the pope to sanction up to twelve marriages in England between couples related within four degrees of kinship. Just forty-eight hours later, on 18 January 1486, Henry VII and Elizabeth of York were married. Little is recorded of the actual ceremony, although Bernard André in his not unbiased biography *Life of Henry VII* wrote: 'Gifts flowed freely on all sides and were showered on everyone, while feasts, dances, and tournaments were celebrated with liberal generosity to make known and to magnify the joyful occasion and the bounty of gold, silver, rings and jewels.'[21] André further remarked that 'great gladness filled all the kingdom', whilst the people 'built fires for joy far and wide, and celebrated with dances, songs, and feasts in many parts of London'.

André also reported that shortly after coming to the throne, Henry commissioned a special state bed in which he planned to consummate his marriage to Elizabeth, an extravagant item of furniture replete with symbolism in which, quite literally, a new royal dynasty was to be created. Crafted from the finest Germanic oak and painted in vivid and rare colours more expensive than gold, the four-poster bed was intricately carved with religious iconography to depict Henry and his new queen as Adam and Eve, surrounded by imagery associated with fertility and marriage, such as fruit and the acorn. Other symbols on the headboard included roses and the royal arms, with the two central figures shown crushing three evil beasts, a cockatrice, a lion and a dragon, beneath their feet. It was a very personal, and yet public, statement, reflecting and representing his righteous victory in war.

Having therefore honoured the oath he had first sworn in front of his supporters in Rennes Cathedral on Christmas Day 1483, within weeks it was announced Queen Elizabeth was pregnant with, it was anticipated, a male Tudor heir. Before the birth, however, Henry was eager to solidify his grip on the kingdom in those parts of his realm still presumed hostile to his rise, and plans therefore were announced for an extensive northern progress in March 1486 'in order to keep in obedience the folk of the North'.[22]

A significant part of Henry's support prior to Bosworth had been drawn from southern-based landowners and lords, whilst the north had been closely associated with Richard III for over a decade before his downfall. Henry's progress, therefore, was clearly a public relations exercise to personally survey – and to be seen in – a region in which he was considered an unknown quantity and to secure the support, or at the very least the compliance, of the northern populace. It was not dissimilar to expeditions made by Edward IV in 1461 and Richard in 1483, both conducted shortly after their respective coronations and intended to ensure influential individuals in the region could be counted on in a time of crisis.

Henry had been careful to avoid changing much of the personnel who traditionally held sway in Yorkshire and beyond during his first six months on the throne. Just a month after Bosworth, he even handed a commission to several figures previously associated with Richard III's regime to protect the region 'in readiness for an invasion of the Scots', albeit only once they had sworn an oath of allegiance that promised they would be the true subjects to their new king and to 'ayde, supporte and defend' the Tudor crown.[23] In December 1485, Henry also authorised the release of Northumberland from incarceration, restoring the Percy earl to his erstwhile position as the most powerful noble in the north.

The king now wanted to personally confront his northern subjects and to assure them, face-to-face, that he fully intended to fulfil the duties of his royal office fairly and without malice, whilst listening to any concerns and addressing their issues. They did not know him, and this was an ideal opportunity for Henry to display the kingly virtues of piety and magnanimity. Henry would be fair to them, if in return they proved supportive of him. It helped, of course, that he travelled north decked in the finest garments he owned, projecting an alluring image of majesty which in itself could often be a factor in securing popular support amongst the commons. On his return journey south, the king instructed his trusty chancellor of the Duchy of Lancaster Reginald Bray to procure, 'in as goodly hast as ye can', materials such as black and crimson velvet as well as cloth of gold for riding gowns with purple and black satin for lining, and it seems likely similar orders were placed for the outbound journey.[24]

Departing Waltham Holy Cross in mid-March 1486, Henry and his vast household headed north to Cambridge before advancing through Huntingdon and Stamford. Upon reaching Lincoln, the largest city in the region and home to a towering cathedral, the progress ground to a halt for the Easter period. Rather than honour his Easter devotions in a private chapel, Henry used the opportunity to display his piety in the public eye – another chance to harness popular support for his reign.

On Maundy Thursday, in imitation of Jesus Christ, the king humbly washed the feet of twenty-nine poor men, one for each year of his life, before presenting several blessed cramp rings made of silver or gold to the people on Good Friday. The rings were believed to provide the bearer with medicinal benefits, and those fortunate enough to receive one would have voiced their gratitude to the generous king who stood before them. On both days, meanwhile, Henry dispensed 'marveolous great summes of mony in grotes' to paupers, prisoners and lepers.[25] All his religious obligations during his stay in Lincoln were performed in the cathedral, and this may have been of some personal interest to the king; it was within this vast structure that his ancestors John of Gaunt and Katherine Swynford, to whom he owed his English royal lineage through their Beaufort offspring, were married in 1396.

It was at Lincoln that Henry first became informed of an uprising in the north.[26] Taking precautionary steps, he withdrew south-east to Nottingham where he was joined by several other lords and their retinues, bolstering his numbers to create a formidable entourage. Thereafter the royal household pushed north to Doncaster, where the king was personally welcomed to Yorkshire on 10 April 1486 by the reconciled Henry Percy, 4th Earl of Northumberland, before continuing to Pontefract and Tadcaster. Here the growing cavalcade crossed the River Wharfe and entered the jurisdiction of the city of York.

Henry's arrival on the periphery of the second-largest city in the kingdom, one uneasily associated with Richard III during his lengthy tenure as President of the Council of the North, marked a crucial moment in establishing the Tudor king's authority in the region, not to mention York's own standing in the eyes of its new sovereign. Both parties, therefore, were keen to make a good impression for their own reasons, with York's officials, not unlike many of the nobles who had ridden north at Henry's side, particularly hopeful of fostering a positive political and personal relationship from the outset of the reign.

Perhaps the most expedient method to cultivate the king's good grace was to welcome his presence to the city with a lavish celebration of his person, and this York accomplished in considerable style,[27] with the mayor, sheriffs and aldermen hoping their efforts would amply demonstrate to the king they were 'gladdit and joyed' by the 'commyng of his moost riall persone'.

Traditionally, the city dispatched two sheriffs with twenty horses to Tadcaster Bridge, around ten miles south-west of York, to attend on visiting kings, but for Henry VII it was considered prudent that the sheriffs would be assisted by two additional aldermen with the number of horses doubled to forty. It was further decreed that, contrary to previous occasions when the mayor and his aldermen, 'clad in long gownys of skarlet', would wait for the royal entourage only two miles outside the city walls, in this instance they would travel an extra four miles to Bilbrough Cross where they would be joined by the council, clad in violet, the chamberlains in murrey-coloured gowns, and a number of citizens on horseback in plain red. Any person unable to procure red gowns or horses for the short journey was expected to line the route between Dringhouses and the city wall, whilst children were to gather by St James' Chapel to greet the arriving procession with cries of 'King Henrie, King Henrie!' as it passed by.

Entry into York itself from the south was through Micklegate Bar, a well-fortified barbican that still stands, and it was here that Henry was greeted with his first pageant. From under 'a place in maner of a heven, of grete joy and Angicall armony', sprang up

> ... a rioall, rich, rede rose, convaide by viace unto the which rose shall appeyre an othre rich white rose, unto whome so being to gedre all othre floures shall lowte and evidently geve suffrantie, shewing the rose to be principall of all floures.

There can be little doubt Henry must have approved of such a splendid image, a visual representation of how the union between Lancaster and York had formed an unchallenged merger that would rule over all it surveyed forever more. It was precisely this notion of peaceful unification after Bosworth that the king wished to convey to the English people, and through their 'craftely conceyvid' gesture, it was apparent the city of York, earnestly or otherwise, was at least prepared to follow official royal policy.

Once the roses had been unveiled, an actor stepped forward and declared himself to be Ebrauk, the mythical founder of York. Henry was lauded for his personal qualities before receiving the keys to the city from Ebrauk, who voiced how contented he was to yield 'his title and his crowne unto the king as moost glad of hym above al othre'. Through Ebrauk's words, the city officials implored the king to 'mynd how this citie of old and pure affeccion, Gladdith and injoith your high grace and commyng, with our concent, knowing you the sufferaine and king'.

Symbolically clutching the key he had received from Ebrauk, Henry and his royal entourage passed through the gate and down Micklegate towards Ouse Bridge, with both sides of the street furnished with the finest of cloths in honour of the royal guest. Upon reaching the southern end of the city's principal river crossing, Henry was greeted with a second pageant. In the middle of the bridge stood six crowned kings, representing the half-dozen previous monarchs who shared a name with Henry. Another king, this one depicting the biblical king Solomon, serenaded Henry at length for his wisdom and justice, before handing over a sceptre and beseeching the recipient to 'reule ye your reame rightwosly, by politike providence, as God haith indewid'.

Crossing the Ouse, Henry was presented with his third pageant at the junction of Ousegate and Coney Street, and this time was greeted by King David, who handed a sword of victory to the new king, who had so been recently crowned on the battlefield. Finally, as the royal cavalcade reached Stonegate in the heart of the city, with the Minster rising gloriously towards the heavens at the northern end, the Virgin Mary appeared to reassure Henry that in York and its people he need have 'no drede nor no dowting'.

The above account of the official welcome to Henry notwithstanding, the general reaction Henry received from the common man is unclear, although the anonymous author of the *Croyland Chronicle* did refer to at least one attempt on the king's life from a nameless attacker before the timely intervention of Northumberland 'prudently quelled this insurrection at its first beginning'. The perpetrators were duly 'hanged on the gallows'.[28]

Henry's visit to York coincided with St George's Day, his first as king, and in a departure from custom, the feast of the Order of the Garter was held in the city rather than at Windsor. The evening before, robed in a 'blew mantel above his sircote and on his hede his cap of maintenaunce', the king heard the Evensong service within York's soaring Minster, another public demonstration of his piety. The following morning, he appeared once more before the masses, this time bearing his crown and surrounded by his nobility. To the common observer, during his time in the city Henry not only appeared to be devout, magnanimous, and regal, fine qualities in any king, but it was clear England's ruling elite was supportive of his reign. This show of aristocratic solidarity undoubtedly had some positive influence on the northerners' attitude to a king they had hitherto been unsure of.[29] Henry, meanwhile, took the opportunity of a captive audience to induct two men who had been integral to his victory at Bosworth, John de Vere, Earl of Oxford, and John Cheney, into the prestigious Order.

The Tudor king had spent a week in total courting the region from his base in York, and – the apparent assassination attempt excluded – was satisfied with his treatment. The purpose of the progress had been to show himself to the people who may have had reservations about his rise to the throne, to break old loyalties and develop a new relationship going forward, one that it was hoped would be mutually beneficial to all. On 18 June, 'in consideration of the state of ruin, poverty, and decay they are in, and of the special affection the king bears them', he made a belated gesture of his appreciation to the city for his reception by granting the mayor and citizens an exemption from their customary annual fees.[30] In return, of course, he counted on their cooperation forthwith.

Once Henry's business in the north had been completed, thoughts turned to the impending birth of the royal child and so the king started his return journey south, via a detour to the West Country to deal with a minor insurrection. True to form, he assumed a central role in this most delicate of matters, determining how and where his first child would be born, energetically ensuring this much-vaunted heir of both York and Lancaster would symbolise, by name and birthplace, the rebirth of a nation beleaguered by several generations of internecine conflict.

As a Welshman born and, until the age of fourteen when he was forced into exile, primarily raised, it was likely Henry was surrounded by the legendary exploits of King Arthur during his youth in Pembroke and Raglan, the tales of this ancient Briton perhaps resonating with a child whose Tudor forebears claimed Arthur as an ancestor. If the Arthurian legend had been popular in Wales for several centuries after the publication of Geoffrey of Monmouth's seminal work *Historia Regum Britanniae* in the twelfth century, it received renewed attention in England in 1485 after the release of Thomas Malory's *Le Morte d'Arthur* through William Caxton's pioneering printing press. Malory's work identified Arthur's famed city of Camelot as 'English Winchester'[31] and Henry wisely recognised an opportunity to associate his heir with the renowned king of legend. At the end of August 1486, he issued orders for the queen's household to decamp to Winchester shortly before the birth of what he confidently expected would be a son, a prince he now intended to name for his supposed royal ancestor. It was nothing short of 'ancestral propaganda',[32] and yet this extreme attempt to tap into popular Arthurian folklore to enhance his fledgling dynasty proved successful. In the early hours of 20 September 1486, within a lavishly decorated chamber in St Swithun's Priory in Winchester, a second Arthur was born.

As the prince was born prematurely, just eight months after the wedding, some members of the royal court had yet to arrive in Winchester for the child's christening, which was subsequently delayed until 24 September. Serving as Arthur's godparents were his step-grandfather Thomas Stanley, Earl of Derby; Thomas FitzAlan, Lord Maltravers and heir to the earldom of Arundel; and the prince's maternal grandmother, Elizabeth Wydeville, the dowager queen of England. Appropriately for a child who supposedly symbolised peace and unity, the ceremony featured input from both sides of Arthur's family tree, whether Lancastrian or Yorkist. All their combined focus now devolved upon the small prince in their midst, garbed resplendently in a mantle of crimson cloth-of-gold that had been furred with soft ermine.

The man responsible for baptising the child was Bishop Alcock, the chancellor who opened the reign's first parliament just under a year earlier.[33] The entire occasion would be another extravagant attempt by the king to further the prevalent narrative emanating from his administration that his victory in battle, followed swiftly by the birth of an heir who, it was forecast, would usher in another Arthurian Golden Age, had rescued the bitterly divided kingdom from dreadful tyranny.

As the court gradually dispersed from Winchester once the ceremony and its subsequent festivities had concluded, Henry could be forgiven for feeling satisfied with how matters had unfolded as he journeyed back to the capital. Just thirteen months into his reign, he had already fathered a healthy male heir, a prince of promise upon which to build his dynasty, and with a beautiful queen who was only twenty years old, there was the potential of many more offspring to come.

Henry VII came to the throne from an unprecedented position; he had been an impoverished refugee with little knowledge of government, estate management, or even England and its people. He was, however, a shrewd man and a natural survivor, and wisely acknowledged that support for his kingship rested heavily upon his ability to be viewed as a moderating force between extreme Lancastrian and Yorkist sentiments, feelings which lingered yet in the hearts of some of his more obstinate subjects. It was in the king's interest to reinforce the notion he had been personally responsible for ending the Wars by uniting the rival houses, and this he demonstrated far and wide by ingeniously promoting the so-called Tudor Rose, a new heraldic emblem that was supposedly an amalgamation of the Red Rose of Lancaster and the Yorkist White Rose.

As far as branding exercises went, the Rose was unquestionably appealing. It was a visual representation of the marital alliance between Henry VII and Elizabeth of York, overt political symbolism embodied by their young son, considered to be the true inheritor of both houses. Heraldry was extremely important in the fifteenth century in establishing one's story, demonstrating to contemporaries where one came from, from whom one was descended, and what one represented. Henry VII alone used the Beaufort Portcullis, the Richmond Greyhound, the Red Dragon of Cadwaladr and, since Bosworth, the Crown in Hawthorn Bush as his own badges. The Tudor Rose, however, represented something greater than just Henry himself; it signified the triumph of the royal dynasty he anticipated would reign over England forever more, foreshadowing an era of prosperity and peace for all.

As the royal family celebrated Christmas 1486 at Greenwich surrounded by hundreds of attendants serving scores of noble courtiers, little did Henry realise the durability of his Rose would soon be severely tested. All was not well in his kingdom, and in truth hadn't been since his victory at Bosworth. Trouble had been brewing beneath the surface for some time, something the cautious king may have recognised and which probably prompted his innovative implementation of the Yeomen of the Guard in October 1485, the first known instance of a personal bodyguard attached to an English king. It was not without merit, for from the outset of his reign, Polydore Vergil observed:

> He began to be harassed by the treachery of his opponents and, assaulted frequently thereafter by the forces of his enemies and the insurrections of his own subjects, he evaded peril not without effort.[34]

Uneasy, indeed, is the head that wears the crown, and after less than a year on the throne, Henry was starting to feel the pressure.

3

Rebels and Traitors

Henry VII's marriage to Elizabeth of York and the momentous, myth-laden birth of Prince Arthur were extravagant celebrations which the Tudor king anticipated would help solidify his tenuous grasp on a crown he had seized, albeit in remarkable circumstances, by might rather than right. Although Henry's unexpected victory at Bosworth was widely portrayed in official legislative records and several chronicle accounts which followed as having peacefully united the realm, it was surely inevitable there would be some degree of resistance from those who had lost any semblance of authority or riches through the downfall of Richard III.

Much of this disgruntlement was restricted to the extremities of the kingdom like the north, parts of the south-west, and across the sea in distant Ireland, and although it would only cause minor disruption to the Tudor regime in the short-term, it was nevertheless disconcerting to royal officials who wished to underscore the supposed prosperous peace of post-Bosworth England.

On 17 October 1485, for example, a fortnight before his coronation, the king wrote to Sir Henry Vernon of Haddon to alert him that 'rebelles and traitours being of litell honour or substance' in Yorkshire were conspiring with the Scots, having made 'insurreccion and assemblies in the north portions of our realme, taking Robin of Riddesdale, Jack St Thomalyn at Lath, and Maister Mendall for their capteyns'. The names themselves evoked disturbing memories of the shadowy figures who helped briefly overthrow Edward IV in 1470.[1]

In February 1486, Robert Throckmorton, sheriff of Warwickshire and Leicestershire, received a special pardon after complaining that 'suche rebellioun and troble' within his remit had made it difficult to collect royal revenue as the king's laws were yet established in those parts.[2] Henry's uncle Jasper, Duke of Bedford, also headed 'into Wales to se that country' around this time, suggesting trouble was brewing in the homeland of the Tudors.[3] The following month, March, a commission was handed to eight people to enquire into the riots and misdemeanours of Giles and Christopher Wellesbourne, with orders to bring the men and any adherents before the king and council if apprehended.

Henry also had to deal with the devastating and sudden effects of a mysterious sweating sickness which took hold in England 'immediately after Henry's landing in the island', a 'baleful affliction' according to Vergil,[4] which 'made great ravages' that claimed the lives of two mayors of London in one year alone.[5] To a superstitious, God-fearing population, it was inevitable some would consider the terrifying epidemic to be a sign of God's disfavour with the new order, and Henry faced a potential propaganda disaster when his feet were barely under the table at Westminster.

Fortunately for the novice king, however, much of Richard III's core support during the latter's brief reign didn't survive the battle, and consequently there wasn't an influential faction in place to exploit such political, social or economic misfortune in the uncertain period that followed Bosworth. Amongst those killed fighting under Richard's white boar banner at Bosworth were John Howard, 1st Duke of Norfolk, Walter Devereux, 7th Baron Ferrers of Chartley, Sir Robert Brackenbury, Sir Percival Thirlwall and Sir Richard Ratcliffe, whilst Sir William Catesby was dispatched shortly afterwards on a chopping block in Leicester. Scores of other influential members of the lower gentry had also been slain alongside their Yorkist king. Other leading figures meanwhile, such as Thomas Howard, 1st Earl of Surrey, and Henry Percy, 4th Earl of Northumberland, were locked up, albeit briefly in the latter's case, whilst Richard's nephew John de la Pole, 1st Earl of Lincoln, was initially reconciled to the ascendant Tudor government.

King Richard's affinity, therefore, carefully cultivated during his decade as the prevailing authority in the north and then his short-lived reign as king, was comprehensively overwhelmed post-Bosworth through either death or reconciliation, with the notable exception of a small band of malcontents who had managed to flee the battlefield still alive with little intention to renounce their master.

One of Richard's closest allies, from his youth in Yorkshire under the guardianship of the Nevilles through to his very last moments on a Leicestershire field, was Francis Lovell, a man of unwavering devotion to his high-ranking friend, whether he was duke of Gloucester, Lord Protector, or king of England. Although Lovell grew increasingly conspicuous as an integral part of Richard's northern powerbase as their careers progressed, he was, by birth, a son of the southern aristocracy as heir of John Lovell, 8th Baron Lovel, and Joan Beaumont.

The Lovells, who also held the barony of Holand, were a well-established gentry family with their principal seat based at Minster Lovell Hall in Oxfordshire, whilst Francis' maternal relations were prominent in East Anglia and Lincolnshire and had been faithful servants of the Lancastrians during the early stages of the Wars of the Roses. Lovell's grandfather John Beaumont, 1st Viscount Beaumont, had even been killed fighting the Yorkists at the Battle of Northampton in 1460, whilst his uncle William, 2nd Viscount, rallied to the cause of Henry Tudor at Bosworth, perhaps even facing off against his Lovell kinsman, who was probably amongst Richard's ranks on that fateful day.

Lovell inherited his father's baronies as a child, and after initially becoming a royal ward of Edward IV was placed in the household of the mighty Richard Neville, 16th Earl of Warwick, in November 1467,[6] having married the earl's niece Alice FitzHugh two years earlier. It was here he found a temporary home within the household of one of England's proudest and wealthiest households.

It is likely that Lovell's stay with the Nevilles also first brought him to the attention of another youngster under Warwick's care in the north: the future Richard III, with whom he soon developed a close and enduring bond. The pair's friendship may have developed as the youngsters navigated between the great northern Neville strongholds, imposing fortresses such as Middleham, Richmond and Sheriff Hutton, whilst learning from the finest tutors the earl could assemble about what it meant to be a noble courtier worthy of earning a king's favour in later life. After Warwick's fall from grace and death in battle at Barnet in 1471, Lovell spent some time in the household of John de la Pole, 2nd Duke of Suffolk, becoming familiar with another Yorkist youth he would later befriend: his guardian's namesake and heir, the earl of Lincoln.

Lovell formally entered his inheritance in November 1477 and served alongside Richard in June 1480, August 1481 and the summer of 1482 as the duke of Gloucester marshalled the north on behalf of his brother Edward IV. He was raised to the rank of Viscount in January 1483 and his rise continued unabated once Richard ascended the throne, first bearing a sword of state during his friend's coronation before being confirmed as Chief Butler of England and King's Chamberlain less than two months into the reign.[7]

Richard III's confidence in Lovell, warmly referred to in documents as 'the king's kinsman' as both men were married to first cousins, was further established not only through the viscount's induction into the prestigious Order of the Garter, but also from the fact that the king visited Minster Lovell during his summer progress of 1483. During his time on the throne Richard did not visit any other courtier's home, making this a singular honour. Most famously, Lovell's connection with Richard III is best known for the mocking rhyme which was pinned to the door of St Paul's Cathedral in July 1484, referencing Lovell's heraldic silver wolf badge alongside those of the king, William Catesby, and Richard Ratcliffe: 'The catte, the ratte, and Lovell our dogge, Rulyth all Englande under a hogge.'[8]

Events at Bosworth Field halted Lovell's rise just as he reached the peak of his career, and his fall thereafter was swift. Many of those who fought for Richard III and survived to live another day submitted to Henry VII after the battle, throwing themselves upon the mercy of their new sovereign and gratefully accepting whatever bones were thrown their way. For Lovell, however, there could be no reconciliation with the man responsible for slaughtering his close friend, and the viscount instead fled through the east of England to St John's Abbey in Colchester, where he desperately claimed sanctuary within the Benedictine monastery.

The choice of location was somewhat unusual when one considers Lovell's connections were chiefly in the north, whilst Colchester was around 130 miles south-east of Bosworth. Across the English Channel, however, lay the Burgundian Netherlands, home of Margaret of York, the dowager duchess and the sister of Richard III and Edward IV. As time would tell, Lovell had correctly deduced that the Netherlands was a potential safe haven for those hostile to the Tudor king. But if flight across the sea at this juncture was his initial strategy, for whatever reason he failed to complete the sailing.

Accompanying Lovell to the Essex coast were Humphrey and Thomas Stafford, two brothers from Grafton in Worcestershire. Like the viscount, the Staffords had been faithful followers of Richard III, and fought for him at Bosworth, only departing the battlefield once it became clear the day belonged to Tudor. Together, the trio now colluded within the confines of the abbey, plotting how to revenge their fallen master and topple the fledgling dynasty which now occupied the throne in his place.

Any hesitancy to act was probably diminished by their collective attainder during Henry VII's first parliament in November 1485, with all three punished for 'traiterously intendinge, imagininge and conspireinge' the destruction of the new king.[9] Furthermore, Lovell's inheritance had already started to be reallocated amongst Henry's supporters; on 2 March 1486, the king's uncle Jasper, Duke of Bedford, was granted Minster Lovell Hall, along with other Lovell property across the counties of Wiltshire, Oxfordshire, Gloucestershire and Shropshire, and five days later John Savage, as a reward for his efforts on the battlefield, received Lovell estates in Derbyshire, Nottinghamshire and Leicestershire.[10] With little to lose, therefore, Lovell and the Staffords pressed ahead with their scheme.

In April 1486, whilst the king was on his way north, the three rebels finally emerged from their sanctuary after eight months in hiding, with Lovell purposefully heading towards Yorkshire where he hoped to stir the former estates of Richard III. The Staffords hurried west to Worcestershire where they likewise anticipated finding some degree of support amongst their neighbours.

When initially informed of the uprising by Sir Hugh Conway during his Easter stopover in Lincoln, Henry refused to believe the news, replying that 'it could not be so' and questioning the messenger's motives.[11] When he reached York, however, it became abundantly clear that the intelligence was indeed correct, and that Lovell had even amassed a respectable force in the region that was preparing to march on the city 'with hostile intent'.[12]

Henry, suddenly mindful of the fact he was vulnerable, even exposed, in a city 'so little devoted to his interests' in spite of the welcome he had received, could not help but be 'struck by great fear, for he had neither an army nor arms ready for his supporters'. Contributing to the unease that pervaded through the nomadic royal household was the attempted attack on the king's person mentioned in the *Croyland Chronicle*, thwarted by the vigilant earl of Northumberland before harm could be done.

Henry nevertheless showed little hesitation in moving aggressively against the threat once he accepted its existence, and decisively conveyed orders to his commanders to muster 3,000 of his retinue to march on Lovell's camp in the Yorkshire countryside, mindful of the fact that a large proportion of those men were only protected by armour hurriedly crafted from little more than leather.

A pitched battle clearly wasn't in the royal interest at this moment, and so Henry dispatched heralds ahead of his advancing force armed with a promise that he would pardon any would-be rebel who willingly laid down whatever weapons they had procured before they struck a blow in anger. Whilst the offer was considered, Lovell, perhaps sensing that his rashly assembled militia lacked the enthusiasm or skill to see through their mission, abandoned his position and snuck away under the cover of darkness. He made his way through the Yorkshire Dales and into Lancashire where he sought refuge for the next few months with a knight 'of great authority in those parts' named Thomas Broughton.

Once the coast was clear, figuratively and literally, Lovell set sail for the Burgundian Netherlands and belatedly claimed asylum under the protection of Margaret of York, who had no qualms in welcoming an intimate family friend who had served both of her royal siblings, Edward IV and Richard III. Without a military leader to command them against the king's advancing men, and perhaps more importantly lacking a viable Yorkist candidate for the crown around whom to rally, the rebels quietly surrendered without further incident.[13] Broughton would later receive a pardon for his part in harbouring a fugitive and was forced to swear another oath of allegiance to Henry, one he would nonetheless break the following year.[14]

The Stafford brothers, on the other hand, grew alarmed at reports emerging from the north that Henry's household had departed York untroubled after their extended break, and were rapidly heading south-west and directly towards their Worcestershire base. Worryingly for the brothers, whereas Lovell had succeeded in raising enough troops to warrant some comment by chroniclers such as Vergil, the Staffords struggled, probably owing to their lesser status as mere knights and the damage the attainders had done to any reputation they may once have held.

Three men the siblings did recruit were Ralph Botery, Richard Burdett, and Humphrey Stafford's illegitimate son John Stafford, all later charged for aiding the rebels. John was accused of stealing horses from a royal stable in Upton-on-Severn, Botery with supplying two pheasants for sustenance, and Burdett with forewarning the Staffords of the king's whereabouts. The latter charge probably related to an instance where one of the king's retainers, Thomas Cokesey, who had been commissioned by Henry to scour the Worcestershire countryside for the rebels, managed to track down their camp to a woodland near Bewdley, albeit arriving shortly after the prey had bolted.

In a frantic attempt to persuade their hesitant peers to join their cause, the Staffords started spreading false rumours in the locality that their attainders had been overturned, even producing forged letters patent and claiming Henry had pardoned them of all offences. They also announced that Lovell had captured the king at York, and such a disingenuous strategy soon paid some dividend, for the Staffords started to amass a small band of adherents who had no qualms about openly plotting Henry's death. The rebels even started championing the name Warwick in public, alluding to the young Yorkist prince held in the Tower of London. It was unquestionably treasonous activity, and all were partaking in a deadly game against overwhelming odds.

The employment of the Warwick name was likely connected to another minor plot uncovered a few miles north of London in early May 1486, adding to the king's growing burden, in which several conspirators armed themselves with ploughs, rakes and woolsacks and attempted to assault some members of the royal household. Although the basic weapons suggest the revolt was poorly planned and trivial in comparison to similar uprisings, the insurgents involved did provocatively wave a ragged staff banner, a well-known heraldic device associated with previous generations of Warwick earls, including the present incumbent's grandfather Richard Neville, the 16th Earl, better remembered as 'the Kingmaker' for his tireless scheming during the earlier phases of the Wars of the Roses. It certainly wasn't escaping the attention of some disaffected Yorkist diehards that there was still a prince of Yorkist blood known to be alive, albeit confined within the walls of the Tower.

Momentarily boosted by a slight upturn in support, the Staffords were even able to briefly enter Worcester after the town guard proved embarrassingly lax in their defence of their gateways, a dereliction of duty which earned the bailiff and commonalty the severe displeasure of their irritated sovereign.[15] Nonetheless, the rebel efforts proved in vain.

By 3 May 1486, the royal cavalcade had reached Nottingham from where the cautious king issued commissions to several of his foremost lords to 'enquire of all treasons, felonies and conspiracies' in Warwick and Worcester. These commissions were to be led by his uncle Bedford, the earls of Lincoln, Oxford, Derby, Shrewsbury and Rivers, and supported by another of the king's uncles, John Welles, 1st Viscount Welles, with the assistance of twenty others. When Henry reached Worcester on 11 May, the commission was repeated and extended to Hereford, suggesting the threat of rebellion had spread.[16]

The arrival of the royal entourage in the locality almost certainly prompted the flight of Humphrey and Thomas Stafford into sanctuary for a second time, this time selecting a church in Culham, a small settlement near Abingdon in Oxfordshire. It was also less than twenty miles from their accomplice's ancestral seat at Minster Lovell, which may have influenced the decision. Henry, however, was unwilling to take any chances.

Just three days later, a force of around sixty men under the command of Sir John Savage, a Yorkist veteran of the battle of Tewkesbury who nevertheless sided with Henry at Bosworth, burst into the church and forcibly removed the Staffords from their place of refuge. One imagines the colour draining from the brothers' faces as they fretfully watched Savage's heavily armed unit hurtling through the nave towards them. Little concern was demonstrated for the rights of sanctuary, or presumably the pleas of the prior to put away their weapons.

The siblings' apprehension raised a complex legal predicament for those judges of the King's Bench recruited to try the case, who now faced the delicate issue of determining whether Henry had been just in ordering sanctuary to be broken by force. Before the case was openly heard, the judges discussed the matter at length in private, anticipating the Staffords' defence would centre around a demand to be restored to their place of refuge. Their initial reaction was to claim the matter was a spiritual issue outside their remit, although this feeble attempt to relinquish responsibility was quickly rebuffed by royal officials, who tersely reminded the justices that 'no franchise can be made without a grant from the king, because none can grant such a franchise, that anyone can have such a place of safety, except the king himself'. The law, it seems, was being doctored somewhat.

With the Staffords' right to sanctuary therefore determined to be a common law matter rather than a spiritual one, the indignant brothers duly appeared before the King's Bench on 20 June demanding to be freed, their cause sponsored by John Sant, abbot of Abingdon. After further consideration of the case amongst the judges, acutely aware the king had voiced his preference for a swift resolution, it was declared that sanctuary could not, and would not, be afforded to those stood accused of high treason against their sovereign, a controversial stance later approved by Pope Innocent VIII. The fate of the Staffords was sealed.[17]

On 5 July 1486, Humphrey, the eldest of the pair, was dragged to Tyburn where he paid for his treachery with his head. Thomas, on the other hand, was granted a pardon at the last moment as it was deemed he had not been acting of his own volition but was rather led astray through the 'evell counsaill and mischeavcous persuasion' of a dominant brother.[18]

The Lovell and Stafford uprising of mid-1486 failed largely because the ringleaders were unable to put forward a viable contender for the throne around whom they could mobilise, militarily or otherwise. It was not enough for many potential supporters to jeopardise their livelihoods for a cause alone, which history had shown to be no substitute for the personal magnetism of a senior royal capable of persuading even the most reluctant of hearts to flock to his banner. Henry IV and Edward IV were just two examples of usurpers who had been able to attract an abundance of support during their respective marches to the throne, as had Henry VII himself to an extent during the Bosworth campaign. Lovell and Stafford had no such candidate prepared to step forward and challenge the Tudor hegemony, and as a consequence their revolt faltered with little fanfare.

The king, meanwhile, had left Worcester on 15 May, returning to Westminster via Hereford, Gloucester and Bristol with much to think about after a gruelling two-month progress around his realm that surely placed significant strain on both body and mind. Henry had not been on the throne for even a year when forced to face down the first concerted threat to his rule, which, although suppressed with little difficulty, proved unsettling for those associated with the royal household.

The birth of Prince Arthur in September, followed by an uneventful winter with little sign of discord amongst his nobility, reassured Henry, but he would soon come to rue the failure of his forces to capture Francis Lovell during the spring of 1486. As the fallen viscount fled the kingdom after the collapse of his aborted revolt, two thoughts would have dominated his thinking as he navigated the rough seas towards Flanders; the first was that he needed a focal point to nominally head any subsequent rebellion, a leader in name if not in person who was preferably of Yorkist descent to counter the hybrid Tudor ascendancy, and secondly, there was the evident readiness of some to invoke the Warwick name when publicly decrying the kingship of Henry VII.

A plan was forming, and Lovell, perhaps unfairly disparaged by Vergil as feeble of spirit,[19] was already boldly plotting his return. For an unyielding partisan of the House of York, utterly devoted to the remembrance, and perhaps more importantly the avenging, of Richard III, there could be no other option. The Tudor usurper had to fall.

4

Insatiable Hatred

It is not known for certain when and how Sir Francis Lovell left English shores, but by January 1487 there were reports that the attainted viscount had reached Malines in Flanders. Once there, he desperately sought the protection of Margaret of York, sister of Yorkist kings Edward IV and Richard III, following a similar path trodden by the latter two after the Lancastrians briefly recaptured the throne in 1471.[1]

Lovell's choice of destination proved to be a wise one. Margaret of York was the proud third daughter of Richard, 3rd Duke of York, and Cecily Neville, through both of whom she inherited English royal blood. From her youngest days, she was acutely aware of her prestigious lineage, presumably more so once her frustrated father openly laid claim to Henry VI's throne in October 1460, by which point his daughter was an attentive and impressionable fourteen-year-old who must have observed many impassioned discussions within the Yorkist household about the duke's supposed hereditary right to be called king. Her father's slaughter at the hands of his enemies outside Sandal Castle in December 1460, alongside her seventeen-year-old brother Edmund, followed by her eldest brother Edward's deposing of Henry VI a few months later, did little to dampen her strong sense of dynastic devotion before she even reached adulthood.

Margaret remained a part of her brother Edward IV's royal household until June 1468 when she was married to Charles the Bold, the fiercely ambitious and wealthy duke of Burgundy who had been reverently referred to in that year's English parliament as 'oon of the myghtyest Princes of the world that bereth no crown'.[2] The union had been initiated as part of Edward's diplomatic strategy to establish stronger cross-Channel trading ties whilst securing the support of the warlike duke against the anticipated military advances of their mutual adversary, King Louis XI of France.

Charles's influence in the political affairs of Europe largely stemmed from the extensive and profitable trade conducted through his lands, a diverse collection of fragmented territories that stretched from the Zuiderzee in the north to Lake Geneva in the south. This included the movement of wine, spices, wool, fish and furs through his territories, the sizable income from which contributed to the magisterial town halls erected in affluent towns such as Bruges, Brussels, Louvain and Ghent. Bruges, in particular, had managed to establish itself as the commercial and financial centre of northern Europe, playing host to vast numbers of merchant traders and bankers and perhaps only rivalled by the great Italian city-states to the south.[3]

Unlike England, the Burgundian territories were chiefly urban, and Margaret's marital arrangements provided her with several towns of her own, including the cloth-rich port-town of Malines, which would become her primary base during widowhood. These towns of the duchess would play a significant role in future conspiracies against Henry VII. Margaret's golden coronet, meanwhile, served as a palpable reminder to everyone who encountered her of her Yorkist ancestry. It was trimmed with pearls and embellished with a collection of precious stones that were set into White Roses of York. A large diamond cross topped with another pearl and white rose formed the centrepiece, whilst the entwined initials of C and M appeared around the base, as did the arms of both England and Burgundy.[4]

Despite such auspicious beginnings, the marriage lasted just nine years before the childless union was brought to a shattering end with the brutal demise of Charles at the Battle of Nancy, where he was waging war against the Swiss Confederates, a collection of states within the remit of the Holy Roman Empire who resented his aggressive expansionist movements and economic embargoes. The duke's short, thickset body was only found three days after his death, frozen in a river with his head severely mutilated almost beyond recognition, firstly by the halberd of a Swiss mercenary and thereafter by wild dogs which had feasted on his naked corpse. Charles was only belatedly identified by his lengthy nails, missing teeth, and assortment of scars from previous battles.[5]

Widowed at thirty with no children of her own, Margaret of York's focus shifted towards guiding her inexperienced stepdaughter Mary through a difficult transitional period for the duchy of Burgundy, bequeathed to a teenaged female heir after four successive warrior dukes. She proved an astute mentor, competently supervising the military defence of the Burgundian Netherlands from persistent French advances whilst counselling the nineteen-year-old duchess to consider taking Maximilian of Hapsburg as her husband once it became clear a union with Margaret's favourite brother George of Clarence was doubtful.[6]

This celebrated union with the eighteen-year-old heir of Frederick III, Archduke of Austria and Holy Roman Emperor, was completed in Ghent during August 1477, conducted under Margaret's watchful eye less than seven months after the death of her own husband, Charles the Bold. The duke's untimely demise, however, proved not to be an isolated moment of heartache for Margaret. In the intervening decade between her stepdaughter's nuptials and the arrival of Francis Lovell at her court, her life was littered with tragedies, each of which must have taken its toll on her character and partly influenced her later decisions.

In February 1478, the dowager duchess's brother Clarence, with whom it was observed she was more affectionate than with the rest of her kindred,[7] was executed by their eldest brother Edward IV, and in March 1482 she suffered a second traumatic personal loss after her beloved stepdaughter Mary was thrown from her horse whilst out riding. She would pass away a few weeks later from an internal injury suffered during the accident. According to the Burgundian diplomat and chronicler Philippe de Commines, the duchess's death was a 'great loss to her subjects, for she was a person of great honour, affability, and generosity to all her people', and there is little doubt Margaret would have grieved deeply.[8] She may not have been her biological mother, but Margaret had overseen much of her stepdaughter's development.

Just over a year later, her brother Edward IV died, triggering the bitter succession crisis within the House of York that saw her nephew Edward V dramatically deposed in favour of her last surviving brother, Richard III, the culmination of a cataclysmic series of events that led to the ruin of her dynasty two years later at Bosworth Field. Margaret's reaction to the Tudor ascendancy was one of outright hostility, regardless of the fact her niece Elizabeth became queen shortly thereafter and her own mother Cecily Neville, who had more reason than most to loathe any Lancastrian resurgence, pragmatically accepted the situation.

Margaret had left England two years after Elizabeth's birth, and other than a short trip across the Channel in 1481, it is likely aunt and niece had little personal connection outside of their Yorkist kinship. For the dowager duchess, the supposed peaceful union between two warring houses was a farce and her loyalty to the memory of her brother Richard III, butchered at Bosworth and unceremoniously put into the ground by the Tudor usurper, proved unwavering. It was the verdict of Polydore Vergil, admittedly prejudiced as a member of the Tudor court, that Margaret of York 'pursued Henry with insatiable hatred' and with 'fiery wrath never desisted from employing every scheme which might harm him'.[9] Biased or otherwise, Vergil had grounds for penning such a judgement.

Margaret's ardent partisanship for the flagging Yorkist cause was driven by several motives, all of which combined to create in the dowager duchess an uncomfortable thorn in the side of the Tudor king, a dangerous nuisance that would endure until her own death in November 1503. With a deep sense of dynastic allegiance that had been fostered from an impressionable age, Margaret's anti-Lancastrian tendencies had been exacerbated not only by her father's and brother's killings in 1460 at the hands of a Beaufort-led army, but also from the flight of her other brothers Edward and Richard to the Burgundian Netherlands in October 1470 after the earl of Warwick briefly restored Henry VI to the throne.

She played a significant role in returning Edward IV to his throne, encouraging her husband Charles the Bold to support her brother's cause whilst energetically raising funds for an expedition from five Dutch towns.[10] She even played host to Richard for a couple of nights in early February 1471, before reaching out to their estranged brother George, making a 'great and diligent effort' in coercing the wayward duke of Clarence to switch sides from Warwick and return into the Yorkist fold, a defection that ultimately took place during Edward's invasion one month later.[11]

There was also economic motivation for Margaret's desire to topple the fledgling Tudor regime. The deaths of her husband Charles and stepdaughter Mary weakened Margaret's political influence in Burgundy, and she suffered a significant financial setback when Henry VII declined to renew the profitable cross-Channel trading privileges she had enjoyed during the reigns of her brothers.[12] The new English king was costing her money.

Through her amiable relationship with her ambitious stepson-in-law Maximilian I, meanwhile, there was an unexpected dynastic aspect to the dowager duchess's scheming that wasn't Yorkist in origin. Through Philippa of Lancaster, the eldest child of John of Gaunt and granddaughter of Edward III, the Hapsburgs possessed a claim to the English throne that was at least as impressive as any claim Henry Tudor was able to profess, if not more.

Furthermore, Maximilian's nine-year-old heir Philip, now duke of Burgundy after the demise of his mother Mary, could also boast separate descent from Philippa through his maternal Burgundian line. If a viable Yorkist candidate could not be found in England, then Margaret undoubtedly had a Lancastrian substitute in mind, a proposal Maximilian was hardly likely to reject, either on behalf of himself or his son. Of more immediate concern to Maximilian, however, was the disturbing threat an Anglo-French alliance would pose to his plans to salvage the Burgundian inheritance for his son.

Francis Lovell's appearance in the Netherlands unquestionably galvanised Margaret of York into action, and his gloomy account of recent events unquestionably fuelled her well-developed prejudice against Henry VII. Lovell's presence overseas happened to coincide with curious rumours circulating in Ireland about the existence of a young man purporting to be Edward Plantagenet, the earl of Warwick supposedly safely confined in the Tower of London. Something was afoot, and it was about to cause the king of England a mighty headache.

*

Edward, 17th Earl of Warwick, was the only surviving son of George, 1st Duke of Clarence, and his wife Isabel Neville, eldest daughter of the kingmaking Richard Neville, 16th Earl of Warwick. Through both his parents, the young Warwick boasted an illustrious lineage that placed him high in the English line of succession from his very first breath, an enviable pedigree that made him a threat to the Tudor ascendancy, whether he was capable of appreciating the fact or not.

Through his father Clarence, the child earl, just ten years old at the time of Henry VII's accession, was descended from Edward III through that king's fourth surviving son Edmund of Langley, 1st Duke of York. He could also boast Lancastrian ancestry through his grandmother Cecily Neville's Beaufort mother Joan, the daughter of John of Gaunt, 1st Duke of Lancaster and Edmund's older brother (Joan had no fewer than fourteen children from her second marriage, of whom ten Survived to adulthood). Through his mother Isabel, meanwhile, Warwick was again descended from Joan Beaufort through his great-grandfather Richard Neville, 5th Earl of Salisbury, and again from Edmund of York in the direct female line. Whichever way it was considered, Warwick was as royal as they came.

The union of his parents Clarence and Isabel, and the subsequent merging of their respective bloodlines in the offspring they produced, had enraged Edward IV, wary of his brother's ambition and not without good cause. Although Clarence had received considerable patronage from his elder brother after the Yorkists wrested the throne from the Lancastrians in 1461, most notably his dukedom and a lifetime grant of the lucrative Honour of Richmond, the headstrong duke nevertheless wavered in his loyalty as the reign progressed.

Frustrated by Edward hindering his attempt to marry Mary of Burgundy, through whom Clarence anticipated one day ruling the wealthy duchy, the duke gradually fell under the malign influence of his uncle Warwick, who himself had grown estranged from the king on account of the latter's foreign policy and proclivity to reward his Wydeville in-laws to the slighted earl's noticeable exclusion. In July 1469, Warwick and the nineteen-year-old Clarence crossed the Channel to Calais without permission and before they returned to England, the duke had married Isabel Neville. Their interests irrevocably entwined, the wayward pair initiated a coup against Edward once back on the mainland, cornering the king in the Midlands and imprisoning him in Warwick's imposing fortress of Middleham in Yorkshire.

Warwick and Clarence's revolt, however, quickly faltered as the pair struggled to maintain law and order in a realm vulnerable without its king at liberty. The pair had no mandate to govern in Edward's stead, and failed to galvanise the nobles to support their actions. The king was duly released from captivity, and although he proved surprisingly magnanimous to his erstwhile captors, Warwick and Clarence soon fled abroad to France where they entered a desperate coalition with the exiled Lancastrian court of Margaret of

Anjou, the robust wife of Henry VI. The result of this unexpected alliance was the deposition of Edward IV in October 1470, with Henry returned to his throne.

Clarence soon developed misgivings about his position, however, having helped remove his brother from the throne without any tangible benefit to himself, other than a promise he would become king in the unlikely event the Lancastrian line failed. By April 1471, the duke was reconciled to Edward with the help of their sister Margaret, and together with their younger sibling Richard, all three brothers of York defeated and killed Warwick at the Battle of Barnet. A follow-up victory at Tewkesbury a few weeks later crushed the remainder of the Lancastrian resistance, and the throne thereafter safely remained in Yorkist hands until the drama of Bosworth Field fourteen years later.[13]

Nevertheless, it wasn't long before 'violent dissensions'[14] once more arose between Clarence and one of his York brothers, on this occasion Richard, Duke of Gloucester, and the fallout would have dramatic consequences for the dynasty. By February 1472, it became clear Gloucester intended to take Anne Neville, the younger sister of Clarence's wife Isabel, as his wife, triggering a bitter feud. Clarence went so far as to defiantly pledge he would 'parte no lyvelod' to his brother.

Gloucester, however, proved tenacious in pursuing the rights of his new Neville wife, and ultimately the king was forced to intercede to command the partition of the inheritance between his squabbling siblings.[15] The rights of the Neville sisters' living mother Anne Beauchamp, the dowager countess and legal holder of the Warwick estates, were coldly disregarded by the acquisitive brothers, 'as if the seid Countesse were then naturally dede',[16] and by March 1474 George was regarded in official records as 'duke of Clarence, earl of Warwick and Salisbury, lord of Richmond, great chamberlain of England and lieutenant of Ireland'.[17] It was an array of riches and responsibility that should have appeased the ambitions of George Plantagenet.

In the meantime, Clarence turned his attentions towards securing the future of his own dynasty. In August 1473, Isabel gave birth to a girl named Margaret, one would believe in honour of the duke's sister, followed on 25 February 1475 by his male heir, Edward. Clarence's joy was brief. On 22 December 1476, about two months after giving birth to a short-lived second son named Richard, the duchess passed away without recovering from the birthing, provoking an outpouring of grief from Clarence, whose behaviour thereafter became increasingly unstable and dangerous.

Two episodes in 1477 hastened his downfall. After Charles the Bold's death in January that year, Clarence again declared his desire to seek a match with Mary, the new Duchess of Burgundy, a proposal opposed for a second time by Edward IV, suspicious of his brother's intentions for the latent Burgundian claim to the English throne. In April, meanwhile, with the help of 'divers riotous persons' numbering eighty men, Clarence abducted one of his deceased wife's former ladies-in-waiting, Ankarette Twynyho, a widow of 'good disposition', from her Somerset manor. She was conveyed seventy miles through the West Country to Warwick where she was thrown into prison, her jewels, money, and goods having also been seized in the process.

Acting as though 'he had used king's power', Clarence ordered Ankarette to be tried in the Guildhall for the murder of Isabel the previous year, accusing the presumably petrified lady of providing his duchess 'a venomous drink of ale mixed with poison'. With the town justices unable to placate the frenzied brother of the king, and understandably fearful of reprisals from the duke's armed entourage, which remained in close attendance, they passed a guilty verdict 'contrary to their conscience', a later investigation reported. The jurors also approached Ankarette when a death sentence was given, 'in remorse and asked her forgiveness'. With Clarence watching on, she was hanged in the centre of Warwick. It was a shameful episode.[18]

Edward IV was enraged when he discovered this deplorable abuse of power, and before the year was out it was observed that each brother 'began to look upon the other with no very fraternal eyes'. Clarence even absented himself from court, and may have been left to his own devices had he not publicly protested in May 1477 the hanging of two astronomers and a member of his household convicted of using necromancy for evil intentions. Such persistent disobedience was enough for the king to order his brother's arrest before the summer was over, with Clarence imprisoned in the Tower of London until parliament assembled in January 1478 for his trial.[19]

Remarkably, the prosecution was led by the king himself, who bitterly decried the 'manyfold grete Conspiracies, malicious and heinous Tresons, that heretofore hath be compassed by dyverse persones' plotting to destroy 'his moost Roiall persone'.

With specific reference to Clarence, the exasperated king alleged that treachery had been 'contryved, imagined and conspired by that persone that of all erthely creatures, beside the dutie of ligeaunce, by nature, by benefitte, by gratitude, and by yefres and grauntes of goodes and possessions', should have been more appreciative of his privileged status, particularly as Edward had 'evere loved and cheryshed' the duke 'as tenderly and as kyndely, as eny creature myght his naturell Brother'.

There was little doubt in the king's mind that his sibling had been 'growyng daily in more and more malice', and was plotting his downfall 'by many subtill contryved weyes', even openly brandishing the petition granted by Henry VI during the brief Lancastrian restoration that declared Clarence to be the residual heir to the throne in the event the senior Lancaster line failed, which had occurred, with Clarence's assistance, at Tewkesbury in 1471.[20]

With nobody willing to speak up for the unrepentant duke, King Edward achieved the outcome he sought. Clarence was found guilty of high treason, with an act of attainder passed against the duke and his heirs. On 18 February 1478, deep within the confines of the Tower, George Plantagenet was put to death in the same fortress as Henry VI had been seven years earlier. The second continuator of the *Croyland Chronicle*, often well versed in the significant events of Edward IV's reign, was uncharacteristically vague about the method of execution[21] although Robert Fabyan, a London sheriff writing during the reign of Henry VII, noted very specifically that the duke had been 'drowned in a barell of malvesye', or Malmsey wine.[22]

Clarence's execution after a decade of insubordination which had periodically manifested itself treasonously was a ruthless necessity on the part of Edward IV to protect his crown against the menace his maddening sibling increasingly posed. The duke's downfall would, however, have far-reaching consequences for the orphaned children he left behind. Margaret was four years old and young Edward just three. Due to his father's attainder, which specifically stated that the 'Honoure, Estate, Dignitie and name of Duke' which Clarence held before his execution was 'forfeit from hym and his heyres for ever',[23] young Edward's inheritance stemmed solely from the lands associated with the Warwick earldom, a title which now fell to him by right of his mother Isabel Neville.

Although openly regarded as the earl of Warwick from the moment of his father's death, Edward was obviously too young to enter his inheritance immediately, and as a result between February 1478 and November 1482 the king granted much of his nephew's estate to his supporters, with the provision it would return to the earl once he reached the end of his minority at the age of twenty-one.[24] The earldom of Salisbury, meanwhile, did not descend to Warwick, and was instead granted to his cousin Edward of Middleham, the son of Richard of Gloucester, in keeping with the notion that the Neville estates were to be granted equally between the sons of Isabel and Anne Neville.[25]

As a parentless child, Warwick became a royal ward upon his father's execution, and this status remained in place until 16 September 1480 when Edward IV granted custody of his nephew to Thomas Grey, Marquis of Dorset and the king's stepson, in exchange for a payment of £2,000. The grant included several lordships across Hampshire, Dorset, Wiltshire and Worcestershire as well as the town and liberty of Tewkesbury, and further handed the marquis the marital rights of Warwick, although one imagines he would not have acted on this delicate matter without the guidance of the king.[26]

Warwick's precise whereabouts and manner of upbringing are thereafter uncertain, but it does appear some of his estates were not being treated perhaps as the young earl may have hoped. On 5 June 1482, Edward IV issued a commission to six men to survey all the lands, woods and parks in several Gloucestershire lordships which comprised part of Warwick's inheritance, for it was alleged the steward Sir Richard Beauchamp was guilty of 'divers wastes' in executing his office.[27]

During the dynastic upheaval in the summer of 1483 after Edward IV's death, Warwick was conspicuously overlooked for the throne after his cousin Edward V was declared illegitimate, evidently on account of his father's attainder. This situation conveniently cleared the path for the duke of Gloucester to assume the throne as Richard III, the only senior male member of the House of York left untainted by accusations of illegitimacy or treason.

Although Warwick was only eight years old at the time, some four years younger than his doomed cousin Edward V and hardly suitable to bear a crown at this juncture, the attainder in place wasn't necessarily an obstacle that couldn't be overcome, should there have been sufficient clamour amongst the commons and lords for such a thing to occur. It was in the power of parliament to reverse any act of attainder, and in 1483 this could conceivably have been a viable option once the children of Edward IV had been deemed illegitimate.

Edward IV himself had claimed the throne in 1461 although subject to an act of attainder, as had Henry VI in 1470 and as would Henry VII two years later in 1485.

Unfortunately for Warwick, who as a child may have been oblivious to such matters, there was little support for his cause, not least from his only surviving uncle Gloucester who appeared content to accept the crown for himself. Any claim Warwick had to the throne of England, therefore, remained void throughout 1483.

There is no suggestion Gloucester, now Richard III, treated Warwick poorly during his tenure upon the throne, although he certainly kept his Yorkist nephew under close observation. Whilst serving as Lord Protector just prior to his bid for the crown, Richard commanded Warwick 'should come to the city', meaning London, and dispensed orders that the 'lad should be kept in confinement in the household of his wife' Anne Neville, who also happened to be Warwick's maternal aunt. It wasn't quite the Tower of London, where Warwick's cousins Edward V and Richard of Shrewsbury, Duke of York, were placed, but there can be little doubt the earl was just as firmly under his uncle's control.[28]

Warwick was present during Richard's coronation festivities, noticeably riding through London on 5 July 1483 amongst a vast entourage which included most of the dukes, earls, viscounts and barons of the realm,[29] and on 21 July also formed part of the royal procession which departed the capital on the new king's perambulation through the northern reaches of his realm.[30] Also present on this journey north was another of the king's Yorkist-descended nephews, the son of his sister Elizabeth, John de la Pole, Earl of Lincoln, though conspicuous by their absence were the two sons of Edward IV. Does this raise the possibility there was no longer any need for Richard to keep the two princes in the Tower in such proximity to his person as they were no longer alive? Perhaps, although there is not enough evidence to be certain. If they were still alive at this moment, it does take a great deal of trust on Richard's part that they would not be sprung from captivity whilst he was away from London.

In the Chancery Rolls, meanwhile, it is also evident that Warwick was referred to more warmly during the reign of Richard III, when he is typically mentioned in grants as the king's nephew rather than a mere earl as he had been under Edward IV.[31] Of course, Warwick was Richard's nephew twice over, by blood and by marriage, which may have had some bearing on his outwardly affectionate treatment of his brother Clarence's sole male heir.

It will never be known what would have become of Warwick in the event Richard III retained his crown at Bosworth. Would the earl, as a grown man fully conscious of his lineage, accept a role subservient to an uncle who, fairly or otherwise, disregarded his claim in the summer of 1483 for his own benefit? Richard, it should be remembered, could never realistically reverse the attainder against the duke of Clarence, or propose the duke's son Warwick to be his residual heir, without sacrificing the legitimacy of his own claim to the throne. Due to the rise of Henry Tudor, these are questions that never required answers.

Shortly after the events at Bosworth Field, on Henry VII's orders Warwick was brought back to London from Sheriff Hutton Castle in North Yorkshire, where he had been placed by Richard III towards the end of the latter's reign. Living under his third king at just ten years old, the helpless young earl remained a pawn with little control over his own destiny. Perhaps the new monarch could relate on some level, having been in a similar position during his own youth in Wales and Brittany.

Warwick's new residence under Tudor rule was the Tower of London, the last place his cousins had been seen alive a few summers earlier,[32] and it wouldn't be surprising to discover that some citizens feared for the boy's future. Like Richard III before him, Henry VII had to appreciate the claim to the throne Warwick possessed, attainder or otherwise, and one of most secure fortresses in the land was considered the appropriate place to hold the young earl whilst the novice king strove to establish his authority.

If it was anticipated Edward Plantagenet would be forgotten, however, Henry and his council were to be frustrated. Warwick's name had been publicly proclaimed during the Staffords' uprising in April 1486, with some rebels even spreading word that the earl had been freed in Guernsey before being delivered to Francis Lovell's care in Yorkshire.[33] In July that year there had also been a vague reference to a son of Clarence supposedly surfacing at the Burgundian court, about which no further information emerged.[34]

On 29 November, meanwhile, Thomas Betanson, then dwelling in St Sepulchre-without-Newgate Church in London, penned a report to his Yorkshire-based master Sir Robert Plumpton about current affairs in the capital, during the course of which he made an ambiguous reference to Warwick. Betanson noted that whilst the king, queen and earl of Derby were in residence at Greenwich, the earl of Northumberland was in Winchester, and the earl of Oxford in Essex, there was 'but little spech of the erle of Warwyk'. He did, however, portentously add, 'But after christenmas, they say ther wylbe more spech of.'[35]

Just who 'they' were, and what it was this unidentified group were referring to, was left mysteriously unspecified. Finally, there was another mention of Warwick in the chronicle of the Flemish writer Adrian de But, who alleged the earl had been seen in Ireland towards the end of the year.[36]

Such persistent gossip about Warwick's whereabouts, combined with concern there was a conspiracy afoot that had yet to reveal itself, caused the apprehensive king to issue summonses to his council in December 1486 to assemble at the Carthusians' convent near his royal palace of Sheen in mid-February, once the Christmas festivities were firmly out of the way.[37] The irony may not have been lost on Henry VII that, like Richard III before him, he was now the one who had growing reason to doubt the loyalty of some of the men he had assembled around him.

Although discussions about how to defend Henry from enemies within and without England were debated at length, the primary outcome of the council meeting was the order to briefly remove the earl of Warwick from his chambers in the Tower and show him in public so that the 'foolish notion that the boy was in Ireland would be driven from men's minds'.[38] Rumours may have placed Warwick across the Irish Sea, or even in the Channel Islands and Yorkshire, but the incontrovertible fact was that Henry had the earl safely guarded in the Tower, where he had been based since the days following Bosworth. It was a logical way to suppress the gossip whilst attempting to nip any plots in the bud.

There could be little question the boy in the Tower was the 'real' Warwick, either. The youngster had been personally known to his uncles Edward IV and Richard III before he came into Tudor possession, not to mention the scores of other relatives still extant at the royal court post-Bosworth, not least Elizabeth of York, John de la Pole, and even Edward's slightly older sister, Margaret.

The person who arguably knew Warwick better than most was Thomas Grey, Marquis of Dorset, who had been granted the wardship of the earl during the reign of Edward IV, overseeing the child's upbringing between the ages of three and eight. If the Warwick in the Tower was some changeling, a puppet kept in captivity by Henry VII whilst the authentic earl moved freely around the coast of England, then surely his Yorkist kinsfolk would have noticed.

As planned, therefore, Edward of Warwick was withdrawn from his apartments at the Tower to appear before the council, where he was inspected and probably briefly interrogated, although given his young age one expects this wasn't a rigorous examination. Once the council was dismissed by the king, the earl was led from the Tower through the streets of London until he reached the doors of St Paul's Cathedral.

Every care was taken to ensure Warwick was shown to the hundreds of citizens who had gathered along the route to catch a rare glimpse of this little-known heir of the notorious duke of Clarence. Once inside the illustrious church, Warwick, 'as he had been instructed', fell to his knees in prayer and took part in worship, before taking time to speak with several significant dignitaries whom the king no doubt hoped could later vouch that they had personally conversed with the earl on this day.

According to Vergil's testimony, some of those Warwick was instructed to speak to were men whom Henry had privately voiced his suspicions about, with the hope they would 'more readily understand that the Irish had based their new rebellion on an empty and spurious cause'.[39] It was a calculated move by the king, and the message from the royal authorities to any would-be conspirators couldn't have been clearer; the earl of Warwick was not only alive and well, but safely in the custody of the first Tudor king.

This very public parading of the earl through the packed streets of London should have brought any rumours of his supposed liberty to a conclusive end. That it didn't raised two very troubling questions for Henry and his councillors – just who was impersonating Warwick, and, more importantly, who were his backers?

5

The Joiner's Son

Henry VII had every right to be concerned about a fresh conspiracy during the early days of 1487. Rumours of the earl of Warwick's supposed appearance in Ireland may have initially been treated with caution towards the end of the previous year, but by February 1487 the king's councillors were certainly paying far closer attention to persistent gossip that a plot revolving around the Yorkist prince was brewing. Henry himself had seized the crown from an improbable position a few summers earlier, and it would have been foolish to disregard a similar threat against him to the one he himself had once posed to Richard III.

The council meeting held in Sheen during mid-February had several outcomes, not least the shrewd decision to parade the genuine earl of Warwick through the streets of London and to attend a service in public at St Paul's Cathedral. Henry, however, was determined not to remain passive to any potential threat and reacted decisively to counteract those he considered potentially associated with a conspiracy centred around Warwick, particularly once he received further insight into the shadowy scheme being hatched against him from a convocation of the Province of Canterbury that assembled at St Paul's on 13 February 1487.[1]

This synod of clergymen, comprising the foremost bishops, deans, archdeacons and abbots of the province as well as the mayor, aldermen and sheriffs of London, were charged with investigating the behaviour of a priest named William Symonds. The details forthcoming from the lowly cleric when he appeared before his more senior colleagues on 17 February were startling.

According to the official record documented in the *Register of John Morton, Archbishop of Canterbury*, the twenty-eight-year-old

Symonds was presented to the convocation where he confessed that he had personally abducted the son of an unidentified organ maker associated with the University of Oxford and transported him across the sea to Ireland. It was there that the child was hailed as the earl of Warwick by his Irish hosts.

Symonds furthermore admitted that this organ maker's son, whose name is conspicuously absent at this stage, had also been present in the company of Francis Lovell at Furness Fells, a hilly terrain in the most north-westerly extremity of England, confirming the fallen viscount's involvement in the shadowy plot. Satisfied with Symonds' testimony, Archbishop Morton, one of the king's most trusted confidants, requested the sheriffs place the priest in the Tower of London as he only had room for one prisoner at his Bishop's Palace in Lambeth, and that spot was already taken by another unnamed conspirator.[2]

If this confession did indeed occur as recorded in the official account, then the royal authorities had unearthed a perturbing plot that involved a priest, an anonymous child in Ireland masquerading as an earl, and the re-emergence of the implacable Francis Lovell. No specific dates are provided to suggest when the organ maker's son was taken to Ireland, nor when he made Lovell's acquaintance in Furness Fells.

Nonetheless, by the end of February 1487, it appears a priest named William Symonds was locked up in the Tower having given up the basics of the plot, perhaps pointedly lodged in the very same fortress as the real Warwick. In the meantime, a 'profoundly disturbed'[3] Henry VII turned his attention to those he suspected of supporting the conspiracy, directly or otherwise. Two of those targeted were Robert Stillington, Bishop of Bath and Wells, and perhaps more unexpectedly, the king's own mother-in-law, and former queen consort of England, Elizabeth Wydeville.

On the surface, it appears highly improbable Elizabeth would be a willing participant in any conspiracy to depose her son-in-law from his hard-won throne in favour of a mere nephew-by-marriage in Warwick, much less an organ maker's son pretending to be the earl. If successful, the plot would also have resulted in the removal of her grandson Arthur from the line of succession, not to mention the deposition of her own daughter as queen.

For what reason then, did Henry VII apparently penalise the dowager queen during this period by transferring all honours, castles, manors and lordships she held into the hands of her daughter, Queen Elizabeth, and overseeing her removal to Bermondsey Abbey where she would see out the last five years of her life in comparative isolation?[4]

Evidence about the personal relationship between Henry and his mother-in-law during the king's eighteen-month reign from August 1485 to February 1487 is vague, but there is reason to suppose relations were not particularly warm. It may be conjectured that Elizabeth Wydeville resented Henry for his hesitancy to crown her daughter, despite having provided him with a healthy male heir. It does also seem conceivable the king harboured his own grudge towards the dowager queen for her reconciliation with Richard III during the spring of 1484, a state of affairs which almost curtailed the fledgling Tudor conspiracy before it had even reached the English mainland. Vergil himself ventured that this latter reason was the grounds for which Elizabeth was deprived of her lands, although the fact that Henry waited nearly two years to take action raises doubts.[5]

Perhaps it wasn't Elizabeth Wydeville herself who had fallen under the king's suspicion, but rather her son from her first marriage, Thomas Grey, Marquis of Dorset. Dorset was not an unknown quantity to Henry, for he had joined the latter's court-in-exile in Brittany during the upheaval of 1483, where his uncommitted conduct hardly endeared him to his future king and brother-in-law. On one notable occasion the following year, the marquis furtively slipped away from the rebel court and fled towards Flanders, intending to return to England having been 'partly subornyd by king Richerds fayre promyses', a consequence of his mother's reconciliation. A search party caught up with Dorset, however, and 'perswadyd' him to return to Henry's side, one imagines under considerable duress.[6] When the rebels invaded England in August 1485, Dorset was left behind in Paris.

Although his noble title was confirmed by the new king in November 1486,[7] the marquis failed to earn Henry's trust thereafter, and would be granted no significant position of influence for the remainder of his life. When rumours of a Warwick-inspired rebellion abounded in the early months of 1487, Dorset swiftly fell under royal suspicion, and with good reason. He undeniably had strong connections to the young earl, over whom he served as guardian for several years during the reign of Edward IV, and as he had also held the marital rights for his ward it was not inconceivable Dorset maintained long-term ambitions to wed one of his daughters to this Yorkist prince, and perhaps in time see his descendants on the throne. He would not have been the first English noble to toy with such thoughts.

Unfortunately, we can only speculate about Henry VII's behaviour towards his Wydeville in-laws during the spring of 1487, or indeed what his queen thought of such matters. The possibility cannot be rejected, of course, that Elizabeth Wydeville's withdrawal to Bermondsey was a coincidental occurrence, and that such a move had been planned for some time, perhaps for financial, medical or religious reasons. What isn't contested, however, is that any influence this dowager queen, or by association her Wydeville kin, once possessed in abundance had by February 1487 been severely curtailed, partly due to the king's uncertainty over their trustworthiness.

Bishop Robert Stillington, on the other hand, proved to be a different proposition altogether. No friend of the Wydevilles due to his role in the deposition of Edward V, the Yorkshire-born Stillington had served as bishop of Bath and Wells since 1465, rising under Edward IV's reign to become keeper of the privy seal between 1461 and 1467 and chancellor between 1467 and 1473, with the six-month period of the Lancastrian readeption excepted. In 1471, he was appointed one of the administrators of the lands of the prince of Wales, the future Edward V, and two years later was recognised as one of the boy's councillors.

In February 1478, however, he fell foul of the king around the time of the duke of Clarence's execution, and was briefly incarcerated himself, although the specific reasons for this treatment remain speculative. The elderly bishop returned to the fore in 1483 when he informed Richard of Gloucester that he knew the marriage of Edward IV to Elizabeth Wydeville to be invalid due to an earlier precontract on the king's part, the damaging ramifications of which led to their children being declared illegitimate and disqualified from holding royal office.

Stillington's role in the rise of Richard III was recognised when he was imprisoned shortly after the accession of Henry VII, although the new king pardoned the bishop on 22 November 1485 after the churchman had petitioned him on account of his 'grete age, long infirmitie, and feblenes'.[8] This pardon did not signal Stillington's retirement from the political arena, however, and he soon fell under suspicion of scheming against the king during the tense months of early 1487. The bishop's arrest was ordered by Henry in March, 'ffore certen grete and urgent caases touchynge owre personne and the quietenesse off thys owre realme'. Rather than surrendering peacefully to the royal authorities, Stillington instead sought refuge behind the walls of the University of Oxford.

The king dispatched a letter to the university on 7 March 1487 imploring them to hand over their guest, whom he suspected of 'usyng certan practyses prohybyte by the lawes off holy church, and othere damnabyll conjurecies and conspiraes' to the 'subversione off the universall wole and tranquillyte off thys owre realme'. The university, much to the king's frustration, resisted his command, prompting him to write again on 14 March advising them they would forfeit any royal privileges if they failed to turn over Stillington. A third letter followed on 22 March, in which an exasperated Henry declared all he received from the university were 'pleasaunte answerys and wordys, and none or lytyl effect off dede'. The king, therefore, tersely warned that he had searched through records and had failed to find any franchises or liberties that permitted the university to provide refuge to those stood accused of treason. If they continued to refuse his orders, he would

> ... not only sende thyder such power as oure entent in thys parties shalbe undowtly executed and fulfylled, but also provide for the punishment of your disobeissaunce in such sharpe wyse as shalbe to the ferfull example of them so presumyng or attempting heraftyr.[9]

Judging by these menacing words, it is clear Henry was under considerable strain from the burden of second-guessing the conspiracy growing against him. He was determined to get hold of Stillington, who it was hoped could shine some light on the shadowy plot. The king's sustained intimidation slowly produced results. The university authorities responded that although they wouldn't forcibly hand over the bishop, neither would they use force to defend him. Shortly thereafter, Henry's men moved in and apprehended Stillington with little incident. Regardless of his age, or self-proclaimed feebleness, the bishop was almost certainly interrogated at length by the king's agents and leading councillors, although there isn't any evidence to suggest he was censured further, which may indicate his role in any conspiracy wasn't as significant as suspected, if he was involved at all. After the drama of his flight into Oxford, Stillington, in fact, disappeared thereafter into relative obscurity and remained of little consequence for the remaining few years of his life.

If Henry thought he had made some headway into exposing the conspiracy with Symonds' arrest and Stillington's interrogation, he was to be sorely disappointed. The king's attempts to 'bring his subjects to their senses without armed conflict',[10] as Vergil eloquently wrote, proved in vain, for in March John de la Pole, 1st Earl of Lincoln, abruptly absconded from the royal court and fled abroad to the court of his aunt, Margaret of York. This was a distressing development for Henry and one which caused considerable alarm amongst his council, which had been unprepared for such a damaging defection. Lincoln wasn't merely a lowly priest like Symonds, or a fallen viscount of moderate influence like Lovell, but rather a grandson of Richard, Duke of York, through his mother, and therefore a Yorkist prince of royal blood.

At the time of his flight, John de la Pole was around twenty-five years old and, much like his cousin Warwick, heir to a prestigious legacy on both sides of his family. Whilst he could proudly claim both Yorkist and Lancastrian descent from Edward III through his mother, Lincoln's paternal ancestry was no less impressive, if not quite as royal. His namesake father was the 2nd Duke of Suffolk and himself the heir of William de la Pole, the 1st Duke and a controversial figure who was for a brief period during the late 1440s the most powerful person in the kingdom. His paternal grandmother, meanwhile, was Alice Chaucer, the granddaughter of the renowned fourteenth-century poet commonly lauded as one of the greatest individuals in the history of English literature.

Although created earl of Lincoln as a child by his uncle Edward IV,[11] it was under the reign of another uncle, Richard III, that John de la Pole truly came to prominence. Lincoln supported Richard through his rise to the throne, for which he was handsomely rewarded, receiving revenues worth £509 a year and being appointed president of the Council of the North, effectively filling the influential position his uncle had vacated upon becoming king.[12]

His prospects received another unexpected boost in April 1484 when Richard's sole heir, Edward of Middleham, died aged only ten, for it was Lincoln who was announced to be his cousin's replacement as Lieutenant of Ireland four months later,[13] a post which possibly suggested the king had his de la Pole nephew in mind when considering potential heirs to his throne. The other obvious choice was, of course, Edward, Earl of Warwick, but if Richard overturned the attainder that prohibited Warwick from the line of succession this would raise the complication that the earl possessed a stronger claim to the throne than the king himself, being the son of his elder brother Clarence. There is no solid evidence that Richard ever legally confirmed who was his heir, and one suspects he would have sought to remarry and father more sons had he survived Bosworth Field.

If Lincoln was a leading light in the reign of Richard III, the latter's premature death at Bosworth significantly reduced the earl's prospects. No longer was he riding high in the confidence of his Yorkist uncle, but rather acclimatising to an uncertain future as a minor member on the privy council of a king he had never met before 22 August 1485. Henry VII brought to the throne his own advisors, men that included his own uncle, Jasper Tudor, Duke of Bedford, his stepfather Thomas Stanley, Earl of Derby, and John de Vere, Earl of Oxford, not to mention highly capably churchmen like John Morton, Archbishop of Canterbury, and Reginald Bray, most of whom had fostered a profoundly loyal and intimate relationship with their king whilst languishing in exile.

In the magnanimous, if politically prudent, spirit of reconciliation, Henry had sought not to alienate those Yorkists who freely submitted to his authority, although naturally much of their influence was thereafter diminished. Contrary to what is often supposed, the first Tudor king did not mercilessly extinguish the post-Bosworth remnant of Richard III's administration in a fit of vengeful fury; William Catesby was the only notable victim dispatched on the block. Others such as Lovell and the Stafford brothers fled rather than submitting, as we have seen, whereas the earls of Northumberland and Surrey were imprisoned until the king could be sure of their commitment.

Pragmatists like Lincoln's own father Suffolk, meanwhile, swiftly ingratiated themselves with the new order, as initially did the earl, who even accompanied the Tudor king on his northern progress in 1486 before assuming a prominent role in the christening of Prince Arthur. Lincoln was also handed a role on the king's council, and it was anticipated the earl would gradually settle, if resignedly, into his new role as just one cog amongst many in the fledgling Tudor regime.

Whether Lincoln was truly open to reconciliation at any stage is unclear, but as his actions would show, persisting in such an insignificant role subservient to the men responsible for his uncle's destruction proved unpalatable. It is possible he found himself uncomfortable amongst the veteran Lancastrians and resurgent anti-Richard Yorkists who made up the rest of the king's council. Shortly after attending the council meeting in February 1487, which ordered Warwick's removal from the Tower in response to rumours the boy was in Ireland, Lincoln slipped away from court and fled across the Channel.

What were Lincoln's reasons for abandoning England? If he had intended to rebel against Henry VII from the outset of the reign, then he certainly bided his time, waiting over eighteen months before making his move. He doesn't appear to have come under any obvious suspicion during that time, particularly as he was part of the council meeting in Sheen focused on dealing with the rebel threat, and his defection appears to have surprised the king, who bitterly complained that he had treated the earl with 'greate and sovereygn kyndnes' at 'dyvers sundry tymes'.[14]

The answer must surely lie in Lincoln's own dormant ambition to wear the crown borne by two of his uncles. As the political uncertainty of early 1487 progressed, the earl had probably come to the realisation he could exploit the situation for his own ends. During the council meeting, Lincoln had been privy to the king's strategy to defend his crown, and it's not inconceivable he may have considered the plans put in place as weak, and susceptible to defeat if vigorously tested. Crucially, Lincoln also knew his cousin Warwick remained safely in royal captivity with little likelihood of having his father's attainder overturned, allowing the scheming earl to use the mysterious imposter in Ireland as a smokescreen to conceal his own intentions to challenge for the throne.

Lincoln had witnessed Richard III and Henry VII accede to the throne in unlikely circumstances in the last four years; there was no reason to think he couldn't emulate those men and likewise rise to become King John II. There doesn't appear to be any other justification for his defection than to advance his own Yorkist claim to the throne.

Lincoln's destination of Malines, home of his aunt Margaret of York's court, wasn't by chance, and in fact indicates a plan for the earl's flight had been in place for some time. This is given credence by a detail in a later parliamentary act accusing John Sant, the abbot of Abingdon who had aided the Stafford brothers the previous year, of committing fresh treason in 1487. Part of the case against Sant recounted how the calculating churchman, along with two other Abingdon men named John Mayne and Christopher Swann, had been guilty of 'conspiryng and ymaginyng the destruction of the Kyng' in January 1487 when the trio raised a 'certeyn some of Money' for the 'helpe and ayde' of Lincoln, 'then beyng a great Rebell, Enemy and Traitour'.[15]

If indeed this was the case, that Abbot Sant and his accomplices were fundraising for the earl's cause as early as the turn of the year, and presumably for weeks or even months beforehand, then it suggests Lincoln's defection had been planned in advance of his defection in March, the moment he openly renounced his allegiance to Henry by fleeing.

As the errant earl entered Malines' bustling port, his attention would have been drawn towards the frenzied activity around the waterfront as scores of labourers busied themselves readying a fleet of ships, with blacksmiths clanging back and forth in their red-hot forges amassing a variety of battle-ready weapons. Buoyed by the likes of Francis Lovell, Margaret of York was already preparing an invasion force, a 'grete Navye' which was intended to strike at the very heart of the Tudor regime she so fiercely despised. This wasn't merely an amateur conspiracy fronted by a shadowy Oxfordshire priest named Symonds and an organ maker's son, but rather a heavily funded, full-scale attack on Henry's crown.

It is unclear if the shadowy plot involving rumours of Warwick's presence in Ireland had its origins in Malines, but Lovell, Lincoln, and Margaret were undoubtedly willing to commandeer the conspiracy which was meant to trigger the king's 'Murder, Deth and Destruction'[16] for their own ends. For Henry, meanwhile, despite parading the real Warwick through the streets of London, rumours of a ten-year-old boy in Ireland using the earl's title were only growing with each passing day. Something was undoubtedly afoot. The question that dogged the king in the spring of 1487 is the same one we are still asking over five hundred years later – just who was this boy and where had he come from?

*

Lambert Simnel has entered the historical record as the curious moniker of the enigmatic young figure credited with impersonating the earl of Warwick, yet in early 1487 the royal authorities had little idea about the true identity of this imposter, other than that he was supposedly the son of an Oxford organ maker. In fact, what little we now know of Simnel only comes from official records produced *after* the conspiracy's eventual failure, and as such their veracity has often been questioned.[17]

The act of attainder passed against the earl of Lincoln in the November 1487 parliament offers the first known reference to the pretender by name, probably uncovered through a series of interrogations of those who survived the conspiracy's anticlimactic end, not least the imposter himself. In the act's preamble, Lincoln is accused of reneging on his oath to his 'most naturall Sovereygne' in favour of a certain 'Lambert Symnell, a child of x yere of age, sonne to Thomas Symnell, late of Oxford Joynonre'.[18]

This November act, therefore, differs somewhat from the earlier conclusions drawn by February's Canterbury convocation by asserting Simnel was the son of a joiner rather than an organ maker, though one imagines an accomplished tradesman could conceivably have been proficient in both jobs, perhaps explaining the discrepancy. That Simnel was an organ maker's son is also mentioned in an Irish ballad produced during the year of the conspiracy.[19] On the other hand, Bernard André, the Frenchman widely regarded as Henry VII's official biographer, later speculated that Simnel was the son of 'a miller or a cobbler' who was otherwise 'not worthy' of inclusion in his work.

More curiously, André believed the pretender was not imitating Edward, Earl of Warwick, but rather his cousin Edward V, one of the so-called Princes in the Tower, although he is alone in this allegation and the fact the king specifically paraded Warwick in response can probably be taken as an indicator that the flawed biographer was mistaken.[20] Vergil, meanwhile, noted wryly that the boy was merely of 'ignoble origin'[21] and frustratingly failed to expand further, a rarity for the usually expansive wordsmith. No reference has been found to the boy's mother, and it is uncertain whether this is because she evaded detection from the authorities, was deemed irrelevant, or had died before the rebellion.

The name Lambert Simnel has an air of eccentricity to the modern ear, one which has ensured this peculiar if brief episode in history has riveted generations of scholars and schoolchildren across several centuries. In truth, however, it is not at all unlikely that it was the genuine name of the young child fronting the conspiracy to topple a king.

Although a name of Germanic origin popular in the Netherlands, where the cult of St Lambert was prevalent, there is evidence that Lambert as a given name was used in England throughout the fifteenth century, although admittedly it could hardly be considered common. Lambert Fossedyke was appointed abbot of Croyland Abbey in 1484,[22] for example, whilst there are various references in the Chancery Rolls to Lambert Brancaster of Norfolk, Lambert Salter of Lincoln, Lambert Pevy of Lincolnshire, Lambert Lee of Sussex, and Lambert May, none of whom are referred to as immigrants from across the Channel.[23] Even during Henry VII's reign, there is a certain Lambert Langtree, who in November 1485 was granted the office of bailiff of Buckby in Northamptonshire, ironically part of the earl of Warwick's estate.[24] The Lambert name may even have been derived from the family name of a female ancestor, perhaps his mother's maiden name, and suffice to say there is plenty of evidence for Lambert as a surname during the period.

Simnel, or its variants Symnell and Symnel, is more difficult to pinpoint, but again there is evidence of its presence during the reigns of the early Lancastrian kings. In June 1406, a Roger Symnell brought a suit of felony against another man in the county of Kent, whilst in October 1417, Richard Symnel of Great Stratton, Lincoln, is referred to in the Patent Rolls concerning a small debt he was owed.[25] Considering the scarcity of this name in fifteenth-century records, it is not inconceivable Roger or Richard, or perhaps even both, were ancestors of young Lambert or otherwise related. Most pertinent, however, is the existence of a Thomas Simnel residing in Oxford in 1479, where he rented property from Osney Abbey – surely this is the very same man referred to in the parliamentary act.[26]

Based on the name Lambert Simnel, therefore, we cannot say with certainty that the boy in Ireland had his origins across the English Channel as is often suspected, and he may very well have been English, born and raised. Matters are however further complicated by an anonymous herald's report written within a few years of the conspiracy's conclusion, in which the pretender's Christian name was given as John.[27]

Provided this herald was an eyewitness to the capture of the pretender in the summer of 1487, one must afford a considerable degree of credibility to his statement. It was these messengers who were specifically charged with recording all relevant information relating to major exploits of their masters, such as battles, where they were expected to gather an accurate list of the participants and to identify the dead. On the other hand, one cannot discount the possibility the child nervously offered the name John out of fear for his life, and only subsequently revealed his true identity as Lambert Simnel later down the line, particularly as John doesn't reoccur in records thereafter. One could even speculate that the boy simply proffered the name of the man who had led the conspiracy, namely John de la Pole, Earl of Lincoln. Unfortunately, the name of this child will never be confirmed, but if one accepts him to have been an imposter as must be considered the likelihood, then there is no reason the name Lambert Simnel should be discounted as genuine.

As for the child's place of origin, Oxford makes a compelling case on several counts. During the 1480s, the city was a bustling metropolis populated by a diverse community which regenerated every university year with a new intake of scholars drawn from around the country and, in some instances, the continent. Littered with colleges, churches and several striking timber-framed houses, Oxford would have been an exciting place for any young child to grow up, offering endless possibilities to rub shoulders in the lively streets and narrow lanes with the finest intellectual minds of the period, many bringing with them extensive connections with those of wealth and status. Lincoln, St Mary's, St Bernard's, All Souls' and Magdalen colleges were all founded during the fifteenth century, whilst in 1478 the city's first book was printed. As an upwardly mobile settlement with a burgeoning economy, there would also have been considerable work for a tradesman proficient in skills such as joinery or organ-making, and this opportunity may have attracted the Simnel family to the city if they were not already native residents.

It is perhaps more than coincidence that Oxford was relatively close to three other places of note, specifically Abingdon, Minster Lovell, and Ewelme, which may have brought the boy Simnel into more prestigious, if conspiratorial, circles. Abingdon, just seven miles south of Oxford, was already associated with rebellion during the reign of Henry VII through its connections with Abbot John Sant and the Stafford brothers, whilst Minster Lovell, ancestral home of Francis Lovell, was fourteen miles to the west. Ewelme, meanwhile, thirteen miles south-east, was recognised as the family seat of the de la Poles. Oxford, of course, was also where Bishop Robert Stillington was arrested in March 1487. If we can't comprehensively reject Lambert Simnel as the authentic name of the child at the forefront of the 1487 conspiracy to unseat Henry VII, then neither can we discount Oxford as his home, easily accessible as it was from the Oxfordshire residences of those plotting against their king.

So, accepting the likelihood that in the mid-1480s there was a child of around ten years old named Lambert Simnel living in Oxford, who most certainly wasn't the captive earl of Warwick, how did he become an integral part of an international plot to unseat the first Tudor monarch? The key to the conspiracy, it would seem, is the priest Symonds. Unfortunately, as with Simnel, there are some inconsistencies in the historical record that frustratingly obscure the truth surrounding the origins of the entire matter.

The convocation which took place in February 1487 clearly confirms a twenty-eight-year-old priest named William Symonds admitted transporting a child across to Ireland. This priest was subsequently imprisoned in the Tower of London on Archbishop Morton's request. Polydore Vergil, however, has the priest's name as Richard Simons, or Symonds in the original Latin text, 'a lowborn priest' who was 'as cunning as he was corrupt'. In Vergil's account, it was at Oxford this priest 'evolved a villainous deed' by which he hoped to 'trouble the country's tranquillity', coaching Simnel courtly manners 'so that if ever he should pretend the lad to be of royal descent people would the more readily believe it and have absolute trust in the bold deceit'.

Vergil also credited Symonds with changing the boy's name to Edward, after it was 'popularly rumoured' that the earl of Warwick had been murdered in the Tower of London, before departing to Ireland where he widely proclaimed the boy to be the real earl. Dates are not included in the account, so frustratingly we are unsure precisely when these events occurred.[28] It is crucial to note, of course, that Vergil was writing using second-hand knowledge recalled more than twenty years later, and the Italian would only have been able to record what he was told, accurate or not.

Why the discrepancy between the two accounts? Could Richard and William have been the same person, and either the convocation or Vergil were mistaken? Perhaps Richard and William Symonds were brothers, with one captured in February and the other after the battle in June? What is odd about the priest theory, other than the troubling inconsistency regarding name, capture and timeline, is that it seems highly improbable a lowly churchman was capable of initiating such a comprehensive conspiracy on his lonesome, a scheme which involved educating a tradesman's child to such an extent he could satisfactorily impersonate a royal prince. Whilst bishops, deans or royal chaplains would encounter royalty or members of the upper nobility on a regular basis, is it conceivable a priest of little standing would possess the knowledge to carry through such an exhaustive tuition? If it was so easy for a mere priest to train an imposter to such an acceptable standard, why wasn't Symonds' scheme emulated several times over until successful?

Curiously, there is no record of a priest or clerk under either name in the Patent Rolls for the previous or following decade,[29] nor in a comprehensive biographical list of English clergymen between 1300 and 1542,[30] and there doesn't appear to be any other tangible evidence for Symonds' existence. André makes no specific mention of Symonds, or even a priest for that matter, although, as we have seen, his understanding of the plot differs somewhat from other records. It wouldn't, therefore, be preposterous to suggest that the priest may never have existed, and in fact was the product of a form of legal fiction on behalf of the royal authorities.

By February 1487, King Henry was under considerable strain from a conspiracy that was clearly afoot around the fringes of his kingdom, and authoritative action had to be taken. To be perceived as a weak or hesitant sovereign was not an option. Can we therefore discount the idea that the king and his council, with the willing cooperation of the convocation of Canterbury, devised the idea of Priest Symonds to allow them to put forth the impression they had the matter under control by spreading news of his supposed capture? Noticeably, the pretender was not named by the convocation, and remained anonymous until he was received into royal hands after the conspiracy's eventual failure. One would expect the priest, through fair means or foul, to have given up such details, if indeed he did exist.

Archbishop Morton was certainly a man capable of fabricating such a deception, having proved particularly calculating during the turmoil of 1483 when he persuaded his captor the duke of Buckingham to turn on Richard III. It had also been Morton who supposedly requested 'Symonds' be moved into the vast Tower of London once his testimony had been heard during the convocation, and one must wonder if this apparent transfer was recorded so that the priest, or at least the spectre of the priest, could fade into obscurity without further scrutiny. If we trust Vergil's account, however, Symonds was not in the Tower in February but later captured after the Battle of Stoke Field in June, and only escaped execution on account of his holy orders.[31] There is no record of this priest thereafter in any account, the presumption often being he was imprisoned for life.

If the priest did exist and was indeed entangled in this confusing web of conspiracy from its inception, then he surely had considerable financial and intellectual backing from the outset and was at best a trivial cog in a far bigger wheel of intrigue. It would not have been cheap to educate and attire a child in the manner befitting a prince, nor to sustain his daily upkeep over several months, perhaps even years. As well as Latin, French, and an enhanced understanding of theological matters, Lambert Simnel would also have been trained how to act in several different social situations, how to respond when questioned about any topic relating to his rank, and how to carry himself so that he always appeared of undeniable royal pedigree whenever seen in public.

Simnel would surely have also undergone intensive genealogical tutelage with regards to his supposed Yorkist relations, with an expectation he could recall details that the real Warwick would know as second nature. This is all information that had to come from someone far closer to royal circles than a rural priest. Furthermore, funds had to be raised for the child to be transported into the north-west of England and across the Irish Sea, and this had to come from someone with greater wealth than a mere churchman of little status and no discernible income.

In this last matter, perhaps Lincoln or Lovell were covertly funding Simnel's training using their Oxfordshire connections, not to mention Margaret of York who may have been channelling resources across the Channel from her Burgundian base. The man most likely overseeing the plot on the ground was the tireless Abbot John Sant, the Yorkist diplomat who had already fallen foul of Henry for conspiring with the Staffords, just as he would once more two years later.

At such a distance of time, it is unlikely we will ever have the answers we so desperately seek as to the precise identity of Lambert Simnel and William/Richard Symonds, if the latter did indeed exist. There is enough reason to suppose, however, that Simnel was an Oxford youth exploited by regionally significant figures like Sant, Lovell, and Lincoln to provoke national revolution in the name of Warwick, who languished in the Tower.

As the summer of 1487 approached, Henry VII did not have the luxury of musing upon such matters. His kingdom and his life were under serious threat, and the enigmatic boy purporting to be the true Yorkist heir was rapidly gaining support and acceptance across the Irish Sea. Messengers now brought tidings to the king that the earl of Lincoln and Francis Lovell had openly allied themselves to the pretender's cause. The conspiracy was gathering pace. A storm was coming Henry's way, and it carried with it Irish and German soldiers primed to conquer England.

6

A Mad Dance

Fifteenth-century Ireland was a fractious and complex land bitterly divided along geopolitical and ethnic grounds amongst three groups: the native Irish families, the assimilated descendants of Anglo-Norman settlers, and later English royal officials. All frequently feuded with each other in an endless struggle for supremacy over the island's governance.[1]

By the time Henry VII acceded to the English throne in 1485, the native Irish had long suffered at the hands of their more powerful continental neighbours, from partial Viking settlement in the ninth century to a series of relentless invasions by the Angevin king of England Henry II in 1172 to impose his overlordship, the latter bringing significant integration with not only the English, but also people of Welsh, Flemish and Breton backgrounds.

Although the island never fell under the complete sovereignty of the English kings, despite their assertion since 1177 to be *Dominus Hiberniae*, or Lord of Ireland, by the late fifteenth century the complicated political landscape was largely dominated by several influential Anglo-Irish families who governed Ireland on behalf of the English king and to the exclusion of the frustrated native Irish. These Anglo-Irish lords, not quite as Irish as the native Gaelic-speaking tribes but neither considered wholly English due to their widespread adoption of local customs and culture, comprised some of the foremost dynasties living in Ireland throughout the fifteenth century, including the FitzGeralds, the Burkes, the Talbots, the FitzMaurices and the Butlers. They largely held territory directly in and around Dublin, a rectangular strip of land known as the Pale, with some estates stretching south-west through the heart of the island and covering bustling towns such as Limerick, Cork and Waterford. They existed, not always so peacefully, alongside prominent Irish clans such as the O'Briens, O'Reillys, O'Neills and Mac Carthy Mors.

Several Anglo-Irishmen also boasted titles in the Irish peerage, which owed fealty to the English crown. The Butlers had held the earldom of Ormond since 1328, and two branches of the FitzGeralds were in possession of the earldoms of Kildare and Desmond, to name the most prominent examples. The principal heads of the House of York, meanwhile, in their capacity as hereditary earls of Ulster through their Mortimer and de Burgh forebears, held estates in the most north-easterly reaches of Ireland which they retained after acceding to the English throne in 1461. The rest of the island, such as the extreme west and south-west which bordered the Atlantic Ocean, along with the remainder of the north and north-west, much of it covered in bogs and woodland, were still in the hands of the native Irish and for the most part ruled autonomously outside the direct influence of the Anglo-Irish.

When one accounts for the destabilising feuding which often erupted between various Anglo-Irish families eager to exert their dominance over one another, Ireland proved anything but straightforward for successive English kings to govern. For Henry VII, in particular, the island would prove a problematic arena throughout the first decade of his reign, owing partly to lingering loyalties to the House of York. In 1487, this fidelity to the White Rose was resurrected in a most dramatic, and volatile, fashion.

Direct English royal involvement in the affairs of Ireland had greatly diminished as the fifteenth century progressed, largely due to the significant distractions of the failing war in France and the bitter internecine conflict between the houses of York and Lancaster which followed thereafter. Few English kings visited Ireland, with no incumbent sovereign completing the short sea crossing since Richard II in the final years of the preceding century. Before that, one must go back to King John's firm-handed campaign in 1210.

The island was typically perceived by the English court to be a wild and uncivilised outpost, home to a barbaric people better ruled on behalf of the king by a Dublin-based lieutenant, who in turn generally delegated his duties to a deputy drawn from the ranks of the Anglo-Irish. These lords, despite their assimilation and appropriation of Irish customs, never wavered in their determination to serve the interests of the crown, and willingly clutched at such opportunities to wield power over their compatriots. One Englishman who didn't neglect Ireland, however, albeit through political necessity as much as personal sentiment, was Richard, Duke of York.

Through his mother Anne Mortimer, York was the grandson of Roger Mortimer, 4th Earl of March, from whom he inherited the extensive Mortimer estates and titles in north-eastern Ireland after the death of his childless cousin Edmund Mortimer, 5th Earl of March. This impressive inheritance included the earldom of Ulster and the lordships of Connacht and Trim, centred around vast, imposing fortresses such as Carrickfergus. In a barely concealed attempt by the leading figures of the Lancastrian court to politically exclude the duke from interfering in matters of English governance, in 1447 the pliable Henry VI appointed York lieutenant of Ireland for a period of ten years, a post the duke reluctantly assumed in person two years later.

Once settled across the sea, York worked assiduously to quell the persistent unrest in Ireland and succeeded in securing the submission of the native Irish in Ulster and Leinster. It was a strategy which partly protected his own ancestral estates from devastating raids and which further helped bolster his political standing in England, where the Lancastrian regime, fronted by the dukes of Suffolk and Somerset, was incurring scathing criticism from all quarters for its handling, amongst other matters, of the war in France. News of York's exploits was energetically spread throughout England by his supporters, with one overly-optimistic report boasting that within twelve months 'the wildest Irishman in Ireland shall be sworn English'.[2] It was a fanciful prediction that was simply unfeasible, but nonetheless such bold propaganda on behalf of the duke of York only served to enhance his growing reputation amongst the English commons as a man in whom the entire governance of England should be entrusted.

Although York returned to the English political scene in 1450, he retained significant personal support in Ireland; after he was attainted in 1459 for raising an army against his Lancastrian rivals near Ludlow, it was across the Irish Sea the duke pointedly sought refuge rather than Calais, where his son Edward had fled with his Neville kinsmen, the earls of Salisbury and Warwick. The Irish parliament quickly confirmed York in his post as lieutenant, in defiance of the attainder recently passed by their English counterpart, and when a messenger arrived from across the sea carrying orders for the duke's arrest, the hapless herald was promptly executed for breaching Irish law rather than enforcing English.

York returned to England in September 1460, but before the year was out the mighty duke was ambushed by a shrewd Lancastrian force and butchered outside Sandal Castle in Yorkshire. His strapping eighteen-year-old son stepped into his father's shoes as the 4th Duke of York, and within three months had acceded to the English throne as the first Yorkist king of England, Edward IV. With regards to Ireland, the young king retained the core of his father's support, although just like England the island was plagued by its own factional discord throughout the 1450s and 1460s. Feuding amongst the Anglo-Irish lords was nothing new as they regularly clashed over control of the Irish government, but in the aftermath of Richard of York's downfall the principal houses assumed opposing sides in the escalating Lancaster–York conflict across the water.

The Butler family pledged themselves fervently to the cause of Henry VI, firstly under James Butler, 5th Earl of Ormond in Ireland and 1st Earl of Wiltshire in England, and after his execution in May 1461 under his surviving siblings John and Thomas. The Butlers were bitterly opposed by the Yorkist-aligned FitzGeralds, one branch of which was fronted by the earl of Desmond and another by the earl of Kildare. In the spring of 1462, an army led by John Butler encountered another commanded by Thomas FitzGerald, 7th Earl of Desmond, on a field outside Piltown, a usually serene setting on the banks of the River Suir around twelve miles upstream from Waterford.

The ensuing battle was the only skirmish of the Wars of the Roses to take place in Ireland, with the Butlers comprehensively defeated by Desmond's forces, a victory for which the latter was rewarded by an appreciative Edward IV with the deputy lieutenancy. His supremacy was to be short-lived, however. In 1467, Desmond was replaced by the ferocious Englishman John Tiptoft, Earl of Worcester, who ordered Desmond's arrest and summary execution for liaising too closely with the Gaelic Irish chieftains. With the Butlers and Desmond FitzGeralds politically neutralised, it was the opportunistic Kildare branch of the FitzGeralds which sought to fill the void vacated by the downfall of their Anglo-Irish brethren.[3]

From the imposing family seat at Maynooth Castle, Thomas FitzGerald, 7th Earl of Kildare, had served as deputy lieutenant for a brief period under Richard of York, and although attainted alongside his cousin Desmond in 1468 he had managed to reverse the judgment passed against him by York's son Edward IV by passionately pleading his case in person. It was a reprieve which would have far-reaching consequences for a future English king, Henry VII, just under two decades later. The Kildare earls' rise was steady once they renewed their relationship with the House of York, with the 7th Earl restored as Irish deputy in 1470, serving until his death seven years later. Perhaps crucially for future events, this lengthy tenure occurred under the nominal lieutenancy of Edward IV's brother George, Duke of Clarence, bonding the FitzGeralds to Clarence, and in time his son Edward, Earl of Warwick.

The 7th Earl's heir was Gerald FitzGerald, a headstrong figure later described by various sixteenth-century English writers as 'open and plain, hardly able to rule himself when he were moved to anger' and a man of no great wit 'without great knowledge or learning, but rudely brought up according to the usage of his country'.[4] These English scribes may have been harsh in their assessment of Kildare, for there are grounds to believe he was an above-average horseman who enjoyed the noble pursuits of hunting and hawking, and was quite possibly proficient not only in English and Gaelic but French and Latin.[5] The 8th Kildare may not have been as cultured as many within the ranks of English nobility, but he was hardly a barbarian as later writers would have it. He was also well placed, by pedigree, property and personality, to govern Ireland competently on behalf of the House of York, rather than stand in its way.

The strength of Kildare's character became evident shortly after inheriting his father's earldom and position as justiciar of Ireland when Edward IV overlooked the young earl for the post of deputy lieutenant, preferring instead to appoint an Englishman named Henry Grey, 4th Baron Grey of Codnor. When Grey crossed the Irish Sea at the end of the summer of 1478 to assume the office, however, he encountered a somewhat frosty welcome from the locals. Led by the bold Kildare, several Anglo-Irish lords refused to recognise Grey's authority and prevented him from accessing his quarters in Dublin Castle by destroying the drawbridge spanning the broad moat. Rowland FitzEustace, 1st Baron Portlester, who happened to be Kildare's father-in-law, even refused to hand over the Great Seal of Ireland, impeding state business as part of a concerted campaign of non-cooperation.

The resulting stand-off between Grey and Kildare, with both men even hosting their own parliaments, created an untenable situation that forced Edward IV to intervene and summon his discordant subjects to London to settle the issue. Surprisingly, it was Kildare, the king's 'right trusty and wellbeloved cosyn', who emerged from the summit holding the post of deputy lieutenant, a role in which he was confirmed later that year during the English parliament.[6] He would not only retain the role until Edward's death in 1483, but also throughout the brief reigns of Edward V and Richard III, ultimately serving three successive Yorkist kings with little further incident.

When it became apparent Henry Tudor was primed to make a move on Richard's throne, Kildare was nothing if not prudent in ensuring his political survival regardless of the outcome of this latest tug-of-war over the English crown. He used his sway with the Irish parliament to ratify his position as justiciar of Ireland, an office over which no English parliament or king had legal right to determine, and protected himself in the process from the menace posed by a Butler resurgence should Tudor emerge victorious.

As it transpired, after his victory at Bosworth, Henry VII was preoccupied early on in his reign with learning the ropes of kingship, and like his Yorkist predecessors proved content to permit Kildare to continue his ascendancy over Irish politics for the foreseeable future. In March 1486, the earl was formally reappointed deputy lieutenant, serving for the first time not under a Yorkist lieutenant but a Lancastrian one in the king's resilient uncle, Jasper Tudor, Duke of Bedford. Kildare's younger brother Thomas FitzGerald, meanwhile, was also confirmed in his post as lord chancellor of Ireland, handing the family clear supremacy over their compatriots.

There was a distant familial connection between the FitzGeralds and the Tudors of which both parties were possibly aware, sharing mutual descent from the late eleventh-century king of Deheubarth Rhys ap Tewdwr, who once ruled a kingdom which comprised much of modern-day West Wales. That said, the FitzGeralds's recent allegiance had unmistakably been to the House of York, and when a fine youth of apparent noble bearing landed in Ireland purporting to be the earl of Warwick, Kildare and his impressionable affinity were quick to pledge their support. Disingenuously sponsored by figures of the calibre of Lincoln and Lovell, there was little reason they shouldn't believe this boy was the grandson of Richard of York.

If Henry VII had been propelled towards the throne on a wave of support from large parts of Edward IV's former affinity, why did the earl of Kildare, his chancellor brother Thomas FitzGerald, and many other Anglo-Irish lords so readily declare for the child it was now claimed was Warwick? Aside from the obvious issue of self-preservation arising from fear the Tudor king would remove them from their posts when he had the opportunity, the answer surely has much to do with Warwick's father, George, Duke of Clarence.

It was during Richard of York's tenure as lieutenant of Ireland that his duchess, Cecily Neville, gave birth to George within the confines of Dublin Castle, the early thirteenth-century fortress that served as a palpable reminder of English royal supremacy on the eastern Irish coast. Kildare's maternal grandfather James FitzGerald, 6th Earl of Desmond, and James Butler, 4th Earl of Ormond, had even been present at the child's baptism. Sponsoring the son of an Irish-born duke descended from traditional Anglo-Irish families such as the de Burghs and de Lacys, therefore, was without question an appealing proposition for Kildare and his allies, not dissimilar to the support the Welsh-born Henry VII had been able to garner during his march through Wales on the way to Bosworth.

Edward of Warwick, it would seem, was quite simply Irish enough to be claimed by men like Kildare as one of their own, a cause worth supporting for the opportunities it could bring their way if successful. Whether they ever considered the fact that their Warwick was not, in fact, Warwick at all is open to debate. If there was any doubt in their minds after they were presented to the youth, then they didn't betray their feelings openly.[7]

It must also be remembered that a new regime invariably brought new ideas and new men, and Kildare, effectively ruler of Ireland for much of the later reign of Edward IV, was ambitious enough to resist being squeezed out of power once the Tudor regime became firmly esablished. In supporting Lambert Simnel, or rather Warwick as he likely believed the boy to be, the earl was simply making a pre-emptive strike against a king he remained unsure of. To Kildare and his allies, it made perfect sense.

*

By late spring 1487, the conspiracy in Ireland focused around the beguiling figure of Lambert Simnel was steadily developing into a well-organised movement. Although specific details are frustratingly scarce, it is clear the child was readily accepted by the local authorities and lords as none other than Edward, Earl of Warwick, and there are understandable reasons for this. Considering the distance from the royal court in London, the Anglo-Irish lords were less familiar with court customs and etiquette that could have exposed the imposter, not to mention any physical variances from the actual Warwick, such as height, weight or other features which may have been noticed by an informed observer.

That the child in Dublin purporting to be the earl enjoyed the support of figures such as the earl of Lincoln, Warwick's own cousin, and Francis Lovell, widely known to have faithfully served two previous Yorkist kings, would have helped persuade most of the impressionable Anglo-Irish lords of his credibility. There is little reason not to accept that, to a man, they believed they were about to play an integral role in returning the Irish-blooded descendants of Richard of York to the English throne, and in the process topple a Welsh-born usurper of whom they had no personal knowledge. In short, they were duped.

The Anglo-Irish weren't the only party recruited to the mounting conspiracy, however. Through the far-reaching agency of Margaret of York, Lincoln and Lovell were able to procure the much-sought-after services of several thousand southern German and Swiss mercenaries under the command of the highly competent colonel Martin Schwartz. How did Schwartz, a self-assured military veteran originating from the Swabian city of Augsburg, enter the picture at this late stage, far from his homeland? Margaret, it would seem, petitioned her stepson-in-law Maximilian I, recently elected King of the Romans and one of the most influential figures on the continent, to assist her nephew Lincoln, and his response was to turn to Schwartz, most recently active in adeptly suppressing a rebellion in Flanders.

Maximilian had assumed control of what remained of the Burgundian inheritance after the death of his wife Mary as their heir Philip was still a minor, but the king faced considered resistance from the Flemish who feared he would reverse their favourable trading terms and terminate much of the economic and political autonomy they enjoyed under the duchess.

In June 1483, several Flemish cities united to form a regency council, which they declared would govern the County of Flanders in the name of young Philip, who was in their possession at the time, rather than be ruled by Maximilian. The authorities of Ghent, meanwhile, provocatively started minting their own coins bearing only the name of the child duke, with no reference to his Hapsburg father.

Maximilian was even humiliatingly deposed as head of the Order of the Golden Fleece, the prestigious Burgundian equivalent to England's Order of the Garter, and barred from entering Bruges with more than a dozen companions. He did, however, retain the support of other parts of the Burgundian Netherlands, and in 1485 resorted to military force to ruthlessly crush the rebellious Flemish cities over the next eighteen months. It was a brutal campaign in which he enlisted the rapacious Martin Schwartz and his mercenary troops.[8]

Schwartz's men were so efficient, if perhaps overzealous, in defeating Maximilian's enemies they were soon handed a fresh assignment, one that would remove them from Flanders where they had gradually become disorderly. It was a mission that would see them depart for Ireland to bolster the dissident Yorkist forces that had started to assemble in Dublin. An arrangement was struck between Schwartz and Margaret of York, with the German colonel handed a commission to supply up to two thousand soldiers, with money provided to procure several ships filled with wagons of weapons and food.[9]

Schwartz's mercenaries were known in their homelands as *Landsknechts*, or 'servant of the country', and were well-trained and heavily disciplined soldiers who had already cultivated a formidable and not wholly unmerited continent-wide reputation in the first few years of their existence. An archetypal *Landsknecht* regiment was largely comprised of robust pikemen bearing halberds upon their shoulders that could measure up to eight feet in length, ably supported by foot-soldiers known as *Zweihänder*. As the name suggested, these soldiers bore hefty two-handed swords providing considerable reach and power in close-combat situations, a scenario in which the strikingly attired *Landsknecht* often excelled.

Once recruited by Schwartz and his captains, the soldiers were compelled to agree to a strict code of conduct known as articles of war, which typically specified they would not flee from the enemy, burn or pillage towns without orders, harm women, children, the elderly or priests, or conduct martial meetings without the permission of their senior officer. Whilst in camp, it was imperative that good relations between the soldiers was fostered, with drinking and gambling to be kept within bounds to prevent any disruptive issues arising. Religious devotions, meanwhile, were always strictly adhered to. The result was a close-knit, well-behaved brotherhood focused solely on the task they had been set, a valuable resource for any master willing to pay the mercenaries' not insignificant wages.[10]

It is not documented when precisely Lincoln, Lovell and the *Landsknechts* departed for Dublin from the court of Margaret of York, but it is known the motley crew arrived in the Irish capital on 5 May after around a fortnight at sea, evident from two letters written by Henry VII. The first was written to the authorities of York on 4 May cautioning them he had 'certain knowleige in sundry wise that our rebelles bene departid out of Flaundres and goon westwardes',[11] followed by a second to Thomas Butler, 7th Earl of Ormond, chamberlain to the queen, in which the king confidently advised he had 'tidings that our rebels landed the fifth day of his month in our land of Ireland'.[12]

The troubled English king had not been inactive himself during this period, and, 'deeply provoked' by Lincoln's defection and the 'rashness of the Irish', pledged to 'prosecute his enemies openly and revenge by force the wrongs they had done him'.[13] Henry had intended his reign to be one which put an end to the civil wars which preceded it, and he was not taking this threat from overseas lightly.

On 4 March 1487, the king handed a commission to Thomas Brandon, the brother of his fallen standard bearer at Bosworth, to take command of an armed force mustered to 'proceed to sea against the king's enemies there cruising', whilst on 7 April an extensive commission of array was handed to the duke of Suffolk, earl of Oxford, and forty-three other persons to raise men to defend the eastern coastal counties of Suffolk, Norfolk and Essex. They were also ordered by a 'special injunction to cause to be repaired and well guarded the beacons on the sea-coast, for forewarning the people of that country of the advent of the king's enemies'. Two days later, a payment of £44 15s was made to William White, recorder of Waterford, for 'certain provisions for the security and safe custody' of the south-eastern Irish city in anticipation of any attempted landing or attack in the area.[14]

Henry was embarking on a progress around East Anglia at this time, and Polydore Vergil mentions that whilst visiting Bury St Edmunds the king was informed that Thomas Grey, Marquis of Dorset and the queen's untrustworthy half-brother, was approaching the royal camp. Henry, who remained unsure of Dorset's commitment to his cause, suspected the marquis of having connections to the conspiracy and ordered him arrested by the earl of Oxford as a precaution. Dorset was taken away from the king's presence and placed in the Tower of London, ironically where the genuine earl of Warwick was dwelling under close guard.[15] Henry was taking no chances, even with his closest in-laws.

The king celebrated Easter that year in Norwich, arriving in the principal city of East Anglia on 10 April.[16] His destination may not have been coincidence. Lying just over a hundred miles north-east of London, Norwich was within reasonable distance of the vast eastern coastline along which Henry must have initially anticipated his enemies would attempt to land. It was also located near to the duke of Suffolk's ancestral lands.

Although Henry doesn't seem to have suspected the duke himself of colluding with the rebels, as shown from his inclusion in the commissions of array, it could not be overlooked that Suffolk was nevertheless father of the traitorous earl of Lincoln, and the king would have been foolish not to personally inspect the region for any palpable evidence there was support for the earl's actions. One can only wonder at the awkwardness of the conversation that passed between Henry and Suffolk over the next few days, as the king undoubtedly grumbled about the duke's wayward son. Suffolk, presumably, could only offer apologies in response whilst reiterating his own loyalty.

On 12 April, which was Maundy Thursday, the king fulfilled his religious devotions by providing alms to the poor and washing the feet of the poor before marking Easter weekend with a myriad of services in the city's striking cathedral, topped so spectacularly with an imposing stone spire that had only been finished seven years earlier. The royal retinue decamped from Norwich before 17 April and moved on to Walsingham, where the king 'prayed devoutly before the image of the Blessed Virgin Mary' so that he 'might be preserved from the wiles of his enemies'.[17]

Thereafter, the king travelled westwards, passing through Thetford, Cambridge, Huntingdon, and Northampton before reaching Coventry on 22 April. Finally, on 9 May, the royal cavalcade reached its destination at Kenilworth Castle, a vast, palatial fortress in the heart of the kingdom that was particularly associated with Henry's Lancastrian forebears, having been extensively remodelled by his great-great-grandfather John of Gaunt and where his half-uncle Henry VI had frequently withdrawn with his queen Margaret of Anjou during the factional discord of the mid-to-late 1450s. It was both a safe haven and a lavish retreat where the king could temporarily unwind, with sprawling lands that could cater for the growing army that was starting to assemble around their sovereign.

Why the move inland? Through means unknown, Henry must have gathered sufficient intelligence that the rebels in Flanders had finally boarded their ships and sailed out into the English Channel. Rather than heading directly for the East Anglian coast as anticipated, however, they had instead navigated westwards along the south coast with little indication they were planning to make landfall any time soon. Uncertain of their destination, the prudent decision was taken by Henry to withdraw into the centre of his kingdom from where he could prepare for all eventualities, particularly as he was now confident there was little threat of revolt in Norfolk and Suffolk. A letter written in May from Oxburgh by Edmund Bedingfield demonstrated Henry enjoyed support in the region, for the Norfolk knight faithfully boasted to his kinsman John Paston he was prepared to serve the king and his lord the earl of Oxford 'to the uttermust off my powere'.[18]

From Kenilworth, therefore, Henry was ideally positioned to confront the rebels once they landed, wheresoever that may be in his kingdom. It was, incidentally, a similar strategy to that which Richard III had adopted two years earlier when preparing anxiously for Henry's landing, akin to a spider in the centre of its web. The Tudor king's seriousness regarding the anticipated invasion was evident in his failure to attend the customary St George's Day festivities at Windsor, upsetting the duke of Suffolk and Lord Maltravers by heading directly to the Midlands instead.[19]

During his journey to Kenilworth from Norfolk, Henry received further intelligence of the rebels' whereabouts, and on 4 May he instructed Thomas Rotherham, Archbishop of York, to urgently broadcast news of a papal bull granted by Pope Innocent VIII, which threatened those who disputed Henry's royal title with excommunication:

> And for diverce causes us moving we pray and require you that ye woll do the bulle of censures graunted by oure holy fadre the pope to be denunced and executed solemnly with all spede and dyligence and with all serimonies and circumstaunce, alswell in te abbey of Fourneis as in the priory of Cartmail, wherin ye shall singerly please us.[20]

The specific mention of Furness Abbey and Cartmel Priory, both on the Lancashire coast, was an indication that Henry fully anticipated the north-west to be targeted by his enemies, or at the very least to be an area ripe for rebellion. He may even have received his information from a double agent operating on the periphery of the conspiracy. The papal bull was duly published on the orders of Archbishop Rotherham, emphatically invoking the authority of Pope Innocent to warn that anyone 'that makes or laburs to make such new trowbles commocions or stirryngs' would 'from the sight of almyghty god and the holy company of hevyn' be cast out and forever damned in the eyes of the Church.[21]

On the same date, Henry had also written from his base in Coventry to William Todd, Mayor of York, advising that he had 'certain knowleige in sundry wise that our rebelles bene departid out of Flaundres and goon westwardes'.[22] By 13 May he was able to write confidently to Ormond that he now knew for certain his enemies had reached Ireland. His decision to move towards the centre of England, therefore, had proved correct.

Across the Irish Sea, Lincoln, Lovell and Schwartz were indeed in Dublin, and readying themselves for a second sea journey in a month. This time, their destination was England, and they were vigorously rousing their collective retinues for the tough mission ahead. Bolstering their numbers were men such as Richard Harleston, a former governor of Jersey, and the Cornish knight Henry Bodrugan, an inveterate troublemaker who had been pardoned by Edward IV in 1472 for 'outlawry', attainted in 1474 for 'divers treasons, riots and felonies', and pardoned again for unspecified offences in 1479, possibly piracy or corruption.[23] According to the parliamentary attainder later passed against the conspirators, another twenty-five Englishmen were also suspected of joining the growing plot around this period.[24]

Increasingly visible at the forefront of the entire enterprise were the 8th Earl of Kildare and his brother Thomas FitzGerald. The latter appears to have assumed a more hands-on role in the conspiracy, even resigning his chancellorship to dedicate himself to a cause he hoped would bring rewards beyond his wildest expectations. It wasn't every day a figure like FitzGerald was gifted the opportunity to help make a king. If Margaret of York brought German and Swiss mercenaries to the pretender's cause, then Kildare was responsible for the enthusiastic recruitment of Irish troops, most notably hundreds of *kerns*, lightly armed footmen treasured for their speed and mobility if not their vulnerability to attack, and *gallóglaigh*, or gallowglass, a heavily trained mercenary band of soldiers lauded for their fighting skills.

When Henry VII was exiled in Brittany during 1483, he fomented support for his cause by pledging a Christmas Day oath in front of the altar at Rennes Cathedral that he would wed Elizabeth of York once safely upon the throne. Around the same period, Henry, then merely an attainted earl of Richmond who had been absent from England for a dozen years, also presumptuously adopted the style of king in any letters he dispatched, and quite probably in person as well. The rebels assembled in Dublin during those tense days in May 1487 went one step further.

On 24 May 1487, most likely within the aged Norman stone walls of the Cathedral of the Holy Trinity in the very heart of Dublin, the child known to history as Lambert Simnel was led in procession through the hushed nave to a throne that had been placed before the altar. Although it is unclear who had made the decision to crown Simnel as the latest king to bear the name Edward, the ceremony was attended by the foremost figures involved in the conspiracy, including Lincoln, Lovell and Kildare. It was presided over by Walter FitzSimon,

Archbishop of Dublin, with assistance from the bishops of Meath, Kildare and Cloyne. The archbishops of Armagh, Tuam and Cashel, along with the bishops of Clogher and Ossory, meanwhile, remained neutral, with Armagh, an Italian named Ottaviano, later recalling how he had personally incurred the wrath of Lincoln for refusing to participate in the coronation to the point he had feared for his life.

Observing events closely were scores of abbots and priors drawn from throughout the isle, as well as most of the Anglo-Irish gentry who appeared content to follow the FitzGeralds' lead.[25] One lord who did not accept the boy-pretender as his king, however, was Nicholas St Lawrence, 4th Baron Howth. As stepson to Joan Beaufort, daughter of Edmund Beaufort, 2nd Duke of Somerset, he was probably influenced by feelings of kinship to the Beaufort-descended English king, and contemptuously regarded the plot to create a king in Dublin as 'but a mad dance'.[26]

Some of what we know about events in Ireland during this period is taken from the *Book of Howth*, a later sixteenth-century eulogy of the St Lawrence family that must, naturally, be interpreted with caution, particularly as the 4th Baron was a notable opponent to the conspiracy. Nevertheless, the book is one of the few detailed near-contemporary sources available, and, according to the author, 'There in Dublinge in Ireland they proclaimed this child King of England, being borne and sitting upon Darsey's shoulders to be seen of all men, for that Darsey was then the highest.'[27]

A second, more detailed contemporary account of matters in Dublin can be found in a curious document known as the *Mayor of Waterford's Letter*, a scornful summary of the Simnel conspiracy written from the only significant Irish town that maintained its loyalty to Henry VII during 1487. This version makes no mention of a towering figure known as Darsey and places the coronation in Dublin Castle, which seems unlikely as this was a secular building. The letter read, in part:

To the great discredit of foolish men, then held for wise, it is remembered, and the posteritie is to take notice of the foolery, that one Lambert, a boy, an organ-maker's sonne, was crowned at Dublin Kinge of England and Lord of Ireland, in the third yere of Henry the 7. The circumstances may not be forgotten. The Earl of Kildare, then governor of the realme, with the assistance of all the lords spritiual and temporall, and commons, of the north part of Ireland, assembled in the Castell of Dublin, crowned the boy and proclaumed him as aforesaid. The crowne they took off the head of the image of our Lady of Damascus, and clapt it on the boye's head. The maior of Dublin tooke the boye in his armes, caried him about the citie in procession with great triumph, the clergie goinge before; the Erle of Kildare, then governor; Walter, Archbishop of Dublin, lord chaunceler, the nobilitie, counsell, and citizens of the said citie, followinge him as their kinge; unto whome, also, all the partes of Ireland yelded obedience.[28]

It was not recorded in either account who performed the actual crowning of the pretender, completed using a borrowed golden circlet from a nearby statue of the Virgin Mary, but as the deed was done within the archbishop of Dublin's jurisdiction it is reasonable to suggest it was FitzSimon who was granted the dubious honour. A passionate sermon was also given that same day by John Payne, Bishop of Meath, declaring the right of the boy they now proclaimed King Edward to rule England and Ireland, a performance that presumably galvanised much support amongst the commons of Dublin as he was carried before them.

The deed done, Kildare thereafter composed a letter to John Butler, the mayor of Waterford, imploring the citizens of his town 'upon their duty of allegianc' to formally submit to the king crowned in Dublin. Butler's answer was conveyed by messenger, which declared both he and the people he represented had elected to remain loyal to Henry VII, believing the pretender, 'whosoever he be', had fraudulently taken upon himself 'the imperiall crowne or name to be kynge of England', despite 'having no right thereunto'.

It was the judgement of the Waterford authorities, Butler continued, that Kildare and his cohorts were little other than 'rude enemyes, traitors and rebells to the right prince and king of England'. It was a defiant response, and one which provoked a violent reaction in Kildare, who ordered the hapless messenger to be hanged in an area known as Hoggin Green to the east of the city.

Once his anger had abated, Kildare instructed his own messenger to travel south to Waterford, demanding 'upon payne of hanging at their dores' that the town's citizens 'forthwith proclaime, or cause the kinge lately crowned at Dublin to be proclaimed, in their citie, Kinge of England and Lord of Ireland'. Butler proved just as resolute as before, upholding his previous stance and declaring his citizens remained 'faithfull subjects to the crowne and dignitie of England, and the true and lawfull kinge of the same, being lord of Ireland'. The mayor went one step further, challenging Kildare and his allies to meet him thirty miles outside Waterford where Butler boldly claimed he would 'answere them with the sword of true loyalty and subjection'.[29]

When they received word of the challenge, the rebel leadership in Dublin showed little desire to deplete their ranks in such a meaningless manner, and instead committed to reinforcing their position in the Irish capital. A parliament was summoned so that the pretender could be recognised as the rightful king of England and Ireland, with orders given for coins to be struck bearing the words *Edwardus Rex Anglie Francie* on one side and *Et Rex Hybernie* on the reverse.[30]

A king, however, needed a kingdom to rule, and by the end of May 1487, the English, Irish, German and Swiss force boarded its ships, uncertain of its prospects but nonetheless driven by thoughts of riches and titles that could be won on the battlefield that surely awaited. The fleet's destination was Lancashire, confirming Henry VII's suspicions, and probably determined by Lovell and Lincoln's connections to the region. Less than two years after the Battle of Bosworth Field had witnessed the unlikely dawn of the Tudors, there was to be yet another concerted, and fierce, challenge for the coveted English crown. Despite the Tudor king's bluster, the Wars of the Roses were far from over.

7

The Fortunes of War

After several days navigating through the typically choppy Irish Sea, hearing wave after wave rhythmically crash against the bow of his ship whilst the sails and battle standards of those aboard fluttered freely in the breeze, it is not difficult to imagine the ten-year-old boy at the centre of the hopeful voyage, and indeed the wider conspiracy, staring fixedly at the Lancashire coast that appeared ever closer on the horizon. Lambert Simnel, or rather King Edward to those onboard, was old enough to appreciate the enormity of the moment, if perhaps not the personal danger that lay ahead. He was but a pawn in a game played out between the adults that controlled him.

As the pretender took his first tentative steps on the soft sand and nervously inhaled the salty sea air, the conspiracy which had been brewing for around a year had reached a critical point in its journey. Once the men, numbering almost eight thousand,[1] had safely disembarked from their ships, packed up their supplies, and started the strenuous slog inland, there could be no turning back. On 4 June 1487, for the second time in just twenty-two months, a disparate army bolstered with foreign mercenaries of various nationalities had landed in England with a brazen determination to slay the incumbent king and wrest from his grip the glittering crown that rested unsteadily upon his head.

Although Simnel was undoubtedly the slight figurehead around whom most of the soldiers rallied, whether for sentimental reasons or simply coin, the true leaders of the expedition remained John de la Pole, the attainted earl of Lincoln, and Francis Lovell, with Colonel Martin Schwartz overseeing the German-Swiss contingent and Thomas FitzGerald supervising the Irish recruits. FitzGerald's brother Gerald, Earl of Kildare, had cautiously elected to remain behind, perhaps an indication that despite his ambitious backing for the campaign thus far he was not prepared to risk his finest troops, or more importantly his own life, for the cause. It was not dissimilar to the calculated strategy adopted by the Stanley brothers throughout the late fifteenth century, with one brother typically assuming an active role in military engagement whilst the other appeared outwardly passive. As a consequence of such careful manoeuvring, the family unit endured regardless of how events unfolded during each battle. For the Stanleys, this had been most evident at Bosworth, when William Stanley appears to have taken the lead.

The precise location of the rebel army's landing in England is uncertain, with Bernard André writing vaguely it took place somewhere 'on the northern coast'[2] and Polydore Vergil believing they made landfall 'according to plan on the west coast not far from Lancaster'.[3] The nearest contemporary source in existence, Henry Percy, 4th Earl of Northumberland, wrote to the city of York on 6 June 1487 confidently asserting the rebels had landed 'at the pile of Fowdrey',[4] one of several islands located off the Furness Peninsula.

The small isle mentioned by the earl, known to later generations as Piel Island, was home to an impressive rectangular fortress constructed in 1327 to defend the local populace from ferocious Scottish raids, and the three-storey keep may have represented an ideal spot for Lincoln and his cohorts to scout whether it was safe to advance on to the mainland.[5] If the army did briefly rest at Piel Island, it would only have been a temporary pause in their journey whilst awaiting a trusted collaborator to appear half a mile across the haven beckoning them to land.

One such figure may have been the prominent local landowner Sir Thomas Broughton, a former retainer of Richard III who had only recently been pardoned by Henry VII for aiding Lovell's earlier uprising with the Staffords the year before.[6] Despite his second chance, Broughton, whom Vergil considered an individual 'of great authority in that part' of the kingdom,[7] could not reconcile himself to the king who had slaughtered his erstwhile master. It was likely through his extensive regional connections and knowledge of the Furness terrain that Lincoln's men were able to safely make their way inland from the coast without encountering any significant opposition. Other men of Lancashire, harshly rebuked by King Henry as 'ill disposed persones and traytours', who joined the conspiracy around this stage included Broughton's brother John, Robert Harrington of Cartmel, and members of the Middleton family, all of whom had been pardoned by an aggrieved king the previous August.[8]

The decision to land near Furness was logical on several counts, Broughton's presence notwithstanding. Not only was it directly across the Irish Sea from the rebels' Dublin base, thus minimising the risk of shipwreck during a lengthier voyage, it also prudently evaded regions likely to remain loyal to Henry, including Cheshire where the king's stepfather Thomas Stanley held sway, or Wales, which was governed on the king's behalf by Rhys ap Thomas in the south and William Griffith in the north.

The West Country, meanwhile, had traditionally been Lancastrian in sentiment throughout the Wars of the Roses, and it was anticipated the conspiracy would encounter difficulty in raising troops in and around that part of the kingdom. Landing on or near the Furness Peninsula, therefore, provided the rebels an opportunity to march across the north into Yorkshire, where widespread support for the cause of a child purporting to be Edward of Warwick was expected from the former retainers of Richard III and Richard Neville, the esteemed 16th Earl of Warwick known as the Kingmaker, supposedly the child's's uncle and grandfather respectively.

The task of unloading the ships probably took several hours, with several wagons full to the brim with all manner of weaponry and armour, swords, spears, morris pikes, bows, guns, harnesses, brigandines and hauberks all having to be carefully removed.[9] For many of the *Landsknechts* and the Irish recruits, this was the first time they had ever set foot on English soil; some would never make the return journey.

A local tradition endures that the army spent their first night in England camping near a village now known as Swarthmoor, supposedly named for the formidable German colonel. Although it is likely the name of the settlement derived from the Old English *sweart*, which meant black, as in the black moor, Martin Schwartz's name is given in the original Latin text of Polydore Vergil's *Anglica Historica* as Swarth, which could have been the basis for the tradition.[10] The rebels had to bypass Furness Abbey to reach the moor, and it is unknown if any assistance was forthcoming from the abbot, who may have been cowed by the threat of excommunication for anyone who acted against the terms of the recently reissued papal bull confirming the king's title.

Refreshed after their sea voyage and assured a royal ambush was not imminent, orders filtered through the ranks to commence their gruelling march through Lonsdale and towards Yorkshire, a destination probably chosen by Lincoln, who had personal experience of the lingering York-Neville allegiances prevalent throughout much of the county. Many of those living in the area at the time would have served under both Richard III and Warwick the Kingmaker. The army's likeliest route took them north-east from Swarthmoor, following the River Leven to Newby Bridge and on to the market town of Kendal, from where they prepared to cross the Yorkshire Dales via Sedburgh.

An alternative route has been suggested, which, although not the most direct course towards their destination, nevertheless avoided some of the more precipitous terrain, albeit it in exchange for navigating the perilous sands of Morecambe Bay. This second route would also have brought the rebels closer to Cartmel Priory, the other religious house threatened by censure if they provided aid in any way to the king's enemies. Considering the sheer number of soldiers present, not to mention the heavy wagons filled with supplies, it would have been foolish to risk crossing the unpredictable sands, particularly as the majority of those present had limited knowledge, if any, of the turning tides that have claimed many lives across the centuries.[11]

If Lincoln directed his army east towards Yorkshire through Sedburgh and across the scenic Howgill Fells, as seems the most reasonable deduction based on knowledge of their eventual destination, then the march was a laborious undertaking for even the fittest of men amongst the caravan. Their route took them through the Yorkshire Dales, the climb rising steadily towards Garsdale Head before descending into Wensleydale, following the meandering River Ure through or near to settlements like Aysgarth, Castle Bolton and Wensley before reaching Middleham. Orders were passed down through the ranks for the troops to proceed slowly at every stage, with Lincoln 'offering no harm to the local inhabitants, for he hoped some of the people would rally to his side'.

It was at Middleham in particular that Lincoln and Lovell probably anticipated raising considerable backing for the pretender they eagerly promoted, playing on the child's supposed kinship with the Kingmaker and Richard III, both popular former lords of Middleham. Although some northerners, such as Edward Frank, Thomas Metcalf, Richard Bank, Richard Knaresborough and Sir Edmund Hastings, abandoned their livelihoods to pledge their fealty to the child they were told was Edward of Warwick, any large-scale outpouring of spontaneous support for the rebels proved elusive.[12]

Nevertheless, when Lincoln 'saw his following was small he resolved none the less to try the fortunes of war, recalling that two years earlier Henry with a smaller number of soldiers had conquered the great army of King Richard'. One does wonder whether seeing large numbers of 'destitute and almost unarmed Irish' alongside strangely attired German and Swiss mercenaries furiously beating their drums drained the enthusiasm of the northerners to join what appeared to be a decidedly non-English affair, the presence of leaders like Lincoln and Lovell notwithstanding.[13] Furthermore, despite their connections with Yorkshire through their association with Richard III and the service they did their former master in those parts, the hereditary lands of Lincoln and Lovell were based in the south, something that also must have impeded each man's ability to muster support.

One person who did provide some degree of assistance at this stage of the march was William Heslington, the abbot of the nearby Cistercian abbey of Jervaulx, lying on the bank of the Ure a few miles south of Middleham. Whether it was food, shelter, money or simple counsel that Heslington supplied the rebels is not specified, but he was later forced to seek a pardon from Henry VII for his misconduct, duly granted in August 1488 during the king's visit to nearby Ripon.[14]

The abbot wasn't the only member of the Yorkshire clergy to fall foul of the king's suspicions; William Beverley, Dean of Middleham and the Chapel Royal under Richard III, was censured for partaking in seditious activity, as was Ralph Scrope, Rector of Wensley, both of whom were later made to pay significant bonds to ensure their future good behaviour. Abbots John Darnton of Fountains and William Sever of St Mary's in York, along with Prior John Auckland of Durham and Archdeacon Ralph Booth of York, also paid fines for their transgressions, suggesting the church in Yorkshire was actively employed by the conspirators to recruit on their behalf.[15]

By 8 June, just four days after landing over eighty miles away in north-western Lancashire, the rebels reached Masham, described by John Leland half a century later as 'a praty quik market town' that possessed a 'faire chirch' with a spire which rose high above the rooftops.[16] It was in this quaint town that the rebel leadership welcomed the morale-boosting news that two influential Yorkshire lords of distant relation, John Scrope, 5th Baron Scrope of Bolton, and Thomas Scrope, 6th Baron Scrope of Masham, had declared for their cause. The former had fought for Richard III at Bosworth Field and now readily defected from Henry VII's side despite his marriage to Elizabeth St John, the half-sister of the king's mother Margaret Beaufort. Having a key northern lord – not to mention an uncle by marriage – switch sides must have caused some uproar when Henry was brought the news.

Masham provided an ideal opportunity for the rebels to replenish their supplies, and it was from here on 8 June that a fascinating letter was composed 'by the king' to the mayor and aldermen of York, explaining that his men were prepared to come to the aid of England's supposedly oppressed subjects:

By the king,

To our trusty and welbiloved the maiour and his brethren and communaltye of our citie of York

Trusty and welbiloved we grete you wele, and forsomoch as we beene commen within this our realm not oonely by Goddes grace to atteyn our right of the same but also for the relief and well of our said realme, you and all othre our true subgiettes which hath bene gretely iniuried and oppressid in default of nowne ministracion of good rules and justice, desire therefor and in our right hertly wise pray you that in this behalve ye woll show unto us your good aides and favourez, and where we and such power as we have broght with us by meane of travayle of the see and upon the land beene gretely weryed and laboured, it woll like you that we may have relief and ease of logeing and vitailles within our citie ther, and soo to depart and truly pay for that at we shall take, and in your soo doing ye shall doo thing unto us of right acceptable pleaser, and for the same find us your good and souverain lord at all tymes hereafter, and of your disposicions herin to ascertain us by this bringer.

Yevene undre our signet at Masham the viii day of Juyn[17]

The letter was almost certainly composed at Lincoln's instigation, particularly when one considers his role as leader of the conspiracy and the tender age of his boy king. It is perhaps notable for the manner in which the pretender boldly uses royal language such as 'our true subjects', 'this our realm' and 'given under our signet', and for beseeching the York authorities to show their favour to this apparent king of Yorkist descent now approaching their city.

In fact, it is similar in composition to a letter Henry VII himself posted across the Channel a few years earlier when it was he who was daringly challenging the English people to sponsor his equally unlikely cause against the incumbent 'tyrant', Richard III. In that instance, enough people responded favourably to Henry to allow him a fighting chance of success, and Lincoln now hoped for a comparable reaction from the leaders and citizens of York. He was counting on bonds he had formed in the city when he briefly ruled the area as Richard's chief lieutenant in the north. He was to be sorely disappointed.

The landing in Lancashire had not gone unnoticed by the royal authorities. The king acknowledged the region was likely to be targeted by his enemies, and he wisely recruited one of the most trusted men in his service, Christopher Urswick, to actively scout the area on his behalf. The thirty-seven-year-old Urswick proved an astute choice for such a sensitive task, partly because he was the son of a lay-brother residing at the suspect Furness Abbey, with further family connections in the surrounding villages.

A Cambridge-educated priest, Urswick had initially entered the household of the king's mother Margaret Beaufort in 1482, serving as her chaplain and confessor before being utilised in the complex international conspiracies between 1483 and 1485 that propelled her son towards the throne. He claimed in January 1486 to have known Henry for around fifteen years, suggesting the priest must have encountered the future king whilst he was exiled in Brittany as a little-known teenager, and he certainly visited the would-be king in person in 1484 when sent by Bishop John Morton to convey a warning that Richard III was encouraging the Bretons to hand him over. Henry's subsequent flight to France may have saved his life.

Urswick returned to England as part of the Bosworth campaign, and was rewarded by becoming the new king's personal confessor. He would also become the recipient of considerable royal patronage across the next twenty years, holding at various points the archdeaconries of Wilts, Norfolk and Oxford, as well as serving as the dean of York and Windsor. As a sign of his reliability and trustworthiness, he was also tasked with sensitive diplomatic matters, including negotiating the Spanish marriage of Prince Arthur in 1489 and partaking in peace discussions with the Scottish and French in 1492.

In May 1487, however, before such exploits, Urswick was sent to Furness by the king 'to find out whether the ports on the Lancashire coast were capable of handling large ships, so that if they proved likely to be useful to his enemies he could at once place his soldiers as to deny them the coast'. According to Polydore Vergil, the steadfast Urswick carried out his orders as instructed before returning to Henry at Kenilworth with his findings. It is he who probably carried confirmation to the king that the rebels had already landed and were making their way towards him.[18]

The arrival of the rebels in the north raised Henry's concerns that they would attempt to take the city of York at the first opportunity, playing on the sorrow the authorities had publicly shown over the death of Richard III two years earlier. The letter from Masham in the name of Warwick had shown this concern to be justified. Having anticipated this turn of events, therefore, the circumspect king had already put preparations in place to make sure the city defences could not be breached with ease. If York fell, it would allow the rebels a foothold in the north whilst serving as an embarrassing black eye for the Tudor crown.

As early as 1 April, Henry Percy, 4th Earl of Northumberland and the most authoritative figure in the north, had written to York's mayor William Todd to advise he had been informed about Lincoln's defection, taking the opportunity to implore the city to 'shew your faithfull diligence for thestablisshment of good and peax', and to subdue 'all ryot and riotous language by any persone committed contrary to the well of the king'. The king himself then entered into correspondence with the city, starting with a letter on 20 April addressed to Mayor Todd and his aldermen to warn them of the threat they potentially faced from the rebels and to caution them to maintain watch both day and night for evidence of sedition amongst their ranks.[19]

Three days later, having perhaps heeded the words of Northumberland and conscious of the king's expectations of them, the city authorities drafted their own letter to the 'moost highe and mighty Christen prince', pledging to be his true and faithful subjects and content to do his bidding for 'the safegard of your moost royall persone'. They did, however, wish to bring to Henry's attention that York was 'gretely decayed', with much of the protective walls having collapsed. The once mighty castle, meanwhile, was in a state of disrepair owing to unfinished renovations. Furthermore, the mayor and his colleagues complained they could only muster half the number of 'good men' they had been able to in the past, and with these disadvantages in mind, beseeched Henry to urgently deliver extra supplies and weapons so they could put up an adequate defence should an attack materialise.[20]

The king's response was positive. It was, after all, to his benefit to ensure York was adequately protected. On 30 April, Henry replied to confirm he had received their request, and supported by the testimony of the city recorder John Vavasour, who had been sent to Coventry to appeal in person, agreed to provide further assistance. Orders were dispatched to several prominent Yorkshire knights, including Richard Tunstall, John Saville, Robert Rither, John Neville, Ralph Bigod and Marmaduke Constable, to raise funds, whilst William Tunstall, Constable of Scarborough Castle, was charged with delivering twelve large guns for the city's use. According to Vavasour's report, the king appeared 'well pleased and content' with the 'politik guyding' of the York authorities, and held the mayor and his brethren in high esteem for their pleasing conduct thus far.[21] On 4 May, Henry wrote to the city once again, informing the authorities he had knowledge the rebels had departed Flanders, yet noting:

> It is thoght by us and by oure counsaill that ye shal not need to have any strength or company of men of werre for this season to ly amonges you, and therefor we pray you that ye woll have sad regard to the good rule and sauf keping of oure citie ther to thappesing of rumours and correcting of evel disposed folkes, with sending unto us of your newes from tyme to tyme.[22]

The king's confidence that York could relax its preparations, however, proved to be premature. By 8 June, the rebels were camped in Masham, a mere thirty miles from the dilapidated walls of York. A violent confrontation between the two armies, one rebel and one royal, was inching ever closer with each passing day.

*

On 6 June 1487, a meeting was held in the Council Chamber within York's magnificent Guildhall, erected nearly forty years earlier on the eastern bank of the River Ouse and where all major decisions were made by the city elders. After a period of tense deliberation, the mayor, aldermen, sheriffs and commons of York reached an agreement 'that they wold kep this citie with ther bodiez and goodes to thuttermast of ther powerz' on behalf of Henry VII 'ayenst his rebelles'.[23] It was a resounding declaration of fealty to, and faith in, the Tudor king.

When the York authorities took receipt of the Masham letter bearing the name of King Edward, they forwarded the incriminating document on to the earl of Northumberland, with a copy urgently sent to Kenilworth Castle marked for the king's attention. The mayor and his brethren assembled once again in the Guildhall to discuss the letter's contents, and concluded that forthwith every warden that kept watch on the city walls should be in armoured harness, and individuals prohibited from entering any of the four principal gateways unless it was certain they were the king's true liegeman. How this was to be determined was left unstated.

It was also agreed to send three chamberlains to meet with Lincoln and Lovell, the two men identified correctly as the actual ringleaders of the conspiracy, and inform them face-to-face that the commonalty of York would ardently resist any attempt by the rebels to enter the city.[24] It couldn't have been the most agreeable of tasks for the three men in question.

York's decision to confront Lincoln probably influenced his next movements. Rather than head towards York as perhaps was the initial plan, the earl instead led his disparate army south through Ripon to Boroughbridge, following the Great North Road until reaching the vicinity of Bramham Moor, fifteen miles west of York and scene of a famous rebel defeat in 1408 during the reign of a previous Lancastrian king, Henry IV.

With the York authorities still unsure of Lincoln's intentions, Henry Clifford, 10th Baron de Clifford, sent word to Mayor Todd that he was prepared to come to the aid of the city with an armed retinue numbering around four hundred soldiers. Clifford's father had been killed in a skirmish with the Yorkists the day before their crushing victory at Towton, and the implacable son, restored to his ancestral lands upon Henry VII's accession, rose to the opportunity to scupper the threat now posed by Lincoln's army.

This desire to wreak havoc on the king's enemies and repay Henry for returning his inheritance probably prompted Clifford's decision to march west out of York towards the rebels shortly after his arrival in the city. With camp established on the edge of the city boundary in Tadcaster, Clifford and his men were taken by surprise when the rebels advanced on his position, triggering a 'grete skrymisse' that forced the humbled baron to flee back to the safety of the city. In a humiliating reversal of fortunes for Clifford, many of his men had been 'slayne and maymed' in the encounter, with those lucky to have survived nevertheless 'spoled and robbed'.[25]

Once back behind York's walls and taking stock of his losses, Clifford was joined by the considerably larger retinue of Northumberland. With a combined force of 6,000 men, they marched back out of the city intending to meet up with the king in the Midlands. They were only six miles into their journey when word reached them that the two lords Scrope had separated from Lincoln and, whether of their own volition or acting under orders, were marching on York with purpose. The Scropes appeared menacingly on horseback before Bootham Bar, the city's north-western entrance, on 12 June, and within earshot of the watchmen loudly declared their support for 'King Edward' before assaulting the gateway.

Bootham Bar had served as an entranceway to York since the Romans had occupied the city, and by the time the Scropes appeared in its shadow it was an imposing three-storey stone structure with a hefty portcullis that barred entry to any undesirables. The city's preparations over previous months and the attentiveness of the armoured guards marshalling the walls were enough to repel the attacks, with official records proudly boasting how 'the comons being watchmen ther well and manly defendid tham' and put the rebels 'to ffliht'. The successful defence even prompted the mayor to ride through the streets of York with a hundred armoured men to issue a defiant proclamation reaffirming the city's loyalty to Henry VII, should anyone present be in any doubt.[26] York was staunchly pro-Tudor in the summer of 1487.

The actions of the principal figures in and around York at this juncture are nevertheless intriguing, and perhaps indicate a degree of uncertainty about where the loyalties of the northern lords outside the city lay as the conspiracy gathered speed. The motivations behind the Scropes' assault on Bootham Bar is difficult to ascertain. It may well have been part of a diversionary tactic to draw Northumberland back to York to clear the route south for Lincoln to advance towards a confrontation with a weakened royal army. The two barons may also have supposed that an attack on Bootham Bar would endear them to Lincoln should his campaign prove successful, whilst not substantial enough an act to condemn them in the mind of Henry VII, who had shown himself generally magnanimous in the aftermath of Bosworth. In effect, they were hedging their bets, a tactic arguably adopted by Northumberland at the same time on the other side.

The earl's swift return to York after receiving word of the attack appears unnecessary, and may have been used as the pretext not to join up with the king's army for the impending battle. If Henry emerged victorious from the confrontation, Northumberland could plead he had earnestly protected the royal interest in the north, but crucially, if Lincoln won the day, he could truthfully explain he had not been present on the battlefield. Such apparent non-committal behaviour had worked for the earl at Bosworth, after all, when he was restored to his estates after a short period of incarceration.

It is not recorded if Lincoln had been personally involved in routing Clifford's forces near Tadcaster, or whether it was simply a detachment of his overall force, but this delay notwithstanding, his swift advance south thereafter continued unabated. Polydore Vergil wrote that the rebels, having put the Tadcaster and York incidents behind them, progressed slowly through the rest of Yorkshire, all the while 'offering no harm to the local inhabitants' since Lincoln 'hoped some of the people would rally to his side'. If an accurate summary of the earl's strategy, it betrays a man eager to recruit more Englishmen to his side, not just to bolster his overall numbers but to add credibility to the crusade. It was imperative the campaign didn't appear to be a foreign invasion, but rather a restoration of the true English royal house to a usurped throne, as supported by the common Englishman.

Lincoln could not escape the fact that the people of York had failed to declare for him, or rather King Edward, which must have been perceived in private to be a frustrating setback. Though there is no reason to doubt Vergil's claim that the earl was frustrated 'when he saw his following was small', he nevertheless resolved to daringly 'try the fortunes of war', presumably gaining some hope from the fact that just two years previously his adversary, 'with a small number of soldiers had conquered the great army of King Richard'. It is true, also, that Lincoln, Lovell, and the other leading figures of the conspiracy had come too far to turn back, marching at the head of a largely mercenary army trained in and paid for warfare and shipped across seas for the purpose. It was the same 'do or die' attitude Henry VII had shown during his own rise to the throne.

With little other option, therefore, it was resolved by the rebels to 'march directly on the king',[27] passing through or near to towns such as Pontefract, Doncaster and Worksop on the way, and perhaps even as far as Southwell a few miles north of the Trent. From the moment they had landed in England, they had covered around 180 miles. Henry VII, meanwhile, was more than prepared to fight for the crown he had won against the odds with considerable effort. Defeat would, after all, have not just meant surrendering his throne, but probably his life, a fate perhaps to be shared by his baby son and other members of his inner circle.

Armed with evidence of the rebels' landing in Lancashire from the trusted testimony of Christopher Urswick, and no doubt kept abreast of developments in Yorkshire by countless other messengers scuttling across the country, Henry resolved to face the threat head-on, and without hesitation initiated plans to 'set out forthwith against the foe wherever he might betake himself'.[28] Lincoln's army could not be allowed to march too far south, and certainly not reach London, which had traditionally been sympathetic to Yorkist causes throughout the Wars of the Roses, for they could conceivably draw support with each mile they covered.

There were precedents; Henry of Bolingbroke in 1399 and Edward IV in 1471, for example, were but two men who had cultivated considerable backing during their respective marches south from Yorkshire, and although Lincoln had thus far failed to garner any significant support, Henry could not take any chances. His predecessor, Richard III, had after all probably allowed Henry to advance too far into the heart of England during August 1485, providing the invader ample time to foster alliances with families such as the Stanleys and Talbots, which facilitated his ultimately victorious campaign. Henry VII was, however, a most prudent monarch, and wasn't about to make the same mistakes as those before him.

The most contemporary account of Henry's movements throughout June 1487 are found in an anonymous herald's report, produced shortly after the conspiracy was brought to a conclusion. The herald's account is detailed and insightful, suggesting the nameless messenger personally accompanied the royal army for part, if not all, of the campaign, or at least was very well informed by someone present during those eventful weeks. According to the report, shortly after being briefed about the rebels' landing in the north-west, the king summoned his council to Kenilworth Castle and set about organising a formidable royal army to crush the mounting threat before it could reach the south.

Foremost amongst those Henry now called upon to protect his crown was the 'noble and coraygious knight' John de Vere, 13th Earl of Oxford, who at his own request was handed command of the vanguard. He was supported by many other 'great coragious and lusty Knyghts' including George Talbot, 4th Earl of Shrewsbury, Edward Grey, 1st Viscount Lisle, the Barons Grey de Ruthyn, Grey de Codnor, Hastings, and Ferrers of Chartley, and the Cheshire knight Sir John Savage. John Grey, Baron Grey of Powis, along with Edward Wydeville, Charles Somerset, Richard Haute and Richard Pole, all knights, were in the meantime appointed the army's foreriders, specifically tasked with riding ahead of the main force to scout the terrain for signs of enemy action.[29]

Henry's next step, in preparation of his departure from Kenilworth and on the sage advice of leading religious figures such as the archbishop of Canterbury and bishops of Winchester and Exeter, was to issue a proclamation demanding the 'goode Rule of his Hooste' as they travelled through the Midlands. An unruly army would hardly endear the king to the local populace, who often beheld a passing royal force with a mixture of wonder and fear. A series of ordinances were therefore devised to ensure the troops would maintain a strict code of behaviour.

Firstly, no soldier of any rank should despoil or steal religious property, nor rob or harm any man or woman they encountered, 'upon Peyne of Deth'. All members of the king's host were strictly prohibited from ravishing any religious woman, nor were they to bring harm to any man's wife, daughter, maiden or servant. They were also expected not to steal, or rather 'presume to take', any meat or victuals belonging to any local person without prior agreement, again on pain of death. Furthermore, the king's men were not to take it upon themselves to secure lodging wherever the convoy came to a halt, but rather wait until accommodation was assigned to them by the royal officials. Feuding or quarrelling with fellow soldiers was strictly barred, regardless of cause, whilst any shouting, horn-blowing or similar anti-social behaviour after curfew was strongly discouraged. Vagabonds and common women, or prostitutes, were also expressly banned from congregating in and around the king's host. Lastly, every man was expected to be at the king's service, on horseback with their horse saddled and bridled, within three blasts of the trumpet. Failure to be ready would be punished with imprisonment.[30]

With the appropriate measures taken to ensure his army's good conduct and the necessary supplies procured for the march ahead,

Henry issued the order for his imposing host to move out of the protective walls of Kenilworth and onwards through Coventry to Leicester, a trek of around thirty miles that would have brought the king close to the Bosworth area where he won his crown two years earlier. One wonders whether this was mentioned in conversation between Henry's closest companions who had been present that day, such as the earl of Oxford, or whether the king merely reminisced privately whilst publicly remaining focused on the mission ahead.

When the army's arrived in Leicester on 10 June, the extensive ordinances Henry had unveiled at Kenilworth were put into action under the supervision of Archbishop Morton, with the observant herald noting that 'ther wer imprisonede great Nomber' of vagabonds and common women who had disobediently been drawn to the soldiers. The following morning, Monday 11 June, the army headed out of Leicester and on to Loughborough, where the stocks and prisons were once more 'reasonabley fylled with Harlatts and Vagabonnds', though thereafter there 'were but fewe in the Hooste' as thoughts turned more seriously to the forthcoming confrontation.

On 12 June, the very day the Scropes were attacking York, Henry continued his push northwards 'and lay al Nyght in the Felde, under a Wode callede Bonley Rice', probably modern-day Bunny in Nottinghamshire which lies just eight miles from Loughborough. The following day, however, the king's patience was tested when, due to the failure of his harbingers to properly scout the terrain, 'ther was no propre Grounde appoyntede wher the Kings Hooste shulde logge that Nyght'. Fortunately, as it was the middle of June, it proved to be a 'wele tempered Day', and after the army 'wandrede her and ther a great Espace of Tyme' looking for ideal spot they finally set up camp near a 'fayre longe Hille'. The king himself did not lie with his troops, and instead rode to a village three miles south of Nottingham named Ruddington, where he lodged in a local 'Gentilmannes Place', who presumably was only too happy to play host to the mighty king of England for a night.[31]

Nottingham in the fifteenth century was one of the largest settlements in the English Midlands, centred around an impressive royal fortress which stood upon a cliff overlooking the town below. It was with good reason that Richard III based himself there prior to the Tudor invasion two summers earlier, but there is little evidence Henry himself made use of a castle that was part of the royal estate. This may have been as the king was fully aware his enemies were loitering in the vicinity and he had little time to tarry, a fact brought home to the royal entourage when several local malcontents were accused of spreading rumours that Henry had fled in fear, a falsehood which led to some being hanged above the Trent from one end of Nottingham Bridge.

After a night spent in the unknown gentleman's house near Ruddington, on the morning of 14 June Henry rose and observed Mass in the local parish church to mark the Feast of Corpus Christi. According to the herald, he then slipped away from the core of his army without explanation to personally welcome the arrival of his stepbrother George Stanley, Lord Strange, who brought with him considerable Stanley resources drawn from their north-west hegemony.

It is unclear if there was any lingering fear within Henry's mind that the Stanleys would fail to support him at this most significant juncture early in his reign, having worked so diligently to place him on the throne in the first place, and it does seem highly unlikely the earl of Derby, the king's stepfather and recipient of considerable reward since events at Bosworth Field, entertained any notion of defection. Henry may simply have chosen to attend to Strange's arrival out of genuine affection, and certainly his return to camp alongside his stepbrother's 'great Host' was a timely morale boost for his own men, who could only marvel at the sight of the Stanley soldiers.[32]

That night, the royal army remained in the vicinity of Nottingham, the king's men based on the southern side of the bridge over the Trent, whilst Stanley's men camped across the water on meadows in the Lenton area of the city. Though there was a 'great Skrye', or scurry, nearby, which prompted several men to flee in panic, perhaps spooked by a non-existent attack, those who remained behind responded in 'grete joy' to see 'how sone the King was redye' with 'his true Men in Array'. It was proof enough that this Tudor king was not going to bolt at the first sign of trouble. He may not have been as well versed in combat as other military-minded kings before him, but Henry VII nevertheless exhibited enough strength of character, even courage, to retain the loyalty of his troops when he most needed their support, and crucially, to inspire them on to victory.[33]

On 15 June, the king received word from his forerunners that the rebels were advancing towards Newark, having passed Southwell on the other side of the Trent, prompting Henry to order his men to follow the south bank downstream towards Radcliffe. The march from Kenilworth to this latest temporary camp had totalled around seventy miles. With knowledge his enemies were now within a day's travel, there was little left for Henry to do but discuss military strategy with his leading commanders, most notably Oxford, who had proven indispensable at Bosworth Field, and thereafter to get some rest. Another slight panic spread through some of the troops that evening for the second night in a row, but the herald 'harde of no Man of Worship that fledde, but Raskells'. The men Henry needed remained by his side.

The following morning, for the second time in just twenty-two months, the king was to send an army into the field to fight to the death for his cause. The only difference on this occasion was that he was not fighting to win a crown, but rather to keep it. For the first time in his tumultuous life, Henry Tudor had everything to lose.

8

The Noble Triumph

On the summer morning of Saturday 16 June 1487, in the vicinity of the rural village of Radcliffe on the southern banks of the Trent, the king of England arose earlier than was usual. His mind was likely anxious about the coming day, and his sleep disturbed. The mental strain of leading an army into battle, in which defeat would result in almost certain death, was enough to make any man restless, and Henry VII was no different to any other member of his force, whatever their rank. The king had, of course, been in a similar position on the morning of the Battle of Bosworth Field two years earlier, but with a wife and son now awaiting his safe return, this experience was hardly a comfort as he prepared to lay everything on the line to overcome the unknown threat he now faced.

Like anyone who stood on the periphery of a medieval battlefield, Henry gravely appreciated he may not live to witness sunset; perhaps he would be hastily slung over a horse and maliciously defiled as Richard III was two years earlier. This understandable fear may have prompted his decision to hear two masses soon after waking, complemented by the melodic chanting of Richard Foxe, Bishop of Exeter and Lord

. Spiritually reinvigorated from his religious duties and physically refreshed after breakfast, Henry had five 'good and true Men' of Radcliffe brought into his presence and charged them with showing his men the simplest route to Newark, cautiously avoiding any groves where an ambush may occur. Two of the men were assigned to John de Vere, 13th Earl of Oxford, so they could guide the vanguard, whilst three were retained by Henry to accompany the main bulk of his army.

The services of the local quintet, however, were ultimately not required, for just before nine o'clock in the morning beside a minor settlement known as East Stoke, Oxford's vanguard finally encountered the rebel force, led nominally by the pretender boy-king Simnel but in truth by John de la Pole, Earl of Lincoln, and Francis Lovell, ably supported by the courageous Irish under the command of Thomas FitzGerald, and Martin Schwartz's hardy German-Swiss mercenaries.[1]

It seems improbable Henry was surprised when informed his vanguard had spotted the rebels; chronicler Edward Hall later mused that the king 'knewe every houre what the Erle did' and 'approached nere hys enemyes soner then they loked for him', and there seems little reason to doubt this.[2] Henry's actions thus far show that he had determined attack was the wisest form of defending his realm. He had aggressively moved toward the threat with each passing day.

East Stoke lay several hundred metres from the meandering Trent, which curved away towards the village of Fiskerton on the northern bank. As the rebels were based in Southwell the day before, Fiskerton, the most direct riverside settlement, likely marks where the rebels made their fateful crossing. Just as Henry had his scouts attentively tracking the whereabouts of his enemies, Lincoln and his cohorts would also have been receiving their own intelligence on the king's location, from which they must have determined that entering the nearby town of Newark was no longer the logical decision. With just the river separating the two forces, the rebel leadership made the decision prior to the morning of 16 June to wade across the water, and once back on dry land on the other side to assume position upon a plateau to the south-west of Stoke village. From this vantage point, the pretender's disparate army patiently awaited the measured arrival of the royal host.

As the two armies sized each other up across the scenic Nottinghamshire fields for the first time, a mixture of fear and excitement would have coursed through the tense bodies of those present on the frontlines, conscious of the fact the next steps they took may be the last of their mortal lives. In Bernard André's *Life of Henry VII*, the blind poet has his patron addressing the troops with 'steady and courageous spirit' just before the battle, and although André's words almost certainly originate from his vivid imagination, it is nevertheless likely the king did encourage his men in a similar manner:

My faithful lords and hardy soldiers who have endured so many dangers with me on land and sea, behold again how against our will we are tested in battle. For the earl of Lincoln – a treacherous man, as you know – is taking up an unjust cause against me completely unprovoked.[3]

Of the forces, it was Henry's that was the more polished, carefully assembled using the vast resources of his nobility and gentry, the majority of whom had no qualms in placing themselves at their king's service. Amongst those accompanying the king from Kenilworth to Stoke were the earls of Oxford and Shrewsbury, Edward Grey, 1st Viscount Lisle, the lords Strange, Grey de Ruthyn, Grey de Codnor, Grey of Powis, Hastings and Ferrers of Chartley, and knights John Savage, Edward Wydeville, Charles Somerset, Richard Haute and Richard Pole.[4] Henry's steadfast uncle Jasper Tudor is often reported to have been present, as he was at Bosworth, but the duke of Bedford is noticeably conspicuous by his lack of mention in the herald's report. Once all his supporters' soldiers had been accounted for, the king's army numbered in the region of 15,000 men.

During the day of battle, the attentive herald mentions that Henry made thirteen knights banneret, an elevated status that permitted the selected knight to lead a company of soldiers under his own heraldic banner, often rectangular in design. Three of those, Gilbert Talbot, John Cheyne and William Stonor, received the honour before the battle commenced, and were soldiers who had first proven their loyalty by joining Henry in exile before he was king, and thereafter proved their military credentials fighting for him at Bosworth.[5]

Talbot was the uncle of the young earl of Shrewsbury and had been rewarded by Henry the previous year with the forfeited Worcestershire estates of the Stafford brothers.[6] Cheyne, meanwhile, a man of considerable stature considered by Vergil to be 'a man of muche fortitude, far exceeding the common sort',[7] was one of a multitude of Edward IV's servants who defected to Henry's side after Richard III's accession. More pertinently, Cheyne had already earnt his king's respect at Bosworth when he was unhorsed by Richard during the latter stages of the battle, a clash which may just have distracted the Yorkist king enough to bring about his downfall shortly thereafter. His dedication to the Tudor cause was unquestioned. William Stonor was another former member of Edward IV's household who abandoned Richard III several months into his reign, even snubbing an impassioned plea from his 'lovyng cosyn' Francis Lovell to remain loyal, which surely added a personal edge to the Stoke campaign for both men.[8] All were men who had capably fought alongside Henry in battle once before, and he clearly entrusted the trio to do so once again. Men like Talbot, Cheyne, and Stoner held the future of the Tudor dynasty in their hands.

On the contrary, the army that declared for Lambert Simnel, or to their mind King Edward, was of a more disparate composition, and noticeably smaller than that which they now sought to overcome. Aside from the four identifiable leaders – Lincoln, Lovell, FitzGerald and Schwartz – the rebel force was generally comprised of men of inferior status and wealth to those they faced. Of the Englishmen known to be present from their later parliamentary attainders, most were minor figures drawn from parts of Yorkshire and Lancashire, including John Beaumond, Thomas and James Harrington, Robert Percy, Edward Frank, Richard Middleton and Richard Harleston, augmented by several members of the Mallary family from Northamptonshire.[9] There were no belted earls or dukes amongst the army, nor viscounts or barons. Any hope of a rebel victory rested in the abilities of the robust German-Swiss mercenaries, and the brave if ill-equipped Irish contingent.

As with other fifteenth-century military encounters, Stoke Field suffers from a lack of irreproachable source material, which naturally makes it difficult to piece together an accurate chronology of events as they unfolded on the morning of 16 June 1487. Perhaps the most vivid account is that of Vergil, which, although not contemporary, nonetheless was partially informed by those who had witnessed events first-hand. According to the Italian, it was King Henry who initially 'offered battle' upon encountering his enemies 'on the level ground' near Stoke, although Bernard André suggests the rebels were waiting 'on the ridge of a mountain', which was probably a plateau today known as Burnham Furlong. What is clear is that Lincoln appreciated he could not avoid confronting the royal army, and in response to the challenge issued on behalf of a king whose authority he rejected, the earl 'led forward his troops and, at a given signal, gave battle', imploring his soldiers to 'remembre his honoure, and their awne lyves'.[10]

As the two forces hurtled towards one another, the frenzied moment represented the culmination of several months scheming across three countries and two seas, and which threatened to trigger a third deposition within two fraught years. One can only speculate what thoughts were racing through the mind of Lambert Simnel as he watched from afar as the two unstoppable forces crashed together, with swords, maces, pikes and javelins on both sides tearing flesh from bone amidst the anguished screams of those unfortunate souls who failed to defend their lives.

It would be interesting to have some insight into what thoughts were racing through the boy's mind as he processed the violence unfolding before him, the screams of the dying rising above the incessant clanging of steel upon steel. Was the gruesome horror too much for Simnel, causing him to turn his face away, or did his immaturity allow him to be moved to innocent excitement at such chaotic scenes he had only ever heard about in anecdotes from his elders? Unfortunately, we will never know.

The battle was a fierce clash in which Vergil asserted 'both sides fought with the bitterest energy', a ferocious release of several weeks' pent-up aggression carefully fomented during their respective marches to this field on the banks of the River Trent. Vergil recounted how 'for some time the struggle was fought with no advantage to either side', commending 'those rugged men of the mountains, the Germans, so practiced in warfare' and who had quickly advanced to 'the forefront of the battle' where they 'yielded little to the English in valour'. The mercenaries certainly operated as a robust and well-practised unit and were expertly marshalled in the heart of the fighting by their leader Schwartz, a commander 'not inferior to many in his courage and resolution'.[11]

The Irish recruits, however, particularly the *kerns*, were woefully 'unprotected by body armour' and despite fighting 'most spiritedly', suffered heavy casualties as the battle unfolded, 'more than the other troops engaged'. Writing five decades after the bloody event, Edward Hall mused the Irish were 'stryken downe and slayne lyke dull and brute beastes' to the 'great discouragyne and abashement' of their fellow combatants, forced to avoid the bloody corpses that started to litter the battlefield.[12] During their march through the north, the *Great Chronicle* reported a confrontation between Schwartz and Lincoln over the latter's failure to stimulate considerable levels of support in England, with the German colonel accusing the earl 'that ye have dyssayvyd your sylf and alsoo me'.[13] The swift capitulation of the Irish troops only served to confirm Schwartz's concern that their force was inadequate for the task expected of them. Perhaps he had been deceived after all.

Although the battle took around three gruelling hours to reach its climax, Henry VII's army was simply far better equipped than his enemies, who were 'smaller in number and inferior in resources'. In the end, only the royal vanguard under Oxford's command had been committed to the fray, and it had proved more than capable of overcoming the threat alone. As soon as troops on the rebel side abandoned their losing cause and started to flee, the subsequent rout was swift and merciless as Oxford's troops 'charged the enemy with such vigour that it at once crushed those of the hostile leaders who were still resisting'.[14]

Similar to previous encounters in the Wars of the Roses such as Towton and Hexham, the slaughter which followed the fighting was dreadful. Those not fortunate enough to be captured were cut down in the mass confusion and panic as hundreds of soldiers, German, Irish and English, desperately fled into the surrounding countryside. Credited by Hall for their 'manly stomakes', their 'courageous hartes', and their 'valyaunt courage',[15] it is likely some made their way through a deep ravine later known, perhaps fittingly, as the Red Gutter. If any were lucky enough to dive into the river, they had to hope they weren't picked off by the archers who hunted them like game from the banks. By the end of the morning's carnage, around 5,000 rebels were slain.[16]

With victory assured for the royal army, 'suddenly the cry of "King Henry!" arose to the skies', and 'with bugles playing on all sides, sounds of gladness filled everyone's ears'.[17] The king, who had probably observed matters on the periphery of the battlefield with the core of his army, was 'greatly pleased that he had overcome his enemies' in such a resounding manner,[18] having lost few men of note. More importantly, he accomplished what Richard III and Henry VI had failed to do in similar circumstances – he successfully defended his crown on the field of battle.

Amongst those lying lifeless on the blood-splattered soil were the mutilated bodies of Martin Schwartz, 'who fell bravely in the fray',[19] and Thomas FitzGerald, fatally wounded fighting amongst the men he had led into battle. The most noteworthy body uncovered, however, was that of Lincoln, cut down and butchered before he could be captured for interrogation by royal officers. According to Vergil, informed by those present, the earl's death vexed the king who had expressly issued a command for the rebel leader to be apprehended alive 'in order to learn from him more concerning the conspiracy'. His troops, however, 'refused to spare the earl, being terrified that by chance it would happen that the sparing of one man's life would lead to the loss of the lives of many'.[20]

Vergil, meanwhile, perhaps reflecting ideas prevalent in the Tudor court during his time of writing nearly two decades later, recorded that the conspiracy's other leader, Francis Lovell, together with Thomas Broughton, the Lancashire knight who had aided the rebels after their landing in Furness, had also been killed during the battle, with Edward Hall even confidently asserting the former had drowned trying to cross the Trent. This is contrary to the contemporary herald's report and the City of York records, which have both men simply fleeing the slaughter.[21] Lovell's fate is unknown, although Francis Bacon's speculative early seventeenth-century biography of Henry VII mentions rumours of the fallen lord living out his days in 'a cave or vault', of which, however, there is no earlier evidence to substantiate such claims.[22] He simply disappeared.

The earl of Lincoln's death prevented Henry from personally grilling the figure who had marshalled an extensive conspiracy intended to unseat him from the throne, and robbed him of the satisfaction of humiliating his rival during a trial in which the guilty verdict was assured. Lincoln's capture need not have signalled his inevitable execution, however. Henry, certainly this early in his reign, was not vindictive in victory, as shown by his magnanimous attitude after Bosworth, from which Lincoln himself had personally benefitted. Perhaps, in exchange for a significant fine of course, the king was open to handing the earl one final chance to truly reconcile himself to the Tudor regime. The intervention and mediation of Lincoln's father the duke of Suffolk, who had proved steadfast in his loyalty to the crown, could have helped.

Two figures in the rebel force known to have survived the climax of the battle were Lambert Simnel – King Edward to his followers – and the shadowy priest who had been visible by the pretender's side since the conspiracy's earliest moments. It is not explicitly stated in any extant source where the pair were situated whilst the battle raged, but with Simnel a mere child and Symonds a member of the clergy, it can be confidently asserted neither participated in the actual bloodshed, and were probably placed at a safe distance from the action. It is tantalising to suggest the pair were guarded by Francis Lovell, who absconded when he grasped the day was lost, wilfully abandoning the child he must have known was a puppet king.

Most of the various sources are in agreement that Simnel and the priest were apprehended once the fighting had ceased. The herald recorded in his official report that after the battle 'ther was taken the Lad that his Rebelles callede King Edwarde', along with Symonds, who escaped with his life only because of his holy orders. The person credited with seizing the pretender was a 'gentil Esquier of the King's Howse' named Robert Bellingham.[23] The *York House Books*, a record of the city minutes, confirm 'the child which they callid ther king was takyn and broght unto the kinges grace'[24] where one can picture the chastened boy sitting through an exhaustive grilling from an inquisitive Henry VII.

The later accounts of Vergil and André again reiterate both boy and priest were seized. The former refers to Simnel as 'the false boy king', noting he was granted his life by King Henry as an 'innocent lad' who was 'too young to have himself committed any offence'.[25] André was less favourable in his judgement, accusing Simnel of being nothing less than a 'miserable kinglet of scoundrels', who when pressed as to what had possessed him to 'dare commit such a great crime' meekly admitted that 'infamous persons of his own rank had coerced him' and that his true parents were indeed 'mean individuals' with 'low occupations'.[26] The one source which seems to contradict the report of Symonds' capture at this point is the earlier February convocation.

As for Simnel's fate once the battle had become a distant memory, Vergil, whose manuscript was drafted before 1513, reported that 'Lambert is still alive to this very day, having been promoted trainer of the king's hawks' after a period working as a turnspit in the royal kitchens.[27] This suggests that the king's intentions in 1497, if indeed the Milanese ambassador's testimony can be trusted, to make Simnel a priest 'out of respect for the sacred unction' never came to fruition.[28] Although the pretender's menial role in the frenzied and hazardous confines of the kitchen would have made for a tough existence, his adult years working with hawks would have been more pleasurable, not to mention financially rewarding.

The ancient art of hawking involved utilising an assortment of birds of prey such as goshawks and sparrowhawks to hunt food for the royal kitchens, typically pheasant, rabbits, hare and geese. Falcons, on the other hand, were usually reserved for the entertainment of those higher in social status, with *The Boke of Saint Albans*, compiled by the Benedictine prioress of Sopwell in 1486, advising that birds such as gyrfalcons and peregrines were usually reserved for kings and princes.[29] Vergil's manuscript specifically notes Simnel was a hawker, known as an *austringer*, and it is unclear if he was involved with the king's falcons as commonly believed, a position of considerable honour.

It is not known how Simnel came to be involved in training the royal hawks, but it is conceivable he displayed signs of a natural affinity with the birds during his employment in the kitchens, and was therefore promoted accordingly. It was the trainer's role to bond with the hawks so they grew accustomed to human interaction, learning to trust their handler enough to return to a gloved fist upon completing their flight and for which they were routinely rewarded with mice and chunks of chicken from a small leather pouch known as a bechin bag.

Training hawks and falcons was a costly exercise, requiring extensive caging known as mews, plus fitted accessories such as hoods, bells and lures. It was a rich man's pastime, and one particularly relished by Henry VII and his son Henry VIII, both of whom Simnel must have served from the royal mews near Charing Cross to the west of London. For his services, he was likely rewarded well, although admittedly there are no known references to his name in the royal chamber books to corroborate this.

If one takes into consideration the scholarly work of the twelfth-century philosopher Adelard of Bath, the pretender's role in tending to the king's birds possibly reveals more about the character of the enigmatic Simnel than any other account. It was Adelard's belief that the ideal proponent of falconry and hawking was a patient and chaste man, armed with good eyesight, a good carrying voice, and a retentive memory, the latter of which Simnel may have already exhibited during his months impersonating a prince. A daring spirit was also considered a valuable asset, which one imagines was held in abundance by the boy who had once crossed England at the head of an unlikely conspiracy and then convinced the king to spare his life.[30]

Aside from knowing Lambert Simnel escaped execution and was put to work in the royal kitchens and later with the king's hawks, little is known about the figure who had almost brought the fledgling Tudor regime to its knees during the summer of 1487. The sixteenth-century Irish *Book of Howth*, not a contemporary source and riddled with inconsistencies, does include an intriguing tale not recounted elsewhere that Henry VII summoned the Irish nobility, led by the earl of Kildare, to London a few years after Stoke, where he admonished them with the cutting remark, 'My masters of Ireland, you will crown apes at length.' Later that evening, the mischievous king supposedly had the child the Irish lords had crowned in Dublin serve them dinner, intending to cause embarrassment to his guests. The charade backfired on Henry, however, as all refused to accept drink from the boy, with the exception of the loyal Lord Howth. It remains, however, a fanciful tale of dubious origin.[31]

Little is recorded of Lambert thereafter, although he was the recipient of 20 shillings for six months' work in the household of Sir Thomas Lovell, the king's chancellor, between Michaelmas of 1522 and 1523, some thirty-five years after Stoke Field. Lovell's household account records he had two falconers in his employ, one of whom was Simnel, with the other named as Richard Breteyn, paid double that given to Simnel as he worked for a full year. It is certainly intriguing to speculate what conversation passed between Sir Thomas and the man tasked with training his birds during their hours in the field, both men having played a role on opposing sides during the Stoke campaign three decades earlier, for which the former had earned his knighthood.[32] Just over a year later, in May 1524, Simnel was one of ninety-seven yeomen provided robes to participate in Lovell's funeral, another indication of their acknowledged association in later life.[33]

Although other details of his later life are absent from the records, including his own date of death, there is the tantalising suggestion Lambert had issue during the reign of Henry VIII. Considering the rarity of the erstwhile pretender's supposed surname, Richard Simnell, a canon of St Osyth's Priory before its dissolution in 1539, could conceivably have been his son.[34] On 25 October 1561, meanwhile, a pardon was granted to 'Robert Symnell late of Donyngton in Holland, co Lincoln, husbandman', perhaps a grandson, who had been imprisoned in Fleet Prison for non-payment of a 40-shilling debt.[35] It will be recalled there is earlier evidence of Simnels living in Lincolnshire during the early fifteenth century, when a Richard Symnel of Great Stratton was himself owed a debt.[36]

The Simnel name certainly endured throughout the Tudor period, and ironically beyond, with a Robert Simnel, who may or may not be the same person as the Donnington Simnel, a bailiff of Colchester in May 1599.[37] Of course, ultimately these connections are unproven, and must, therefore, remain conjecture, with Lambert Simnel's fate, much like his origins, obscured by the mists of time. One does wonder, however, if in later years Simnel wistfully looked back on his few weeks as 'king of England', and the adventure that accompanied it, prior to its brutal and bloody conclusion. At the very least, he must have been thankful Henry VII had not ended his life as soon as he was captured, on the block or worse.

As for what became of Priest Symonds, the tutor of a would-be king doesn't merit a mention in the works of Vergil, André or the herald after the battle of Stoke, although Edward Hall supposed he was 'comitted to perpetual pryson and miserable captivitie', a reasonable assumption for a wayward traitor who initiated a wide-ranging conspiracy which undoubtedly rattled Henry VII.[38] Edward, the authentic earl of Warwick, meanwhile, remained under close observation in the Tower of London for the foreseeable future.

*

The morning after what had proved a comprehensive royal victory, around 3 a.m. to be precise, a breathless servant of the city's recorder John Vavasour wearily made his way through the deserted streets of York, bearing news of how 'Almighty God had sent the king victorye of his ennymies and rebelles'. Urgently seeking an audience with Mayor William Todd, along with the city's aldermen and councillors, the messenger recounted to his captive audience what had transpired seventy-five miles to the south, prompting his listeners to depart to the city's grand cathedral 'to make lovinges to our saveour for the tryumphe and victory forsaid, singing solemplye in the high qwere of the said church the psalme of *Te deum laudamus*'.[39] One envisages similar journeys by a host of messengers were completed throughout England, each conveying news that the reign of Henry VII, for the time being at least, endured.

Once the congratulatory backslapping had ended on Stoke Field – and according to unverified tradition Henry had triumphantly planted a banner upon the ridge earlier occupied by Lincoln's forces – orders from the royal camp commanded the dead on both sides were to be gathered and buried in crudely dug ditches, although not before the lifeless bodies were stripped of armour or weapons that could be recycled by the victors. It is likely the king was shown Lincoln's corpse before the earl's body was disposed of, if only to confirm his adversary had indeed perished during the day's violence.

Satisfied with how the battle had unfolded, from Stoke the jubilant king and his conquering army removed themselves to Newark, around five miles away, where he conferred celebratory knighthoods upon fifty-two men in recognition of their valour during the day's events. In addition to the three knights banneret created prior to the battle, another ten were honoured afterwards, namely John Arundel, Thomas Cokesey, Edmund Bedingfield, John Fortescue, Humphrey Stanley, James Blount, Richard Delabere, John Mortimer, William Troutbecke, Richard Croft, and James Baskerville.[40] That evening's festivities, raucous one imagines if the considerable payment of £42 by the king to a 'wel-beloved' merchant for wine is taken into account, probably took place in the royal fortress which rose nobly above the River Trent.[41]

It was from Newark the king composed a letter to Mayor Todd, which opened with the customary, if defiant, statement, 'By the king.' Henry's words are the most contemporary insight we have into his mindset immediately after the battle, and his desire to piously offer thanksgiving to God probably betrays his considerable relief at the victory:

> Trusty and welbeloved we grete you wele, and forsomoch as it hath liked our blissed salveour to graunte unto us of his benigne grace the triumphe and victorye of our rebelles without deth of any noble or gentilman on our part, we therefore desire and pray you and sithen this said victorye procedeth of hyme and concernyth not oonely the wele and hounour of us but also of this our royme, nathelesse charge you that calling unto you in the moost solempne churche of our citie ther your brethren thaldremen and othre, ye do lovinges and praisinges to be yevene to our said salveour after the best of your powers.[42]

After a suitable period of rest in Newark, Henry and his household headed north-west to Lincoln, while as a warning to anyone in the region with thoughts of rebellion on their minds the king 'punished several of his captives with death'. That the names of the condemned are not provided by Vergil suggests they were men of little standing. Henry was mindful not to neglect his religious devotions at this time. He summoned to his presence his trusted servant Christopher Urswick to receive another sensitive mission. Urswick was commanded to take the royal standard, which Henry 'had used against the enemy whom he had defeated', to Walsingham in Norfolk 'to offer thanks for the victory in the shrine of the Blessed Virgin and to place the standard there as a memorial to the favour he had received from God'. It is uncertain if this was the same standard which tradition dictates he planted on the battlefield, but Urswick, we are assured, 'diligently performed' his duty.[43]

The king's next movements were designed to reinforce his suspect authority in the north and secure peace with Scotland before overseeing the legal destruction of his vanquished enemies, dead or alive, through the workings of parliament. From the city of Lincoln, therefore, Henry and his court briefly retreated to Kenilworth before packing up in mid-July 1487 and heading north once again, this time to York.

Although his chief purpose was to 'reform the territory bordering on Scotland' and ensure 'there was no refuge or place of safety for rebels' within his neighbouring realm, there can be little doubt Henry also took the opportunity to personally remind 'all who were suspect' in Yorkshire and beyond of their duty to remain loyal to the crown.[44] In the words of Edward Hall, the king was determined to 'wede oute, and purge his land of all sedicyous seede'.[45]

The *York House Books* reported that Henry arrived into the city around 4 p.m. on 30 July, 'accompanyed with many lordes and nobles of his realme' and riding at the head of a vast retinue numbering around 10,000 men. For his second visit to York in fifteenth months, the king was ceremoniously greeted outside Micklegate Bar by the city authorities, including the recorder John Vavasour, who commemorated his royal guest's arrival with a reverential oration:

Moste high and mighty Christen prince and our moost drad souverain liege lord, your true and faithfull subgiettes, the mayer, aldermen, shereffes and common counsaill, with thool body of this your citie in ther moost humbly wise welcomes your moost noble grace unto the same, yeving due lovinges unto almighty God for the grete fortune, noble trihumpe and victory which it hath pleased his godhead to graunt unto your highnesse in subduyng your rebelles and ennymes at this tyme, besuching almighty God to continewe your moost noble grace in the same.[46]

Henry's residence whilst in York was the splendid archbishop's palace, which stood in the shadows of the towering cathedral, and on 1 August he visited the Coney Street house of Thomas Scot to observe the city's famed cycle of Mystery Plays, a series of lavish Biblical pageants celebrating the feast of Corpus Christi and which were performed at his own request. That same day, he bestowed knighthoods upon Mayor Todd and an alderman named Richard York, presumably for their support in holding the city during the recent crisis. The following day, a squire named Roger Layton was condemned for 'certain poyntes of treason committed by hyme ayenst the kinges highnesse', as was Thomas Metcalfe, although only the former paid with his head.[47]

Henry remained in York until Monday 6 August when he resumed his extensive northern progress by briefly visiting Newcastle before commencing the lengthy three-hundred-mile trek south to London, passing through Durham, Richmond, Ripon, Pontefract, Newark, Stamford, Huntingdon and St Albans with only a short detour to

Warwick to collect his queen.[48] On 3 November 1487, after an absence of nearly eight months, Henry arrived on the outskirts of his capital to be met 'on Horsbak ful wel and honorably' by the mayor, sheriffs, aldermen and selected commons of the city. That afternoon, the king, 'as a comely and roiall Prince, apparailled accordingly', entered London's teeming streets, 'hogely replenyshede with People in passing great Nomber', until he reached the western door of St Paul's Cathedral. There can be no question, after his struggles, Henry was greatly encouraged to see his subjects had 'made great Joye and Exaltation' as he passed by.[49]

Six days later, the second parliament of what was proving a lively reign assembled in Westminster, having been summoned two months earlier 'for the consideration of divers urgent and important matters touching the state and defence of the kingdom and the church of England'.[50] As well as the more mundane aspects of late fifteenth-century governance, the parliament dealt with the fallout from the rebellion, providing the only official account on record. The meticulous act[51] passed against the rebels provides a clear indication of parliament's wrath against those who had mobilised against the king, with particular ire reserved for the slain earl of Lincoln, who despite 'the greate and sovereygn kyndnes that oure Sovereygne Leige Lord that nowe ys, at dyvers sundry tymes, contynuelly shewed to the said late Erle', nevertheless 'conspired and ymagynged the most doloruse and lamentable Murder, Deth and Destruction of the Roiall persone of oure said Sovereygne and Leige Lorde, and also distruction of all this Realme'.

The earl's 'malicious purpose' to unseat the king started the moment he 'traiterously departed to the parties beyond the See, and ther acompanyed hymselfe with many other false Traitours, and Enemyes to our said Sovereigne Leige Lord'. The act described how Lincoln had 'prepared a grete Navye for the Counties of Brabon, and arryved in the Portes of Irland' where he conspired at length with Henry Bodrugan and John Beaumond. On 24 May 1487 in Dublin, 'contrarie to his homage and faith, trouth and allegiuance', Lincoln

> ... trayterously renowned, revoked and disclaymed his owne said most naturall Sovereygne Leige Lord the Kyng, and caused oone Lambert Symnell, a child of x yere of age, sonne to Thomas Symnell, late of Oxforde Joynonre, to be proclamed, erecte and reputed as Kyng of this Realm, and to hym did feith and homage, to the grete dishonour and despite of all this Realme.

The act went on to recount in almost incredulous terms how Lincoln departed Ireland for Lancashire on 4 June, and 'in hostyle maner' passed 'from place to place' until he arrived at Stoke Field, where he 'levied warre ayenst the persone of his Sovereygne and natural Leige Lorde'.

With such vivid recitation of events declared before parliament, it is little surprise that Lincoln, along with the rather restrained figure of just twenty-seven others, was attainted 'by the advyse of all the Lordes Spiritall and Temporall, and the Commons'. All those declared rebels would be 'reputed, jugged, and taken as Traytours, and convicte and attaynte of High Treason'. The earl, of course, had not left the battlefield alive, but all castles, lordships, manors and goods that had been in his possession were forfeited to the crown, legally passing into the hands of the very person he had conspired to destroy.

Despite the gravity of the act, however, in time Henry proved surprisingly lenient with many of the rebels who survived the Stoke Field campaign. The two Scrope barons, for example, were pardoned in 1489,[52] as were seventy-eight others between August 1487 and August 1489.[53] He also dealt gently with the Irish nobility, although through political necessity as much as magnanimity. Though he initially requested Pope Innocent VIII to excommunicate all Irish bishops who had 'lent assistance to the rebels, and to a spurious lad',[54] Henry acknowledged he could not afford to alienate the lords further, particularly the influential earl of Kildare, who had not only felt confident enough in his position to crown a rival king but even to dispatch his brother into England with an Irish army.

On 25 May 1488, almost a year after the battle, Richard Edgecombe, a respected comptroller of the Royal Household, was handed a commission to cross the Irish Sea to formally receive the submission of the Irish, with power to dispense 'general pardons for crimes' to thirty-two people, including Kildare, the archbishops of Armagh and Dublin, the bishops of Cloyne, Meath and Derry, seven abbots, three priors, seventeen other lords of lesser ranks, and for good measure the citizenry of Dublin and Drogheda.[55] It nonetheless took Edgecombe two months to come to terms, but all did ultimately swear fresh oaths of fealty to Henry VII.

The king's moderate policy proved astute; he could not be seen to be excessively lenient to those who had defied his authority, with financial punishments and sporadic executions employed to discourage future misbehaviour, but vengefully targeting those areas that had supported the rebels risked permanently alienating large numbers of his subjects.

One man who notably did not receive a pardon, however, was Lincoln's chief co-conspirator Francis Lovell. In fact, nobody appears to know what happened to Lovell at all, and aside from a grant of safe conduct given by James IV of Scotland, his fate remains as uncertain as that of the Princes in the Tower.

The year 1487 had not been an easy one for Henry VII; his crown, even his life, had come under considerable threat from hostile forces within and without his kingdom, although the resilient king succeeded in overcoming his enemies' 'unrighteous fury'.[56] The first six months of the year had been preoccupied with interpreting the rebels' intentions and preparing for their advance before defeating them in a hard-fought battle. During the second part of 1487, meanwhile, focus shifted to solidifying the Tudor grip on the crown whilst steadily eradicating any lingering danger. To that end, Henry, 'for the perfyght love and syncere affeccion that he bare to his queen', took advantage of his nobility's presence in the capital for parliament, and arranged the belated coronation of his wife Elizabeth.[57]

Putting aside any obvious affection for the woman who had provided him an heir just eight months into their marriage, the stirring spectacle was a convenient opportunity for Henry to very publicly reassert his emergent regime's authority after two failed rebellions within a year. It was also a chance to remind his subjects, loyal or otherwise, just whose grip remained on the crown. Little expense was spared by the king, with the festivities starting in earnest on 23 November 1487 when Elizabeth, 'royally apparelled, and companynede with my Lady the Kyngs Moder', Margaret Beaufort, was conveyed upstream from her royal apartments in Greenwich.[58]

For the queen's journey by water, she was encircled by an ostentatious water pageant that spanned the breadth of the Thames, with 'Barges freshely furnyshed with Baners and Stremers of Silk richely besene' on every side. One particular boat, known as the *Bachelers Barge*, outshone all others for it supported 'a great red Dragon spowting Flamys of Fyer' into the river, whilst the air was filled by joyful music courtesy of trumpets, clarions and minstrels, arranged for Elizabeth's 'Sport and Pleasure'. Those watching the remarkable spectacle from either bank must have been astounded as the barges sailed past one by one, an exhilarating blend of sound and colour emanating from the water.[59]

The river pageant terminated at Tower Wharf on the northern bank of the crowded Thames, where Elizabeth was ceremoniously guided through the heart of the Tower of London to her husband, who personally welcomed his queen 'in suche Maner and Forme' that it proved 'a very good Sight, and right joyous and comfortable to beholde'.[60] Although this wouldn't have been the first time Elizabeth had visited the fortress since her brothers' disappearance during the summer of 1483, one does wonder whether she paid her missing siblings any thought two nights before a coronation she would never have undergone had their whereabouts been known.

The following morning, the queen departed the Tower for Westminster dressed in a kirtle of white cloth of gold covered with an ermine mantle, fastened by a gold and silk lace embellished with tassels to protect her from the autumn chill. Her 'faire yelow hair' hung loosely down her back, and atop her head sat a golden circlet richly garnished with precious stones. With her younger sister Cecily bearing her train, Elizabeth was carried through the freshly cleaned and richly decorated streets of London in a litter furnished with large feather pillows and covered with more cloth of gold. All along the route, she was greeted with the sight of children dressed as angels and virgins, who sang sweet songs as she passed.

Riding near the royal litter in positions of honour were Henry VII's most trusted men, figures like Jasper Tudor, Duke of Bedford, and the earls of Oxford and Derby, each of whom had been instrumental in propelling the king to his throne. Another prominent noble accompanying the procession was the duke of Suffolk, who presumably was mindful to conceal any grief he felt over the death of his traitor son Lincoln just a few months previously.

It is intriguing to note that amongst the procession were six henchmen very visibly guarding the queen, each riding a palfrey covered with cloth of gold embroidered with white roses and suns, symbols closely associated with Elizabeth's father Edward IV and the House of York in general. This would not have been sanctioned without the consent of King Henry, keen to brand his dynasty with the increasingly ubiquitous Tudor Rose, but demonstrates the wily monarch was willing to encourage the Londoners' known affection for the Yorkists, in the hope it would generate support for his own line through the agency of his beloved wife.[61]

The coronation took place the following morning, 25 November, during which Elizabeth was dressed in another kirtle covered with ermine mantle of purple velvet, her head again topped with a golden circlet covered in pearls and other precious gems. In a similar manner to her husband two years before, and her mother twenty-two years earlier, the queen was led through the abbey to the altar where, after a series of religious rituals and prayers, she was anointed and crowned by Archbishop Morton.

Observing matters covertly from a 'goodlye Stage coverede and well besene with Clothes of Arras' was the king, and his mother Margaret Beaufort. With them also was the fourteen-year-old Lady Margaret of Clarence, sister to the earl of Warwick in whose name the rebellion earlier that year had occurred. Perhaps keen to ensure her Yorkist blood was carefully managed in future generations to prevent yet another dynastic complication arising, the king had arranged around this time for young Margaret to marry one of his most steadfast supporters, a Welshman named Richard Pole whose aunt on his maternal side happened to be Margaret Beaufort. In a smaller way, this union may also have been designed to signal the reconciliation between the York and Lancaster factions. The strategy would not work – the Poles ultimately proved to be a problem for his son, Henry VIII, under whom Margaret would be shamefully executed in 1541. Back in November 1487, however, the impressionable young teenager innocently savoured the sumptuous feast which followed her cousin Elizabeth's coronation, seated alongside the newly crowned queen and the other guests in Westminster Palace's Great Hall. Once every course had been sampled, including swan, goat, boar, and a re-dressed peacock with its plumage intact, 'the Quene departede with Godds Blessing, and to the Rejoysing of many a trwe Englishe Mannes Hert'.[62]

Henry VII had done everything he possibly could to secure his position upon the throne as the Christmas festivities of 1487 approached; he had crowned his Yorkist queen, which he anticipated would ensure the continued loyalty and integration of her father's former household, could count on the support of most of his nobility, whether willingly or reluctantly, and had cultivated a firm working relationship with both church and parliament. He had crushed his enemies on the field of battle, and although he couldn't have known it at the time, Stoke Field proved to be the final battle in the tumultuous period of English history known as the Wars of the Roses.

Most importantly, he had a healthy baby son to one day succeed him, and by March 1489 had successfully negotiated the Treaty of Medina del Campo with King Ferdinand of Aragon and Queen Isabella of Castile, which agreed in principle the future marriage of Arthur to the Spanish *infanta*, Katherine of Aragon. It was a considerable coup that injected the fledgling Tudor regime with a much-needed dose of continental credibility and recognition.[63]

It had been a stuttering start to the reign of the first Tudor monarch, from which Henry emerged more confident and self-assured in his ability to rule. He now resolved to place fears of pretenders and rebellion to the back of his mind to focus on governing the realm on his own terms, with his own men. Henry forthwith surrounded himself with those he trusted implicitly, men like his lord privy seal Richard Foxe, his high treasurer John Dynham, and the chancellor John Morton, all of whom would remain in their roles until the turn of the century.

In his *Life of Henry VII*, Bernard André considered his patron to be an 'invincible king', but entering the third year of his reign, little did anyone realise that just four years later a fresh threat would appear menacingly on the horizon. A new pretender, one 'raised from the dead',[64] was about to emerge from the shadows to challenge Henry's position. This time, the Tudor king was faced with a foe far more evasive, enigmatic, and enduring than Lambert Simnel.

9

Werbecque of Tournai

The remarkably well-dressed young figure, armed with a sharp mind and blessed with flowing blond locks, confidently glided through the streets of Cork, Ireland, during the winter of 1491, attracting curious glances with every step he took in public. Aged in his mid-teens, he had arrived suddenly, and without warning, in the town. There was an unmistakeable air of majesty about the stylish visitor who now walked amongst the inquisitive locals. All naturally pondered his identity.

Rumours soon circulated that this fashionable stranger in silk was not merely a wandering soul from some distant noble family, but rather a prince. Further speculation even suggested he was none other than Prince Richard of Shrewsbury, the duke of York and youngest son of Edward IV who had vanished without trace from the Tower of London during the political turmoil of 1483.

A later mid-sixteenth-century sketch by an unidentified Flemish artist, possibly Jacques Le Boucq, if accurately copied from an earlier original, offers some explanation why such rumours took hold; in the vivid drawing, part of a hefty manuscript of black and red chalk portraits known as the *Recueil D'Arras* after the city in which the collection is stored, there is certainly a passing resemblance between Edward IV and the youth, staring hopefully into the distance as though contemplating what the future held in store.

The clean-shaven sitter possessed a strong jaw and cleft chin, with a full lower lip, a long thin nose and a high forehead. This alleged prince did, however, have a fairer shade of hair than the mighty Yorkist king it was claimed was his father, as shown by the artist's inscription of '*blon*', or blonde, on the sketch itself. It will be recalled, however, that Elizabeth of York, his apparent sister, was similarly described as having fair yellow hair at her coronation in 1486, so hair colour alone should not be taken to definitively settle the matter either way. Once dressed in expensive silks and presented to a crowd not often acquainted with such fine attire, it is certainly plausible the wearer passed without much difficulty for an English prince.[1]

History has remembered this enigmatic figure who arrived in Cork in 1491 as Perkin Warbeck, the second of the famed pretenders who sought the English crown during the reign of Henry VII. But who was this Perkin Warbeck, and how did he come to claim to be Prince Richard, who had disappeared from public view several years earlier and was presumed dead?

According to Warbeck's own testimony given to royal officials after his eventual capture in 1497, he claimed to have been born in Tournai to John Osbek, the controller of the town, and Kateryn de Ffaro. His paternal grandfather's name was given as Deryk Osbek, after whose death his grandmother married a man named Petir Flam, Tournai's receiver and dean of the Boatmen's Guild on the vibrant River Scheldt. His father's sister was Johane, or Jane, and he briefly lived with his aunt and her husband John Stalyn at their home in the St Pyas section of town. His maternal grandfather's name was given as Petir Ffaro, and he served as keeper of the keys for St John's Gate.[2] Though Vergil later claimed Warbeck was a commoner born into poverty,[3] this background, if accurate, suggests a family of educated public servants who formed an integral part of the city's governing classes, moving with ease throughout the higher echelons of Tournai society and earning enough to be comfortable, if not wealthy.

Tournai during the fifteenth century was one of the largest settlements in the region, a 'fair and strong town' according to Philippe de Commines, formerly part of Flanders but annexed to France in the fourteenth century. Predominately French-speaking, despite their Flemish past and proud independence, the citizens traditionally 'bore a great affection' to successive kings of France, and had even been courted by Joan of Arc in June 1429 during her spirited campaign against England, when she appealed to the 'gentle loyal Frenchmen' of the city to provide aid. That Warbeck, who was never said to be French by birth, was nevertheless later referred to as a 'French lad' by Gerald FitzGerald, 8th Earl of Kildare, is perhaps indicative of his upbringing in Tournai. In the interests of trade, however, the merchants of Tournai, which would have included members of the Osbek and Ffaro families, worked to preserve their political neutrality with their Flemish and Burgundian neighbours, ensuring their income and trading connections suffered minimal disruption during the ever-changing geopolitical situation of the period.[4]

According to Warbeck, if his confession is given credence, during his early teens he was sent by his mother to Antwerp for six months to stay with her cousin John Steinbeck, an officer of the town. It was expected that he would learn the Flemish language to complement his natural French, a useful skill should he enter the family trade. Briefly returning to Tournai because of intermittent political turmoil in Flanders, Warbeck said he returned to Antwerp under the guidance of a merchant named Berlo, but after falling gravely ill was moved once more to board with a skinner. Significantly, this latest residence was located near the house of the English merchants.

After recovering from his five-month-long illness, Warbeck continued his nomadic life by accompanying Berlo to Barowe, modern-day Bergen Op Zoom. He spent two months lodging in an inn bearing the 'sign of the old man' before moving on to Middelburg in the Province of Zeeland to stay with John Strewe, from whom he was tasked with learning an unspecified language, possibly English. Warbeck recalled that he remained under Strewe's care between Christmas and Easter, certainly enough time to start developing some proficiency in the language he was studying, and it is during this period in Middelburg he first encountered the company of Sir Edward Brampton, a Portuguese Jew born Duarte Brandão who had risen high in Yorkist circles during the reigns of Edward IV and Richard III.[5]

Brampton had emigrated to England during the 1460s where he quickly converted to Christianity, taking his new English name from Edward IV before dutifully entering royal service. Brampton soon established close relations with his new master and the wider House of York, providing 'good service to the king in many battles' for which he was rewarded in 1472 with letters of denizenship and property in London. He later served as an esquire of the king's body and governor of Guernsey, and after Edward's death in 1483 continued to serve Richard III, under whom he was knighted in August 1484. The same month, Brampton was granted the considerable sum of £100 'in consideration of services to be rendered' for 'certain indentures', although what these mysterious services were remains a matter of speculation. They may or may not be concerned with the fate of the Princes in the Tower.[6]

After Henry Tudor invaded England and deposed Richard III at Bosworth in August 1485, Brampton resurfaced across the Channel under the protection of Margaret of York in Flanders before returning home to Portugal, forfeiting the English lands and grants he had accumulated over the previous two decades for his service to the Yorkists. During this post-Bosworth period the paths of Warbeck and Brampton appear to have briefly crossed, or rather re-crossed if one believes the pretender was indeed the same Prince Richard the Portuguese had known during the lifetime of Edward IV.

According to Warbeck's thorough confession, he claimed he left his family behind in Tournai after his stay in Middelburg so he could accompany Brampton's wife back to Portugal. This probably occurred sometime after Easter 1487 when he left Strewe's household and is corroborated by the Portuguese knight's own testimony almost a decade later, given during an inquisition that took place in Setúbal on 25 April 1496.[7] Though Brampton's account may have been clouded by a desire to ingratiate himself with the English king in anticipation of future opportunity in the land he had once lived, he was unequivocal that the pretender claiming at that time to be Richard of York was little more than a youth from Tournai named Piris, the son of a boatman whose name, given in the Iberian fashion, was Bernal Uberque. He could not be one of the Yorkist princes for they had been killed, Brampton said – 'the worst evil in the world'.

The Portuguese was able to provide further insight into the background of Warbeck, claiming the family lived below the St Jean Bridge in Tournai and that the boy had been placed in the household of an organist for several years before he ran away, the start of a dramatic lifetime on the run that would eventually bring him into direct conflict with the English king. Brampton's testimony also agreed that Warbeck had relocated to Middelburg, where the knight understood the teenager had found employment with a craftsman who sold needles and purses.

Brampton's knowledge, it seems, originated from his English wife Margaret Beaumont, who was living opposite the craftsman during this period. Margaret had an assortment of French boys in her service, with whom Warbeck started associating, supporting the idea he was naturally proficient in their language from his Tournai upbringing. When Brampton summoned his wife home to Portugal, he claimed that Warbeck found out from the French boys and boldly invited himself along for the voyage. This was corroborated by the pretender's own confession the following year.

Brampton, however, said he rejected Warbeck upon the latter's arrival in Lisbon, claiming he had no use for another French servant in his employ, and instead found the adventurous youth a place in the household of a gentleman named Pero Vaz da Cunha, the one-eyed knight whose name was given as Petir Vacz de Cogna in the pretender's own recollection.

Brampton next encountered Warbeck during the marriage festivities of Prince Afonso in the autumn of 1490, where the youth was conspicuous in an opulent doublet with sleeves of brocade covered by a silk gown. Lisbon must have been an exhilarating and energetic place to live during the late 1480s, particularly for someone with a bold spirit like Warbeck, absorbing the extraordinary accounts of various explorers freshly returned from their latest travels around west and southern Africa.

It was the Age of Discovery, and the boy who had recently arrived from the Burgundian Netherlands must have been seduced by the opportunities further afield, for both testimonies agree that Warbeck soon voiced a desire to leave the Iberian Peninsula. It was Brampton's understanding the youngster, who folded up all his clothes for the voyage, including the brocade doublet and silk gown, initially attempted a return to Flanders but having missed one ship's departure impulsively boarded another that was bound for Ireland first. It was the expensive outfits that Warbeck took with him, Brampton surmised, that led the Irish to presumptuously assume he was of more princely bearing than a mere boatman's son. Warbeck would give the name of the man who took him to Ireland as the Breton merchant Pregent Meno.

Brampton wasn't the only figure interrogated during the Setúbal sessions in 1496, assembled to try and find out who this pretender harassing the English king truly was. Rui de Sousa, a high-ranking household knight of Manuel I of Portugal, testified he had met Edward IV's son Richard of York when visiting England during the late king's reign, and had considered the boy to have been the most beautiful creature he had ever laid eyes upon. When pressed about Perkin Warbeck, who had assumed the persona of that same boy in recent years, de Sousa agreed that this pretender had arrived in Portugal in the company of Brampton's wife before entering the service of Pero Vaz, who treated him as a page. Like Brampton, de Sousa also noted Warbeck's attire during Prince Afonso's wedding, but when probed if he personally considered this youth to be the same royal boy he had once encountered in England, he answered no, for Prince Richard had been more beautiful.

A herald of the Portuguese king named Tanjar, meanwhile, was similarly quizzed about his knowledge of Warbeck, responding he had not only seen him living with Pero Vaz but knew him to be a native of Tournai, the same town from which the herald himself originated. Tanjar recounted how on one journey to his homeland he was visited by a boatman called John Osbeque, who queried if he had come across his son, whose name the herald understood to be Piris, in Lisbon. The father provided a list of distinguishing marks that could identify the boy, about fourteen going on fifteen years old, including a mark under his eye, an upper lip that was slightly raised, and thin legs. The herald admitted he had indeed encountered such a youth in Portugal.

With the Portuguese thereafter losing sight of Warbeck upon his departure to Ireland, the pretender's own confession claimed that when he arrived in Cork, the locals, presumably because of the fine clothes in his possession and in which he may even have been dressed, accused him of being Edward, Earl of Warwick, a charge he strenuously denied. His hosts were not convinced, however, for Mayor John Lewelyn ordered the well-dressed stranger to swear upon the Gospel and a crucifix he wasn't the son of the duke of Clarence, nor any other of his blood. Warbeck recalled he was then approached by a pair of Englishmen, Stephen Poytron and John Atwater, who declared he was in fact the bastard son of Richard III, a possible reference to someone known as John of Gloucester, which again was denied.

Poytron and Atwater supposedly counselled Warbeck not to be afraid of revealing his royal identity, promising to aid and assist him in any quarrel he had with the usurper occupying the English throne, Henry VII. The visitor says that he was, after some resistance, forced to learn English as well as how to adopt a princely bearing. After a short period, his new accomplices, who now also included John Taylor and Hubert Burke amongst others, encouraged Warbeck to assume the persona of Richard, Duke of York, the younger of the so-called Princes in the Tower. Once he agreed, the pretender was widely proclaimed around Cork to be the rightful heir of the House of York, ready to reclaim the throne that had been taken away from his elder brother in 1483.[8]

The aforementioned account is the gripping tale of Perkin Warbeck's nomadic life covering the period from his childhood through to his sudden appearance in Ireland, as recounted by his own confession post-capture and elaborated upon by the testimonies of various Portuguese knights. Although there are some minor discrepancies, the accounts do roughly concur – Warbeck was a native of Tournai who spent time moving between various households in Flanders before heading to Portugal with the wife of Edward Brampton. A chance encounter provided him the 'opportunity to continue onwards to Ireland where the silk clothes of his master evidently made an impression on a group of English dissidents living in Cork. His name was consistently given as Piris by the Portuguese trio, whilst his father's name is variously recorded as John Osbek, Bernal Uberque, and John Osbeque, the surnames of which are undeniably similar.

Lending further credibility to Warbeck's 1497 confession that he was merely an imposter is the fact that many of his mentioned relations are found in the fifteenth-century archives of Tournai; Pierart Flan, known as Petir Flam in the confession, and Pierart Faron, or Petir Ffaro, are found in municipal records for 1459, whilst in 1474 is a record for Jehan de Werbecque, son of the late Diericq de Werbecque.[9] A separate document uncovered in the late nineteenth century also provides the family name as Werbecque, with the son's name recorded as Pierrechon, or Pierre, not too dissimilar from how the pretender was later known by the Portuguese and English.

His mother's name, however, is not Kateryn de Ffaro in this latter record, but rather Nicaise or Caisine, which is certainly a puzzling discrepancy for which there is no present explanation.[10] Even the merchant who supposedly conveyed Warbeck to Ireland, Pregent Meno, can be clearly traced in the historical record, having been granted a sum of £300 from the customs of Dublin and Drogheda in 1495 and the constableship of Carrickfergus the following year, perhaps as a reward for information provided about the origins of the pretender.[11]

It may be conjectured the confession was forged by Henry VII's royal officials, shrewdly utilising the names of a genuine Tournaisis family to conceal Warbeck's Yorkist pedigree. This would have been a risky tactic, however, and could have been exposed at any moment, raising more questions to answer about the pretender's identity and the royal suppression of evidence. The story is certainly believable.

Several years prior to the confession and the Setúbal testimonies, however, Warbeck's recollection of his earlier life to his captive audience in Ireland and further afield couldn't have been more different. The clearest example of the story Warbeck and his supporters started to publicly spread is found in a Latin letter written from Dendermonde, Flanders, two years later on 8 September 1493. This document was addressed to Queen Isabella of Castile and was composed in the name of Richard Plantagenet, second son of Edward IV and Duke of York.

In the letter, Warbeck, as Richard, declared that his brother of pious memory Edward V had indeed been 'miserably put to death' as earlier rumours had suggested, but he himself had been spared by the unidentified lord who had received orders to destroy him. Who had given the order to murder this prince was left unstated. The anonymous would-be killer instead took pity on the innocent eight-year-old boy, and in return for a promise upon the sacraments not to reveal his name, birth, or royal lineage for several years to come, he was spirited away to safety, albeit 'deprived of country, inheritance and fortune'.

The letter continued, claiming that Warbeck, or rather Prince Richard as he was in this account, was then sent away under the care of two unnamed protectors, who were at the same time his jailors and governors. He thereafter led a miserable nomadic life 'in the midst of extreme perils' for nearly eight years during which he was concealed in various places throughout western Europe. In time, however, one of his protectors passed away and the other returned to his home country, leaving the boy alone and without income. It was thus he chose to emigrate to Portugal, although without giving reason why, and onwards to Ireland where he was 'received with great joy and honour' by the earls of Kildare and Desmond. It was only here in Cork that his true identity was revealed.[12]

The age given by Warbeck in the letter to Castile regarding his disappearance, eight but nearly nine, is a curiosity, for it was incorrect. In the summer of 1483, the presumed disappearance date for the two princes, Prince Richard would have been nine years old, his tenth birthday occurring in August. Whilst acknowledging the possibility Warbeck, if truly the prince, did not accurately know his age due to the nature of his wandering lifestyle away from close family, it must also be considered a blunder that might just have betrayed the author's deception.

It does seem inescapably opportune that Edward V, the elder of the two siblings and senior in rank, is reported murdered, which obviously cleared the path for Warbeck to advance his own claim as Richard unhindered. None of those who had helped in the apparent escape from the Tower were named, which must also raise questions about their existence. Omitted from the letter are any specific memories of this past life Warbeck could have used to persuade the reader he giving a truthful account, such as intimate recollections of his parents, Edward IV and Elizabeth Wydeville, or other notable incidents that would have been emotionally stirring, such as colourful Christmas celebrations or the worrisome period he spent in sanctuary with his anxious mother in 1483.

Unlike the 1497 confession by Warbeck, this earlier account of his supposed escape is frustratingly vague and its veracity must surely be questioned. In particular, the impulsive behaviour of a compassionate assassin who failed to undertake his duty to kill the prince, instead inexplicably permitting a potential threat to the throne to abscond overseas, stretches the bounds of credibility.

When considering the convenient timing of Warbeck's appearance in Ireland, around November 1491, attention must be paid to a French-sponsored plot revolving around the captive Yorkist prince, Edward, Earl of Warwick, which occurred shortly before the pretender's emergence. On 15 September 1491, John Taylor, an Exeter merchant and former customs agent under Edward IV, wrote a letter from his refuge in Rouen, Normandy, to John Hayes, a native of Tiverton in Devon. Taylor implored Hayes to recall unspecified conversations the pair had once exchanged in St Peter's Church, Exeter, and the nearby Dominican friary, before claiming:

> Sir, ye shall understand, that the Kynges grace of Fraunce, by th' advyse and assent of his Counsell, woll aide and support your maisters son to his right, and all his lovers and servants, and take theym as his frendys, bothe by land and by water, and all they may well be assured savely to come unto Fraunce, both bodyes and goodes, and suche as have no goodes they may come hedre and be releved, if they be knowen for true men to the quarell; and over that, he woll geve help of his own subgiettes, with shippes, gold and silver, to come into England, and with suche nombre as shall be thought by you, and by other youre maisters sonnes freinds, necessarie and behofull for his helpe and sucour, and they to be redy and land at such tyme and place, as ye with othre shall appoint.[13]

Taylor, like Hayes, had once been in the employ of George, Duke of Clarence, and the master's son mentioned in the letter referred to that duke's only son, Warwick, who remained under close royal supervision in the Tower of London four years after the collapse of the Lambert Simnel plot. Taylor was an ardent York loyalist, having also served Richard III during his brief reign, and was dismissed from his customs post just a few months after Henry VII's accession. Prior to his dismissal, however, he had managed to develop a wide range of useful contacts across a lengthy career, relationships with many continental ports that would hold him in good stead in coming years.[14]

With opportunities for advancement appearing unlikely under Tudor rule, Taylor fled his homeland for France, and his letter home to Hayes now promised the collusion of Charles VIII in a plot against the English king. For this apparent pledge of support, Taylor wrote that the French monarch 'woll aske nothing in recompence, but to do it for the wrong he dyd, in making Henry Kyng of England', referring to the latter's recent support for Breton interests, 'and for the gode will he oweth unto the sonne of youre maister, for they be nere of kyn'. That Charles was in fact nearer in kin to Henry was unmentioned. Other conspirators cited in the letter included Hayes's fellow Devonians William Ward of Topsham, Thomas Gale of Dartmouth (who had also lost his office as a result of Henry's victory at Bosworth), John Allen of Pole, and John Affright, notably a servant of Anne Beauchamp, Countess of Warwick and grandmother of the present earl.

That Taylor surfaced in Ireland around November 1491, near Warbeck's own arrival, indicates the two were already associated in some manner, and suggests the former had resorted to an alternative plan after accepting the futility of advancing the earl of Warwick's cause whilst he remained firmly in Henry VII's control. In effect, he had substituted a genuine Yorkist prince with a fraud. Henry certainly suspected the conspiracy's origins to be in France, raising a complaint to Pope Innocent VIII on 8 December 1491 that the French had incited 'certain barons in Ireland and in our kingdom to rebel against us', despite his inclination to be 'desirious of peace'.[15]

Later Tudor writers such as Bernard André, Polydore Vergil and Edward Hall, for their part, firmly placed culpability for Warbeck's sudden appearance in Ireland on Margaret of York, the dowager duchess of Burgundy. André believed the redoubtable sister of Richard III and Edward IV had 'conceived a new and unprecedented scheme' against Henry VII in which she hoped to 'channel her undying hatred' onto his subjects to provoke a popular uprising. Vergil mused that Margaret was 'under the influence of envy' and 'cherished such a deep hatred of King Henry, that it seemed she would be content with nothing short of his death', invoking her 'cunning and craft' by despatching Warbeck, whom she had personally instructed in English affairs 'so that afterwards he should readily remember everything and convince all by his performance that he sprung from the Yorkist line'. For Hall, Margaret was a 'diabolicall duchess', but if Warbeck's confession was at all accurate, all three were mistaken and possibly influenced by her later involvement.[16]

Regrettably, the origins of Perkin Warbeck remain a frustrating cause of speculation, which in the absence of unbiased, independently corroborated sources are dependent on which of the above accounts one personally gives more credence. To accept the version provided by Warbeck himself, that he was a son of the Osbek, or Werbecque, family of Tournai, is to believe his testimony after capture was truthful and not manufactured by a nervous Tudor regime eager to obscure his actual background, which, if royal, had the potential to reignite years of bitter conflict.

This account is supported by the Setúbal testimonies of the Portuguese knights in 1496 and knowledge in Tournai circles that a Warbeck family truly existed. The counter-argument is that such evidence, although outside the English king's jurisdiction, may have been manipulated to his benefit, although this is highly implausible. Henry VII was a powerful figure by the mid-1490s, but still just one participant in a never-ending chess game of political one-upmanship amongst his fellow potentates, rather than someone able to drive policy to his own advantage.

What is, however, undeniable is that Warbeck arrived on the political scene at the very moment Anglo-French relations under Tudor rule were at their lowest ebb, a consequence of Henry VII's determination to support Brittany against France's expansionist ambition. The pretender's cause was heavily backed at its outset by Charles VIII and France, and their motivation for doing so is transparent.

To trust the well-spoken and intelligent figure[17] who arrived in southwestern Ireland in 1491 was indeed Richard of Shrewsbury, Duke of York, is to accept at least one of the so-called Princes in the Tower escaped from the fortress unscathed, exonerating their uncle Richard III of at least one count of child-murder and perhaps solving part of English history's most infamous cold case. This latter theory must be considered the more far-fetched of the two, featuring anonymous conspirators and a convenient backstory, and yet cannot necessarily be wholly discounted in light of conclusive evidence to the contrary.

Dominic Mancini, for example, only made specific reference to rumours of Edward V's death, with no mention of his brother Richard,[18] whilst Warbeck did supposedly master the English language and court etiquette to such an extent it was passable around those with first-hand knowledge of such matters. Both these curiosities can be explained of course; Mancini may simply have neglected to mention the younger boy due to his inferior status, and the Warbecks of Tournai were certainly no paupers, as is often supposed for a family of boatmen – any child of theirs would have received an appropriate education.

Nevertheless, this subject proves an unsolvable conundrum, even after five hundred years of assiduous academic scrutiny by those eager to uncover the truth behind this enigmatic figure popularly remembered as Perkin Warbeck, or perhaps more correctly Piris Osbeck or Pierrechon Werbecque. The two most well-known sources about the issue, Warbeck's 1493 letter to Isabella of Castile signed Richard, Duke of York, and his contradictory confession post-capture four years later in which he sought to correct earlier claims, have both been treated with scepticism by historians, and we therefore remain none the wiser as to who he truly was. The matter has effectively been reduced to one of personal intuition upon reading all the assembled evidence.

As 1491 drew to a close, and word reached the astonished royal court in London about events in distant Cork where a Yorkist prince had apparently been 'raised from the dead',[19] Henry VII was faced with a similar challenge, except it was one which posed an immediate risk to the welfare of himself and his family. This latest adversary, regardless of his background, was about to become a very significant problem for the naturally cautious Tudor king, and crucially, from the outset of what would prove a complex conspiracy, Henry simply did not know who he was truly dealing with – pretender, or brother-in-law?

*

By the winter during which the elegant if mysterious figure of Perkin Warbeck was creating a stir in the streets and taverns of Cork, Henry VII had occupied the English throne for just over six years. Having crowned his queen, fathered three children, overseen three parliaments, and wrangled with some of Europe's foremost rulers in that time, all whilst successfully repelling several attacks on his sovereignty including a hard-fought battle at Stoke Field, the king would have been forgiven if he yearned for a period of quiet in which to rest his weary mind. It had certainly been a frantic few years since defeating Lambert Simnel's rebel forces in June 1487, a period in which Henry had focused his attention on nurturing his credibility as king both within and without his realm.

The second parliament of the reign had dissolved on 18 December 1487, and aside from confirming the attainders of the rebels who had mobilised against Henry at Stoke Field, was responsible for passing a judicial act creating a new committee separate to the king's council, which handed certain privy councillors statutory authority to bypass the traditional common law process, in effect allowing them to deal swiftly with matters considered contrary to public order and the security of the king. The act, frequently if erroneously known as the Star Chamber Act, was intended to supplement any defects in the legislative process for 'the policy and good rule of this realm' by permitting any two of the chancellor, treasurer and lord privy seal to meet with two chief justices, a bishop and a lord temporal to 'punish divers Misdemeanours' that breached the peace, including murder, robbery, perjury, debt, slander, unlawful assemblies and corruption.

An appeal made to this dedicated court by a plaintiff would result in the defendant's examination under oath. Punishment could include fines, imprisonment, whipping, branding, cutting off of ears, or any other public humiliation deemed appropriate to the offence committed. The act was a direct response to the various threats Henry had experienced during his short tenure upon the throne, and provided the vigilant king with an additional legislative weapon to deter new outbreaks of disorder that threatened his position. Other outcomes of the parliament included canvassing papal support to suppress the misuse of sanctuary by rebels, agreeing additional provisions to improve the strategic garrisons of Berwick and Calais on the periphery of the king's realm, and a grant of taxation to help bolster the general defence of England.[20]

Henry's reasonable concerns about matters of defence were hardly assuaged by the lynching of his chief northern lord Henry Percy, 4th Earl of Northumberland, in April 1489. The earl's violent downfall occurred after the king secured a parliamentary subsidy earlier that year to levy a tax totalling around £100,000, a burden which prompted a Cleveland man named John Chamber to raise a protest march on York declaring 'they wolde pay no money'. Henry was sensitive to rebellion in the north more so than any other part of his realm, and commanded Northumberland not only to confront the protesters but to ensure the tax was thoroughly enforced throughout the region and all sums collected. The earl responded to the request and encountered the tax rebels near Topcliffe on 28 April, but before he could accomplish his duty he was deserted by his retainers, and 'ayenst al humanyte' was 'cruelly murdred and distroid'.[21] Some believed it to be in response to Northumberland's failure to aid Richard III at Bosworth.

Compounding matters for the alarmed king was the consequent emergence of another collection of rebels under the direction of

Sir John Egremont, an illegitimate and disenfranchised relation of Northumberland whom Vergil considered 'ambitious for power'. By 6 May 1489, the mob under Egremont's command had assembled near Sheriff Hutton, one of the great Yorkshire strongholds of the Nevilles, before turning south towards York, entering the city on 15 May with the aid of Thomas Wrangwash, an alderman once associated with Richard III. Intending to overrun the rebels before they gathered further support as he had two years earlier, King Henry wasted little time in mobilising his troops under the command of the earls of Oxford and Surrey, who headed north 'with a greate arme' that prompted Egremont's men to flee 'in all directions as a cowardly crowd usually does'.[22]

Although the rebel knight evaded capture and sought refuge in Flanders, often a place of sanctuary for Yorkist dissidents, Chamber was one of six men hanged in York, an unambiguous warning to the northerners that the king's patience was wearing thin. Even so, Henry did not wholly discard his natural inclination to show restraint when punishing his enemies, and issued pardons to another 1,500 miscreants, albeit often with punitive bonds to guarantee their future good behaviour.[23]

During these final years of the decade, Henry was also preoccupied with imposing himself in political affairs on the continent, a complicated arena populated by a host of scheming rulers scrambling to advance their interests, dynastically or economically, to the detriment of their rivals. He himself had been the beneficiary of such politicking earlier in his life, firstly safeguarded by the Bretons for over a dozen years before being propelled towards the English crown by the money and ships of the French, and some hardy soldiers of Scotland. It was with some frustration therefore that in 1488 Henry was reluctantly pulled towards defending the interests of Duke Francis II of Brittany against the increasingly expansionist policy of the French regency council, who, 'greedy to extend their rule' on behalf of the underage Charles VIII, prepared to wage war to annex the duchy.[24]

Henry had reason to be indebted to both king and duke, and therefore endeavoured to serve as an intermediary in the escalating conflict, dispatching his dependable almoner Christopher Urswick to address both camps in a futile effort to resolve the thorny issue. According to Vergil, the English king instinctively 'preferred a pacific rather than warlike solution', but in this matter was forced to accept that in lieu of peace 'it would not be to his advantage that Brittany should be occupied by the French'. His efforts were undermined by the rash actions of his queen's uncle Sir Edward Wydeville, 'an impetuous man, trained to arms and incapable of languishing in idleness'.

Without royal approval, Wydeville assembled a band of soldiers numbering four hundred and covertly departed his base on the Isle of Wight to sail to Duke Francis's rescue, but his unauthorised crusade proved disastrous; on 28 July 1488, a Breton force bolstered by Wydeville's recruits was routed by the French near Saint-Aubin-du-Cormier, with the renegade English commander just one of many who perished on the battlefield. Though Henry eventually 'made up his mind to support the duke' and forfeit any pretension of negotiating a cross-Channel peace, Francis II was exposed by this latest military setback and reluctantly yielded to his powerful adversary, signing the Treaty of Sablé on 20 August and formally accepting his status as vassal to the French king.[25]

Less than a month later, the elderly duke was dead, succeeded by his vulnerable twelve-year-old daughter Anne. Faced with the renewed prospect of the French overrunning Brittany, in effect expanding their presence along the entirety of the Channel and disrupting the profitable Anglo-Breton trade, Henry VII responded by openly pledging his support for the Bretons by ratifying his own pact, the Treaty of Redon, on 14 February 1489, the terms of which stipulated he would provide 6,000 men for the duchy's defence. It was the taxes raised for this venture that triggered events which led to the lynching of the earl of Northumberland in Yorkshire two months later.

Matters were further complicated in December 1490 when Maximilian I, King of the Romans and father of young Philip, the underage duke of Burgundy, married the Breton duchess Anne by proxy, a union the French considered a violation of the Sablé agreement. Henry VII could only observe from afar as Charles VIII's regency council launched another military campaign against the Bretons, gradually seizing control of the duchy and its teenage duchess, whom the French king himself married on 6 December 1491 at the Château de Langeais, conveniently ignoring her earlier union. His English counterpart, meanwhile, had only served to anger the French by meddling in the Breton affair, and they now sought to respond in kind, having strengthened their domestic position.

Henry VII enjoyed greater success elsewhere; in July 1486, he secured a three-year truce with Scotland to protect his northern border, and on 27 March 1489 the Treaty of Medina del Campo was signed with the Spanish, which not only promised a future union between Prince Arthur and Katherine of Aragon, but also secured a formidable ally if relations with the French continued to deteriorate and head towards war. Henry also engineered a working relationship with Maximilian I, who for four years between 1488 and 1492 offered no palpable support for Yorkist plots despite the malign influence of his stepmother-in-law Margaret of York, preferring to concentrate on his own political agenda in opposing French expansion into his territory. During Christmas 1490, Maximilian was even inducted into the Order of the Garter, a clear indication of friendship and cooperation between both rulers as they sought to frustrate French belligerence together.[26]

Matters in Henry's personal life also gave the king cause for optimism as the tumultuous decade neared its conclusion. On 28 November 1489 at Westminster Palace, Queen Elizabeth gave birth to a daughter christened Margaret for her paternal grandmother, followed by a second son on 28 June 1491 named Henry after his father.[27] Labour during the fifteenth century was a hazardous feat of endurance that could, and often did, claim the lives of both mother and child, and Henry we can imagine certainly exhaled with considerable relief once the danger had passed. Queens, after all, were no more exempt from death during the childbirth process than the common woman, but unfortunately the burden was very much upon their shoulders to secure the future of their dynasty with heirs, whatever the risk.

A set of ordinances arranged under the supervision of the king's mother Margaret Beaufort nevertheless ensured the queen was as comfortable as could be for each of her pregnancies, if restricted by strict protocol considered appropriate to her rank. The chambers designated for the royal births were heavily decorated with rich cloth of Arras, with only one window exempt to allow a small degree of natural light to fill the room during the daytime. The bed, the centrepiece of the room and where the queen would give birth to a prince or princess, was as expected an object of unsurpassed luxury, consisting of a woollen mattress, sheets crafted from fine Rennes cloth, fustian cloth pillows filled with down, a head-sheet made using cloth of gold, and a scarlet counterpane furred with ermine and embroidered with crimson velvet. The floor throughout the chamber was carpeted, whilst the queen was provided a chair of estate she was free to use at her pleasure and from where she could receive spices and wine brought by her servants, all of whom had to be female.[28]

Fortunately for all concerned, Elizabeth emerged from each of her pregnancies during this period in full health, and by the summer of 1491 the royal couple had an encouraging nursery of three healthy children, the next generation of the Tudor dynasty and each representative of the physical union between York and Lancaster. As Henry and Elizabeth cast their proud eyes upon the brood they had created whenever visiting the nursery at Greenwich, they could hardly have predicted it would be the youngest of the trio who would eventually succeed his father and become one of Europe's most infamous, and immortal, kings; at the time, however, young Prince Henry's status was little more than that of 'spare heir'.

Despite such optimism for the future of his reign, the unexpected emergence of Perkin Warbeck, *alias* Prince Richard, across the Irish Sea towards the end of 1491 proved deeply concerning for Henry, particularly as he had already endured one distressing Irish-backed insurrection that almost toppled him from his throne. Fortunately for the resilient king, the response in Ireland for the latest Yorkist pretender in their midst was somewhat lukewarm, and certainly more restrained than the warm embrace which greeted Lambert Simnel in Dublin a few years earlier.

Warbeck, 'not unpleasant in appearance' according to Vergil, and whose 'mind was sharp and artful',[29] undoubtedly raised curiosity amongst the Corkonians he encountered on the streets of their city, and, aided by the reassurance of sponsors such as John Taylor and John Atwater, garnered some degree of support for his claim. There was little reason why the average citizen would doubt the dramatic story presented to them that this majestic figure was a Yorkist prince, particularly after learning one of those offering support to the teenager was Maurice FitzGerald, 9th Earl of Desmond. His cousin Gerald FitzGerald, 8th Earl of Kildare and prominent above all other Anglo-Irish lords, was also suspected of extending the hand of friendship to Warbeck, a fact alleged by the pretender's own words in his later 1493 letter to Isabella of Castile.[30]

Unlike the Simnel affair, however, in which Kildare had assumed a leading role alongside his brother Thomas, the earl's participation was more subdued this time around, with no armies raised or coronations organised. He may not have been involved at all, with his name merely used by the conspiracy's leaders to lend credibility to the cause and open a potential breach between king and lord that could be exploited in future. In a letter to the earl of Ormond in 1493, Kildare protested his innocence, bemoaning how 'I am accused to the kyng, as I understand, that I sholde have layn with the French lad' before avowing, 'I never lay with hym ne ayded, comforted, ne supported hym,' which he defiantly swore his fellow lords could confirm.[31]

It is not inconceivable Kildare was telling the truth, particularly considering the lack of any solid evidence to the contrary other than Warbeck's own testimony, and perhaps he had opted to honour the terms of his earlier pardon having already witnessed his brother slain during the previous plot to dethrone the king. The earl's reference to Warbeck as 'the French lad' also suggests he may have suspected, or even known, that the pretender's origins lay in France, and that as a foreign fraud he wasn't worthy of his support.

Despite the success of the earl of Lincoln in amassing a considerable Irish army on behalf of Simnel in 1487, it is clear Warbeck and his advocates failed to provoke a similar outpouring of support during their own sojourn in Ireland. There are multiple reasons for this; the most obvious one is that, despite his demeanour, appearance and attire, many of the lords were simply not convinced this teenager before them was truly Prince Richard. It is unlikely most of them had ever personally seen Edward IV in person, much less his son prior to the 1483 disappearance, and they were therefore ill placed to say with certainty Warbeck indeed resembled the prince.

The brutal collapse of the Simnel campaign, where a large section of Irish society had rallied to the pretender's cause only to be humiliated and punished, also weighed heavily on minds, even if they accepted Warbeck for who he said he was. Landowners like Kildare had little desire to forfeit their hereditary estates by breaking fresh oaths, whereas bishops and other clergy were likewise keen not to risk excommunication by flouting the pope's express wishes that Henry's right to reign was respected.

A further reason why Warbeck's tenure in Ireland was not as fruitful as he and his supporters had perhaps hoped is the energetic response of the English king, who acted more swiftly than he had against Lincoln and Simnel in 1487. Having been made aware of Warbeck's presence in Ireland around November 1491, by the end of the month Henry had dispensed orders for James Norwiche, a Doctor of Theology, to cross the sea and investigate the conduct of the Irish bishops[32] whilst on 6 December he issued a commission to James Ormonde and Thomas Garth 'to send an army' into the counties of Kilkenny and Tipperary in order 'to suppress his rebels and enemies' and 'arrest and commit to prison all delinquients'. The former's power was extensive; not only was Ormonde empowered to make statutes and issue proclamations on behalf of the government, but his authority temporarily superseded that of the lieutenant.[33]

Henry's urgency for their departure is palpable from a terse letter he wrote to his treasurer John Dynham two days later declaring his 'great mervaill' at learning that Garth had yet to receive his bows and arrows for the campaign, whereas Ormonde had only been handed a quarter of the funds he had been promised.[34] The king strengthened Ormonde's standing less than a week later by granting the knight, an illegitimate son of the late 6th Earl of Ormond, all castles and lordships in the counties of Meath, Kilkenny and Tipperary for a two-year period, a consciously political act considering the lands belonged to the earldom of March, a title closely associated with the House of York but now merged with the crown.

On 13 February 1492, meanwhile, Henry ordered a ship known as the *Margarete of Barstaple* to be fitted with guns and gunpowder, with the expectation that the vessel would patrol the southern Irish coast to monitor the 'state and condicion' of the rebels now known to be dwelling there.[35] Finally, on 11 June 1492, the king replaced Kildare as deputy lieutenant with Walter Fitzsimons, Archbishop of Dublin, an indication he remained uncertain of the earl's contribution to the conspiracy and which prompted the Irishman's letter to the earl of Ormond the following year protesting his innocence.[36]

Whether he was accepted as the duke of York or not by his Irish hosts, Warbeck and his backers were plainly aware after several months they had not cultivated enough support in Ireland to make a move against Henry, and if they were serious about advancing his claim to the English throne had little choice than to seek aid elsewhere before they were overrun. The options were limited.

The Spain of Ferdinand and Isabella and the Burgundian Netherlands under Maximilian I's influence were on amiable terms with Henry, as was Scotland, which could offer little assistance despite letters from Warbeck and the earl of Desmond appealing to James IV for help.[37] The only obvious destination therefore was France, from where the entire conspiracy likely originated through the determined efforts of John Taylor, formerly resident in Normandy and who maintained links with the French court. Warbeck's 1497 confession mentioned that an embassy from Charles VIII, led by a French-speaking Burgundian named Stephen Fryon and the French naval commander Loyte Lucas, arrived in Cork and promised this supposed duke of York and prospective contender for the English crown an enthusiastic welcome across the Channel.[38]

Fryon was a fascinating character with a storied career, having entered the service of Charles the Bold in the 1470s before transferring his services to Edward IV, who appointed him secretary in September 1480. He was retained by Richard III in 1483 to deal with matters 'in the Gallic tongue', and when Henry VII came to the throne Fryon initially adapted once again to a new master, operating as the new king's French secretary. Around 1489, however, he defected across the Channel to Charles VIII's court.[39]

Armed with intimate political knowledge of various European courts and first-hand experience of the etiquette required when dealing with kings and princes, Fryon was well-placed to tutor Warbeck during the voyage to France, refining the youth's behaviour and mannerisms so that day by day he appeared more prince than imposter. If Warbeck's roots were truly in Tournai and the surrounding area, he may even have developed a natural rapport with a teacher who shared a similar background, aiding his process of transformation from Perkin of Tournai into Richard of York. Even if one accepts the boy was a Yorkist prince by birth, it is likely Fryon's guidance would have proved invaluable in finessing his knowledge after years away from home.

It had been less than seven years since French patronage had played a crucial role in Henry VII's rise from unknown Welsh exile to king of England, but the once fruitful relationship between the two royal cousins was firmly consigned to the past by the start of the 1490s. England and France, not for the first or last time, were in open conflict with one another, and for Perkin Warbeck, whomsoever he truly was, this escalating feud provided a window of opportunity. He grabbed it with both hands.

10

War of Necessity

As the dawn of the sixteenth century approached, relations between the kingdoms of England and France remained as uneasy as they had been for previous generations, a cross-Channel enmity complicated by centuries of tenuous cooperation, regular intermarriage between royalty and, on several instances, protracted warfare fuelled by dynastic ambitions. What affected England often had an impact on France, and vice versa, with the result that generation after generation, individual rulers from both sides fervently sought to gain advantage over their rivals through any means at their disposal.

This inimical state of affairs between two nations that, on the surface, appeared to have much in common, had its origins in the remarkable rise of William II, Duke of Normandy, who invaded the south coast of England at the end of September 1066 and defeated the Anglo-Saxon Harold Godwinson two weeks later at the Battle of Hastings, ushering in a new Norman dynasty of English kings in the process. William's claim to the English throne stemmed from a promise he said he had received from the recently deceased king Edward the Confessor, his father Robert's first cousin. Though successful in his overseas venture, as duke of Normandy William still owed fealty to the French king Philip I. This conflicting status, equal on one hand as a fellow king yet subservient on the other as a mere vassal, introduced a new dynamic in Anglo-French relations that triggered considerable hostility on both sides of the Channel that has lasted, to varying degrees, to the present day, an unintended consequence of the Norman Conquest.

Poor relations between England and France were further exacerbated when Henry II, son of Empress Matilda and Geoffrey V,

160

Count of Anjou, acceded to the English throne in 1154, the first monarch of what later became known as the Plantagenet dynasty, named for a sprig of broom called *planta genista* that Count Geoffrey supposedly wore in his hat. Inheriting the kingdom of England through his mother and the duchy of Normandy and the counties of Anjou and Maine through his father, Henry II had also secured control over the duchy of Aquitaine two years earlier after his contentious marriage to Duchess Eleanor, who had previously been married to Louis VII of France. Henry II's marriage and inheritance therefore placed at his disposal a vast dominion stretching from the Scottish border in the north to the Pyrenees in the south, covering parts of Ireland and Wales and ensuring he was a significant geopolitical threat to successive French kings of the House of Capet.

Henry II's continental expansion proved unsustainable and crumbled during the reigns of his sons Richard I and John, in the latter of which Normandy was lost. Louis, son of Philip II of France, even invaded England in 1216 in an unsuccessful attempt to conquer the kingdom from that side of the Channel, as had occurred 150 years earlier. The two sides continued to clash throughout the thirteenth century until the Treaty of Montreuil was ratified in 1299, the terms of which partly approved the future marriage of Isabella, daughter of Philip IV of France, to Edward of Caernarfon, heir of Edward I of England, a union ultimately concluded on 25 January 1308 once the latter had become king. Isabella was just twelve years old at the time.

Although the marriage between a French princess and English king was intended by both parties to introduce a period of prolonged amity, within a generation war once more raged between the two kingdoms. Between 1314 and 1328, three of Isabella's brothers, Louis X, Philip V and Charles IV, each became king of France before passing away without legitimate male issue. For over three centuries the French throne had passed through the male line only, and upon Charles IV's demise, the crown passed not to Isabella or her English son Edward III, for it was agreed women could not transmit a claim, but rather to a cousin who acceded as Philip VI, the first of the ascendant House of Valois.

From the outset of Edward III's reign upon the English throne, the status of Aquitaine proved a contentious issue. The duchy had been conquered by the French shortly before Edward became king, and in 1329 he was compelled to pay homage to Philip VI in his capacity as duke to reclaim his inheritance. Relations between the two kings further deteriorated after Edward III provided refuge to Robert III of Artois, a friend-turned-foe of Philip's, and when in 1337 the French monarch declared Aquitaine would be confiscated in response, war was inevitable. Edward openly challenged Philip's right to the French throne, turning a political and economic dispute into a decidedly dynastic matter, and in June 1340 he crossed the Channel with a sizable army, triggering a brutal conflict of several distinct phases known to history as the Hundred Years War.

This bitter and protracted war only served to further divide England and France, galvanising nascent nationalist fervour in both kingdoms and prompting French king Charles VII to refer to 'our ancient enemies the English' in 1436, after nearly a century of intermittent conflict.[1] The sentiment was unquestionably echoed amongst the English, who had grown increasingly hostile to their continental neighbours. Several ferocious and bloody battles were contested throughout the fourteenth and fifteenth centuries, including Crécy in 1346, Poitiers in 1356, Agincourt in 1415, Baugé in 1421, Verneuil in 1424, Formigny in 1450 and Castillon in 1453. The latter resulted in the distraught English finally relinquishing their lands in Aquitaine three hundred years after Eleanor brought the duchy to England via her marriage to Henry II. There had been famous victories and agonising defeats on both sides, but by the middle of the fifteenth century, it was the English who had been humiliatingly expelled from their continental possessions, Calais excluded.

As France prospered unencumbered by marauding English armies for the first time in several generations, recriminations within England over the devastating military losses in recent years compounded by spiralling financial issues opened fresh conflict, manifested by a vicious civil war which erupted amongst the noble classes who gradually mobilised into two distinct camps – York, initially fronted by Richard, Duke of York and the Neville father and son, earls of Salisbury and Warwick; and Lancaster, nominally led by Henry VI but guided by Queen Margaret of Anjou, Edmund Beaufort, 2nd Duke of Somerset, and a score of other magnates such as the Percy earls of Northumberland.

Louis XI, who reigned over France between 1461 and 1483 and was known by foreign contemporaries as 'the Universal Spider' on account of his scheming nature, persistently manipulated the desperate situation across the Channel to his own advantage.

He provided refuge to his Lancastrian cousins, including Jasper Tudor, Henry VII's uncle, and even helped reconcile Richard Neville, Earl of Warwick, to Margaret of Anjou in 1470 so that the previously implacable enemies could organise a joint invasion of Yorkist England. Henry VII, perhaps above all others, had himself benefitted from opportunistic French machinations in 1485 when his disparate army featuring French recruits sailed from Normandy largely funded by the regency council governing on behalf of the-then underage Charles VIII, continuing the meddlesome policy of his father, the cunning Louis XI.

By the early 1490s, however, it was Henry's turn as king of England to be a victim of French intrigue, a consequence of his support for the Bretons and contrary to the optimistic truce negotiated between the two kingdoms on 12 October 1485, two months after his accession and in which he amiably referred to the young French king as his 'most Derrest Cousyn'.[2] Cautious about Charles VIII's expansionist policy and the risk it potentially posed to England, Henry had already set plans in motion throughout 1491 to aggressively defend his realm. This, it should be noted, was months before Warbeck's presence in Ireland became known and certainly prior to the pretender's subsequent departure for France, which would only serve to exacerbate existing hostilities between the rival kings.

On 16 February 1491, for example, a commission was handed to John Gaye, master of *The Regent*, and five other men to recruit hardened sailors and soldiers to counteract the danger posed by the king's enemies who were 'daily congregating' around the English coast, whilst on 26 April a similar directive was entrusted to William Fortescue, William Copleston, Richard Lake and John Wheeler. On 2 May, Thomas Prate was ordered to convey artillery two hundred miles from the Tower of London to Dartmouth in Devon, suggesting Henry was anxious about an attack from the south-west. Nine days later, Stephen Bull of *La Margaret of Depe* also received a commission to head out to sea, and was again recruited on 24 October when he was appointed with 'armed power for the protection of the fishermen on the coasts of Norfolk and Suffolk from the king's enemies at present on the sea', with all costs borne by those who wanted to continue their trade under protection.[3]

When parliament assembled on 17 October, the king's foremost intention, 'with the Grace of God', was to appeal to the commons, and beyond that to his subjects, to agree that war with France was the wisest course of action in defending the realm from an antagonistic foe. He was aided in that matter by the persuasive words of Archbishop Morton's opening address, which declared such action must be considered acceptable where the cause was just. Parliament agreed with the case presented, and 'for the necessarie defence' of the kingdom granted a subsidy of two fifteenths and tenths from every city, town and burgh in England, a fractional tax levied on the value of all moveable goods, with the smaller amount for rural communities and the larger for urban settlements.[4]

Emboldened by parliament's support and pledge of funds, on 6 December 1491, the very date he handed a commission to James Ormonde and Thomas Garth to cross to Ireland to quell the unrest there caused by Warbeck's sudden appearance, Henry VII ordered Thomas Howard, 1st Earl of Surrey, the abbot of St Mary's Abbey in York, Sir Richard Tunstall, Sir Henry Wentworth, Sir Nicholas Knyfton and John Beverley to travel throughout Yorkshire gathering the tax.[5] Two days later, he wrote to Pope Innocent VIII complaining about French attempts to provoke the Scottish into attacking their English neighbours, for which they had provided money and provisions, whilst taking the opportunity to defend his own armament in response.

The king's detailed missive to Rome further explained how he had pleaded with the French to withdraw their forces from Brittany 'and treat their business not by force of arms, but by law and amicable adjustment', but the only terms forthcoming after a round of negotiations were considered 'disgraceful'. After France persisted with their 'incessant, vigorous, and calamitous war' against the Bretons and 'gradually usurped the whole duchy', Henry alleged they had also been inciting certain barons in Ireland to rebel against their king, presumably meaning men such as the earl of Desmond and possibly the earl of Kildare, and with the arrival of Warbeck across the Irish Sea known shortly before this letter was dispatched, he certainly had suspicions the impetus for the burgeoning conspiracy had its roots within Charles VIII's court. In short, according to the English king, the French were plotting 'all the mischief they can against us and our neighbours and confederates', which included Maximilian I and Burgundy.

Arguing that he had exhausted all 'peaceful means' in avoiding conflict and failed to obtain terms that were 'just and fair', Henry VII believed he had little recourse than to 'repel these manifold wrongs' by waging a 'war of necessity, having left nothing whatever untried for the maintenance of peace and friendship'.

This was, the English king was keen to assure the Holy Father, despite the fact nothing was more abhorrent to his sensitivities than the 'slaughter of men and the shedding of Christian blood'. His language became increasingly combative as the letter neared its conclusion, beseeching Pope Innocent VIII that such 'intense and insatiable coveting of the dominions of others cannot be borne' and that this 'violent thirst for annexation' and 'insolent lawlessness' by the French could not be left unbridled, for in time it may astonishingly threaten even the Holy See.[6]

Having worked on parliament and pope in canvassing widespread support for war at the end of 1491, Henry wasn't done with his propaganda efforts once the Christmas festivities of that year were concluded. On 10 January 1492 from his palace at Sheen he wrote another letter warning against the 'intense ambition' and 'insatiable covetousness' of the French, this time addressed to the commanding regent of Milan, Ludovico Sforza. Henry sternly warned Sforza about France's 'great thirst and desire for domination', led by a king who was 'so covetous of empire that the whole world would not suffice him', and declared how he was prepared to 'undertake a war' in alliance with Maximilian I and the king and queen of Spain, the latter buoyed by the recent fall of Muslim Granada. To his great cost in coming years, Sforza resisted the English king's overtures.

When word reached the English court later that year that Warbeck had not only departed Ireland but had been enthusiastically welcomed at the French court of Charles VIII, Henry had little option but to advance his plans and live up to the threats he had issued with increasing severity over the previous twelve months. Though 'constitutionally more inclined to peace than war',[7] Charles's burgeoning friendship with Warbeck was interpreted within England to be yet another affront to Henry's authority, and in order to maintain his standing he had to be seen to respond aggressively to such disrespect for his kingship.

It helped, of course, that by declaring war on the French Henry hoped to be seen continuing the well-trodden path of prestigious predecessors such as Edward IV, Henry V and Edward III in commanding an army overseas, capitalising upon their revered reputations amongst the common Englishman to enhance his own status by association. He even ordered new coins to be minted bearing the arms of France in the centre of the increasingly ubiquitous Tudor Rose, as well as commissioning horse trappings embroidered with the fleur-de-lys, a traditional French royal symbol.[8]

By the spring of 1492, war with France was no longer an unexpected course of action, as Henry's letters to the Pope and Sforza attest, but the motive for mobilising an army to cross the Channel had unquestionably shifted, from protecting Breton interests and maintaining the status quo to aggressively defending his own position in direct response to French plans to potentially provide military backing to Warbeck and his cohorts. Henry knew from personal experience how a pretender could thrive with only meagre resources and a determined following, and so resolved to nip any French-backed conspiracy in the bud. In short, the matter had turned decidedly personal for Henry, as it was now his crown rather than Breton sovereignty that was at stake.

It is evident from another letter written by William Paston on 18 February 1492 that preparations for war were progressing steadily, for Paston described how the king was sending ordinances daily to the seaside where tents and pavilions were rapidly under construction, with many gentlemen busy gathering horses, harnesses, carts and other supplies that would prove useful for the forthcoming campaign.[9] It was Paston's understanding his king planned to depart for France around Easter, but by May the growing royal army remained in England when indentures were agreed with twenty-six people, including the earls of Kent, Devon and Surrey, Viscount Welles, and several other lords and knights such as Sir William Stanley to provide further men-at-arms, lances, billmen and archers, both mounted and on foot, to serve with Henry for up to a year if necessary.[10] At the same time, three large breweries were erected in Portsmouth to supply the English troops who had started assembling in the town – much to their pleasure, one imagines.[11]

It was not until mid-June 1492 that a fleet of thirty-five ships left the south coast under the command of Sir Robert Willoughby, bound for Cherbourg on the northern tip of Normandy. After years of solid service under Edward IV, Willoughby had been one of Edward's former servants who joined Henry Tudor in exile in 1483, returning to England two years later during the Bosworth campaign, after which he rose to become the new king's councillor and a member of the prestigious Order of the Garter. He was now entrusted with fronting a preliminary expedition, with a remit to cause considerable disarray around the Cotentin Peninsula. When 1,500 English troops under his command temporarily disembarked near Barfleur, they managed to torch forty-five French vessels in the town's sizable harbour before being repelled.[12]

Henry VII was not complacent, however. On 2 August 1492, patents were issued to the sheriffs of Kent and Sussex, the mayor of Canterbury, the lieutenant of Dover, and the warden of the Cinque Ports, charging them to have their men ready at only an hour's notice,[13] suggesting the king's plans had almost reached fruition, if later than initially expected. In the same month another small force under Edward Poynings was sent across to besiege the town of Sluys, which fell to the English in October.[14]

Charles VIII could not ignore the escalating menace the English posed towards the north of his kingdom, but was nevertheless keen to focus his attentions, and his armies, elsewhere. In 1489, Innocent VIII had deposed and excommunicated Ferdinand I, King of Naples, over a monetary dispute, and instead offered the vacant crown to Charles, who claimed the throne through his paternal grandmother Marie of Anjou, daughter of a previous king, Louis II. Though the pope did ultimately reverse his decision, Charles's ambitions had nevertheless been boosted by the prize briefly held out to him, and the French king resolved to press his claim militarily, which he could hardly do without first neutralising the mounting English threat.

At the end of August, therefore, Charles extended an offer of peace to Henry, pledging to reimburse the English monarch for any costs incurred through the latter's support for the Bretons, a proposal that was firmly rejected. Henry desired greater concessions and – aware of Charles's desperation – would not be easily appeased. Military preparations in England therefore continued unabated until finally, in the first week of September 1492, the English king and his army moved purposefully from Windsor to Dartford, beginning their journey towards the Kent coast in preparation for the crossing.

From Dartford, Henry travelled through Sittingbourne and Canterbury to Sandwich, where he boarded a ship called *The Swan*, arriving in Calais on the morning of 2 October. Privy Purse records show that the king rewarded the mariners of *The Ship* with a payment of £6 13s 4d, whilst the minstrels who entertained him aboard were paid 13s 4d.[15] Accompanying Henry and *The Swan* through the Strait of Dover were around seven hundred other ships, carrying 14,000 men under the command of the duke of Bedford and earl of Oxford, the largest army assembled by any English king for a foreign expedition during the fifteenth century.[16] With the various standards of the king and his noblemen fluttering proudly high above the decks, the war fleet must surely have been a grand sight to behold.

October was late in the year to launch an extensive military campaign, for the harsh weather and lack of natural sustenance often created logistical difficulties absent, or at least less troublesome, during warmer summer months. Though naturally pragmatic and disinclined to war, Henry's preparations had been too thorough to postpone or even abandon the enterprise at this late stage, however. Disembarking in Calais, the last part of the continent still under English jurisdiction and where the ships could be unloaded without fear of ambush, his army pushed south-west until by 18 October 1492 they had reached the gates of Boulogne, the nearest French town of note, which was promptly besieged.

Although Boulogne possessed 'a resolute garrison' which 'energetically defended' the harassed town,[17] Henry's men bombarded the citizens into submission and captured Charles's attention. French envoys were once more dispatched to the English camp, though this time armed with an improved proposal it was hoped would prove more acceptable.

The English king deliberated upon the terms, and on 27 October sought the input of his lords, counsellors and captains, requiring their 'good feithfull and trew Counsell' in determining the best course of action, not just for his personal honour but also for the prosperity of England. The proposal was debated at length by twenty-four lords in total, led by the earls of Dorset, Shrewsbury, Kent and Devon, before they responded in writing that having considered the 'fair Advancement of the Season' in which the king's men suffer daily 'greate Seknesses', it was deemed 'most necessarie, hehofull, and honourable' to accept the terms 'without any Denigration of his Honeour Royall'. It was further expressed that Henry had firmly kept his promises thus far, to his considerable cost, having 'greately Jeopartid his Person Royall, making Werr and redy to geve Batell to his Enmye in Person'. It was unanimous; the king should accept the peace offered.[18]

Writing several years later, Polydore Vergil hinted that some English troops were 'immeasurably grieved' at this decision, and were 'indignant and angry with Henry, as though he had made peace with the enemy through fear'. Although it is expected there must have been some rumblings of discontent amongst the frustrated rank and file, who had perhaps hoped that the spoils of war would improve their personal circumstances, their king nevertheless judged 'a diplomatic victory to be no less glorious to a commander than a military victory', and in this instance it must be conceded it was a reasonable stance to assume, and one supported by his own lords.[19] No one could argue the terms secured were not generous, vindicating Henry's decision not to treat rashly at an earlier stage of negotiation, and to his undoubted pleasure surpassed those conceded to Edward IV at Picquigny in 1475.

On 3 November at Étaples, therefore, the English king formally agreed to halt his invasion of France in exchange for reimbursement of 620,000 crowns spent on defending Breton interests along with arrears of 125,000 crowns from the Picquigny agreement. It amounted to a colossal total of 745,000 crowns, which would be paid at a rate of 50,000 a year, increasing his annual income by half. The French proved as good as their word; the payments, which Vergil perceptively labelled 'an enormous sum of money', endured throughout the remainder of Henry's reign.[20]

Perhaps of utmost importance for Henry, however, at least in the immediate term, was that he procured a promise from Charles VIII that no further support would be proffered to any rebels, including most notably Perkin Warbeck. As far as Henry was concerned, his aborted crusade could be regarded as nothing more than a resounding success. Money equalled security, as did disrupting the overseas haven of rebels conspiring against his rule, and this had been achieved without needless bloodshed or extracting years of punishing taxation from his people for a war recent history had shown couldn't be won. Furthermore, Henry had shown his fellow European rulers that the English were, after decades distracted by internecine conflict between rival factions, once more a cohesive force that demanded respect. The king departed Calais satisfied, and returned to London on 22 November 1492 more than content with what had been accomplished.

For Perkin Warbeck, however, his brief French sojourn under the protection of Charles VIII was at an end. According to the letter he wrote to Queen Isabella of Castile the following year, Warbeck claimed that when he was in Ireland, 'The King of France then sent for him, promising him aid against Henry Richmond, usurper of the Crown of England' and upon arriving across the Channel was indeed shown 'the greatest honour' by his new host.[21] This account was corroborated by the pretender's 1497 confession in which he reiterated how an embassy had been sent to Cork beckoning him to France[22] and, given the context of Charles's growing frustration with the English king's meddling in Brittany, there seems little reason to doubt the veracity of these words.

After a lengthy voyage from southern Ireland, sailing around the Cornish coast and the Isles of Scilly and then into the English Channel, Warbeck was greeted at Harfleur by the Scottish-born Seigneur d'Aubugny Bernard Stewart. He had docked at the very same port where Henry himself had departed in August 1485 for the Bosworth campaign, upon which Stewart actually served as one of the commanders. It is not inconceivable Stewart spent a considerable amount of time in Henry's company both before and during their journey to England and into battle, and one wonders how this capable lord regarded Warbeck upon their introduction, the young man who now sought to overturn the great Tudor victory he himself had helped achieve. Regardless of any personal sentiment for Henry VII, however, if we assume any did indeed exist, in 1492 Stewart was nevertheless duty-bound by his service to Charles VIII to aid and protect Warbeck, and this he accomplished with utmost professionalism. Assisting him was another Scottish emigrant in the employ of the French king, Alexander Monypeny, Seigneur de Concressault, the French ambassador to James IV of Scotland, tasked with overseeing Warbeck's bodyguard.[23]

According to the account of Vergil, Warbeck was 'kindly received' by Charles VIII and 'honoured with a retinue and all the other dignities which were fitting for a man of royal descent', as he was purporting to be.[24] Surrounded by a small band of faithful adherents, including John Taylor and George Neville, the latter having served Richard III as an esquire to the body,[25] together they shadowed the main royal court throughout the summer of 1492 and into the autumn, observing escalating tensions between England and France with more than a passing interest.

Little is recorded about Warbeck's tenure in France, but it is not unlikely he developed some rapport with King Charles, who at just twenty-one may have welcomed another youthful figure around court. If Warbeck, styled the Duke of York by his hosts, did indeed remain with the king's household throughout his stay, he would have visited lavish royal residences such as Amboise and Vincennes, partaking in pursuits like hunting and hawking whilst socialising with the higher echelons of French society. This acceptance into such esteemed company represented a significant step-up for Warbeck in terms of prestige and patronage, for public recognition from a sovereign as powerful as Charles, however cynical that may have been in private, was of far greater consequence for his wider ambitions than similar acknowledgment from a handful of Irish lords with limited international influence. As was widely known, the French had succeeded in helping propel a pretender towards the English throne in 1485, whereas the Irish had failed at great cost two years later.

To the French monarch, however, Warbeck was only ever of minor importance, a convenient goad to irritate his English counterpart whilst he remained fixed on his own expansionist project, defending hard-won gains and preparing for future glory. Tangible support in the form of men, money and artillery had yet to materialise for Warbeck several months after his arrival, prompting him to later rue how 'the promised aid was not given' for him to be able to seriously launch a challenge for the crown.[26]

In hindsight, this lack of support from the French proved beneficial to Warbeck's ambitions, for it is unlikely he would have garnered much sympathy in England if he had invaded with an army that was not only French-backed, but overwhelmingly French in composition; even Henry Tudor in 1485 could boast considerable numbers of Englishmen amongst his ranks, something Warbeck could not emulate. When the treaty at Étaples was signed in November 1492 and Charles VIII was compelled to withdraw any support for English rebels, Warbeck, 'his hopes dashed',[27] duly packed up whatever belongings he had accumulated and prepared to leave the kingdom.

Henry VII could be forgiven for trusting Warbeck and his companions would thereafter fade into obscurity having lost the backing of the French crown, but much to the English king's vexation, the reverse occurred. Upon being informed they were no longer welcome in France, the pretender and the small clique which had formed around him accepted an unexpected invitation to join the Burgundian court.

When Henry VII accepted the terms put forward by the French ambassadors at Étaples, he failed to consult with his ally Maximilian I, an oversight that had significant consequences for Anglo-Burgundian relations over the next decade. A vital precursor to the invasion of France had been the promise of cooperation with the King of the Romans, who had secured funds and men from the German princes to launch a simultaneous attack from the east. As the English were laying siege to Boulogne, Maximilian's army were in the process of capturing Arras on their way to meet up with Henry and continue pushing into France together. When he resorted to peace before this assemblage of armies could take place, however, Henry had effectively withdrawn from the alliance without discussion, prompting an irate Maximilian to turn his ire on his erstwhile partner and even the score.

If the English king had neutralised one foreign adversary, then at once he had created another. Similarly, where Warbeck had lost one friend, he now found another hand extended to him. On 12 December 1492, having possibly used bribery to cross the border,[28] Warbeck returned to the Netherlands for the first time in several years, his flagging cause soon revived through the enthusiastic patronage of another benefactor who had already proven hostile to Tudor rule – the resolute Margaret of York.

11

My Only Son

There is no documented evidence Margaret of York was personally acquainted with Henry VII, but by 1493 the formidable dowager duchess of Burgundy and headstrong sister of Richard III and Edward IV was certainly no stranger to the English king. He was a man she had pursued, in the scornful words of Polydore Vergil, with 'insatiable hatred' and 'fiery wrath' ever since his victory at Bosworth Field eight years earlier.[1]

Margaret's support throughout 1487 for Lambert Simnel and the bold conspiracy energetically fronted by her nephew John de la Pole, Earl of Lincoln, was widely known among contemporaries, and though her influence was politically neutralised between 1488 and 1492 by Maximilian I's subsequent alliance with England, the breach in relations between Henry VII and her Hapsburg stepson-in-law after the Anglo-French Treaty of Étaples offered a fresh opportunity for the former duchess to assail the Tudor regime once more. When Perkin Warbeck was informed Charles VIII of France was rescinding his support, it was to Flanders he and his supporters desperately turned, and Margaret enthusiastically welcomed into her circle the young pretender who professed to be another of her nephews, this time Richard of Shrewsbury, Duke of York.

It was the considered opinion of early sixteenth-century writers such as Vergil, André and Hall, perhaps mirroring the observations of their king, that the origins of the Warbeck conspiracy could be traced to Margaret of York's scheming, but there is little evidence to suggest that she was actively involved in the plot prior to December 1492, when the pretender departed France for her court. This is certainly supported by both Warbeck's 1493 account as Prince Richard, and his later 1497 confession, in which Margaret only plays a secondary role until this juncture.

According to the vague content of the letter despatched to Queen Isabella in August 1493, Warbeck recalled that he only crossed to Margaret's court when forced to leave the protection of the French king.[2] In the confession four years later, meanwhile, he recounted simply that he 'went into ffraunce, and from thens into fflaunders'[3] without any indication he had previously been a resident of Flanders, other than briefly during his childhood years. The probability is that late 1492 was the first time the Warbeck conspiracy reached the Netherlands, with Margaret, and soon Maximilian I, recognising an opportunity to retaliate against the English monarch for his alliance with Charles VIII. For the Yorkist dowager duchess and her Hapsburg stepson-in-law, it was purely an economic and political decision to get involved, rather than one of dynastic principle.

Vergil and Hall were in no doubt about Margaret's elation in receiving Warbeck and offering him refuge, which doesn't seem an outlandish assumption. According to the former, she welcomed her supposed nephew 'as though he had been raised from the dead', and that 'so great was her pleasure that her happiness seemed to have disturbed the balance of her mind'.[4] Hall, meanwhile, reported she did so 'wyth suche gladnes, with suche rejoysyng and such comfort', that she 'fell into such an unmeasurable joye, that she had almost lost her wytte and senses'.[5]

Information is scant about Warbeck's early months under Margaret's care at her court in Malines, modern-day Mechelen, but it is clear she quickly resolved to advance his cause using any means at her disposal. A prosperous city resting on the River Dijle, Malines had been the base of Margaret's husband Charles the Bold for much of his tenure as duke of Burgundy, and as one of the largest settlements in the Netherlands possessed a lively trading port from which its inhabitants derived much of their income. The richest of her dower towns, Margaret's primary residence was a splendid two-storeyed red-brick building featuring a solitary hexagonal tower and a stone balcony, procured from the bishop of Cambrai in 1477 and progressively upgraded to become one of the finest palaces in the region. Wealthy in widowhood, she used her income to embellish her home with numerous tapestries, paintings and books, whilst gardens, shooting galleries, tennis courts, marble fireplaces and hot baths in the Roman style provided a level of comfort few could match.[6]

It was here in Malines that Margaret of York roundly declared Warbeck's Yorkist credentials as Prince Richard, publicly congratulating him on his unlikely survival and taking pleasure in affording him the opportunity to repeat the dramatic tale of how he had fled certain death, so that 'she might convince all that he was indeed Richard the son of her brother Edward'. Thereafter 'she started to treat the youth with great respect and for her sake the Flemings likewise all exalted him', and soon 'the more the deceit was given an appearance of truth, the more people professed that they believed the youth had escaped the hand of King Richard by divine intervention and had been led safely to his aunt'.[7] As the story was repeated without contradiction, there was little reason at this stage the people of Flanders should doubt what they were told.

Warbeck's supporters, meanwhile, collected during his sojourns in Ireland and France, also accompanied the pretender to Malines, and this small band of brothers was soon introduced to Hugues de Meleun, governor of nearby Dendermonde, one of Margaret's dower towns, and a knight of the Golden Fleece, the exclusive Burgundian equivalent to the English Order of the Garter. As a local man with extensive local connections, Meleun's mission was to assist Warbeck in settling in Flanders, and he was notably mentioned in a letter two decades later as the person known to have conducted all Warbeck's affairs during the period.[8]

At the height of summer 1493, Warbeck remained based in Dendermonde, from where on 25 August, as 'Richard Plantagenet, second son of Edward formerly King, Duke of York', he composed his letter to Queen Isabella of Castile, his 'most honoured Lady and Cousin', explaining his sudden reappearance. Its intention was to implore her, and by association her husband King Ferdinand of Aragon, to pledge their weighty support to his cause. After briefly recounting the tale of his escape from London, his wanderings through the Continent and his arrival in Ireland, Warbeck described his invitation to France with the promise of receiving aid against 'Henry of Richmond, the wicked usurper of the kingdom of England'. Though Charles VIII and his council hesitated in their support, preferring friendship with Henry VII, other continental leaders, as well as some in England, were more forthcoming, it was claimed:

> But on his failing to afford me the promised assistance, I betook myself to the illustrious Princess, the Lady Duchess of Burgundy, sister of my father, my dearest aunt, who, with her known humanity

and virtue, welcomed me with all piety and honor; out of regard also to her, the most Serene King of the Romans, and his son, the Archduke of Austria, and the Duke of Saxony, my dearest cousins, as likewise the Kings of Denmark and Scotland, who sent to me their envoys, for the purpose of friendship and alliance. The great nobles of the kingdom of England did the same, who execrate the proud and wicked tyranny of this Henry of Richmond.

It is unclear at this point in Warbeck's story whether Maximilian I or his underage son Philip, Duke of Burgundy, whom Henry had only recently referred to as 'his most dear cousins',[9] had agreed to support Margaret's *cause célèbre*, but after six months in Flanders, one must assume at the very least all parties had engaged in some form of discussion about the pretender's prospects. The same principle can be extended to the kings of Denmark and Scotland, John I and James IV respectively, who likely exhibited some degree of curiosity towards the young man claiming to be a Yorkist prince in exile. Warbeck, as Prince Richard, ended his letter by flattering Isabella, and besought her support in exchange for future gains:

> But, most Serene Princess, Lady and Cousin, since, on account of our relationship, and your renowned virtues, by which you surpass all other princes of the world, in justice, actions, and prosperity, you ought no less than other princes to compassionate our condition, and succour us with pious love, I pray and implore your Majesty will use your influence with your Serene Spouse, that, together with your Clemency, he may be induced to pity the numerous calamities of our family, and in my right, which is also yours, to further me and mine with his favor, aid, and assistance. For I promise, if the Divine Grace should restore me to my hereditary kingdom, that I will continue with both your Majesties in closer alliance and friendship than ever King Edward was, and that I and my kingdom will be ever ready to fulfil your pleasure, no less than your own realms.[10]

We cannot ascertain if such wide international backing was as forthcoming as claimed by Warbeck in his letter, though it isn't inconceivable Margaret drew on all her contacts to reach out to various continental rulers, not least her calculating stepson-in-law Maximilian I. In fact, she herself also composed a letter to Isabella of Castile, justifying her support for the young man she now unequivocally recognised as her nephew, the sole surviving son of Edward IV.

According to Margaret's version of events, the Irish earls of Desmond and Kildare had written to her advising her nephew Richard had been miraculously discovered alive, and they implored her to support his cause in recovering the throne for the House of York. If accurate, her claim that Kildare was involved contradicted the earl's own protestations to the contrary. Although initially believing such news from Ireland to be little more than 'ravings and dreams', once the pretender arrived in France she sent to him 'certain men who would have recognised him as easily as his mother or his nurse, since from their first youth they had been in service and intimate familiarity with King Edward and his children'. When these anonymous messengers returned to her court, all swore that Warbeck was indeed the prince they had once known, declaring they would willingly endure 'every torment and great physical pains' should they be mistaken. When Warbeck finally arrived in Malines, Margaret claimed:

> I recognised him as easily as if I had last seen him yesterday or the day before (for I had seen him once long ago in England). He did not have just one or another sign of resemblance, but so many and so particular that hardly one person in ten, in a hundred or even in a thousand might be found who would have marks of the same kind. Then I recognised him by the private conversations and acts between him and me in times past, which undoubtedly no other person would have been able to guess at. Lastly, I recognised him by the questions and conversations of others, to all of which he responded so aptly and skilfully that it was manifest and notorious that this was he who they thought had died long ago.

She added, for her own part, 'When I gazed on this only male Remnant of our family – who had come through so many perils and misfortunes – I was deeply moved, and out of this natural affection, into which both necessity and the rights of blood were drawing me, I embraced him as my only nephew and my only son.'

Isabella and Ferdinand were unmoved, and the letter did not provoke the response Warbeck and Margaret hoped for. It was instead filed away with the nonchalant, non-committal note, 'From Richard, who styles himself King of England', and two years later, on 20 July 1495, it was further noted in official records that Isabella had apparently shown the dowager duchess that the 'whole affair was an imposture'.[11]

Margaret's enthusiastic sponsorship of Warbeck has often been interpreted as confirmation of his identity as a genuine Yorkist prince, but this isn't necessarily so. It cannot be discounted that Margaret, like many others during the 1490s, was fooled by Warbeck's flawless performance, perhaps a misapprehension made easier by her own overwhelming desire to believe at least one of her nephews yet lived. If an imposter, Warbeck certainly proved himself capable of upholding the pretence for several years, and with the correct tuition may even have perfected his act between his first appearance in Cork and his arrival in the Burgundian Netherlands.

It must also remain a possibility Margaret knew Warbeck to be a fraud, but nevertheless considered it preferable to place a boatman's son from Tournai upon the English throne instead of the Welsh usurper who had wrested the throne from her youngest brother Richard III, regardless how this affected her niece Elizabeth, Henry VII's Yorkist queen. The long-term plan may even have been to use Warbeck merely as the device to depose Henry to enable the crown to be handed to the sole Yorkist prince still known, beyond doubt, to be alive – Edward, Earl of Warwick. If she truly wanted to topple the Tudor king, as evident through her actions during his reign thus far, Margaret could hardly bolster his position by rejecting the youth in her presence as an imposter.

One does additionally wonder if the dowager duchess was simply lonely at this stage of her life, the idea of once more rallying to the aid of a 'nephew' requesting her help giving her some fresh purpose as she approached her fiftieth year. Margaret had lost her husband in 1477, stepdaughter in 1482, all three of her brothers by 1485, three nephews by 1487, and had no children of her own – Warbeck suddenly provided her a reason to fight on, to hope that the fallen House of York may yet rise again. We may never know the precise motivation behind Margaret's wholehearted support for Perkin Warbeck, or whether she truly had any misgivings about his identity, but there can be little doubt that his appearance motivated her to once more strive to make life as difficult as possible for the English king she would not recognise.

What is clear is that during 1493, Margaret of York assumed a leading role in Warbeck's life as his chief mentor, using her own intimate knowledge of her paternal house to finesse the pretender's image, filling his mind with names, dates, and brief scraps of information that could be used in future to convince others of his authenticity. It must be noted, however, that Margaret had been exiled from England, save for a fleeting visit in 1480, for over a quarter of a century and her information may have been antiquated, not unlike how Henry VII was considered more French than English in behaviour after his own fourteen year stint abroad prior to becoming king.

Margaret may also have fulfilled a motherly role to the young man now under her guidance. If the pretender was indeed Prince Richard, this may have been particularly poignant, for the previous June Elizabeth Wydeville had passed away at Bermondsey Abbey. There is no extant evidence to gauge Elizabeth's thoughts regarding this boy who had surfaced purporting to be the younger of her lost royal sons, but again one must assume that messengers or visitors to the abbey at a very minimum brought tidings of his appearance.

Perhaps the news raised fresh hope in the ageing Elizabeth that at least one of her boys lived on, or maybe it merely reopened painful memories that caused fresh grief and heartbreak; we can never know. What is telling, however, is that Warbeck, or rather Richard, does not merit a mention in Elizabeth's will at all, and no known reference was made by Warbeck about his supposed mother's demise, which perhaps supports the theory the pretender was not actually her son. Where was the public lamentation, which in itself could also have acted as a propaganda exercise? The one son of Elizabeth known to be living at the time of her death, Thomas Grey, 1st Marquis of Dorset, was however included in the will as one would expect, and even named as one of her executors.[12] Even in her dying moments, without having to please anyone, Elizabeth Wydeville did not recognise the pretender claiming to be her son.

*

In the meantime, as Perkin Warbeck settled into life at Margaret of York's court, Henry VII observed matters from afar with escalating concern and growing suspicion. A king proactive in dealing with any and all threats against his person, it was not in Henry's character to remain passive in response to developments across the Channel, particularly since he had wrongly anticipated the Treaty of Étaples would halt Warbeck's crusade in its infancy. Richard III had failed to deal with threats adequately, no matter how trivial, and it cost him his life – his successor would not follow suit.

Throughout 1493, therefore, Henry responded in typical energetic fashion, particularly once rumour of this 'twice borne' Prince Richard 'devyded all England and drewe the realme into Partakynges and several faccions' so that 'the myndes of all men were vexed either with hope of gayne and preferment, or with feare of losse and confusion'.[13] He could not afford to be caught off-guard.

In March 1493, by which time Warbeck's location was widely known to be Flanders, Henry sought to ensure any further Irish scheming was neutralised by dispatching another expedition across the sea, whilst the following month he departed London once more and headed north-west to Kenilworth, the same commanding Midlands fortress into which he retreated during the height of the Lambert Simnel plot. There was nowhere, it would seem, the first Tudor king felt safer than behind Kenilworth's robust walls, in the very heart of his kingdom and surrounded by his closest allies, men he knew and trusted from his time in exile.

Across the next few months, several commissions of array were issued throughout the realm, 'touching all offences, conspiracies and conventicles', covering in particular the counties of Shropshire, Herefordshire, Gloucestershire, Worcestershire and the Marches of Wales, suggesting the king was wary of malcontents mobilising in those parts.[14]

He was right to be concerned; at the end of May, a knight named Humphrey Savage and a Middlesex yeoman called John Burton attempted to provoke Londoners into revoking their allegiance to their king and instead declaring for the pretender they believed was Prince Richard of York. Worryingly for Henry VII, Savage was part of a prominent Cheshire gentry family who had supported his rule since Bosworth Field, with Humphrey's brother John even commanding his left flank during the battle, and as a maternal nephew of Thomas and William Stanley he was hardly far removed from the royal inner circle. Having failed to secure the levels of open support he had perhaps anticipated, however, Savage fled into sanctuary at Westminster Abbey, and would later pay for his transgressions with his head.[15] On 27 May, meanwhile, four other men were captured, taken to Tyburn, and 'there ffor treason hangid',[16] a timely warning to the capital's citizens not to waiver in their allegiance to their king, as previous generations of Londoners had done throughout history.

By July, Henry claimed to have finally learnt enough about the supposed prince to start openly questioning the legitimacy of his claim, based on information garnered from scores of spies working tirelessly across the continent. One of the men who may have been the source of such details was Pregent Meno, the Breton merchant responsible for transporting Warbeck into Ireland in 1491. He was rewarded the generous sum of £300 by Henry in 1495, for reasons unspecified.[17] Edward Brampton, the Portuguese knight who later testified that Warbeck was a fraud, may also have been contacted at this time, as could have been the French, now on amiable terms since the treaty.

By whatever means Henry received his information, on 20 July 1493 from his base at Kenilworth he was able to write to his councillor Sir Gilbert Talbot not only warning of rebel activity but also providing the first known reference to Perkin Warbeck, a boatman's son from Tournai. The king's disdain for his wife's aunt, Margaret of York, was also palpable, whom he attacked from the very first line:

> Trusty and well-beloved, we greet you well; and not forgetting the great malice that the Lady Margaret of Burgundy beareth continually against us, as she showed lately in sending hither of a feigned boy, surmising him to have been the son of the Duke of Clarence, and causeth him to be accompanied with the Earl of Lincoln, the Lord Lovel, and with great multitude of Irishmen and Almains, whose end, blessed be God, was as ye know well.
>
> And foreseeing now the perseverance of her malice, by the untrue contriving eftsoon of another feigned lad called Perkin Warbeck, born at Tournay, in Picardy, which at first into Ireland called himself the bastard of King Richard; after that the son of the said Duke of Clarence; and now the second son of our father, King Edward the IVth, whom God assoil; wherethrough she indendeth, by promising unto the Flemings and other of the archduke's obeissaunce, to whom she laboureth daily to take her way, and by her promise to certain aliens, captains of strange nations, to have duchies, counties, baronies and other lands, within this our royaume, to induce them thereby to land here, to the destruction and disinheritance of the same, and finally to the subversion of this our royaume, in case she may attain to her malicious purpose, that God defend.

Henry's letter thereafter counselled Talbot to 'resist her malice', requesting him to have eighty men on horseback 'defensibly arrayed' in preparation, with many archers, bill-men and lancers to be ready 'upon a day's warning' for 'service of war'. The king clearly expected another invasion of his realm and therefore called upon his most loyal subjects to be ready. One suspects similar letters were widely dispatched amongst those he intimately trusted.[18]

Henry never publicly deviated from this account of Warbeck's Tournai background, which was further expanded upon in the pretender's 1497 confession. This was for good reason; to be seen giving credence to the idea Warbeck was a Yorkist prince was to simply risk alienating any support for his own claim to the throne, which had been accepted by many Englishmen in lieu of any surviving sons of Edward IV. Henry treated the matter as expected – with contempt and derision, astonished that 'anyone could have fabricated such a fiction as to make a transparent untruth gain such currency as truth, and to make many of his magnates consider it as established fact'.[19]

In July Henry also dispatched a diplomatic embassy into the Burgundian Netherlands to plead with Duke Philip, the fifteen-year-old step-grandson of Margaret of York, and ordered his council 'to geve no credite, nor them selfes suffre any more to be blynded or seduced with suche mere impostures and craftie illusions', by 'a craftye merchant, whiche had falsely feigned hys name and stock'. Led by Sir Edward Poynings and William Warham, the latter a future archbishop of Canterbury and 'a man of great modestie, learnyng and gravite', their task was to secure a promise no further aid or assistance would be extended to Warbeck by either Philip or Margaret, and to accept that the pretender was unworthy of recognition.[20]

As with the French the previous year, Henry hoped to frustrate Warbeck's ambitions by targeting those who were financially and logistically propping up his campaign, but on this occasion, it was the English king left displeased by the outcome of the summit. Warmly received by Duke Philip and his council, Warham was given the floor and delivered an elegant oration to his hosts, demonstrating 'the mynde entent and desyre of the kynge hys master', stressing that the young man in their midst claiming to be a prince of York was, in fact, merely the son of a boatman. If not of low birth, then he certainly was not of royal birth. Having delivered his king's message, at the end of his address Warham tersely rebuked Margaret of York, who was present for the tense proceedings, 'sayinge that she now in her olde age, within fewe yeres had produced and brought foorth two detestable monsters', referring to her well-known support for Lambert Simnel several years earlier.

With tensions heightened, Warbeck, 'more vexed and encombered with the thinges declared in thys oracion', stepped forward to defend himself and his patroness against these 'tauntes and jestes', whilst Warham's invective only served to 'angre and trouble' Margaret, who thereafter 'determyned clerely to arme and setforward pretty Perkyn agaynst the kynge of England with speare and shilde, might and mayne'.[21] According to Vergil, who may have taken his information from some of the Englishmen present that day, the incensed dowager duchess 'would have harmed William had he not taken care'.[22]

After hearing the argument put forth by the English ambassadors and withdrawing to debate the contentious issue in private, Philip and his council answered that as they were desirous of retaining the love and favour of King Henry, they agreed to 'neither aide nor assist Perkyn nor hys complyces in any cause or quarell'. There was, however, a caveat; should Margaret persist in her schemes, 'it was not in their power to let or withstande it, for because she in the landes assigned to her for her dower, might frankely and freely do and ordre all thynges at her awne wyll and pleasure'.[23] Put simply, the council claimed they did not have the jurisdiction to intervene in the private affairs of the dowager duchess, who was entitled to act as she saw fit within her dowry lands. It was a diplomatic strategy that promised much but delivered little. The ambassadors duly returned to England, and by the end of August debriefed Henry personally at Northampton.

Throughout the summer the circumspect king continued to plan for an invasion of his realm, sending 'some knights with carefully picked troops to guard the coast and ports' all along the eastern coast, tasked with preventing anyone from entering or exiting England without royal permission. All roads and footpaths near the shore were to be observed at all times, and any significant assembly of men was to be reported without delay, as were any other general signs of conspiracy.[24]

Henry must have been reassured by his plans, for in August he abandoned the protection of Kenilworth and returned to London. In fact, his next step was to go on the attack by initiating harsh economic warfare with Flanders by means of a trade embargo, ordered to take effect from 18 September. The king's intent was clear – if he could not convince Duke Philip and his council to voluntarily hand over Warbeck, he would financially crush them into submission.

According to the terms of the royal proclamation which was sent to all major parts of the kingdom from Cornwall in the south-west to Northumberland in the north, 'for divers great and urgent causes' the king commanded that 'no manner of Englishman, denizen, nor yet any stranger, of what estate, degree, or condition he or they be' was permitted to convey unto the lands of the duke 'any manner of goods or merchandise grown or made within this his realm'. Furthermore, without first obtaining a special licence, they could no longer import from Flanders 'upon pain of forfeiture of all such goods and merchandise'.[25]

It was an excessive if calculated reaction, and one which demonstrated Henry VII regarded Warbeck to be a genuine threat in the hands of the right individuals, particularly as such drastic measures impacted negatively on the English economy as well as the Flemish, when Duke Philip's council responded in the following spring with their own retaliatory sanctions. It was a commercial war waged over a political dispute fuelled by dynastic ambition, and one deeply unpopular on both sides of the divide.

In England, the financial pressure provoked an outburst of violence within the trading community; on 15 October, a riot erupted in London when merchants from the Hanseatic League, who had been exempt from the restrictions and continued to profit from their riverside base in Dowgate, were attacked by around eighty resentful locals who had lost their jobs as a result of the economic downturn. The violence was of such magnitude the mayor was forced to mobilise his troops, armed with guns and crossbows, to defend the Hansa merchants and protect their headquarters from widespread looting. During the inquest which followed, those accused of fuelling disorder protested that the 'restreyntys made by the kyng soo long and soo offtyn' caused them to 'decay and wax irk of the world' for they could not buy or sell their wares. As they were no longer capable of affording their daily expenses because of these restraints, they had turned to revolt.[26]

By aggressively targeting the Flemish economy, Henry only served to antagonise Duke Philip whilst hardening the already solid resolve of Margaret of York to pursue Warbeck's claim. Deposing a king of England could not be accomplished using the limited resources of both parties, particularly once the financial downturn took hold, so overtures were sent to the duke's father Maximilian I, and the driven King of the Romans needed little encouragement to collude against his erstwhile ally. Maximilian, Margaret and Philip all had legitimate grievance with the English king, and it was Warbeck who benefitted.

When Henry VII agreed peace with Charles VIII at Étaples, Maximilian interpreted the act as betrayal. The English king had voluntarily entered an alliance with someone who had not only reneged upon a promise to marry Maximilian's daughter Margaret of Austria in 1490, but who had then proceeded to marry the heiress that had been betrothed to the King of the Romans himself, Anne of Brittany. Henry could not reasonably expect to cooperate with Charles and retain the friendship of Maximilian, and when the opportunity arose for the latter to exact a measure of revenge against the English king, he seized it with both hands.

A meeting between Maximilian and Warbeck was scheduled for the end of 1493 in Vienna, where the former was preparing to bury his recently deceased father Frederick III, the Holy Roman Emperor. It was a summit which proved deeply concerning to Henry VII on two accounts; first, if Warbeck convinced Maximilian of his legitimacy, the pretender would secure a valuable sponsor for his cause who could be exploited to gain further support, and second, the death of Frederick III heralded the start of Maximilian's reign as archduke of the reunited Austrian territories, extending his influence across a significant part of central Europe and bolstering his position as one of the most commanding rulers of the day. For Henry, any prospective alliance between Warbeck and Maximilian caused far greater alarm than that between Warbeck and Margaret of York, or even the Anglo-Irish lords. It was Maximilian's input, after all, through the supply of money, troops and ships, which had triggered Lambert Simnel's invasion in 1487.

To facilitate the meeting, in October 1493 Warbeck was introduced to Maximilian's cousin Albert III, Duke of Saxony, and together the pair commenced an arduous autumn journey from Malines. Passing through the various city-states and principalities which comprised the Holy Roman Empire, on 5 November they entered Vienna, a grand metropolis near the Danube long regarded as the *de facto* capital of the Hapsburg dynasty, over which Maximilian now presided as family head. Barely had Warbeck settled into his new environs when a gentleman named Ludwig Klinkhammer, in conversation with Sigismund of Tyrol, remarked upon the pretender's supposed likeness to Margaret of York; whether Klinkhamer genuinely observed a resemblance or was merely attempting to garner some goodwill is undetermined.[27]

When Maximilian and Warbeck met in person, to convince his host that he was the genuine prince he claimed to be, the pretender displayed three marks on his body which would supposedly be recognisable to anyone who knew Prince Richard as a child before his disappearance. This, it seems, along with the enthusiastic assurances of Margaret of York, satisfied Maximilian of the young man's authenticity.[28] It should be noted that Maximilian had never met Henry VII but had cultivated a good working relationship with both Edward IV and Richard III during their respective reigns – for someone espousing a pro-Yorkist cause and with a grudge against the present Tudor king, he was an easy sell.

Attending the funeral of a Holy Roman Emperor was a considerable honour for any continental ruler, but for Warbeck in particular, now openly recognised in Vienna as Richard, Duke of York, it represented an astounding propaganda victory for what had been a flagging cause. Perhaps most satisfyingly of all, there was little Henry VII could do back in England. Warbeck, in fact, was treated by many as though he was England's official representative at the burial ceremony on 7 December, assuming an esteemed position alongside similar luminaries from France, Hungary, Burgundy and the Holy Roman Empire itself, socialising with Europe's elite and surely canvassing support for his claim to the English crown over an exquisite banquet. There is no indication how successful he was in pressing his case, but the opportunity alone was worth the trip, for each dignitary he encountered would have taken news of his existence back to their homeland.

From the moment Warbeck attended Maximilian's father's funeral as an honoured guest, Maximilian I was no longer able to publicly retract his support for the pretender, or to denounce him as an imposter with a convincing act. To be seen backtracking would have been a humiliating climbdown, tantamount to admitting that he had been duped by a mere boy from Tournai. Maximillian was no fool, and neither would he be regarded as so, and from November 1493 onwards he never wavered in his support of Perkin Warbeck. To his mind, Warbeck was simply Prince Richard.

The pair tarried in Vienna until the spring of 1494, likely spending considerable time in each other's company and deliberating over future plans, before returning at a leisurely pace to the Netherlands together, navigating through the continental heartland via towns such as Innsbruck, Cologne, Aachen and Maastricht. By the time Warbeck re-entered Antwerp, he was unabashedly sporting the White Rose emblem of the House of York, and according to Jean Molinet, a French historiographer in the employ of the duke of Burgundy, assumed residence in the English Merchant Adventurers House, which had been abandoned because of the trading dispute.

Not everybody was content with Warbeck's presence in Antwerp, however; when an armorial shield bearing the royal arms of England was erected outside the house, with a banner publicly declaring his title to be Richard, Prince of Wales and Duke of York, son and heir of Edward IV of England, two infuriated Englishmen loyal to Henry VII flung a pot of ordure at the offending item. When Warbeck's own supporters reacted violently to this attack, the English pair fled the town, though not before an innocent bystander was slain during the furious confusion.[29]

Depending on his true identity, Warbeck may or may not have been a stranger to his latest surroundings. As previously mentioned, in his confession post-capture he declared that during his early teens he had spent time in Antwerp with his cousin John Steinbeck, returning several months later when he boarded with a skinner near the English merchants' house, possibly the very same one he now occupied as Prince of England. If the confession was accurate, the dramatic change in his circumstance within a matter of years surely provoked a wry smile from Warbeck in private.

The pretender's burgeoning friendship with Maximilian I and Duke Philip took another step forward in Malines on 24 August 1494, the feast day of St Bartholomew, when Warbeck rode to church alongside the Hapsburg father and son, appearing glorious in robes fashioned from cloth of gold. He was conspicuously surrounded by household staff dressed in murrey and blue, the traditional livery of the House of York. On 6 October, meanwhile, Warbeck again rode in state with Maximilian, this time to Antwerp's Church of Our Lady, where he witnessed the sixteen-year-old Philip publicly swear his oath as Duke of Brabant, on this occasion accompanied by a guard of twenty archers bearing the White Rose badge.[30] A statement was being made.

As he had done upon discovering Warbeck had sought refuge at the court of Margaret of York, Henry VII sprang into action once more after it was revealed that Maximilian had taken the young pretender under his wing. In February 1494, several men were arraigned on suspicion of treason at the Guildhall in London.[31] On 21 July, the king wrote to the town of Grimsby warning of the potential threat of invasion. Similar letters were presumably dispatched to other leading seaports along the eastern coast of England, counselling each of them to remain vigilant against potential agitators operating within the region whilst preventing any suspicious persons from exiting the realm without licence.[32] Though he expected the assistance of his subjects in protecting the crown, Henry was mindful of the fact that he himself had secured his crown through the inactivity of many nearly a decade earlier.

That same month, Henry also attempted to reason with his adversary's backers, sending John Writhe, Garter King of Arms, across the Channel to instruct Margaret of York, Duke Philip, and Maximillian I that their pretender was an imposter rather than a prince, unworthy of their support. When Writhe's message fell on deaf ears, the bold messenger left their presence and wandered through the streets of Malines loudly declaring to the crowds that Richard of York was a fraud and their rulers had been deceived. Only the threat of imprisonment halted his rowdy behaviour.[33]

On 10 August at Sheen Palace, another herald, Roger Machado, Richmond King of Arms, was sent overseas, this time armed with instructions for the French king, Charles VIII. Henry was keen to project a self-assured image to his contemporaries, careful not to betray any sign of weakness that could be exploited whilst his attention was diverted. To this effect, Machado was instructed to inform Charles that though there were rumours Maximilian and Warbeck were preparing an invasion, this was something the English king could 'scarcely believe, seeing that it is derogatory to the honour of any prince to encourage such an imposter'. The pretender was further referred to contemptuously by Machado as 'garçon', a boy who was of 'no account' for his king 'cannot be hurt or annoyed by him; for there is no nobleman, gentleman, or person of any condition in the realm of England, who does not well know that it is a manifest and evident imposture'. In response to Charles's offer of assistance at this current time, Henry extended his 'cordial thanks', but politely declined.

For the avoidance of doubt, before he departed Machado made it known to his French hosts that according to the English king's sources, this latest pretender was merely 'a native of the town of Tournai, and son of a boatman, who is named Warbec', and therefore was held 'in great derision, and not without reason'. Maximilian, it was asserted, only supported the imposture 'on account of the displeasure he feels at the treaty' made between the kings of England and France.[34] That the French had previously sponsored Warbeck, and may even have initiated the conspiracy, was discreetly overlooked.

Henry's confidence was, of course, an act. Though he claimed England was in as 'good, prosperous, and peaceable condition, as it had ever been within the memory of man', and that many within the kingdom considered Warbeck to be a fraud, the enduring presence of this shadowy pretender three years after his initial appearance amid a persistent undercurrent of restlessness in certain parts of his realm undoubtedly caused concern within the royal household. Contrary to the claims of Richmond Herald, his master certainly was taking account of Warbeck's machinations, and giving the evolving conspiracy the full attention it merited.

The wavering loyalties of the inconstant Anglo-Irish lords, meanwhile, who had largely rallied for Lambert Simnel seven years earlier and in more recent times had been responsive to Warbeck's brief appearance in Cork, remained at the forefront of Henry's mind. Though the English king had sent soldiers into Ireland in December 1491 to discourage rebellion, the enduring scheming of the earls of Kildare and Desmond necessitated an additional 'fleet with an armed force' led by Roger Cotton to be dispatched in March 1493, empowered to 'enter Ireland and war with rebels'. Though this increased military presence temporarily quelled the threat of revolt, with Kildare and Desmond amongst those issued pardons, just one year later the latter was once more openly conspiring against Tudor authority.[35]

Recognising the need for drastic measures to bring the Irish to heel, in October 1494 Henry sent Sir Edward Poynings into Ireland armed with a fresh set of instructions that would have far-reaching consequences for Anglo-Irish relations. He was accompanied by fellow Englishmen Henry Deane, bishop-elect of Bangor, and Sir Hugh Conway, who were appointed chancellor and treasurer of Ireland respectively.[36]

As deputy lieutenant, Poynings's mission involved centralising the island's governance under royal officials to safeguard the Tudor crown from the ambitions of overmighty Irish lords, and in particular to ensure Warbeck could not be afforded treatment similar to that once granted to Simnel. Poynings, a man of 'great wisdom and manhood',[37] proved an astute choice for such a delicate mission, having extensive military and diplomatic experience; he had participated in rebellion against Richard III in 1483 before joining Henry in exile for two years, and at Bosworth Field was dubbed a knight banneret before conducting several ambassadorial missions for the new king thereafter.

Landing near Dublin, one of Poynings's first tasks was to issue writs calling a parliament before personally spearheading a military expedition against 'the wilde and savage Irishmen' who lived in the woods and marshes beyond English jurisdiction. These Irishmen were suspected of being 'aiders and avauncers of Perkyns foolishe enterprice' after the pretender had shown himself to them during his time on the island, 'easely persuadygne theim to beleve that he was the same very person whome he falsely fayned'.[38] Despite thorough preparation, the mission had to be aborted when Poynings received word of the 'guile and deceit' of Kildare, his supposed ally in the venture. The earl was accused of conspiring with the native Irish to have the English deputy lieutenant assassinated, and arrested. Rather than being locked up in Ireland, where he was presumably a flight risk, Kildare was shipped across the sea and held in the Tower of London.[39]

Undeterred by the hostile environment, Poynings's parliament convened on 1 December 1494 in Drogheda during which several controversial acts were passed designed to bolster the security of the English crown in Irish lands. It was decreed that forthwith 'no maner of person' should have any authority in Ireland other than by 'the King's will and pleasure', with no parliament permitted to meet in future unless under licence from the Great Seal of England rather than that of Ireland. Any new statutes, meanwhile, could no longer be passed unless they were sanctioned not just by the Irish governor, but also by Henry VII and his council in England. They certainly could not crown another king, as they had done with Simnel in 1487, and all acts or processes passed in the name of that 'pretenced kinge' were revoked. In short, any autonomy the Irish parliament once possessed was removed at a stroke, ensuring it could not be misused in future to work contrary to the king's welfare.[40]

Henry's most significant response to Warbeck's infuriating presence in Flanders under the protection of Maximilian I, Philip of Burgundy, and Margaret of York, however, was to establish his own, official, duke of York in the autumn of 1494. The person he chose for this prestigious honour was his three-year-old namesake son, 'the right and excellent prince', Henry. Considering the boy's tender age and the timing, the purpose was clear – how could Warbeck across the Channel be given any credence as the duke of York when, right here in England, before all the lords and prelates of the realm, was the duke himself, the present king's second son? A new duke of York could not, after all, be created if the previous incumbent was believed alive.

Departing Sheen on 27 October, King Henry, Queen Elizabeth, and Margaret Beaufort travelled to Westminster where the following morning orders were sent for the young prince to be brought in state from the royal nursery at Eltham to join his parents and grandmother. Greeted in London by the mayor, aldermen, and various leaders of craft guilds, all in their finest liveries, the boy was conveyed through the streets with 'great honnour, tryhumphe, and of great astates'. It must have proved a thrilling spectacle for a child who would develop a deep enthusiasm for court pageantry and showmanship in later life.

Before he could be made duke, Prince Henry had to be knighted, a process which occurred two days later in an elaborate overnight ceremony. Dining in state, the king was attended by all the prospective knights, including his young son who was handed the responsibility of bearing his father's towel. After dinner, all the knights-in-waiting retired to their chambers where they climbed into 'royally dressed' baths, which symbolised their spiritual cleansing. Due to his age, the prince's bath was kept in the king's own chamber, separate from the others, and when the elder Henry entered the room, he dipped his hand into the warm bath water, making the sign of the cross on his son's bare shoulder before tenderly kissing the same spot.

This process was repeated by the king in the two other chambers for all the other knights, before all dried as they lay in their beds. Slipping on simple hermit robes, the group were then led down through the palace corridors to the chapel where each took their spices, for which the sergeant of the confectionery was paid a noble by each recipient. Suitably refreshed, a vigil was thereafter kept throughout the night, a considerable undertaking for a three-year-old boy.

In the morning, having heard mass, Prince Henry and his companions handed their gowns to a group of minstrels before returning to their beds, where they were permitted several hours' sleep until the 'tyme wos come that it was the kyngis pleasir that they schuld arise'. The earls of Oxford, Northumberland and Essex, along with Lord Daubeney, were sent to awaken the prince, who was dressed in another simple shirt. He was led back through the Westminster's corridors, past St Stephen's Chapel, and to the foot of the stairs that led to the Star Chamber.

With William Courtenay bearing the prince's sword before him, William Sandys carried the child into the king's presence, where Oxford presented the sword and spurs to his monarch. King Henry commanded the duke of Buckingham and marquis of Dorset to place the spurs on his son's heels, before he personally girded the prince with the sword, completing the rituals that created young Henry a Knight of the Bath. In a touch of fatherly affection, or at least in recognition of the prince's tender age, the boy was lifted onto the table to observe the remainder of the ceremony.

The following day, 1 November, the king woke for prayers before returning to his chamber to put on his robes of estate and crown. Entering the parliament chamber, he assumed position under his royal canopy, crafted from the finest velvet and embroidered with his coat of arms and other assorted dynastic emblems. Henry knew the importance of projecting his majesty, and at this critical juncture in his reign appeared before his subjects an imposing and wealthy figure of power, every inch God's anointed sovereign on Earth. Present before him were most of the leading magnates and prelates of the realm, London's mayor and aldermen, and a collection of judges and court officials. All had been assembled to witness the joyous moment the king created his son the duke of York.

When the king was seated, John Writhe, the same Garter King of Arms who had so recently travelled to meet with Warbeck in Flanders, entered the chamber and presented the letters patent formally creating Prince Henry duke of York, followed closely by Suffolk bearing a rich sword held upwards, Northumberland holding a rod of gold, and Derby, the child's step-grandfather, grasping a cap of estate furred with ermine and topped with a coronet. The earl of Shrewsbury was given the honour of carrying the prince into the room, who when put down was guided up to his father by Dorset and Arundel. Oliver King, Bishop of Exeter and the king's secretary, read the patent aloud, and once the ceremony was concluded, the king directed his lords and clergy to depart the chamber in procession. According to one observer, it was 'the best ordred and moost preysed of all the precessions' and one which featured a crowned Queen Elizabeth and the king's mother, Lady Margaret Beaufort, amongst its participants.

Three days of jousting followed to celebrate the occasion, during which Westminster was furnished in the 'most tryhumphant' manner. On 9 November, the king and queen, 'richely empairelled' and seated upon cushions of cloth of gold in a stage covered with blue Arras cloth decorated with fleurs-de-lys, watched the tournament alongside their second son, in whose honour the jousters competed.

An observant chronicler was overwhelmed by the pageantry, reflecting, 'There schuld you have syen the good riders, the well doying horsses, whatt gambadys, the changelyng of bellis, the glisteryng of spangils', singling out George Neville, 5th Baron Bergavenny, in particular for springing his small black horse so high above the ground and 'so oftyn tyme'. Participating on the first day of competition were the earls of Suffolk and Essex, Sir Edward Burgh, Edward Darell, Sir Robert Curson, Thomas Brandon, John Peche, Matthew Baker, Guillam de la Rivere, Henry Wynslow, William Craythorne and the Breton Roland de Velville. It was, the impressed chronicler mused, a 'tryhumphant sight to see'.

After several courses of supper and a variety of dances, it was Peche who was adjudged the best-performing knight on the first day, for which he was presented a gold and ruby ring from the king's eldest daughter, 'the right high and excellente princesse' Margaret. Two days later, a second tournament was held, and to Prince Henry's delight one side bore his newly granted livery of blue and tawny. It was Suffolk who claimed victory this time, and as champion was rewarded with a gold and diamond ring, although the valiant Brandon was handed a gold and ruby ring for his efforts. In what was clearly a family affair, both were again presented by Princess Margaret. On the final day of jousting, held on 13 November, the competition was furiously fought by all combatants until 'with honnour every man departed the feld', with Burgh and Essex receiving a diamond and emerald ring respectively.[41]

A sumptuous feast marked the end of the festivities, with the king, queen, Margaret Beaufort, the two dukes of Bedford and Buckingham and marquis of Dorset in attendance, along with ten earls, twenty-five lords, one hundred knights, the archbishops of Canterbury and York, and eight bishops. Also present were the ambassador of Naples and several Irish or Scottish lords, whom Henry expected to report home in detail what had transpired. It was a glittering array of the leading figures in the realm, and the king's intention was to show all that he presided over a united court, at the centre of which in November 1494 was the newly created duke of York, a child named Henry, not Richard.

Henry VII, however, had learnt through great difficulty from childhood that not everything was always as it seemed. Life had taught him to be suspicious of even the most outwardly loyal of subjects, and to be wary of those who professed friendship to his face when they maintained hatred in their heart. Throughout the celebrations of the previous fortnight, he had been careful not to betray his innermost thoughts to those around him, for the king had recently received word that one of his most intimate courtiers, a man integral in placing him upon the throne in the first place, had betrayed him.

Though measured in his responses around court and appearing content, even happy, with his world, inside Henry seethed, and set in motion plans to ensnare the snake in his midst. He had witnessed the brutal end of Richard III in person, and was determined not to suffer a similar fate. For that, Henry had to strike first, and strike hard.

12

The Devilish Enterprise

Westminster had been the scene of boisterous rejoicing during the first fortnight of November 1494, but even before all the royal guests had packed up their belongings and started the journey back to their estates, a series of arrests were discreetly made around the capital, with more anticipated in the weeks thereafter. Those rounded up were suspected of colluding against Henry VII in favour of the pretender loitering in Flanders, Perkin Warbeck, and were thoroughly interrogated by scrupulous royal agents who sought to expose fresh details of intrigue brewing both within and without England for the last three years.

Among those seized were several prominent churchmen such as William Worsely, the long-serving Dean of St Paul's, Thomas Poynes and William Richford of the Dominican Order, and Dr William Sutton, Parson of St Stephen Walbrook. There were knights, too, such as William Daubeney, clerk of the Jewel House during the reign of Edward IV, Thomas Thwaits, formerly treasurer of Calais, Robert Ratcliffe, Simon Mountford, Thomas Cressner, Robert Holbourn, and Thomas Astwood, whilst early in 1495, the East Anglian lord John Ratcliffe, 9th Baron Fitzwalter, was also apprehended.[1]

The arrest of Fitzwalter was concerning for Henry, for he had been close to the king from the outset of the reign; as well as serving as steward of the king's household, Fitzwalter had been appointed a joint high steward at the coronations of both Henry and his wife Elizabeth. He had also been given control of several Suffolk and Norfolk manors formerly belonging to Richard III, was named steward of the Duchy of Lancaster in Norfolk, Suffolk and Cambridgeshire, and was one of two chief justices of all forests south of the River Trent – in short, the baron had a proven track record as a dependable royal official, and accordingly had been afforded close proximity to the unsuspecting king.[2]

The re-emergence of Thomas Howard, 1st Earl of Surrey, into East Anglian politics after his release from imprisonment in 1489, however, and the continuing dominance of John de Vere, 13th Earl of Oxford, in the region, may have persuaded Fitzwalter to seek an alternative master under which to prosper. By 14 January 1493 in Windsor, he was prepared to offer men to bolster Warbeck's cause, a private promise that when later exposed would trigger his downfall.[3]

No one outside the king's most intimate circle, however, could have anticipated the finger of suspicion would thereafter be pointed towards another member of his royal household, an influential figure integral in putting a crown atop Henry's head almost a decade earlier. As lord chamberlain, it was also someone who had long been entrusted with controlling access to the vulnerable monarch in private – his step-uncle, Sir William Stanley.

As Henry VII celebrated Christmas Day with his wife and children at Greenwich, he did so fully informed by his network of spies that members of his own household had been colluding in the overseas scheme to depose him. It is likely he had known of this conspiracy for several months but had patiently bided his time until he was certain of the finer details before launching his pre-emptive strike. The visit of an unnamed courier on 19 December, who 'brought the tidings' for which he was rewarded £3, perhaps influenced the king's next move, for one week later he decamped upriver to the Tower of London with orders for his court to join him.[4]

Details are vague about the moment of Stanley's arrest, or what words passed from his mouth when confronted, but it appears he was apprehended shortly after the king assumed residence in the Tower, with a trial scheduled just a few weeks later to determine his fate. It was a turn of events that shocked many in England for the Stanleys were widely regarded, with good reason, to be part of Henry's inner circle, the culmination of a lengthy career among the country's elite. There appeared little discernible reason why one brother would now turn traitor at the age of nearly sixty, other than a genuine belief one of the sons of Edward IV yet lived.

As second son of the 1st Baron Stanley, Sir William did not possess the same level of influence, or indeed inheritance, as his elder brother Thomas, now earl of Derby, to whom he would always be expected to play second fiddle. William nevertheless succeeded in carving out a respectable career for himself throughout the second half of the fifteenth century, earning recognition as a wealthy knight of 'grete strength' in Cheshire and Lancashire who could boast 'excellent substaunce in movable goodys'. After his downfall, a search of his property at Holt Castle in north-east Wales uncovered significant amounts of coin, along with many 'Rich Joyallys of gold and sylvyr, and harneys sufficient ffor a grete hoost of pepull'.[5]

Stanley's rise early in the Wars of the Roses was allied to that of the House of York and specifically Edward IV, to whom he pledged his loyalty from the outset of dynastic conflict. He was present for the Yorkist victories at Blore Heath in 1459 and Towton in 1461, and during the brief Lancastrian readeption in 1470 pointedly had his household in Nantwich ransacked by supporters of Henry VI. He would avenge that insult in 1471 when he was present once more on the battlefield fighting for York at Tewkesbury, unquestionably a key supporter of the White Rose.

Stanley's service to Edward IV allowed him gradually to accumulate an ample north Welsh estate that complemented his brother Thomas's lands in neighbouring Cheshire and Lancashire. An indication of the level of trust between the Yorkist king and Stanley is evident when he was appointed steward of the heir Prince Edward's household, a prestigious and influential office to possess. Under Richard III's reign he would be installed as chief justice of North Wales, but nevertheless betrayed that king at Bosworth in anticipation of greater reward under Henry VII. It is believed Stanley coveted the earldom of Chester, which would have solidified his authority in the region, but to his frustration this title was bestowed upon Prince Arthur in 1489.

Though confirmed in his north Welsh offices after Bosworth, as well as appointed lord chamberlain of the royal household and chamberlain of the Exchequer,[6] elevation to the peerage evaded Stanley. Though he became England's richest knight during this period, vexation at rising no further appears to have been enough to provoke leanings toward treason by the mid-1490s, particularly once rumours of Richard of York's miraculous survival gathered pace around the continent. It was the opinion of Edward Hall forty years later that after a decade of solid service to Henry VII, Stanley simply started to 'grudge and disdeyne the kyng his high frend' for what he perceived was a lack of recognition in driving the Tudors to the throne.[7]

Ultimately, William Stanley's loyalty to the Yorkist cause was reserved for Edward IV and his progeny, as shown by his betrayal of Richard III in 1485 and failure to support Lambert Simnel's Warwick plot in 1487. Once a pretender who had yet to be conclusively ruled out as a son of his former master emerged, Stanley's head was turned. It is perhaps telling that during the inventory of Holt after his arrest, one item of note that was found that helped seal his fate was a livery collar which featured an array of suns and roses, Yorkist badges associated with Edward IV.[8] It was a dangerous item to retain with a pretender at large. Though it may have been William who crowned Henry at Bosworth, rather than his brother Thomas as often supposed, with one chronicle even having him declare, 'Sir here I make yow kyng of England', old loyalties evidently died hard in the fifteenth century.[9]

Stanley's downfall was largely due to a northerner named Robert Clifford, whose crucial testimony just after Christmas 1494 forced Henry's hand in ordering the arrest of his step-uncle. Like Stanley, Clifford had been another 'most devoted follower' of Edward IV, despite his father and brother losing their lives fighting for the Lancastrians at St Albans in 1455 and Towton in 1461 respectively. Clifford was quickly reconciled to the new Yorkist king, however, serving as Edward's esquire throughout the late 1470s and early 1480s, before continuing in royal service under Henry VII, by whom he was appointed chamberlain of Berwick in 1486.[10] In 1491 he was handed a commission to raise funds for the forthcoming French campaign, for which he also served as an interpreter.[11] In short, Clifford was a solid, if undistinguished, official of the crown, one of the many dependable cogs that helped the early Tudor wheel to turn.

By January 1493, when he held a surreptitious discussion with Lord Fitzwalter about providing men for Warbeck's cause, Clifford's loyalty to Henry VII had started to waver, and along with William Barley he fled the kingdom that summer for Flanders. Somewhat predictably he was warmly welcomed by Margaret of York, who was 'exceedingly pleased' to receive fresh news of growing conspiracy in England against the king.[12] When the defectors were introduced to Perkin Warbeck, they quickly perceived him to be the 'true and unfeyned' duke of York, with Clifford supposedly convinced 'he was extracted of the blood royall, and the very somme of kyng Edward'. He even penned a letter to old friends in England wishing to 'put them out of all doubte' about the young man's identity,[13] and was also overheard commenting on Warbeck's authenticity to a woman whilst ambling in Calais.[14]

After William Warham and Edward Poynings returned from their embassy that same summer of 1493 without securing the pretender's capture, Henry VII responded by sending several moles into Flanders over the next year charged with feigning support for Warbeck so that they could unearth further details about the conspiracy. Part of their remit was to convince Clifford and Barley to return to England, 'promisynge to theim franke and free pardone' if they abandoned the 'develishe enterprice'.[15] Clifford, at least, was gradually worn down by their persistence.

Perhaps mindful of the fact that the English appeared to know enough about the plot that it was destined to be exposed, Clifford decided 'for his own self interest to change his mind'[16] and prudently accepted the offer of a deal whilst it was available to him. He was officially pardoned by 22 December 1494.[17]

Two men, William Hoton and Harry Wodeford, were sent to escort Clifford home safely, a mission for which they were rewarded with a not insignificant sum.[18] The *Great Chronicle* reports the trio escaped Flanders 'not withowth some daunger', which suggests it had not been a simple extraction.[19] With Clifford's testimony, however, by the end of 1494 Henry was confident enough to send Richmond Herald back to France to inform Charles VIII that not only was he was in good health, but loved and obeyed by all his people, which was certainly glossing the reality. Additionally, he had little concern for the '*garçon*' in Flanders, Warbeck, who had so far proven himself 'incapable of hurting or doing him injury'.[20]

With Clifford back in London, on 12 January 1495 he was 'thoroughly interrogated' in the king's presence, with Vergil reporting the rebel-turned-defector 'excused his own conduct and revealed the whole extent of the conspiracy and all that had been arranged in Flanders'. More importantly, Clifford identified the leading members of the plot, which, he testified to his stunned audience, included Sir William Stanley.[21] The informant declared that he and Stanley had freely discussed the claim of Warbeck, a conversation during which the chamberlain 'sayde and affirmed there, that he would never fight nor beare armure agaynst the young man, if he knew of a truthe that he was the indubitate sonne of kyng Edward the iiii'.[22] If the words weren't overtly treasonous in themselves, they certainly suggested the man Henry VII had long entrusted 'with all his affairs'[23] was only committed to his master until a more favourable alternative advanced his cause. The king, most understandably, demanded a fidelity from his closest servants far greater than that which Stanley appeared willing to provide. His loyalty, it seemed, came with conditions.

Edward Hall would later claim Henry was 'greatly dismayed and greved' by news of Stanley's wavering heart, whilst Vergil added the king 'greviously mourned' Clifford's testimony and 'could not be persuaded at first to believe Robert's statement'. Both were writing much later than the revelation, however, and one must assume the circumspect sovereign was kept fully abreast of Stanley's shady activities prior to this January 1495 summit. Clifford's 'indisputable evidence' merely confirmed existing suspicions and allowed Henry to order his chamberlain 'to be arrested and examined'.[24]

Widespread commissions of oyer and terminer were issued from Westminster on 25 January, covering most counties south of the River Trent and headed by the king's aged uncle the duke of Bedford, the duke of Buckingham, the marquis of Dorset, the earls of Arundel, Oxford, Northumberland, Shrewsbury, Suffolk, Essex, Surrey, Kent, and Wiltshire, and capably supported by dozens of knights, all of whom were collectively charged with investigating every aspect of the conspiracy. One person of note also recruited to inspect for treachery was Thomas Stanley, the king's stepfather and elder brother to the disgraced William. As the earl of Derby and one of the premier nobles in the kingdom, it was his noble duty to help uncover evidence of conspiracy against his king, information that would be used to condemn his own sibling.[25]

The trials of those arrested across the previous two months commenced on 29 January in London's Guildhall, with proceedings overseen by the city's mayor and members of the king's council. On the first day, those apprehended in November were inspected and the following day sentenced to death, although the churchmen were pardoned in recognition of their holy orders. Two other defendants, Thwaits and Sutton, were also spared by the judges, sent back to the Tower rather than losing their heads on the block. Mountford, Ratcliffe and Daubeney were not as fortunate, and were beheaded on 4 February on Tower Hill, with Cressner and Astwood reprieved only at the last moment, which 'gladded moche people for they were both yong men'. One day later, a Breton named Pety John, a Dutchman named Hans Troy, and Robert Holbourn were hanged, drawn and quartered.[26] Lord Fitzwalter, meanwhile, condemned by the testimony of Clifford and the most notable of the November arrests, was more leniently punished than his co-defendants and instead handed a sentence of life imprisonment in Guînes, near Calais. A botched escape in November 1496, however, eventually saw him executed.

The star defendant, William Stanley, was arraigned before the chief justice of the King's Bench and the council in Westminster, and during his examination 'he nothinge denyed, but wisely and seriously did astipulate and agree to all thinges layed to hys charge'. If Stanley supposed that accepting guilt would earn the king's mercy and save his life, his arrogance was misplaced for he was nevertheless 'adjudged to dye'. Henry could have intervened on his chamberlain's behalf at any moment, but despite apprehension that his stepfather Thomas Stanley, 'in whome he had found great frendship, would take this mattre greveously', the perceptive king understood that to show clemency at this crucial juncture could encourage others to take up arms against a king they perceived to be weak.[27] Stanley had to die; it had to be made clear that disloyalty would be punished. Around eleven o'clock in the morning on 16 February 1495, the fallen knight and hero of Bosworth was solemnly led from his chamber in the Tower to a scaffold that had been erected upon nearby Tower Hill, 'and there byhedid'.[28]

Stanley's offence was hardly the most severe ever committed against a Plantagenet or Tudor monarch; but in the environment of the mid-1490s, raddled with suspicion, as Henry VII grew ever more uncertain about the allegiance of several former Yorkists he had retained in his service, ill-advised comments were enough alone to be condemned, particularly since the English law of the day stipulated that even imagining the king's death was considered treasonous. If Henry couldn't depend on Stanley, whose own words had suggested he could repudiate his loyalty in the event an acceptable Yorkist alternative presented himself, then such a figure intimately connected with the royal household undoubtedly posed a risk that couldn't be nonchalantly dismissed.

Henry had grown to know Stanley well during the decade they had existed in close tandem, and the king must have detected an aspect of his chamberlain's character that was unnerving, something that did not allow forgiveness to be an option. Whatever the motive, Henry acted decisively to eliminate the threat before the matter could escalate into the sort of predicament that cost his predecessor his life. There was, however, one sign of regret on the king's part; he personally paid for Stanley's burial at Syon Abbey.[29]

*

The execution of William Stanley and swift conviction of several other conspirators was a bitter, if not quite fatal, blow to Perkin Warbeck's hopes of launching a successful invasion of the English mainland, and at once removed several crucial allies who had expressed willingness to support the deposition of their current king in favour of the pretender lurking overseas. Furthermore, Henry VII's widescale operation in weeding out scheming traitors in his midst, and even putting his chamberlain to death with little hesitancy, served as a significant deterrent to other would-be defectors sheltering in England.

Warbeck's already sizeable task had certainly been done no favours by the January 1495 trials, yet, to the weary king's dismay, the efforts of his council and shadowy agents failed to bring the plot to a conclusive end, as evidenced by the arrest of two Suffolk yeomen, William White and John Pilkington, near the royal palace of Greenwich on 20 February. They were picked up for distributing letters bearing the name Richard Plantagenet.[30]

Henry's actions in breaking Stanley only served to drive Warbeck, the Richard Plantagenet of the letters, deeper into the embrace of the king's foreign rivals, who for their part remained keen to capitalise on England's domestic woes. There is evidence that, regardless of the arrests in London, plans were progressing well in Flanders as the Christmas period of 1494 approached.

Between 10 and 23 December in Antwerp, the pretender put his name to a document which pledged that when he assumed control of England as Richard IV, he would repay Margaret of York the 800,000 crowns she had already advanced him as well as another 81,666 crowns that remained outstanding from her 200,000 crown dowry of 1468. He would also return to her possession the Hertfordshire manor of Hunsdon, which had been seized by the Tudor king after the fall of her brother Richard III, and for good measure grant her the town and castle of Scarborough on the north-eastern English coast. The deed was witnessed by Robert Clifford, and one must assume that when he returned to England shortly thereafter he freely informed Henry VII of the agreement.[31]

In Malines, meanwhile, on 24 January 1495, the day before Henry VII issued commissions to his leading nobles in England to investigate the conspiracy, Warbeck concluded another agreement, one which resembled a will. This document stipulated that in the event the pretender captured the English throne but died without legitimate issue, the crown would pass into the hands of Maximilian I, and thereafter his son Philip, the latter retaining a distant Lancastrian claim through his mother. If there was an overriding incentive for the ambitious King of the Romans to press Warbeck's claim and depose Henry VII, then the prospect of extending the Hapsburg domain across the English Channel was surely it.[32]

There was another, more pressing, reason for Maximilian's continuing support of Warbeck as 1495 progressed. Having invaded Italy the previous autumn, by the end of February 1495 Charles VIII of France had marched his formidable army through the heart of the Italian peninsula, passing through Genoa, Florence, Siena and Rome before capturing his intended prize, Naples. Whilst the French king exuberantly celebrated his conquest for several weeks, the threat Charles posed to other nations galvanised a number of European potentates to establish a defensive political and military alliance designed to resist a belligerent common enemy. Though not worded as such, this Holy League, or League of Venice after the location where the agreement was signed on 31 March 1495, was in effect an anti-French movement led by the chief signatories – Pope Alexander VI, Ferdinand of Aragon (who was also King of Sicily and maintained his own dynastic claim to the crown of Naples), the new duke of Milan Ludovico Sforza, the Republic of Venice, and the Hapsburg father and son, Maximilian and Philip. It was an innovative, pan-continental proposition.

Both France and the League courted the support of Henry VII, who nevertheless initially adopted a neutral stance to his two suitors. The English king sympathised with the League's concerns and maintained a keen interest in Italian affairs due to the prosperous trade exporting wool and cloth whilst importing wines, spices, and silks, but he could not commit to the cause whilst Maximilian and Philip harboured, and indeed encouraged, Perkin Warbeck.

This reluctance to join the League infuriated the King of the Romans. Rather than reaching out diplomatically to Henry as Ferdinand of Aragon attempted, Maximilian instead boldly declared he would replace the English king on his throne with a candidate more amenable to his objectives, even boasting he already had a suitable Yorkist pretender in his pocket.

For Maximilian, sponsoring Warbeck was no longer merely a matter of goodwill for a youngster he may genuinely have liked – it had manifested into a serious political manoeuvre which he intended to use to manipulate the English king into reversing his decision. If Henry persisted in his refusal to wage war against the French, Maximilian swore he was willing to help provoke revolt in England to achieve his aims.[33]

Spurred on by Maximilian and Margaret, and with loans secured from merchants who had been encouraged to gamble on the unlikely venture,[34] Warbeck gradually accumulated enough funding to establish a modest force, with the decision taken to prepare an assault on England, even after news reached Flanders of William Stanley's execution. There was little other choice – not to attempt to reclaim the throne he called his birthright potentially exposed the pretender to accusations he may not be the true Yorkist prince after all; nor was there the guarantee of continued support from the Hapsburgs, who were under increasing pressure from the League to desist. In a climate where political allegiances could change on a whim, the window of opportunity, as Henry Tudor and Lambert Simnel had discovered with different outcomes in 1485 and 1487 respectively, could not be ignored.

As preparations for Warbeck's departure advanced, Margaret of York attempted to bolster his cause by composing a letter to the pope with the guidance of several theologians. She requested the Holy Father remove the threat of papal sanction against those who rejected Henry VII's kingship, asserting that kings of England traditionally ruled by right of blood and not through battle or with parliamentary assent. As a legitimate scion of the House of York allegedly endured in the person of Prince Richard, Margaret expected that papal endorsement of Henry's reign should be rescinded with immediate effect, and that any person compelled to help restore the Yorkist line to the throne should not be subject to punishment by the Church. They would, she asserted, be merely performing a pious duty.

Margaret's bold appeal to the pope served to demonstrate how desperate the conspiracy had grown. It is fair to assume they were struggling to cultivate fresh support in England after the downfall of Stanley and his cohorts, and it was hoped by removing the Church's support for Henry they could encourage more people to declare for Warbeck without fear of condemning their soul. The appeal was not granted.[35]

Warbeck's army and fleet were given over to the command of a Hainaulter courtier named Roderigue de Lalaing,[36] a competent captain who had served Maximilian I on previous missions and who now hoped to surpass the modest achievements of Martin Schwartz eight years earlier. Aside from Lalaing, there doesn't appear to have been any other commander present on the expedition with extensive military experience, which placed Warbeck at a disadvantage when compared with Simnel's force in 1487; as well as Schwartz, the earlier campaign at least boasted the earl of Lincoln and Thomas FitzGerald amongst its number. Warbeck himself exhibited little evidence of martial bearing, and though that was not dissimilar to Henry Tudor's lack of expertise in 1485, the latter ensured he was guided by hardy veterans of warfare who could, and indeed would, guide him to victory. Warbeck, therefore, was at a significant disadvantage before he even boarded his ship.

His disparate force was lightweight, a 'great crowd of rascals and thieves' according to Vergil;[37] Hall believed they only desired to 'lyve of robbery and rapinge'.[38] Whatever the motivations of those present on the enterprise, by the end of June 1495 Warbeck's modest army nevertheless sailed from Zeeland. They were possibly bound for East Anglia; the same destination Edward IV had initially intended during his own invasion in 1471.[39] Perhaps owing to the calm sea off the Kentish coast shortly into their crossing, and the form that county had for rebellion, on 3 July a significant part of the pretender's fleet instead made landfall near Deal, where according to the later act of attainder they 'there and then trayterously reared and levied Batell and Warre, in Pleyn Feld'.[40]

What occurred on that summer day in 1495 can be gleaned from several sources, all of which fundamentally agree that the mission was an utter failure. Whilst Warbeck remained safely aboard his ship, not unlike Henry during the latter's own failed landing near Devon in 1483, around three hundred of his men, a 'grete multitude of people' armed with bows, bills, halberds, spears and crossbows each 'compassyng the deth and destruccion' of the king, made it on to the beach. They planted their banners with purpose and probed the area for a royal army.

It was not King Henry's men the rebels encountered, however. Without warning, and it would appear without expectation, they found themselves ambushed from all sides by the men of Kent, some from the town of Sandwich and some from Canterbury, who 'at one stroke vanquyshed' the ill-prepared invaders. The locals, having previously shown themselves 'not tymerous nor afraide of their awne mynde in troubleous seasons to move warre against their princes', had determined on this occasion it was not 'expedient nor profitable' to turn on their king. It was their conclusion that Warbeck was indeed little more than a 'peinted ymage', a 'feyned duke' only supported by 'Alienes and straunge people'.[41] Their lot would be best served by remaining steadfast to the Tudor crown.

Those not slain by the heavily armed villagers or drowned whilst desperately attempting to flee the assault back to their ships were rounded up and held prisoner. A report sent to King Ferdinand and Queen Isabella two weeks later by Spanish ambassador De Puebla claimed over 150 rebels were killed in the botched operation. Eighty more were captured, amongst them eight captains, including two Spaniards, Don Fulano de Guevara and Diego the Lame.[42] A letter sent by the Corporation of Yarmouth on 11 July to Norfolk landowner Sir John Paston recorded four of those captains' names as Wight, Belt, Corbett and Mountford, the latter the son of Simon Mountford, who had been executed earlier that year for his role in the Stanley conspiracy.[43]

The entire defence of Deal Beach, and indeed England beyond it, had been accomplished 'without the intervention of a single soldier of the king'.[44] Henry 'greatly thanked' the men of Sandwich, Canterbury and Kent 'for theyre true servyces'.[45] Those captured, meanwhile, were tied in ropes and taken to London by John Peche, the Sheriff of Kent, where they were handed over to his London counterpart. Some were imprisoned in the Tower with others placed in Newgate, and starting on 30 July, over fifty were hanged at Tyburn. As a gruesome warning to others that loyalty to the king was the recommended course of action, more were executed along the coasts of Kent, Essex, Sussex, Norfolk and Suffolk.[46] At least one English rebel, however, managed to escape captivity on the way to his execution, slipping away from his captors during a stopover in Chelmsford and fleeing back to sanctuary in Westminster Abbey. His fate thereafter is unknown.[47]

How did Warbeck, whether fraud or prince, perceive such horrific slaughter from his floating vantage point, particularly as he appears to have been a novice to the brutal reality of warfare? Could he hear the screams of his followers as they were butchered up and down the beach? Did he feel guilt for being the reason hundreds of men were routinely slain for supporting his cause? If merely a boatman's son from Tournai, conscious of his pretence, then surely he must have been deeply affected that such death could have been avoided had he simply disclosed his true origins and brought the dishonest scheme to an end. If, however, he was indeed the son of Edward IV, returning home to claim his lost birthright, then the violent welcome could hardly be more disheartening.

When it became clear Warbeck's hapless men had been utterly overwhelmed at Deal, the order was given to raise anchor and flee the area before the king's fleet arrived to eliminate the remnants of his force. Both Hall and Vergil suggest the pretender briefly returned to Margaret of York's court, though the Spanish ambassador mentioned in his near-contemporary report home, 'It is not probable that they would return to Flanders, because the whole of that country is almost ruined, in consequence of their staying there,' a reference to the economic blockade imposed upon Duke Phillip's lands by Henry.[48]

It seems likely the Spaniard was correct in his judgement, and Warbeck's depleted army instead sailed westwards around the south coast of England and into the Celtic Sea. A later patent suggests they briefly spent time near Youghal on the southern Irish coast, where a ship called *le Cristofre of Plymmouth* was seized by the rebels. Sixty tons of Spanish iron was liberated from the vessel and peddled in Youghal and Cork, raising much-needed capital for the deflated pretender's cause.[49]

Whilst Warbeck had been planning his assault on the English mainland, fresh trouble had erupted in Ireland when Maurice FitzGerald, 9th Earl of Desmond, once more rebelled against royal authority. His latest grievance stemmed from the fact that Henry had stripped him of the constableship of Limerick Castle in favour of someone whose loyalty to the crown was beyond doubt: Sir James Ormond.[50] Desmond's crusade against Tudor rule culminated in laying siege to Waterford, notably the only royal Irish settlement which had remained loyal to Henry during Lambert Simnel's 1487 uprising.

On 23 July 1495, Warbeck appeared in Waterford harbour with eleven ships under his command. Sensing an opportunity to damage the English king's authority in Ireland, the pretender now put his men at Desmond's disposal. He had, however, underestimated both the hardy souls of Waterford and the terrain around the town. Some of his men alighted their ships to the south of their target, hoping to advance by land into Waterford, but found their progress thwarted by the impassable Kilbarry Ponds. Two of his ships, meanwhile, reached Lombard Weir near the centre of the town, but when they docked the men aboard found themselves overwhelmed by the hostile Waterfordians. Those not killed in the initial onslaught were dragged into the marketplace to be summarily beheaded by their captors. Their bloody heads were spiked by the Irish in gruesome triumph.

Cannon fire from the fifty-four-foot-high Reginald's Tower, meanwhile, sank at least one of Warbeck's fleet, 'the noise and cry being great'. When Edward Poynings, Henry VII's deputy in Ireland, appeared on 3 August with a horde of Anglo-Irish troops in tow, Warbeck and Desmond wisely, if humiliatingly, retreated 'with dishonour and great loss of their people'. The pretender's whereabouts for the next few months, other than a brief respite in Cork, are uncertain, but it is clear he kept his head down whilst considering his next move. For their continued loyalty and tenacious resistance, Waterford was granted the motto '*Intacta manet Waterfordia*' – the untouched, or untaken, city. It was a fitting reward.[51]

*

Throughout Perkin Warbeck's exploits during the summer of 1495, the two kings most concerned by his voyage, Maximilian I and Henry VII, anxiously awaited news at their respective courts. Though the former was preoccupied with an intense Diet in the city of Worms covering Imperial reforms and matters relating to the Italian Wars, he ensured messengers were employed to keep him fully informed about the Yorkist conspiracy.

The English king, meanwhile, was also busy exploring the kingdom he hoped to rule for many years to come, having commenced a comprehensive northern progress of England in early June. Henry's intended route was to include a visit to the extensive Stanley family estates in Cheshire and Lancashire, including Lathom, where he hoped 'to recreate his spirites and solace him selfe with his mother'.[52] He would, of course, also take the opportunity to cast his wary eye over the surviving Stanley set-up, and ensure any treasonous activity within the family had died with William Stanley at the start of the year. The Stanleys had brought down Richard III, and, his mother's marriage to the family head Thomas Stanley notwithstanding, Henry probably needed personal assurance the earl of Derby remained on side.

By 3 July, the date the pretender appeared off the coast of Deal with his fleet, the royal caravan had reached the Gloucestershire town of Tewkesbury, over 180 miles away and the scene of abject sorrow for the Houses of Lancaster and Beaufort twenty-four years earlier.[53] That the king had left London, a city which had often sympathised with the Yorkist cause during the Wars of the Roses, when intelligence from his sources indicated an invasion was imminent, suggests two things: firstly, Henry was confident the threat could be overcome without his personal involvement, unlike that of Simnel in 1487 when he joined his army on the battlefield in full armour; and secondly, he had complete trust in his closest advisors to suppress the matter should Warbeck and his army advance on the capital. It helped, of course, that he had prudently put a number of measures in place before departing on his journey.

With Warbeck and his supporters attempting to divide Yorkist loyalties and cause a split amongst Henry's support, on 27 March

1495, the castle, manor, lordship and town of Fotheringhay in Northamptonshire, a principal seat of the House of York and where Richard III had been born, were granted to the king's Yorkist queen Elizabeth. In a conscious link with the past, she was to hold the property under the same terms afforded to her grandfather Richard, Duke of York.[54] The timing was no doubt intentional, with Henry keen to remind any potentially wayward subject that the legacy of York had been firmly integrated into his own fledgling dynasty over the previous decade. The blood of the White Rose, after all, coursed through the veins of his own children, and it was to them that all Yorkist support should be directed, not to questionable pretenders abroad.

At the same time, Henry also sought to remind his subjects that the House of York, as a ruling dynasty, had been destroyed by his own forces at Bosworth ten years earlier. In July 1495, the king commissioned a Nottingham tradesman named Walter Hylton to erect a modest alabaster tomb for Richard III over the latter's grave near the altar in Leicester Grey Friars, for which a payment of £50 was authorised in two instalments. A separate fee of £10 was issued to James Keyley two months later for work on the tomb, and the finished article remained in situ until around 1538 when the friary was suppressed. Richard III's posthumous reputation had suffered in the early years of Tudor rule, during which he was widely derided as an unnatural tyrant who had been punished by God for unlawfully usurping the throne from his nephew. Henry now changed tack, somewhat, by officially recognising Richard's reign with a tomb above his grave. His reasons were clear; by openly commemorating his predecessor, not only did Henry hope to assuage any lingering animosity towards him from Richard's affinity for the latter's hasty burial, but to remind them that to transfer their loyalties to Perkin Warbeck was to ignore the fact that it was Richard himself who had overseen the delegitimisation of Edward IV's sons in the first place. It was worth a shot.[55]

Dynastic propaganda notwithstanding, Henry was also wisely prepared for Warbeck militarily. That same month, he handed over the considerable sum of £476 5s 4d to his royal armourer for the equipping of five ships, whilst on 27 April, Henry Wyatt, Keeper of the King's Jewels, and William Hatcliffe were appointed to inspect and review soldiers who had been selected to cross the Irish Sea, their wages to be collected from the treasurer of Ireland, Hugh Conway.[56] Another payment of £350 2s 9d was made to John Reding in July for supplying four more ships in Plymouth and Fowey, capable of conveying 470 men to sea. For good measure, the *Pycard* of Chester was also procured for a month to ferry even more men into Ireland, where Desmond and his rebels were increasingly active.[57]

In late spring, meanwhile, Henry had sent his cousin Sir Charles Somerset to the Burgundian court in yet another attempt to persuade young Duke Philip and his council to abandon their support for Warbeck. According to the account of Jean Molinet, who may have been present, Somerset merely succeeded in triggering a fresh diplomatic incident. When he was brought into the hall for the summit, the Englishman reverently bowed to all present, with the notable exception of the pretender.

When queried by Margaret of York why he failed to show respect to the young man she claimed was her nephew, Somerset responded he knew the true duke of York to be dead, and would be pleased to show her the very chapel in which this son of Edward IV was buried. Given that nobody seems to have ever revealed the last resting place, if any, of the Princes in the Tower, this was likely a bluff on the part of Somerset, and his goading drew an aggressive reaction from an infuriated Warbeck, who interjected that the knight would rue those words once he became king of England.[58]

Despite such hubris, it was Henry VII, not Perkin Warbeck, who emerged from that fraught summer with his continental reputation enhanced and domestic position strengthened, if personally bereft after the death of his three-year-old daughter Elizabeth in September.[59] The pretender had chanced his arm invading England with a hastily assembled multinational force that featured only a handful of Englishmen, chiefly drawn from the yeoman class, and his gamble proved a comprehensive fiasco – his men failed to make it further inland than Deal Beach, let alone threaten London and overturn a regime that had been in place for a decade. Warbeck had not even been able to capture Waterford in Ireland, a country hardly steadfast in its allegiance to Tudor rule. The summer had been a humiliating experience for the self-proclaimed rightful king of England, and Perkin now desperately sought refuge along the western Irish coast as both friend and foe slowly resolved their differences in his absence.

The failed invasion, along with the ever-present threat of another French military expedition into Italy, encouraged the Holy League leadership to once more pressurise their partner Maximilian I to consider receiving Henry VII, more secure than ever upon his throne, into the alliance. The King of the Romans reluctantly opened discussions with his English counterpart early in the new year, though he did not find the negotiations a foregone conclusion. Not only did

Maximilian unreasonably expect England to invade France on their own by Easter, but he obstinately refused to abandon Warbeck's cause. Unsurprisingly, Henry rebuffed the proposal, and, as someone courted by both France and the League, refused to be bullied into terms not to his advantage.

Ferdinand and Isabella of Spain spent several months attempting to soften Maximilian's terms, concerned Henry would lose patience and reach an agreement with the French. The deadlock was finally broken in July 1496, a year after Warbeck's botched invasion, when the English king, having received a personal plea from Pope Alexander himself, sent the archdeacon of Buckingham, Robert Sherbourne, to Rome to formally declare his entry into the League. News of Henry's alignment with the League was broadcast in Venice, Milan and Rome itself, with bonfires lit in jubilation and church bells ordered to be rung for three consecutive days. According to one ambassador, it was reported that Henry had brought 'the greatest satisfaction' to the other members who had 'long loved and reverenced' the English king. The appreciative pope even arranged for a sword and cap of maintenance to be sent to London as a mark of his gratitude.[60]

Henry had also agreed terms with Maximilian's son Philip of Burgundy earlier that year, concluding a fresh Anglo-Burgundian treaty in London on 24 February 1496 which sought to reverse much of the economic damage incurred by the recent trade war. As with Maximilian and the Holy League, the far-reaching influence of Ferdinand and Isabella was also at play here; Philip was in the final stages of negotiating marriage to Juana, the third child of the Spanish monarchs, and the duke's prospective in-laws championed peace with England.

The treaty Henry secured was considered so favourable to English interests, it was long regarded derisively amongst the Flemish. In the short term, however, the most crucial consequence for the English king was the article which stipulated that each party would not harbour rebels of the other, with the added clause that should Margaret of York provide shelter to any English dissidents in future, unlike on previous occasions Philip would intercede rather than making futile excuses.[61] Aged seventeen and soon to be married, it was time for Philip to look to the future and not become distracted by a past which no longer served his financial, political, or dynastic interests.

The eighteen months spanning 1495 and the first half of 1496 had proven an uneasy time for Henry VII, but he emerged having accomplished much. He had executed his chamberlain William Stanley and several others for conspiring against him, fended off an invasion of

Kent without having to use his own troops, sent Edward Poynings into Ireland to subdue seditious activity, commissioned Europe's first-ever dry dock in Portsmouth to grow his earning capacity, negotiated a fresh Anglo-Burgundian treaty with favourable terms, and earned the pope's gratitude by joining the Holy League. At each step along the way, he had tenaciously weathered the storm to maintain his grip on his crown, and even strengthen it in defiance of the plots and schemes of his enemies and rivals.

Whether measured politically, economically, or dynastically, the king was in a good place at the end of his first decade on the throne. Despite all these accomplishments, however, no doubt to his consternation Henry had not been able to apprehend Perkin Warbeck, or crush the dogged conspiracy around him that longed for the restoration of the pure White Rose. Whilst the pretender remained at large, one imagines the naturally cautious king had a nagging doubt in the back of his mind as the weeks and months went on, even if he put on a brave face in public. To someone as thorough and circumspect as the first Tudor, complacency was clearly not a character trait. Whilst Warbeck remained at liberty, Henry knew this thorn in his side would remain.

Warbeck was indeed persistent; after sailing out of Waterford harbour in August 1495 and licking his wounds following another humiliation, his immediate whereabouts are unknown. It is likely he sheltered somewhere in western Ireland, though his hosts are unknown. By November, however, the chastened pretender re-emerged under the protection of yet another foreign ally, a third king after Charles VIII and Maximilian I who opportunistically extended the hand of friendship along with a resounding pledge of support – James IV of Scotland.

13

Shame and Derision

James IV was an ambitious young king with lofty continental aspirations, conducting himself with such confidence it prompted the Spanish ambassador Pedro de Ayala to report home that he 'esteems himself as much as though he were Lord of the world'.[1] Aged twenty-two as 1495 drew to a close, the energetic Scottish king was even prepared to engage England in a costly war to raise his profile and that of his crown.

The timely appearance of Perkin Warbeck on Scottish soil late in the year provided James an ideal opportunity to draw Henry VII into conflict, contrary to an active treaty in place. For the floundering pretender, meanwhile, he once more encountered a willing royal patron prepared to provide much-needed shelter whilst publicly espousing his claim to be true and just. Timing, as always, was crucial for the success of any venture, and in this particular instance, Warbeck and James entered one another's worlds at the most opportune moment to breathe fresh life into their respective causes. Quite simply, they couldn't achieve their aims alone.

James IV had acceded to the Scottish throne in contentious circumstances in 1488, having personally assumed an integral role in the downfall of his father despite his tender age of just fifteen. After nearly twenty-eight years wearing the crown, James III had grown deeply unpopular with much of his nobility, his reputation tarnished through a dogged insistence on pursuing an English marital alliance for much of his reign and increasing dependence on a small collection of favourites. As seen in England earlier in the fifteenth century, this latter policy often proved contentious to the traditional order.

The Scottish king's standing amongst his peers suffered further from rancorous relationships with his two younger brothers, Alexander, Duke of Albany, and John, Earl of Mar; by the end of 1479, Mar had died in uncertain circumstances in Edinburgh, whilst Albany, who long opposed friendship with the English, had fled to France professing fear for his own life. A series of border raids meanwhile damaged Anglo-Scottish relations, and by April 1480, far from coexisting in peace as James III had desired, both kingdoms were once more in a state of war.

Somewhat ironically considering his previous anti-English stance, the exiled Albany soon entered the service of Edward IV, and in June 1482 the Scottish duke signed an agreement in Fotheringhay not only pledging his loyalty to the king of England, but also laying claim to his brother's crown. Edward assembled an army, spearheaded by his capable brother Richard, Duke of Gloucester, the future Richard III, and that summer the English invaded Scotland with Albany in their midst, intending to topple James III.

Before the plan could hold, however, it was frustrated by James's own nobility. Though the Scottish king elected to march south to meet the threat head-on, an action which would likely have ended in catastrophe against a superior force, James was seized by his men. He was led back to Edinburgh and locked up in his imposing castle upon the rock that overlooked the city below.

When Gloucester, Albany and the English entered the Scottish capital at the end of August, they discovered there was nobody to treat with. Despite James III's unpopularity, it was also clear Albany did not have the support of his countrymen to force a change of king, and, lacking money or supplies for a lengthy siege, Gloucester and his army withdrew home. They stopped only to force the surrender of the border town of Berwick, which was accomplished 'not without some slaughter and bloodshed' in the words of Edward IV.[2] Though Albany did briefly hold sway as lieutenant-general, James III was released from captivity and remained on the throne thereafter for another six years. His wayward brother barely lasted six months before he was conspiring once more, ultimately fleeing the kingdom once more to France where he died a few years later.[3]

Having fended off a serious assault on his crown, within three years James III's principal opponents of 1482, Albany, Edward IV, and Gloucester, were all dead and the king again attempted to foster positive relations with England, by now ruled by a receptive Henry VII who was untainted by previous Anglo-Scottish machinations. James III's revival of his stubborn policy to seek an alliance with his kingdom's ancient enemy, together with his unwise promotion and reliance on a handful of favourites, prompted a fresh outbreak of factional discord in early 1488. Opposition this time around was fervently led by the earls of Angus and Argyll, capably supported by the influential Hume and Hepburn families who were locked in their own dispute with the king over his plans to suppress Coldingham Priory. The figurehead of their revolt would be another member of the king's own family.

James III had three sons: his namesake heir James, Duke of Rothesay, another James, Earl of Ross, and John. To his eldest son's frustration, his father exhibited strong preference for his second child, which he demonstrated by twice angling for a prestigious marriage for Ross with one of Edward IV's daughters, before raising his earldom to a dukedom in the January 1488 parliament. There is little evidence to suggest James III intended to alter the succession of the crown so that it bypassed Rothesay, but the concern the heir felt as his father's reign progressed is perhaps understandable. Others were certainly aware of Rothesay's growing anxiety. In February, he was encouraged by the earls of Angus and Argyll to abandon his father and align himself with the rebels. Foreshadowing his later boldness, the headstrong youth seized the opportunity.

James III responded to this brazen rejection of his authority by raising his own army, and advanced on Stirling where he intended to crush his rivals and forcibly retake possession of his wayward heir. The two forces engaged at Sauchieburn, two miles south of the town, on 11 June 1488, and despite fewer numbers the rebels overwhelmed the royalists. Though bearing the sacred sword of Robert the Bruce, who had won a famous victory over the English at nearby Bannockburn 174 years earlier, James III was slain during the fighting. In Scone Abbey on 24 June, ironically the anniversary of Bannockburn, the dead king's son was crowned James IV.[4]

Fifteen years old when he ascended the throne, the new king, 'of noble stature, neither tall nor short, and as handsome in complexion and shape as a man can be',[5] only attained his majority seven years later in 1495. Though 'not having hitherto busied himself with state affairs', he wasted little time asserting himself in political matters, whether domestic or international.[6] Whereas his father had eagerly pursued an English bride for himself and his second son Ross, James IV instead professed an ambitious desire to retake Berwick whilst boldly seeking a marital alliance with the Spanish, for which he was prepared to repudiate a long-standing treaty with France. He also haughtily demanded entry into the Holy League.

James pledged that if the Spanish monarchs rejected his overtures he would invade England and forcibly distract Henry VII from his own involvement in League matters, which would have had a knock-on effect for the principal partners in the continental enterprise. Though ambassadors would journey between Spain and Scotland throughout 1495 attempting to placate James and reach an agreement, in truth the Scottish king's blackmail had little effect on the Spanish monarchs; they in fact had no daughters free to marry, and their strategy was to merely procure peace between England and Scotland rather than enter any dynastic union.[7]

In October 1495, the Scottish ambassador Archbishop Robert Blackadder returned home from one particular posting in Spain, whilst his Spanish counterparts, Martin de Torre and Garcia de Herera, tarried in England on the way north to continue the ongoing discussions. Their sealed instructions from Ferdinand and Isabella had been sent on ahead of them, however, and embarrassingly for the Spanish embassy were opened by James IV, who had grown suspicious about their intentions. The incandescent king discovered the Spanish deception, that there was no daughter to marry and he was merely being hindered from attacking England. James's response was to follow through on his earlier threats of war should he not get his way. It was into this anti-English maelstrom Perkin Warbeck resurfaced in November.

Though this autumn was the first time Warbeck had physically entered Scotland during his four-year crusade, the Scottish were certainly aware of the pretender's seditious activities, which filtered into the country through messengers, merchants and foreign envoys. There had also been direct contact between the two parties; in March 1492, whilst in Ireland at the outset of his campaign and canvassing for wider support, Warbeck had written to the Scots in vain seeking financial or military assistance, though by the summer of 1495 a modest Scottish force was placed at the pretender's disposal as a favour to Maximilian I and partook in the failed invasion of Deal.

Another connection between Warbeck and Scotland may have occurred four months before his arrival at the Scottish court. Throughout July 1495, the Irishman Hugh O'Donnell of Tyrconnel had been based at James IV's court. Returning home in August it was possibly he who conveyed a message to Warbeck that should he cross to Scotland he could be sure of a warm welcome.[8] As an aside, there was also a curious and as yet unexplained summit in November 1488 between James and forty-two Englishmen who had arrived from the court of Margaret of York. This meeting occurred a year after the failure of the Lambert Simnel conspiracy and a full three years before Warbeck's initial emergence in Ireland, and though it cannot be connected directly with the latter, this suggests some fresh plot behind the back of Henry VII was already afoot.[9] Could word have been passed to the Scottish court at this time that there was a boy from Tournai who, with the right support, might just one day sit upon the English throne? It shouldn't be dismissed.

In any case, what is clear is that by the autumn of 1495 James IV was the latest European ruler to identify Warbeck as the ideal partner, or indeed catspaw, to advance his own cause. On 16 October in Edinburgh, a council of forty men met to formally discuss inviting the floundering pretender into Scotland.[10] The outcome, influenced heavily one would imagine by the king's will and his mounting fury at warm Anglo-Spanish relations, was to extend the hand of friendship to this adversary of the English king, and by 6 November preparations for his arrival were underway at Stirling Castle. Just two days later, James wrote to Spain once more, hoping this latest development would encourage the alliance he desperately sought. The Spanish monarchs remained unmoved.[11]

On 20 November 1495, four and a half months since the debacle at Deal and barely three since the failed Waterford siege, Warbeck and what remained of his retinue swept through Stirling. The rising Ochil Hills to the east and the soaring Grampian Mountains to the north offered a formidable if scenic vista as the visitors climbed up the crag atop which awaited one of the most imposing fortresses in the kingdom. Considering the time of the year, the wind would have been bitter and some of the highest peaks visible in the distance, such as Ben Vorlich, Ben Ledi, and Stuc a'Chroin, may even have been capped with snow. As Warbeck's party made their way through the winding lane that took them up to the castle high above the town, a local guide perhaps pointed out in the distance where the famous battles of Bannockburn and Sauchieburn had taken place, the very site where Scotland had maintained its independence and also where the present king had seized his crown.[12]

Though there are no known contemporary accounts of Warbeck and James's first encounter, Edward Hall did write half a century later that the pretender recounted his survival story to a fresh audience, bringing the dramatic tale up to date. Once his hosts had had time to digest the tale they had just heard, Warbeck turned and addressed the king directly, exhorting James 'heartely with prayer' that he 'helpe and releve me now in my extreme necessite'. If by James's 'ayde and succour' he should obtain the crown of England, Warbeck promised that all future English kings of his line 'shalbe so much obliged and bound unto you' for the rest of time.[13]

Having heard Warbeck's plea, James turned to his council for guidance, and whilst 'the more prudent of them produced many arguments to show that the affair was nothing but a deceit prepared by Margaret and that therefore this young man should not be trusted', others were 'only too pleased to be given the opportunity of fighting the English', though they did concede 'the facts of the case to be uncertain'. Those wanting war with England proved more persuasive, and the king, 'either genuinely misled or pretending to be convinced' according to Vergil,[14] thereafter took to openly calling his guest Richard, Duke of York, the rightful heir to the English throne. It was a vital moment for Warbeck after numerous setbacks, and to his great relief he was forthwith paraded around the Scottish court 'in great honour'.[15]

On 6 December, having spent a fortnight getting to know one another, King James and Warbeck demonstrated their blossoming friendship in public when they celebrated St Nicholas Day together, not unlike how the pretender had once accompanied Philip of Burgundy to church during his time in Flanders. The intention was to project a visible bond between guest and host, and that connection may have been genuine; both were around twenty-two years old, ambitious to achieve lasting success, and orphaned, or in Warbeck's case if he wasn't truly a son of York, several years estranged from his Tournai parents. Friendships had been formed from far less common ground.

On 23 December, the two Spanish ambassadors who had tarried in England, allowing James to discover he was being deceived, finally reached Scotland. They were summoned to Stirling Castle, where upon arrival they were shown into the gardens. With Warbeck a keen observer, James openly lambasted the pair for the schemes of their king and queen, Ferdinand and Isabella, with the Scottish monarch bitterly complaining it was clear they only had the interests of Henry VII at heart. He was correct in his accusation, and vowed retribution for being misled. That retribution would centre around Perkin Warbeck.

From Stirling, the pretender accompanied James to Linlithgow for Christmas where, under the name Richard Plantagenet, he served as a witness to a royal charter, a formal recognition of his status as an English prince-in-exile. To ensure his stay in Scotland was as comfortable and safe as could be, Warbeck was also handed a personal guardian, a thirty-year-old prior named Andrew Forman who already possessed a 'great deal of influence'. The rising churchman was a diplomat with extensive international experience to draw on, having spent time in places such as London and Paris that no doubt helped him develop a rapport with the young man he had now been assigned to look after.[16]

In early January 1496, the royal household, with Warbeck in tow, departed Linlithgow for Edinburgh, and it was likely during the heart of a cold Scottish winter the pretender was given a remarkable gift by his latest host – a bride. Lady Katherine Gordon, regarded by one approving contemporary chronicler as 'a woman of goodly personage and beawty',[17] was the daughter of George Gordon, 2nd Earl of Huntly, by his third wife Elizabeth Hay, herself also of noble stock. Huntly, who inherited the earldom in 1470 along with extensive lands in the north-east of Scotland and Berwickshire in the south, had previously been wed to Annabella Stewart, a great-aunt of James IV, which meant that Warbeck's new bride was distantly related by marriage to the Scottish king, if not his close cousin as is often wrongly claimed. There was no blood connection.

In the circumstances, a daughter of a veteran Scottish earl was a reasonable match for Warbeck in lieu of other royal candidates, but hardly a match which alone can be taken to confirm his Yorkist credentials, as some historians have striven to claim. It was, however, an act designed to provoke the English king and further impair Anglo-Scottish relations – precisely what James IV intended.

It is unclear who provided the impetus behind the union, but in his early twenties, Warbeck was certainly of marriageable age and may have expressed interest in eventually producing legitimate offspring to transmit his claim to the English crown, particularly in the event he should perish pursuing his cause. It is also reasonable to suggest his advisors felt a Scottish match would solidify the burgeoning alliance, making it more problematic for James to suddenly repudiate his support, as had happened in France and Burgundy beforehand. Vergil, meanwhile, later speculated it was James IV who shrewdly sought the match to ensure Warbeck, if triumphant, 'would be put even more in his debt'.[18] Whichever scenario led to Perkin Warbeck marrying Katherine Gordon, the outcome was the same either way; the separate causes of the Scottish king and the Yorkist pretender had been very publicly bonded together to become one and the same.

There is a fascinating, if formulaic, letter which survives from December 1495, purportedly written by, or at least on behalf of, the pretender. In the letter, Warbeck passionately declares his yearning for the virtuous Lady Katherine, 'the brightest ornament of Scotland' and in whom he vested all his hopes. If sincere, it suggests he wasn't averse to the match:

Most noble lady, it is not without reason that all turn their eyes to you; that all admire, love, and obey you. For they see your two-fold virtues by which you are so much distinguished above all other mortals. Whilst, on the one hand, they admire your riches and immutable prosperity, which secure to you the nobility of your lineage and the loftiness of your rank, they are, on the other hand, struck by your rather divine than human beauty, and believe that you are not born in our days, but descended from Heaven.

All look at your face, so bright and serene that it gives splendour to the cloudy sky; all look at your eyes as brilliant as stars, which make all pain to be forgotten, and turn despair into delight; all look at your neck, which outshines pearls; all look at your fine forehead, your purple light of youth, your fair hair; in one word, at the splendid perfection of your person; and looking at, they cannot choose but admire you; admiring, they cannot choose but love you; loving, they cannot choose but obey you.

I shall, perhaps, be the happiest of all your admirers, and the happiest man on earth, since I have reason to hope you will think me worthy of your love. If I represent to my mind all your perfections, I am not only compelled to love, to adore, and to worship you, but love makes me your slave. Whether waking or sleeping, I cannot find rest or happiness except in your affection. All my hopes rest in you, and in you alone.

Most noble lady, my soul, look mercifully down upon me your slave, who has ever been devoted to you from the first hour he saw you. Love is not an earthly thing, it is heaven born. Do not think it below yourself to obey love's dictates. Not only kings, but also gods and goddesses have bent their necks beneath its yoke.

I beseech you, most noble lady, to accept for ever one who in all things will cheerfully do your will as long as his days shall last. Farewell, my soul and my consolation. You, the brightest ornament of Scotland, farewell, farewell.[19]

The union between this lady of noble birth and her devoted slave was celebrated on 13 January 1496 with a series of jousts in which the competitive king himself enthusiastically participated, injuring his hand in the process. There is no suggestion Warbeck competed, though he was presented with a fine white damask 'spousing' gown for the occasion. Other royal gifts included a purple damask-covered suit of armour, six servants, two trumpeters, a French armourer named Laurence, and an annual pension of £1,344.[20]

After a tough and ultimately disappointing summer that culminated in the farce at Deal and failure to capture Waterford, Warbeck's first three months in Scotland offered considerable promise for the future. As he sat and observed the Scottish king crash into his opponents during the jousting tournament, perhaps next to his beautiful wife and generally revelling in the joyous atmosphere around him, the pretender must have felt some degree of contentment that had been lacking in recent years. Still in his early twenties, Warbeck's personal life was starting to take shape and thoughts now turned, not for the first time, towards England, and finally capturing the crown he still maintained was his by right.

*

James IV and the newly married Warbeck left Edinburgh shortly after the wedding celebrations had ground to a halt, and headed across the Forth to Falkland, Fife, to see out the winter. Despite their tight alliance, which had been bonded beyond doubt by the wedding, the Scottish king nevertheless retained hope he could reach his own agreement with the Spanish monarchs, even as he advanced plans to invade England against their wishes. Any overtures for a treaty, however, even using Warbeck's presence in his court as leverage, were snubbed by Ferdinand and Isabella. In April 1496, the Spanish king and queen wrote to their ambassador in Scotland that though their sole purpose remained to 'win over the King of Scots, and to make him friends with the King of England, so that he may no longer show favour to him of York', a reference to Warbeck, it was their intention merely to 'put him off some time longer with vain hopes, in order that he may not begin war with England'.[21]

War with England, nevertheless, was the path James IV was hurtling towards, and that same month he notified his nobility of a planned muster later in the year at Lauder, Berwickshire, the same location incidentally where his unpopular father had been seized by his own nobility in 1482. Throughout the summer of 1496, weapons and artillery were gathered, along with tents and pavilions, all stored in Edinburgh Castle. Two ships were also procured from a pair of Bretons and handed to the Hainaulter Roderigue de Lalaing, who was first appointed by Maximilian and continued to provide a link with the Burgundian court, in secret defiance of the treaty with England that had recently been agreed.[22]

As the preparations for the invasion neared completion, Warbeck and James formalised their alliance in a document that was signed on 3 September 1496. Amongst the articles agreed was a proposition that should the pretender ever become king of England, he would pay his Scottish counterpart 50,000 marks over two years, negotiated down from 100,000 over five years. Controversially, Berwick would also be returned to the Scots.[23] In truth, it is likely James's objectives for the invasion, constrained by the financial reality of raising and sustaining an army in the field for any great length of time, did not stretch beyond recapturing Berwick and weakening English border defences in anticipation of future incursions. If Warbeck did realise his lofty ambition someday, however, the Scottish king wisely ensured he would be well rewarded for his support.

That same September a three-man embassy arrived in Scotland from the French court, led by the Scots-born Seigneur de Concressault, Alexander Monypeny, the very same figure who had personally welcomed Warbeck to France back in 1492. Charles VIII had tasked Monypeny with investigating the causes of the conflict and determining which side was at fault for the deterioration in relations. If possible, he was also to try and procure Warbeck and return him to France for safekeeping, which would in turn allow the French king to try and persuade Henry VII to withdraw from the Holy League in gratitude.

Charles VIII, however, had failed to foresee that the envoy he had charged with carrying out his instructions would be swayed by James IV's insistence that blame for the conflict lay with the English, who had regularly destroyed his ships and cattle. Monypeny's existing relationship with Warbeck also affected his impartiality; though claiming in an official capacity the French had evidence of the pretender's lowly origins, he professed in private conversation he was doubtful of their validity, and soon enough was observed 'everie day in counsaill' with 'ye boye', Warbeck. In short, the negotiator sent to Scotland to act as an arbitrator had, quite frankly, 'don bot litill gud' in the matter for either his French master or the English king.[24]

Regardless of external influence from the Spanish or French, James IV proved firm in his determination to invade England, though his defiant adversary was more than prepared to face down the latest menace to his reign. Having likely received word Warbeck had left Ireland from two messengers that were rewarded with 40s at the start of October 1495,[25] Henry VII set about protecting his northern border in anticipation of the pretender's next movements.

On 18 November 1495, mere days before Warbeck surfaced in Stirling, Thomas Howard, Earl of Surrey and the king's lieutenant in the north, was charged with arraying the men of Yorkshire to be ready, should the Scottish mobilise for war.[26] Several messengers meanwhile were sent throughout the kingdom, from Newcastle in the north to Cornwall in the south-west, bearing royal proclamations which one imagines denounced Warbeck and the Scottish whilst reiterating Henry's right to rule.[27] The king knew from experience, having successfully overwhelmed the Lambert Simnel affair earlier in his reign, the absolute importance of preparation.

Surrey was an astute choice for defending the north; regarded by Vergil as 'a lusty and noble young gentleman' who was 'endowed with prudence, dignity, and firmness',[28] the earl was the son and heir of John Howard, 1st Duke of Norfolk, alongside whom he was one of the few aristocrats who fought without reservation for Richard III against Henry at Bosworth Field. Though his father fell in the battle, Surrey survived the defeat, albeit with injuries, only to be attainted in the new king's first parliament. He spent the next four years languishing in the Tower of London, uncertain of his fate.

It was only in May 1489 that Henry VII ordered Surrey to be released, restoring his erstwhile adversary to his earldom, if not his lands or his father's dukedom. Rather than resume life as a southern lord, Surrey was sent into the north to quell the tax revolt that had peaked with the murder of Henry Percy, 4th Earl of Northumberland. Whilst some former Yorkist adherents, particularly those who had served Richard III, wavered in their loyalty as Henry's reign progressed, Surrey instead devoted all his energies to providing assiduous military service to the fledgling Tudor regime, earning his new master's trust by protecting the north rather than using it to fuel rebellion.

Save for Perkin Warbeck's marriage to Katherine Gordon early in the new year, Henry detected little movement from beyond the border until March 1496, when he received a Scottish spy who was rewarded with 6s 8d. It is likely the English king discovered through this informer that James IV was advancing his preparations for war, prompting Henry to place the mayors of York, Newcastle and Berwick on high alert. Each had permission to raise additional men to defend their cities if deemed necessary.[29] On 23 April, meanwhile, a widespread commission was issued to nobles like the king's brother-in-law Thomas Grey, 1st Marquis of Dorset, and the earls of Arundel, Shrewsbury, and Derby, to muster the men of Sussex, Surrey, Kent, the Cinque Ports, Hampshire, Worcestershire, Lincolnshire, Derbyshire and Staffordshire, 'in view of the warlike preparations of the king of Scots'.[30]

Although the summer passed without incident, in September, the month Warbeck concluded his agreement with James IV, defensive measures in northern England continued to intensify. Surrey instructed the mayor of York to raise another sixty men for the specific purpose of resisting the Scots when they finally made their move, with similar directives presumably disseminated throughout the region. The leading landowners of the north, the bishop of Durham, Richard Foxe, the lords Clifford and Greystoke, and a dozen other prominent Yorkshire gentlemen, were also charged with guarding the borders, if not out of loyalty to the crown then certainly to protect themselves, their estates, and their tenants from the Scottish storm headed their way.[31] This had been a calculated decision by Henry, wisely gauging that to dispatch a southern-based army into the hostile north risked provoking latent Yorkist sentiment. At such a perilous juncture in his reign, the king had chosen to put his faith in his northernmost subjects to defend his crown.

At the same time, Henry was only too conscious of the role Ireland had played in the conspiracies against him over the previous decade, and though Warbeck had failed to capture Waterford the previous August, the English king sought to ensure once and for all the unruly island could no longer be used as a refuge for rebels. Just a month after the Waterford siege, 'alle men women and childyr born wythyn the said Cuntre of Ireland' but now residing in England were ordered to present their names, ages and occupations to the king's exchequer, an authoritarian edict intended to expose any potential rebel sympathisers living on the mainland.[32] The pragmatic route to harmony in Ireland, however, or at least cooperation, came from an unexpected source – Gerald FitzGerald, 8th Earl of Kildare.

Having provided substantial support to Lambert Simnel in 1487 and suspected of aiding Perkin Warbeck in some capacity four years later, the mighty earl had hardly endeared himself to Henry VII during the first decade of Tudor rule. As a result of continuing tensions between the English king and Kildare, the latter had in fact been held prisoner in the Tower of London since March 1495, forcibly removed from his homeland in an attempt to quell the unrest which

Henry was struggling to subdue. In his absence, however, Kildare's supporters, led by his cousin Maurice FitzGerald, Earl of Desmond, had routinely attacked the countryside around the English-governed Pale of Dublin, a direct assault on royal authority that showed no signs of abating. Kildare's brother James FitzGerald had even succeeded in capturing the strategic Carlow Castle from Henry's men, a source of embarrassment for the king.

By the start of 1496, there existed a general collapse in law and order throughout the island that required urgent addressing before it could be exploited by Warbeck and the Scots. Whilst the pretender had failed to make headway in Ireland the previous summer, as he knew well from his dealings elsewhere in Europe, the political scene of the period was certainly fluid. Henry's response was to turn to the man he currently had under lock and key in the Tower.

In March 1496, the month Henry received word from his Scottish spy that preparations for war were underway north of the border, an indenture was drawn up between the earl of Desmond and the English king. One of the key articles in the agreement stipulated that in return for the earl handing over his young heir to the Corporation of Cork for three years as a surety, Henry pledged to release Kildare and restore him to his full inheritance, reversing the attainder earlier passed against him.[33]

The later sixteenth-century *Book of Howth* recounts an extraordinary meeting which subsequently took place between Henry and Kildare in London. The earl protested that he was unable to answer any charges put to him, for he was not as learned as his chief accuser John Payne, Bishop of Meath. The king, good-naturedly, advised him to select any counsellor in England to speak on his behalf instead, assuring the earl he would honour his choice. The person Kildare choose was Henry himself, which provoked an outbreak of laughter from the bemused king. Bishop Payne, however, was not impressed, and uttered dismissively in response to the earl's forthrightness, 'He is as you see, for all Ireland cannot rule yonder gentleman.' Henry's measured retort was supposedly, 'Then he is meet to rule all Ireland, seeing all Ireland cannot rule him.' Though these exact words may have been an invention of the writer, as events would show in the coming months and years, the idea of Kildare being the only figure capable of quelling the Irish for Henry had some element of truth.[34]

The terms of Kildare's release, signed by the earl and the king's council on 6 August 1496, pledged to end the 'great and haynoux

Right: The Tower of
London, where the
Princes disappeared
in 1483.

Below: Site of the Battle
of Bosworth.

King Henry VII at a Battle of Bosworth re-enactment event.

Henry VII's Battle Standard at a Battle of Bosworth re-enactment event.

Right: Westminster Abbey, where Henry VII was crowned king in 1485.

Below: Henry VII and Elizabeth of York's First State Bed. (By permission of Ian Coulson of The Langley Collection)

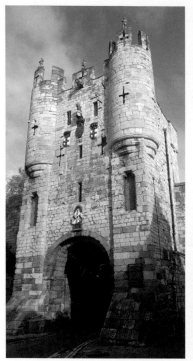

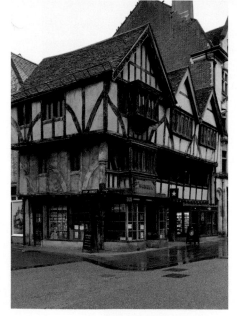

Above left: Micklegate Bar, York, where Henry VII was welcomed in 1486.

Above right: Site of Winchester Cathedral Priory, where Prince Arthur was born in 1486.

Left: Medieval Oxford, alleged birthplace of Lambert Simnel.

Right: Christ Church, Dublin, where Lambert Simnel was crowned in May 1487.

Below: Furness Abbey, suspected of aiding the Simnel conspiracy.

Kenilworth Castle, Henry VII's base against Simnel's invasion.

The Battle of Stoke Field site where the fighting reached its climax in June 1487.

Right: Stoke Field memorial stone commemorating the deaths of the rebels.

Below: The Battle of Stoke Field recorded in the Beaufort Book of Hours, used by Margaret Beaufort to record momentous family events. (British Library Royal MS 2 A XVIII f.30v)

Newark Castle.

Above left: Perkin Warbeck drawing from Recueil d'Arras.

Above right: James IV of Scotland, supporter of Warbeck.

Right: Tournai Cathedral, which the Warbeck family would have known.

Below: River Scheldt, Tournai, from which the Warbeck family made their living.

Margaret of York's Palace in Malines (modern-day Mechelen), where she recognised Warbeck's claim.

The city of Malines, which provided refuge to Yorkist rebels during Henry VII's reign.

Right: Reginald's Tower, Waterford, which resisted Warbeck's attempt to land in 1495.

Below: Stirling Castle, where Warbeck met James IV of Scotland in 1495.

Above: Linlithgow Palace, where Warbeck celebrated Christmas 1495.

Left: Falkland Palace, where Warbeck lived with Katherine Gordon in early 1497.

Above: Beaulieu Abbey, where Warbeck surrendered in October 1497.

Right: Taunton Castle, where Warbeck met Henry VII for the first time.

Left: Modern-day Austin Friars, London, beneath which lie the remains of Perkin Warbeck.

Below: The only remaining part of Richmond Palace, built by Henry VII.

Above: Henry VII
and the Tudor
children after
Elizabeth of
York's Death. (The
National Library
of Wales, Peniarth
MS 482D f.9r)

Right: Henry
VII on his
deathbed. (The
British Library, BL
Add.MS 45131,
f.54)

Above left: Victorian stained-glass window of Henry VII, St Mary's Church, Pembroke.

Above right: Henry VII statue, Bath Abbey.

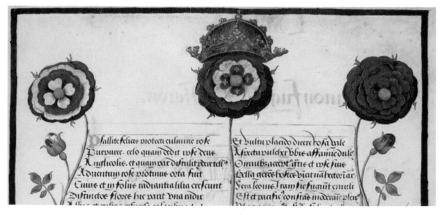

The Tudor Rose (centre), devised by Henry VII to show the union of York and Lancaster. (British Library Royal 11 E XI f.2)

discord' that existed in Ireland between various factions, most notably the FitzGerald and Butler families, and introduce a 'perpetuell and a more assured amytye concorde and love' than had hitherto existed. Henry even secured a promise from Kildare that the latter would uphold the key statutes put in place by Poynings's 1494 parliament, in effect recognising English lordship over the island. The earl furthermore swore he would apprehend any rebels operating in Ireland, regardless of their kinship to him, and provide stout defence against any Scottish or French invaders should they materialise in the coming months or years.

In return, Kildare would be reappointed deputy lieutenant and was even given a bride closely related to the king, Elizabeth St John.[35] The daughter of Oliver St John of Lydiard Tregoze, Wiltshire, the elder half-brother of the king's revered mother, Margaret Beaufort, Elizabeth was Henry's first cousin; she was pointedly referred to in the indenture as the king's 'nighe kynneswoman and of his noble blodde'.[36] All things considered, Henry had undertaken a complete reversal of policy, negotiating a political and matrimonial alliance with an adversary that he anticipated would be instrumental in the defence of his crown against a more complex threat in Perkin Warbeck. It was a gamble, but so had been placing trust in the earl of Surrey several years previously, and that had proven an astute decision. The man who had arranged the Dublin coronation of Lambert Simnel in May 1487 would now be entrusted, a decade later, to hold Ireland against the latest pretender to challenge Tudor rule.

Sailing for Ireland at the end of August 1496 and emboldened with a royal pardon, Kildare landed near Howth on 17 September and immediately strove to 'raise up the weak and pull down the strong'. He swiftly secured the submission of large parts of Leinster and Ulster, and his efficiency in dealing with those unruly parts of Ireland prompted one English gentleman on the island to write home that the king 'coude hafe put no mane in auctorite here that in so short space and with so little coste coude hafe set this land in so good order as it is now'.[37] Incidentally, one of the people specifically excluded from the pardon that Henry issued to sixteen other people besides Kildare that summer was John Atwater, one of Warbeck's most ardent supporters from his initial 1491 landing in Cork. The English king had clearly not forgotten, nor forgiven, his role in the conspiracy's origins.

Henry VII's intelligence about Warbeck and James IV's plans, and why he had been able to efficiently deploy his defensive resources throughout 1496, can be attributed to a spy he had embedded deep in the heart of the Scottish court – John Ramsey, formerly 1st Lord Bothwell. Ramsey was an intriguing character who had no qualms about revealing sensitive information to the English that was exploited to hamper the plans of his king and country. A close confidant of James III despite his low birth, Ramsey was raised to the peerage in 1484 and appointed master of the Royal Household two years later, and was employed by his royal patron to negotiate with the English in 1485 and 1486. He had even been present at Henry VII's coronation as Scotland's formal representative.

Highly regarded by James III in both a professional and personal capacity, Ramsey unsurprisingly harboured deep resentment towards those who had violently dethroned his friend in 1488, exacerbated when he was stripped of his lordship during James IV's first parliament. For the next eight years, he sought refuge in England where he became known to Henry VII. The year of his return to Scotland, 1496, was perhaps not coincidentally the year James IV and Perkin Warbeck were known to be preparing their invasion of England, though Ramsey appears to have been welcomed home without raising suspicions about where his loyalties lay.

Two of Ramsey's letters to Henry VII survive, written in early September 1496 and remarkably detailed about what his Scottish compatriots were up to. In the first letter, the spy revealed he had 'ben busy' regarding a secret matter for Henry Wyatt, captain of Carlisle Castle, with Lord Buchan, the Scottish king's great-uncle, hopeful of fulfilling the task himself. It was, however, considered a difficult mission to complete as Warbeck was protected in the night by James's own guards. The reference to the pretender's sleeping arrangements and mention of his protection strongly suggest this was an assassination plot. Ramsey also mentioned briefly encountering the king's brother Ross at St Andrews, whom he claimed was pleased by Henry's gift of a crossbow and to whom he commended his service humbly, pledging not to join James's march south. Ross proved as good as his word.[38]

More concerning for Henry VII was the revelation that on 28 August a man arrived at the Scottish court from Carlisle seeking an audience with Warbeck. Ramsey claimed this visitor had been sent to the pretender by Randall Dacre, brother of Thomas, 2nd Baron Dacre, the former supporter of Richard III now charged with protecting the western border against the Scots. There were also other reports of men from Northumberland entering clandestine discussions with their Scottish counterparts, information which corroborated Henry

Wyatt's letter to the English king a year earlier warning of wavering loyalties in the region, particularly around the towns of Carlisle and Bewcastle. Henry may have permitted himself a wry smile, however, when told that when James IV discovered the Irish earl of Desmond had submitted to the English king rather than commit to Warbeck, he could 'scarsly beleve it'.[39]

The second letter from Ramsey, dated 8 September and written from Berwick, was a comprehensive account of the Scottish preparations for war, and in truth was a remarkable betrayal of his own countrymen and king. Assuring Henry he was doing everything in his power to persuade James IV to abandon his sponsorship of the 'feynt boy', Ramsey nevertheless conceded the Scottish king was wholeheartedly committed to invading England in one week, his force bolstered by the 1,400 men which by now represented Warbeck's personal retinue. Amongst that number was Rodcrigue de Lalaing, who contributed two ships, some horses, and sixty German mercenaries. Ramsey, however, detected a coldness in Lalaing's demeanour towards the pretender, declaring upon arrival he was in Scotland only to serve James IV 'and for non oder mans saik', adding he had been 'put to great trouble' on Warbeck's behalf already. When quizzed by the pretender about Margaret of York's welfare, Lalaing responded simply, 'Well.'[40] Warbeck, it would seem, did not command complete respect amongst some of his men.

Ramsey also revealed in his letters that James IV was struggling to fund the war effort, for which he had already been forced to sell his chains, plates and cupboards. It was thought the Scottish king did not have enough money to keep his army in the field for more than a week. Specific details of the artillery amassed at Edinburgh Castle were disclosed, and as Ramsey considered James 'oute of reason, and sa litill inclinit to gudness', the spy beseeched Henry to let him know him what 'gud and exceptable serves' he could forthwith provide.[41] The English king had made a payment of £10 to Ramsey for unspecified services four months earlier, and if this was the cost of his intelligence, it seems Henry had struck an informative bargain.[42]

Despite thorough planning on both sides, however, when the time came the Scottish attack proved anti-climactic; far from a war, it was in truth little more than an enthusiastic, if bloody, raid. As late as 14 September, already deep in the traditional campaigning season, Warbeck and James IV tarried in Edinburgh where both made offerings at the altar in Holyrood Abbey to mark the Feast of the Exaltation of the Holy Cross, and only once their religious duties were completed did they start their march towards the border.[43]

With Ellem the designated muster point, the royal host moved east to Haddington before advancing south across Lammermuir Hills to Johnscleuch, Duns and Langton. On 20 September, at the head of a 'greate nombre of Scottes'[44] that had met as commanded, the Scottish king and the pretender pushed on to the banks of the River Tweed, cautiously crossing the water into English territory. Despite the potential support for Warbeck in the western march around Carlisle, James IV elected to remain to the east, which suggests he was prioritising his own objective to recapture Berwick over what was in his partner's interest.

It was around this point Warbeck issued a bold proclamation which was spread widely on the English side of the border.[45] As well as admonishing Henry's conduct as king, it was notable for being the first time the pretender adopted the manner and style of a king. No longer was he merely the duke of York, but rather 'Richard, by the grace of God, king of England and of France, lord of Ireland, prince of Wales'. It served as an open challenge to the loyalties of the border English – just who was their king, and if presented the choice, where did their allegiance lie?

In the lengthy pronouncement, Warbeck, or rather King Richard IV as he now claimed to be, reiterated his well-established survival story, recounting for the benefit of those who remained unaware how 'by God's great might' he had fled the Tower of London as a child. Having been 'secretly conveyed over the sea to other countries', he had now resurfaced to reclaim his birthright.

During his apparent years in the wilderness, Warbeck lamented to his audience how 'one Henry, son to Edmond Tydder, earl of Richmond created, son to Owen Tydder, of low birth, in the county of Wales', had invaded from France in 1485 'and entered into this our realm' where 'by subtle false means' he stole the crown that was his by inheritance. Regarding Henry his 'extreme and mortal enemy', Warbeck used the opportunity to invoke sympathy for his plight, claiming the Tudor king had maliciously

> ... imagined, compassed, and wrought all the subtle ways and means he could devise to our final destruction, insomuch as he hath not only falsely surmised us to be a feigned person, giving us nicknames, so abusing your minds, but also, to deter and put us from our entry into this our realm.

If Warbeck was indeed a fraud, then this was a remarkably disingenuous statement, accusing Henry VII of lying about what was, at heart, an astonishing deception. The pretender continued his attack on the English king's behaviour, alleging he 'hath offered large sums of money to corrupt the princes in every land and country' whilst encouraging turncoats in Warbeck's retinue 'to murder our person'. He also specifically expressed his frustration at Robert Clifford's defection from 'our righteous quarrel', whilst attempting to appeal to the commons' sense of economic injustice by alleging Henry 'hath subtilly and by crafty means levied outrageous and importable sums of money upon the whole body of our realm, to the great hurt and impoverishing of the same'.

There was more: Henry was a bloodthirsty tyrant, guilty of causing 'divers nobles of this our realm whom he hath suspect and stood in dread of, to be cruelly murdered', specifically men such as John Radcliffe, Lord Fitzwater; Robert Chamberlain; Simon Mountford; Robert Radcliffe; William Daubeney; Humphrey Stafford, and of course, Sir William Stanley. Warbeck naturally made no mention of the schemes which brought about each man's downfall.

If that wasn't damning enough, Warbeck drew attention to Henry's treatment of 'our right entirely well-beloved cousin Edward, son and heir to our uncle duke of Clarence', whom the king 'hath long kept and yet keepeth in prison', and reproved him for marrying the daughters of Edward IV to his friends of 'simple and low degree'. Meanwhile, the traditional nobility had been displaced by other 'villains of simple birth' who were spreading 'misrule and mischief' throughout the realm, and for good measure Henry was also guilty of 'breaking the liberty and franchises of our mother holy church to the displeasure of Almighty God'. Thereafter came the vague charge that the king had also overseen manifold treasons, abominable murders, manslaughters, robberies and extortions, 'to the likely destruction and desolation of the whole realm'. It was quite a list.

Now, with the 'right high and mighty prince our dearest cousin the king of Scots' at his side, who proffered support 'without any gift or other thing by him desired or demanded', which was not strictly true, Warbeck readied himself to enter 'into this our realm of England, where we shall shew ourselves openly unto you', the people he vowed to rule justly. To allay any concern his heavily Scottish army would tear through the north of England, Warbeck promised that if James IV witnessed Englishmen 'resort lovingly' unto the pretender, the Scottish king would command his troops to return peaceably across the border; it was almost blackmail – support me or the Scottish will raid your lands.

To conclude his extensive invective against the English king, Warbeck vowed to be the man who could put Henry VII to 'lawful execution' so that the 'disinheriting of rightfull heirs' and the 'injuries and wrongs in anywise committed and done unto the subjects of our realm, both spiritual and temporal, shall be duly redressed, according to right, law, and good conscience'. Those who provided 'aid, succour, and comfort' to Warbeck, 'with their powers, with their lives or goods, or victual our host for ready money' so he could achieve this, he would 'enter upon them lovingly as their natural liege lord, and see they have justice to them'. Addressing the Englishmen of the north in particular, if they freely attended upon him, he promised 'ye shall find us your right, especial, and singular good lord, and so to see you recompensed and rewarded'. For those who remained loyal to Henry, however, he threatened, 'We shall come and enter upon them as their heavy lord, and take and repute them and every of them as our traitors and rebels and see them punished.'

The rousing proclamation and entry into England at the head of a highly organised and capable army should have been a momentous occasion, after several false starts, for Warbeck, who had persisted in his often flagging cause for at least half a decade to reach this very point. If he wasn't truly the son of Edward IV, the crossing marked the first known moment the pretender stepped foot on English soil, and if genuinely a Yorkist prince, clambering up the grassy banks south of the Tweed must have brought an emotional end to over ten years of absence.

Unfortunately for Perkin's aspirations once he had dried himself, and despite the fact he 'gave great assurances that great reinforcements would be forthcoming' when 'they heard he was raising his standard', just like at Deal, few Englishmen appeared willing to flock to his banner.[46] When the Scottish army completed the crossing, it was coolly met by a suspicious populace who after centuries of bitter conflict were deeply antagonistic towards their northern neighbours. After a decade of Tudor rule, these border men of the north were unmoved by this pretender who claimed to be their rightful king, demanding their allegiance with the threat of punishment as traitors. Some may have believed in his claim, but that fact alone was not enough to prompt a switch of allegiance and a return to the uncertainty of dynastic conflict. Some of the older generation may have recalled the blood shed in this part of the world during the battles of Hedgeley Moor and Hexham in 1464, and accordingly shied away from any part in this apparent resurrection of the wars which had once plagued England.

Word had, no doubt, been spread throughout the region by royal officials on behalf of Henry VII that earlier in the year an inquisition in Setúbal, Portugal,[47] had exposed Warbeck's apparent identity as 'Petyr Osbek', a youth of Tournai rather than a son of York, rumours which inspired to be 'made of hym sundey Roundellis and songis to his shame and derision'.[48] Warbeck was being openly mocked in England before his arrival, and this naturally may have affected his ability to summon men to his side. He was publicly portrayed as a joke by the Tudor regime, even if military preparations proved Henry was taking the threat seriously.

Whoever one believes Warbeck truly was, his conduct once across the border hardly evoked memories of the great Edward IV, a general of 'princely and knightly courage'[49] who led his army into battle no less than five times during the internecine wars that plagued his early reign. At the crucial moment of entering England after several nomadic years of campaigning, when he was expected to galvanise his men and secure the affections of those he encountered as he moved south, Warbeck stalled, distraught at the ferocity of the Scottish onslaught and troubled there 'had been no movement in his support among the English'.

Vergil reported that the appalled pretender desperately appealed to James IV to 'harry his people no further and to damage his native land with no more flames', a request the Scottish king dismissed with disdain. Instead, he countered that it appeared Warbeck was 'meddling in other people's business and not his own' for he had 'called England his country and the English his countrymen, but none had rushed forward to lend their aid'. It was thus, Vergil mused in his account of the invasion, James 'exposed that man's foolish impudence'.[50] How could he justifiably claim to be king, after all, if no one seemed willing to respond to his call to arms?

Whether such a heated confrontation took place between James and Warbeck is uncertain, but the latter did abandon the front line less than twenty-four hours into the campaign, turning his back on the army ostensibly raised in his name and fleeing back to Edinburgh. The House of York had a proud military record, often even grasping honour in defeat, but Perkin Warbeck, it would appear, did not have the stomach for a mere raid, let alone the heart required for the horror of a full-scale pitched battle. He rode in the opposite direction.

James IV, on the other hand, later described by the Spanish ambassador Pedro de Ayala as someone who 'loves war' and 'courageous, even more so than a King should be',[51] pressed on undeterred, having 'sent forward some cavalry to find out whether or not the English were prepared for war'. When his scouts reported back to the king's camp that all appeared quiet, the Scots advanced further into England without Warbeck and 'laid waste the fields' of the Tweed and Till valleys before they 'pillaged and then burnt the houses and villages'. Howtel and Braxton Towers were destroyed, whilst other defences in the settlements of Duddo, Twizel and Tilmouth were also razed. Any natives who resisted the Scottish onslaught were 'cruelly killed'.[52]

By 24 September, James's force was assembled outside the formidable Heton Castle, with the Scottish king personally leading the siege, ordering his men to mine beneath the walls for two days in order to breach the stout defence. Around midnight on the 25th, perhaps hours before the castle capitulated, James received word that the forces of Richard Neville, 2nd Baron Latimer and a veteran of Stoke Field ten years earlier, were marching north from Newcastle to counter his invasion. Content with the havoc he had caused in just a few days, the Scottish king gave the signal to his men to return across the Tweed.[53]

From James IV's viewpoint, the raid into enemy territory had been a success; he had 'devastated so savagely the English countryside with fire and steel',[54] obliterating several strategic towers in the process, and made 'greate bost and brag'[55] that enhanced his standing with his subjects. This had likely been the extent of his objectives from the outset, despite promises otherwise made to Warbeck, who was simply the tool needed to justify military action. For the pretender, however, the mission was once more an abject failure, brutally exposing his lack of support amongst the English and his own inadequacy as a warrior.

Back in Edinburgh on 18 October, Warbeck, as 'Rychard off England', wrote a letter to an aged Spanish knight named Bernard de la Fosse, a man of 'grete wisdom' retained by both Edward IV and Richard III. He also happened to be the father of a soldier who had long been part of Warbeck's retinue, Anthony de la Fosse, which was presumably how the pair came into contact. 'Credibly enformed of the grete love, favour and kyndenes' the Spanish knight had once shown his 'most drad lord and Fadyr' Edward IV, he now hoped he could benefit from the same 'pollitique conselles that ye in sundry wises ful lovingly gave' the first Yorkist king. His principal motive for writing to Fosse, however, was in the expectation this 'lovyng, feithfull and kynde' former counsellor to the House of York could be swayed to 'move and stir' a hitherto dismissive Ferdinand of Aragon to his cause.[56]

It was a desperate ploy that Warbeck couldn't hope would bear fruit; just two days earlier, the Spanish monarchs had in fact ratified the new terms of the Holy League, which consented to Henry VII's accession into the alliance, and were pressing on with negotiations to conclude the much-vaunted union of the Houses of Tudor and Trastámara through the marriage of Prince Arthur with the Spanish *Infanta* Katherine.[57] Even if Fosse intervened with his king, the pretender was wasting his time with the Spanish.

Warbeck also penned another letter that same month to Ireland pleading with the earl of Desmond to provide fresh assistance to his cause. Unfortunately for the pretender, for the first time since his initial appearance in Cork six years earlier there was no support forthcoming from the Irish, a direct consequence of Henry VII restoring the earl of Kildare to power in the island. There were no current grounds for the Irish lords to revolt against the Tudor government. With Scottish support also fading after the September campaign, if not actually withdrawn, Warbeck's prospects once more appeared uncertain. He had been offered a bold route into England yet baulked at the chance, retreating at the precise moment he should have been relentless in pursuit of his target. Any momentum the pretender had regained in Scotland after previous disappointments frustratingly ebbed away.

As for Henry VII, a king whose spirit according to the admiring Vergil was 'brave and resolute and never, even at moments of the greatest danger, deserted him',[58] it was not in his nature to squander the opportunity to enhance his standing in light of Warbeck's failure. On 31 October, the mayor and aldermen of London were assembled upon London Bridge in their finest liveries where they 'reverently ressayvid' an orator sent from the papal court of Alexander VI. The visitor brought with him from Rome a cap of maintenance and a richly garnished sword, very visible signs of favour from the Holy Father in recognition of the English king's entry into the League. With 'grete tryumff', the blessed items were paraded through the city with pomp to the bishop of London's palace, where the delighted king was expectantly holding court.

The following morning, the first day of November and All Saints' Day, Henry led a grand procession from the bishop's palace into St Paul's, with the cap and sword proudly borne before him. Once seated inside, Archbishop Morton spoke at length from the west end of the choir for more than an hour, during which the king was lauded as a 'protectour and defendour of the Chyrch of Cryst'. It was a defiant and very public refutation of Warbeck's earlier accusations and marked with a series of 'grete ffyris' in the city's most important streets.[59] The visiting papal orator, meanwhile, was rewarded by his grateful host with £33 6s 8d for his efforts, and after he had departed Henry ordered a customised case to be constructed to house the revered cap and sword.[60]

Having his religious virtues extolled in such dramatic fashion before his subjects notwithstanding, Henry's mind had already turned to military matters as the autumn transitioned into winter. Warbeck may not have been comfortable on the front foot, but the English king had no such apprehension about making a move on his enemy to protect his crown. The time was nigh for Henry VII to turn the screw on the Scottish and flush out the pretender they yet sheltered.

14

Mortal War

If 1496 had started with considerable promise for Perkin Warbeck's prospects, with a new bride for private companionship and an enthusiastic royal benefactor willing to fund an invasion of England, the back end of the year proved a frustrating anti-climax for which he had to shoulder much of the blame. The confidence that had permeated through the pretender's court in the run-up to the September campaign had dissipated the moment he abandoned his troops on the frontline and retreated to safety. If not cowardly behaviour, it certainly wasn't in keeping with the daring attitude shown by those who had successfully seized the crown before him, men like Henry IV in 1399, Edward IV in both 1461 and 1471, or even Henry VII in 1485.

As another Christmas approached, Warbeck had failed to make any significant progress on the previous year's festive period, having only served to antagonise the Tudor king into pledging a severe military response in the coming months. Perhaps most worryingly for the pretender, having struggled in recent times to cultivate wider support for his cause, James IV's hitherto staunch backing was also starting to wane. As time went by, Polydore Vergil observed that the Scottish king 'paid less and less attention' to the pretender and his supposed claim to the English throne, 'since the facts in no way correspond with his false statements and promises'.[1] Whilst he did continue to draw his pension from the Scottish exchequer after the raid and undoubtedly retained some degree of diplomatic value to the Scots, it is clear Warbeck was no longer at the forefront of James's thoughts. In fact, the pretender started spending more time thereafter with his wife Katherine Gordon at Falkland Palace than in the king's company.

In the aftermath of the Scottish raid on his northern border, meanwhile, Henry VII had responded quickly to the attack by issuing a harsh proclamation to his subjects on 25 September 1496. In his official address, the Tudor king reported that James IV, 'of his willful headiness, and without cause', had crossed the Tweed a few days earlier before committing 'great cruelty to man, woman and child' on the English side of the border. Unwilling to turn a blind eye to such provocation, Henry wished it broadcast widely that 'war between the King's highness and the said King of Scots is open and at large'.[2] It is likely this elicited approval from the populace.

A war council was summoned to Sheen by Henry to discuss military reprisal, followed by a larger general council meeting in Westminster on 24 October 1496, where he formally requested funding to launch a retaliatory invasion.[3] As a king regarded as a 'lover of peace' by one chronicler,[4] throughout his reign Henry had sought to secure his northern border by establishing a peaceful relationship with his Scottish counterparts, and had twice offered English brides to James IV as an inducement, namely Katherine, a daughter of the king's cousin Eleanor Beaufort, and his own daughter Margaret Tudor.[5] On this occasion, however, 'fearing least his enemies should be encouraged and inflated with this great gaine of spoyles and prayes, he determined by dent of sworde and mortall warre to revenge and reforme the manifest injurie and apparaunt wrong to him by king James and his people done and committed'.[6] 'Mortal war', not peace, would be Henry's approach henceforth in dealing with the Scots. Patience with threats was clearly wearing thin within the Tudor royal household.

The king's council, which comprised several nobles as well as the realm's leading ecclesiastical minds, concurred with Henry that military action was a necessary evil, having themselves been 'enraged by such Scottish effrontery'. It was entirely appropriate, therefore, to 'punish that country and its men for the crime that had been committed'.[7] To support the proposed campaign, the council requested 'greate sumys of money' amounting to £120,000 to finance a two-pronged land-and-sea invasion scheduled to take place the following year, 1497. It was a war fund that was around twenty times James IV's entire annual revenue.[8]

The colossal figure was ratified by the parliament that assembled in Westminster Hall on 16 January 1497, a process aided by the rousing speech given by Cardinal John Morton, the influential mainstay of the Tudor reign to date. Morton reminded his audience how James IV had 'entred and invaded' England the previous autumn, committing 'grete hurte' to innocent men, women and children in the north, 'amonge many other myschevous and cruell Dedes'. Henry VII himself then addressed parliament, 'persuadynge with many strong argumentes and reasons invincible' that war was inevitable, a fact to which those assembled 'dyd wyllingly agree and gladly assent'.[9]

Though the final total raised proved to be less than half that pledged by parliament, it nevertheless proved more than adequate for the king's needs. In December 1496, £4,575 was spent rigging Henry's navy, and the border garrisons were strengthened with hundreds of troops to deter any fresh Scottish raids over the winter. Money was also expedited to Durham and Newcastle for the establishment of a large northern army to fall under the personal command of Giles Daubeney, who had also recently replaced the disgraced William Stanley as lord chamberlain, the most senior position in the king's household. Another £3,000 was sent northward for soldiers' wages that same month, followed by further instalments of £4,000 in March 1497 and £6,300 in May.[10]

Henry VII also ensured Carlisle, which he considered 'oon of the chief keyes and fortresses to the defens of this our Reame', was suitably defended against threats both external and internal. Instructions were sent to the mayor to prevent any local lord from retaining his citizens, nor to permit anyone to leave the town wearing armour. William Senhouse, Bishop of Carlisle, was also tasked with receiving fresh oaths of fidelity from the townsfolk, with anyone disobeying the king's will to maintain the peace to be reported to the council for punishment. Henry clearly remained uncertain of Carlisle's allegiance to his rule, and, with the cautionary words of Henry Wyatt the previous year still fresh in mind, opted to take no chances with one of his most strategically important towns.[11] During the earlier Scottish raid, James IV headed east towards Berwick; there was no guarantee if he and Warbeck invaded again that they would not head west to Carlisle.

Between September 1496 and February 1497, numerous commissions were granted by the king to advance preparations for his retaliatory campaign. On 28 September, Hugh Furnesse was ordered to assemble gunners, carpenters, smiths and other assorted workmen for the construction and repair of artillery, whilst on 15 November, two commissions were issued to establish storehouses in Berwick and elsewhere along the Scottish March, including three beerhouses for the troops. On the same date, orders were dispatched to ensure four ships, *Mary Rose*, *The Magdalen of Dover*, *The Anne of Dover*, and

Anne Tugoe, were suitably prepared to convey sailors and soldiers to Scotland when required, on top of the three ships, *The Regent*, *The Mary Fortune*, and *The Sweepstake*, already placed at Robert Willoughby de Broke's disposal for the sea invasion.[12]

Further commissions catered for the collection of grain, stores and coal, as well as significant quantities of timber to craft the thousands of arrows the campaign was expected to need. In January, meanwhile, a gentleman named Humphrey Metcalf was assigned to inspect and seize any ships moored in the ports of Yorkshire and Northumberland that could be used to transport soldiers into Scotland. A similar directive covered the ports of Kent, Sussex, Hampshire, Dorset, Devon, Somerset and Cornwall.[13] In February thoughts specifically turned to the recruitment of men for the campaign, with Thomas Dacre, 2nd Baron Dacre and Lord Warden of the West Marches, personally ordered by Henry VII to raise troops 'since our enemy of Scotland, with a great array of our rebels and traitors has hostilely invaded our kingdom'.[14] Willoughby de Broke, Robert Poyntz, William Willoughby and Maurice Berkeley were also empowered that same month to raise a further 2,000 men in the south-west counties to take north.[15]

By June 1497, Henry had also recruited a cosmopolitan array of gunners numbering around two hundred, with several arms depots established throughout the kingdom, including at Kenilworth, Portchester, Newcastle, Berwick, Portsmouth, and the Tower of London, though this last location had been beset by damp and rats, which had damaged some of the horse harnesses.[16] In total, the king had managed to raise a well-prepared and heavily provisioned army numbering around 10,000 men. Emboldened by the moral and financial support of parliament and his nobility, it was clear Henry was set on overwhelming his enemies.

Even though Warbeck was no longer at the forefront of James IV's mind, the Scottish king did not cower from news brought to him by a spy about the extensive preparations of the English, and after a low-key Christmas he determined that attack was the shrewdest form of defence against an adversary much stronger militarily and vastly wealthier. On 12 February, therefore, James launched another raid into England, pillaging roughly the same area he had weakened five months earlier. When he returned north shortly thereafter, the Scottish king left his armour behind in the border town of Hume, intending no doubt return to the front line in due course for the impending war.[17] There is little to suggest Warbeck was present on this particular occasion, which wouldn't be surprising given his previous conduct.

Throughout the spring of 1497, Spanish embassies in both London and Stirling made last-ditch attempts to heal the widening rift between Henry and James in the vain hope that united they could be turned on the French. In late March, a letter from Ferdinand and Isabella to Roderigo de Puebla counselled the ambassador to dissuade Henry from his war, which could prove 'so hazardous an enterprise', for despite superior numbers he should heed the fact that often throughout history 'the few conquer the many'. The English king, after all, 'knows by experience how quickly a kingdom may be won and lost', and in any event, the Spanish understood James's enthusiasm for Warbeck's cause had dwindled since the previous autumn's raid and so 'the ill-advised affray' should be forgotten. De Puebla's mission may have prompted Henry to send a fresh delegation up to Scotland in May to satisfy his Spanish allies, but any efforts to seek a truce were rebuffed.[18]

At the very moment Henry VII stood ready to unleash the full might of his meticulously assembled forces against the obdurate Scottish king, a wholly unanticipated threat to the security of his crown emerged. It came not from the north of his kingdom, or even from overseas, but rather the extreme south-west, 'a rebellion of serious dimensions in an area where it might have least been feared'.[19] It caught the king and his council completely by surprise.

The Duchy of Cornwall had been created in 1337 by Edward III for his eldest son Edward, the 'Black Prince'. All subsequent eldest sons of the incumbent king became duke upon birth, including most recently Henry VII's son Prince Arthur, yet the Cornish people had long remained somewhat distinct from the rest of the country. Since the Norman Conquest, Cornwall had been ruled by, or at least on behalf of, successive English kings, yet the people dwelling beyond the River Tamar retained much of their own culture, customs and folklore, not unlike the Welsh across the sea to the north. This difference was evident to foreign observers such as the Venetian ambassador Lodovico Falier, who in 1531 considered the typical Cornishman to be 'poor, rough and boorish' with a language so different from English 'that they do not understand each other'.[20]

A notable peculiarity of Cornish administration was the Stannary law, introduced by King John and later confirmed by Edward I in 1305 and Edward III in 1337 to oversee mining of the region's tin, considered 'of the purest quality' and the sale of which brought in 'a large sum of money' for everyone involved.[21] This law provided the tinners of Cornwall certain rights that they held dear, including exemption from ordinary taxation and the right to be tried in matters of justice by their fellow miners only, similar in nature to soldiers and the martial law. When in May 1497 Henry VII ordered a local provost to collect a tax from which the Cornishmen had for generations been exempt, a local revolt exploded and quickly escalated into a regional uprising that threatened national stability.

Aside from impinging on their traditional rights, the Cornishmen, whom Vergil described as living 'in a part of the island as restricted in area as it is poor in resources' and who 'with difficulty sought their livelihood in digging tin from the bowels of the earth', claimed they could simply could not 'bear the weight of the tax imposed for the Scottish war'. The first person of note who emerged as a leader amongst the rebels was a blacksmith from St Keverne named Michael Joseph, dubbed *An Gof* in his native tongue after his trade, followed by a lawyer from Bodmin called Thomas Flamank, 'both daring scoundrels' in Vergil's estimation, though Edward Hall nevertheless later conceded they possessed 'high courages and stoute stomackes'.[22] They may have seemed simple people to those living in distant London, but they were undoubtedly tough.

Following the example of previous rebellions, the protestors, who quickly grew to include members of the local gentry and clergy hit hardest by the detested taxation, directed their rage towards those they believed were misadvising the king out of 'cruelty and malice', in particular Cardinal Morton, Richard Foxe, Bishop of Durham, Oliver King, Bishop of Bath, Reginald Bray, and Thomas Lovell. Collectively, the group were dubbed the 'authors of the great oppression' by the rebels, and said to deserve nothing less than death for leading the king astray.[23]

Perhaps buoyed by the surge of support which engulfed the southernmost part of Cornwall, the rebels elected to march to London and petition Henry VII in person, with Hall suggesting Joseph and Flamank reassured their supporters 'not to be afearde to folowe theim in this quarrel' for they would 'do no damage to any creature, but only to se ponyshment and correccion done to such persons which were the aucthours and causers' of such 'unreasonable exaccions and demands'.[24] By the end of May, the swelling horde had reached the gates of Exeter where they forced their way into the city, before moving on quickly to Taunton. It was around this juncture the Cornish started to attract wider support from throughout Somerset, including from an unanticipated source: James Tuchet, 7th Baron Audley.

Audley's motivation for joining the uprising is not immediately clear when one considers he had recently been recruited by Henry VII to raise one hundred troops for the Scottish war and had otherwise loyally served the Tudor regime for its decade in power, which included bearing Prince Arthur's train at the infant's baptism and taking up arms for the king at the Battle of Stoke Field and thereafter in France. It is true the baron did have lengthy connections to Edward IV, having been created a Knight of the Bath at his heir's investiture as Prince of Wales in 1475, for example, but Audley had been typical of many members of the first Yorkist king's affinity who freely transferred their allegiance after his death to the man who pledged to marry Elizabeth of York. Though it is perfectly reasonable that Audley's head was turned in 1497 by the persistent rumours that one of Edward IV's sons had survived, the baron had also gradually grown dismayed by the prominence of some of Henry VII's favourites in his native south-west as the reign progressed, men rising high in the Tudor administration like Giles Daubeney, the king's chamberlain, and John Cheyne. Like other defectors throughout the reign, Audley's decision was likely driven by personal ambition as much as honouring former loyalties.

By the first week of June 1497, Joseph, Flamank, Audley and their amalgamated force reached the city of Wells, and from here it is likely they initiated some form of communication with Perkin Warbeck, who was shortly to leave Scotland bound for the English south-west via Ireland. If the uprising's origins had been solely concerned with opposing the harsh Scottish tax levied on an impoverished populace, by the time they assembled beneath the towering western front of Wells Cathedral, the protestors were showing willingness to wage dynastic war to achieve their aim. Numbering around 10,000 men, the rebel force turned eastwards towards London, with Joseph and Flamank passing through Winchester and Guildford whilst Audley sought to galvanise support in Salisbury. As two of Henry VII's faithful commanders in the West Country, Daubeney and de Broke, were deployed elsewhere finalising preparations for the Scottish war, there was simply no figure of authority in the region to oppose their advance.

When the king was first notified of Cornish disillusionment with the taxation, he could hardly have expected the anger to manifest itself in an armed revolt which was marching menacingly through the south-west and towards his capital, attracting further support along the way. Vergil reports Henry was 'moved by sorrow and anxiety' when he learned of the rebellion, for he knew he could not fight a war on two fronts, and 'since the danger seemed equally threatening from either direction he was for some time uncertain which he should deal with first'.[25] After ruminating upon the matter at length in private, Henry elected to deal with the most imminent threat first. Giles Daubeney and his troops were diverted from their northern mission and charged with confronting those 'unnaturall Subjects' who had 'trayterously moved, sterred and ledde' a great number of rebels out of Cornwall, Devon and Somerset who intended to cause 'the death and destruction' of his noble blood.[26] The much-desired Scottish war would have to wait.

By 13 June, the rebels were approaching the town of Guildford when they chose to lodge overnight on an area known locally as Guildowns. Daubeney and the bulk of his retinue had made swift progress when they received their summons from the king and were themselves based just over twenty miles to the north-east on Hounslow Heath. Tasked by Henry to halt the rebels' progress, Daubeney dispatched around five hundred mounted spearmen to assault the enemy camp and scatter them, but it proved to little avail. The royal force was itself overwhelmed by the superior numbers, and the rebels pushed on, intending to reach Kent where, like Warbeck two years earlier, they hoped to exploit the county's traditional penchant for rebellion; much like the pretender, however, they found little enthusiasm for their cause in one of the more prosperous parts of the Tudor realm. Nevertheless, upon reaching Deptford, their force numbered a healthy 15,000.[27] When Joseph, Flamank, and the Cornish had originally set out on their march, the intention had been merely to present their grievances to the king and hopefully escape the taxation they resented; as their numbers swelled along the way, however, their courage had grown and their words became tougher. A pitched battle to bring the revolt to a conclusion was inevitable.

Whilst the rebels unloaded their baggage, put down their weapons, and set up their camp at Deptford just across the Thames from London, the king was still at Woodstock in Oxfordshire, though preparing his return to the city to personally oversee its defence against the threat now perched on its doorstep. Advancing south, Henry and his household passed through Abingdon to Wallingford, where he sent a messenger to nearby Ewelme to command Edmund de la Pole, Earl of Suffolk, to provide military aid to Daubeney. Suffolk was the younger brother of John de la Pole, the rebellious earl of Lincoln killed fighting the royal army at Stoke Field a decade earlier, and though Suffolk would in time wage his own dynastic conflict with the Tudor king, at this crucial moment he responded loyally to the request.

From Wallingford, Henry pressed on to Reading before turning east towards Windsor and Kingston, reaching Lambeth on the afternoon of 16 June. Rather than seek safety in the Tower of London as the city's mayor had been expecting, the king instead chose to stay at Lambeth Palace, less than four miles from where the rebels were still camped at Deptford.[28] He had, however, ensured his family were secure; Queen Elizabeth had been staying with Prince Henry, the officially recognised six-year-old duke of York, at Margaret Beaufort's Coldharbour home, but all were moved into the Tower when it was known the rebels were advancing on Guildford.[29] There is no mention in the *Great Chronicle* of the royal couple's other children, Margaret and Mary, though one imagines they were also moved to safety, probably with their mother and brother. Having twice been taken into sanctuary in Westminster Abbey by her own mother in 1470 and 1483, Elizabeth likely understood some of the anxiety her offspring were feeling as they awaited the outcome of the revolt and sought to assuage their fears whilst hiding her own. The heir, Arthur, meanwhile, was out of harm's way in Ludlow in his capacity as prince of Wales. As Henry regularly issued rewards to the queen's servants from his Woodstock base throughout early June, it is clear that even though he wasn't with them in person, his family's wellbeing was nevertheless on his mind during this tense period.[30]

At Lambeth, Henry's host joined that of Daubeney's and 'many of his lordes' to create one vast royal army numbering around 25,000. On the night of 16 June, the king was even observed wandering 'in the ffeelde, and abrewing and comfortyng' his soldiers for the battle that lay ahead, offering words of encouragement to the men he expected would die for him in the coming days.[31] In the rebel camp, meanwhile, some of the troops grew nervous about opposing the king in the field, and 'in grete ffere and agony' attempted to desert their positions and surrender. Although their defiant captain Joseph *An Gof* attempted to prevent his men from leaving, by the following morning several hundred had managed to slip away under the cover of darkness.[32]

The two armies finally came face-to-face upon a plain near Blackheath during the morning of 17 June, when around 6 a.m. Sir Humphrey Stanley, 'with a Company of lusty Speris', launched a surprise attack on one flank of the unsuspecting rebels. His assault was followed shortly thereafter by a second charge from John de Vere, the hardy earl of Oxford who had been instrumental in previous Tudor triumphs at Bosworth and Stoke Field. Despite nearing fifty-five years of age, Oxford still possessed considerable vigour on the battlefield, and proved a menacing prospect to the rebels that now scattered before him.

Though the Cornish archers 'in playne Feld inbatteled theymselves in Armes' against Savage and Oxford,[33] once Daubeney entered the fray with fresh troops the day slipped away from the rebels. With additional men entering the battlefield under the command of nobles including the earls of Essex, Kent and Suffolk, those created knights banneret for the day like Welshman Rhys ap Thomas and the king's cousin Charles Somerset, plus two of the rebels' original targets, Thomas Lovell and Reginald Bray, a royal victory was assured.

The Cornish were poorly armed and far from home, with no hope of reinforcement. In Vergil's words they were overwhelmed 'at the first onslaught', and 'stricken with terror'; many simply downed weapons and yielded before they were slain where they stood.[34] When Henry received word that the fighting had commenced, he rode with great speed from his base at Lambeth only to reach the field of battle once the day was already won; not that he would have been too troubled to have missed the action. The outcome was what mattered.

Unlike at Stoke Field, all three rebel leaders, Audley, Flamank, and Joseph, were apprehended 'lyve and unhurt', though 'moche of their people' were slain. Many more taken prisoner, their hands bound together whilst they were mocked by their captors. Content that the threat had been contained, Henry VII chose to head back to London and by two o'clock that afternoon was joyously received by the mayor William Purchas and his aldermen outside St Magnus Church, situated on the northern side of London Bridge.

After accepting the mayor's kind words, the king 'gave cherefull thankes for his good diligence of kepyng and orderyng of the Citie', before drawing his sword and dubbing Purchas a knight in reward, as well as the sheriff and recorder. From the bridge, Henry continued in procession to St Paul's where, not for the first time, he reverently gave thanks at the altar for another military victory that, for the time being at least, preserved his crown. Religious duties observed, the king thereafter pressed on to the Tower to be reunited with his wife and children.[35]

Unlike after Warbeck's failed landing at Deal, Henry showed considerable restraint when dealing with the captured rebels and proved content to 'accept and admit them into his grace and favour', though many rewarded such clemency by promptly re-arming once they arrived home in Cornwall.[36] The three principal leaders, however, werc tried and sentenced to death. On 27 June, Flamank and Joseph were led from the city to Tyburn, where they were hanged, drawn and quartered. As a concession to his noble rank, Audley was beheaded the following day on Tower Hill. All three heads were spiked upon London Bridge, whilst the four quarters of Flamank's body were hooked on to the four main gateways of the capital. Joseph's were sent to his native south-west. It was a gruesome message.[37]

*

Having obtained another military victory on English soil, his third after Bosworth in 1485 and Stoke Field in 1487, when Henry VII found a moment to analyse recent events he would have been relieved to discover his war-hungry Scottish counterpart had not taken the opportunity to pillage northern England, a few minor raids notwithstanding. Perhaps dismayed by the recent battle, Henry brought to a halt his advanced plans to invade Scotland and instead sought to secure a prosperous peace rather than further endure the gamble of war.

From Sheen on 5 July 1497, the English king dictated a set of detailed instructions for Bishop Richard Foxe[38] who was tasked with heading back across the border to negotiate a fresh deal. The bishop's primary objective was to 'demaunde and requyre' James IV 'delyvere unto us of Perkyn Werbek', and if met with some resistance was to stress to the Scottish king that the pretender was 'not the parson that he surmysed to be when he opteyned his salveconduct'. It would not, therefore, damage James's honour to surrender Warbeck, as he had been tricked by an imposter. If this condition proved unacceptable, then he was invited to travel south to Newcastle to meet Henry in person to continue the discussions.

In the event James proved amenable to turning over Warbeck, there were other conditions attached to the peace. It was Henry's will that James be bound upon pain of ecclesiastical censures to ensure he did not renege on the deal, providing 'men of good estate and condicion' to be sent to England as hostages, and that restitution be made 'unto our subjectes for the damages that thei had by the throwyng doon of their castelles and fortilaces' during earlier Scottish raids. In return, Henry was willing to 'restreign our armye', in spite of the 'greate preparacions that we have made' to 'our inestimable charges and costs'. In private, however, Henry empowered Fox to agree any deal that delivered Warbeck into English hands, which serves to underscore the increasing frustration of the king and his desire to bring this exasperating episode to an end.

The problem Foxe encountered once he received his instructions, however, was that Warbeck was no longer available to be surrendered. On 6 July, the very day after Henry VII composed his letter to the bishop, the anxious pretender, with the final instalment of his Scottish pension in his purse and accompanied by his wife Katherine Gordon, set sail from Ayr harbour on the western coast. James IV was not present to bid them farewell, and there appears to have been little of the grand ceremony which greeted Warbeck's arrival in the country nineteen months earlier. It is known that he did leave behind a brown horse to settle any outstanding debts he had incurred.[39]

According to the Scottish treasury accounts, the ship Warbeck boarded was known as the *Cukow* and was a French merchant vessel rather than a warship – more suitable for short voyages rather than to launch a military invasion. For the journey out of Scotland, it was stocked with provisions such as wine, bread, salt beef, mutton, cheese, and fish, and carried around thirty of Warbeck's followers, including one of James IV's own captains, Robert Barton. Katherine, referred to in the Scottish records as the duchess of York and likely leaving her native country for the first time on what was an uncertain adventure, was at least provided some cloth by the king from which to fashion a sea-gown.[40]

Why had Warbeck chosen this precise moment to leave Scotland, to once more sail into the unknown? There is little evidence James personally forced the pretender to leave, but the Scottish king was probably not displeased to rid himself of a complicated drain on his expenses, not to mention a barrier to sealing a potentially advantageous peace with England when the time was right. It is plausible Warbeck's head was turned during this period by the cautionary words of Ambassador de Ayala, who preyed on the pretender's paranoia that any sudden accord between Henry VII and James IV would render him vulnerable to capture as one of the conditions of peace. It should not be discounted either that Warbeck had recently received word that the Cornish had risen in revolt, and came to reason that his best hope of successfully invading England lay through the south-west, capitalising on the region's rampant anti-Tudor sentiment, which had been lacking in Kent and Northumberland during his previous campaigns.

Whatever the motivation for leaving Scotland, during the first week of July Warbeck and his small crew sailed out into the Firth of Clyde and headed south. It is unclear what the initial plan or destination was, but on 25 July, after three weeks at sea, he surfaced once more in the very harbour where his cause first received public attention – Cork.[41] If Warbeck supposed he still had wide support in this corner of southern Ireland, he was mistaken.

Though John Atwater, the former mayor who had fervently championed the pretender since his initial appearance in 1491, still extended the hand of friendship six years later, the combined opposition of the FitzGerald earls of Kildare and Desmond ensured the region was hostile to him this time around. Despite Warbeck's desperate attempts to rally support around Cork, the king's risky pact with Kildare, which had included the earl's restoration as deputy lieutenant, proved durable. Seventy miles along the coast, the royalist town of Waterford predictably rebuffed the pretender's overtures.

Warbeck's activities during this brief visit to Ireland are difficult to ascertain, but at some point during August he abandoned any hope of capturing Cork. Pursued by some of Kildare's men, he fled to Kinsale harbour where a handful of ships awaited his arrival. Heading out into the Irish Sea, one contemporary account suggests that Warbeck's vessel was swiftly detained by English sailors who suspected he was onboard. Even though the ship was thoroughly searched, and the captain advised there was a 1,000-mark reward for the pretender's capture, Warbeck nevertheless avoided detection by hiding within a cask of wine.[42] If the story is accurate, it is as improbable an escape as young Henry Tudor's own escape from his Yorkist captors when a disturbance in the marketplace of St Malo, Brittany, created an opportune diversion, during which he was able to find sanctuary in a nearby church.

His freedom assured for the time being, once the English sailors disappeared from view empty handed, a shaken Warbeck and his modest flotilla continued their spirited voyage, finally bound for England for what would prove the final campaign of his storied crusade to seize the crown. Perhaps like Henry Tudor in 1485, the pretender had simply tired of running, hiding, and conspiring, and felt it was time to face his destiny, for better or for worse. He could still, at this moment, have sought a different destination, though the options were more limited than ever.

As for James IV, his thirst for military glory had not abated once Warbeck left his shores, as shown by the escalation in Anglo-Scottish hostilities throughout the rest of the summer despite Bishop Foxe's attempts to negotiate peace. In early August, whilst the pretender was trying in vain to raise support in Ireland, the Scots crossed the Tweed once more to besiege Norham Castle. Failing to breach the defences, James lifted the siege on 10 August and returned to Edinburgh, only to discover two days later that the earl of Surrey had crossed the border with a vast English force of his own to launch a retaliatory attack on Ayton Castle, five miles north of Berwick.[43]

Heading back into the field to confront the threat, according to a report Henry VII wrote to the mayor of London on 28 August, James boldly challenged Surrey, 'a wyse man and hardy knygth', to single hand-to-hand combat with the status of Berwick on the line, an offer nonchalantly declined by the considerably older earl, who nevertheless thanked the Scottish king 'Rigth hertely for thonour'. Recognising the English had a superior force, James 'ffled shameffully' rather than fight a pitched battle, prompting Surrey to dismiss his men after just five days on Scottish soil, having been 'vexed grevously all that tyme with contynuell Rayn and cold wedyr'. The 1497 Anglo-Scottish war therefore reached a disappointing conclusion, 'full gretly to owir dyspleasure', Henry complained, as he was certain his soldiers had as many supplies as any force ever assembled by an English king to accomplish the objectives set.[44]

With no Warbeck to deliver, and appetite for war diminishing as summer drew to a close, a fresh round of negotiations between the two parties proved more fruitful. At the end of September in Ayton, a seven-year peace was finally agreed, later extended to endure for as long as both kings lived.[45] The treaty eventually paved the way for James to marry Henry's eldest daughter Margaret, a match which resulted in the union of the two kingdoms a century later in 1603, though neither side could have foreseen such far-reaching consequences back in 1497 when focus was merely on halting the tit-for-tat attacks.

As Henry VII surveyed the situation from his rural Oxfordshire retreat at Woodstock Palace in September, he must have been somewhat contented with what he had achieved that year thus far. Despite frustration at Surrey's withdrawal from Scotland and the continuing failure to apprehend Warbeck, the northern border was at least secured after a year of back-and-forth raiding, whilst Ireland also had proven itself steadfast under duress for the first time in his reign. Trade had resumed with the Hapsburg Netherlands, and despite his induction into the Holy League and papal appreciation, Henry's relations with the French remained cordial.

Henry's staunchest allies throughout his recent tribulations had been Ferdinand of Aragon and Isabella of Castile, the Catholic monarchs of Spain. Both had consistently refused to entertain any notion of sponsoring a conspiracy against the English king, and in January 1497 signed the agreement marrying their daughter Katherine to Henry's heir Arthur, a match ratified in London the following July. At Woodstock on 15 August, the betrothal was formally concluded with Ambassador de Puebla standing proxy for the Spanish *infanta*, with the stipulation Katherine would only sail for England once Arthur reached fourteen years of age.[46] In what had proven a tough year, with the Cornish rebellion and the Scottish war, this marked one of Henry's greatest achievements to date, the promise of tying his fledgling dynasty to one of the mightiest in Europe.

The English king also worked on cultivating his reputation in other areas outside trade, war and marriage. As a youth, Henry had spent a considerable amount of time living abroad at the Breton and French court, and therefore was perhaps not as insular as some of his predecessors, displaying a natural curiosity about the world beyond lands he ruled. To that effect, in March 1496 he had issued a commission to the Venetian explorer Giovanni Caboto, better remembered as John Cabot, 'a very good mariner' with 'good in skill in discovering new islands', to search for fresh territories under the English royal banner, and on 24 July 1497 the sailor made landfall in what is today known as Newfoundland. Henry was 'much pleased' by this discovery, issuing Cabot a reward of £10 before announcing plans for a return expedition to probe further.[47]

The most important event of 1497, at least in the short term, had of course been the defeat of the Cornish rebels, who had marched to within a handful of miles of London Bridge. Though the royal forces ultimately routed their enemy at Blackheath, on a different day a reversal of fortunes could very well have toppled Henry from his throne.

Whilst convalescing at Woodstock on 3 September, Henry hosted the Venetian and Milanese ambassadors, Andrea Trevisano and Raimondo de Raimondi, and after his recent travails used the opportunity to project an impressive display of majesty for his attentive guests, conscious they would report home their findings in detail. Henry could not, and certainly would not, be viewed as weak by his fellow potentates, nor his subjects for that matter. Image could, after all, be power.

When the two ambassadors were shown into Woodstock's Great Hall, they were met by the tall, slender king leaning against a high gilt chair covered with cloth of gold. Considered attractive by Vergil, with a cheerful face, particularly when speaking, Henry cut a resplendent sight in his violet-coloured gown extravagantly lined with cloth of gold. Around his neck he wore a rich collar bearing multiple jewels, whilst upon his head was a costly cap embellished with one large diamond and a precious pear-shaped pearl. Stood beside his father during this impressive reception was the eleven-year-old prince Arthur, who Raimondi thought appeared taller than his years and 'of remarkable beauty and grace'. Several other lords and prelates were present, not least the ever-dependable Cardinal Morton. At the other end of the hall, the ambassadors also paid their respects to Queen Elizabeth, 'a handsome woman' also dressed in cloth of gold, and the king's mother, Margaret Beaufort.

After exchanging some pleasantries followed by a warm Latin oration by the cardinal, the ambassadors were treated to a private two-hour summit with the king, whom Trevisano perceived to be 'gracious, grave, and a very worthy person'. Raimondi meanwhile reported approvingly to the duke of Milan, 'Your lordship has heard from many of this king's wisdom and ways. I can testify to this, and need add no more.' All things considered, the Milanese ambassador believed that as of September 1497 'the kingdom of England has never for many years been so obedient to its sovereign as it is at present', a fact he ascribed to Henry's wisdom, 'whereof everyone stands in awe', and his significant wealth.[48] The Tudor king, as he no doubt intended, evidently succeeded in making a positive impression upon his guests, which was little surprise to someone like Vergil, for the king's 'hospitality was splendidly generous' and he was particularly 'fond of having foreigners at his court'.[49]

Despite emerging from the summer in such an apparent position of strength, however, to Henry's fury, Perkin Warbeck continued to remain elusive, six years after first surfacing in Cork. Even when some of his sailors came within feet, possibly inches, of the pretender on a vessel off the Irish coast, he miraculously evaded capture. Though the Irish, Scottish, French and Burgundians withdrew their support for him one by one, none had handed Warbeck over into English custody. Even as his support base withered as a result of Henry's shrewd foreign policy, Warbeck's enduring presence around the periphery of England was troubling for the king, as demonstrated by a conversation that took place in the Midlands shortly after the Battle of Blackheath. When urged by his companion to pray for King Henry, a figure named Master Butlar was overheard musing, 'We ned nott pray for the kyng bename,' but rather just for the rank of king, for it was 'hard to know who is Ryghetwys kyng'.[50] There was respect for the crown, and what it represented, but not for the present incumbent himself.

Henry VII had gone to considerable lengths throughout his reign to establish his credibility as king of England, having seized the crown as a relative unknown in August 1485. He arranged his coronation to take place one week before the first parliament of the reign assembled, and during that parliament ensured his status was recognised publicly by all three estates of the realm, as well as in the law of the land. Despite honouring his pledge to marry Elizabeth of York to unite the two warring houses, Henry did not crown his queen for two years, only doing so after he had defeated the Lambert Simnel conspiracy as a concession to Yorkist sympathisers amongst his support. Astonishing sums of money were freely spent to mark family occasions such as weddings and births, with visiting ambassadors and religious feasts further used by the king to project the grandness of his crown. The ubiquitous employment of dynastic imagery, meanwhile, such as the Lancastrian Red Rose and Welsh Dragon, were designed to connect Henry with past glories, as was his campaign to have his uncle, Henry VI, sanctified by the Church.

Henry's preoccupation with creating his story and then projecting it widely was motivated solely by a desire to cast away any doubt in the minds of his subjects that he was the man to rule their kingdom. News that men such as Butlar still questioned who was the righteous king a dozen years into the reign must have infuriated Henry. Despite his efforts, it was clear that as long as a supposed Yorkist prince remained at large, some would never accept Henry as their righteous king.

With four thriving children to care for, and a prosperous kingdom that was now at peace with most of Europe, Henry knew he had to bring the faltering pretender to heel in the coming months. It was essential to secure his position, and that of the Tudor dynasty. There could only be one righteous king, and for that to be confirmed beyond any doubt, Perkin Warbeck had to be destroyed.

15

Final Conclusion

On 7 September 1497, a small flotilla of ships, just two or three according to various sources, sailed into Whitesand Bay off the coast of Cornwall, the hundred or so people on board nervously monitoring the crescent-shaped beach for any presence of royal troops anticipating their arrival.[1] Barely two miles to the south was Land's End, *Penn an Wlas* in the local tongue, the most westerly point of the kingdom of England, and almost three hundred miles from London. When he set foot on the golden sand, Perkin Warbeck must have felt as far away from seizing the English crown as ever. Even now, several years into his crusade for a throne he had yet to come close to capturing, the enormity of what he was trying to achieve surely raced through his mind as he sized up the steep climb from the coast. Still, he was at least in England, which itself was progress.

Beside Warbeck for the tense voyage from Ireland had been his Scottish wife Lady Katherine Gordon and an intimate multinational band of hardy supporters, who to their credit had yet to desert the man increasingly ridiculed in his supposed homeland as a lowly imposter of little standing. The pretender had been through difficult situations before, whether abandoned by his royal benefactors for their own purpose or observing with dismay from afar as vital supporters like William Stanley and Robert Clifford were exposed by the Tudor machinery.

His situation in early September 1497 was more desperate than ever, with the odds of success for his latest assault on England considerably longer than they had been when his men landed in Kent in July 1495 or when he himself had briefly crossed the Scottish border one year earlier; at least on those occasions Warbeck had something resembling a competent and organised army, the first heavily backed by Burgundian cash and the other by Scottish soldiers under the command of their war-hungry king. The modest force which disembarked at Whitesand Bay could claim parity with neither. Cornwall was certainly not a chance destination, however.

Although Henry VII had comprehensively defeated the Cornish rebellion in a resounding manner three months earlier at the Battle of Blackheath, executing the three principal leaders, Michael Joseph, Thomas Flamank, and Lord Audley, before imposing severe financial punishment on many more participants, the king failed to quell the unruly spirit of the Cornishmen who continued to simmer with resentment and an unbridled thirst for vengeance. During the summer, Warbeck had been made aware that the West Country was a fertile breeding ground for fomenting anti-Tudor support, and his landing in the region was a calculated decision to exploit such sentiment and raise the area for a second rebellion. This time, the movement would feature him at the helm as the rightful heir of York intending to overturn Tudor tyranny. Whitesand Bay itself may even have been pinpointed by Warbeck's advisors as an ideal location to disembark as it lay just thirty miles from the St Keverne hometown of Joseph, where Cornish rage towards the king who had executed the local champion was perhaps at its most intense. It was the pretender's intention to harness that fury and concentrate it against a ruler many in the region had never even laid eyes upon, twelve years into the reign.

As well as Lady Katherine, one of those who accompanied Warbeck from Scotland appears to have been the Breton Guy Foulcart, who several years later demanded compensation from James IV for persuading him to convey the pretender to Cornwall in his vessel. At some point after landing, Foulcart was apprehended by the English, his goods seized and he was forced to pay a heavy fine, the source of his understandable anger towards the Scottish king.[2] Also forming part of Warbeck's invasion force was the implacable John Taylor, a native of Exeter and former adherent of both George, Duke of Clarence, and Richard III. Taylor was an ardent Yorkist loyalist who had been connected with the conspiracy since its outset, personally welcoming Warbeck ashore in Cork in the winter of 1491, and having spent many years in exile now sought to attract support in a region he knew intimately. The pretender's three captains, meanwhile, were John Heron, a former mercer of London who had fled the city because of debt, and two men named Skelton and Astley, a trio the chronicler Edward Hall later disparaged as 'men of more dishonestie then of honest estimacion'.[3] To Warbeck in September 1497, however, their contributions were undoubtedly valued, regardless of their character.

One of the pretender's first acts upon disembarking from his vessel was to find a safe location for his wife to await the outcome of his forthcoming campaign. Presumably on the recommendation of friendly Cornishmen amongst his host, he settled on the parish of St Buryan. Situated four miles inland and roughly half-way between Whitesand and Penzance, St Buryan had been founded by King Athelstan in 936, who conferred upon the parish the sacred privilege of sanctuary, exempt from ordinary legal process and permitted to provide refuge to fugitives who sought its protection.[4] If the feelings Warbeck declared for Katherine in the letter he wrote to her prior to their marriage in Scotland were genuine and at all reciprocated, the parting between husband and wife must have been an emotional one.

As Warbeck disappeared out of view in the distance, Katherine, whom Henry VII's court poet Bernard André would later praise on account of her 'admirable character',[5] was uncertain if she would ever lay eyes upon her man again, and one can only speculate what her innermost thoughts were about the unlikely mission upon which he now embarked. Would he be killed, or would she become a queen? These were unanswerable questions which she must have nervously pondered as she acclimatised to her new surroundings in Buryan, and a basic life that she no doubt hoped would be temporary; south-west Cornwall may have had topographical similarities to her native Scotland, but Katherine was far from home and anxiously awaiting her fate.

When Warbeck, Taylor, and the rest of his steadfast band of followers entered Penzance, the most westerly market town in all the realm, they brazenly attempted to stir support for their cause amongst the citizens. It is interesting to speculate what the Cornishmen made of the pretender's claim to be their true king, or perhaps like the Scottish before them whether they even cared about the intricate details of hereditary right. Which man occupied the throne and by what reason he did so probably had little effect on the daily lives of people this far from the seats of government in Westminster and London.

It is of course possible many were unable to comprehend the strange language of the invaders, preferring to speak their own native tongue, but were nevertheless minded to follow these plotters who stood before them, as they provided an opportunity to resume their hostilities against Henry VII, who these tin miners, blacksmiths, and farmers now openly regarded with disdain. Some of the Cornish dissidents were later identified by parliament, including three gentlemen, John Nankevell,

Walter Tripconny, and Humphrey Calwodeley, and seven yeomen, all drawn from communities in the west of the duchy.[6] They may have had different reasons for rising against the king than Warbeck, but when presented with the opportunity 'voluntarily supported' the pretender and 'with one voice acclaimed him as their leader'.[7]

As the Yorkist rebels became acquainted with their Cornish dissident allies, three battle standards were raised above the heads of the amalgamated force. One featured a red lion, another depicted a little boy emerging from a tomb, and the third bore the image of another boy escaping the mouth of a wolf.[8] Emboldened by a mutual cause, the army started their arduous march through the peninsula, the curious banners attracting further support in each village they passed through. The cry no doubt went out that Henry VII, an enemy of Cornwall, would fall at the hands of this son of York who had returned from the dead. By the time Warbeck and his men reached Bodmin, just over fifty miles from Whitesand Bay, it was speculated he had accumulated between three and five thousand men, and though a London-based chronicler dismissed them as 'men of Rascayll' who were for the 'most parte naked men', that is poorly armed, it was nevertheless not a number that could be dismissed easily by royal officials.[9]

It was at Bodmin, another chronicle claimed, that Warbeck 'made his proclamacions and namyd hym sylf kyng Richard the iiiith and secund sone unto Edward the iiiith late kyng', having presumably waited until he had a substantial captive audience assembled before him to witness such a stirring pronouncement.[10] The irony could not have been lost on some present, for on 3 November 1483 another pretender had been declared king by his supporters in the same place – Henry Tudor.[11] Perhaps some who had proclaimed Henry king now did the same for Warbeck.

Galvanising his support 'with fayre woordes and large promises',[12] the self-styled king and his burgeoning force continued their march across the secluded moorland north-east of Bodmin, having 'decided to proceed methodically against the enemy, and to capture wherever he went fortified places which might usually serve in his defence'.[13] To this end, Warbeck led his men through Launceston, across the River Tamar and towards Exeter, the largest city in the region.

Henry VII discovered Warbeck had landed in Cornwall on 10 September, and two days later urgently sent Richard Empson to his principal nobleman in the West Country, Edward Courtenay, 1st Earl of Devon. In Empson's hands was over £666 to raise as many troops as possible to thwart the rebels' advance.[14] Devon was a suitable choice for what would prove a crucial duty; the Courtenay family were highly influential as the most significant landowners in the region, and though they briefly lost sway during the mid-fifteenth century on account of their adherence to the flagging Lancastrian cause during the years of Yorkist ascendancy, had swiftly regained their supremacy under Henry VII. Devon had been one of the men who had joined the would-be king in exile in Brittany, and later fought for him at Bosworth and at Stoke Field. Rewarded by becoming a knight of the Garter, Devon had earned his king's trust throughout the reign thus far, and was now called upon once more to stand firm to defend the Tudor crown.

King Henry was prudent to act with haste, for just the following day, 13 September, Devon wrote to the king from Okehampton warning that the decision had been made not to draw Warbeck's larger force into battle but instead to retreat behind the walls of Exeter, 'for the defens and sauf keping therof'. It wasn't ideal, of course, and suggested the initial royalist estimation had misjudged the might of Warbeck's host.

The king, however, responded at length three days later on 16 September to his 'right welbeloved cousin' Devon showing appreciation that the earl, 'of youre wisedoms', had 'taken soo wise a direction, ffor moore acceptable it is unto us to haue oure saide Citie surely kept' than for any misfortune to befall him and his men. Henry shared with the earl his strategy to ensnare Warbeck so that he could be 'broughte unto us a lyve', something the king declared was 'the chief thing we desire'. A dead Warbeck could not be interrogated to divulge information about the king's enemies.

Henry's plan involved Devon holding the city of Exeter against the oncoming threat at all costs, but once Warbeck had passed on, the earl should 'take with you all the nobles of your said company with theire retynewes to folowe and for to be at the bakkes of our said rebelles and traitours'. As well as shadowing Warbeck, Devon was also directed to send before him 'a certain nombre of wel horsed men' to aggravate the rear lines of the pretender's force and ensure they stay together in tight formation, whilst doing his utmost to prevent the rebels from replenishing their supplies along the way. This way, Henry mused, Warbeck and his men would in due course be shepherded unaware towards the potent royal army of his Giles Daubeney which was headed their way, and with the latter 'being beforn theym and ye behinde theym shal encombre the said Perkyn' so that he could be taken 'without any stroke or perill'.

Writing from his chamber in Woodstock, the king was certain his plan would work, and was firm that Devon should 'folowe oure mynde' on this point without excuse. As a final point, and to ensure neither Warbeck nor his wife Katherine could flee on the ships that brought them to Cornwall, the earl was directed that if the fleet be found it should be captured, burnt, or otherwise rendered unfit to sail.[15] It was this last condition that may have prompted the Breton Guy Foucart's later complaints to the Scottish king after his vessel was confiscated.

The day after Henry composed his instructions, Warbeck and his Cornish army reached Exeter as predicted, arriving around one o'clock in the afternoon. Failing to persuade Devon to yield the strongly garrisoned city, Warbeck 'concentrated all his forces to break down the gates', focusing in particular on the north and east entrances either side of Rougemont Castle, even setting them ablaze to try and force an entry.[16] The flames may have concerned the residents within the city, but they held firm through the night. The following day, 18 September, Devon updated the king that Warbeck had made 'fresh assaults' upon the two gates that morning with particular emphasis on the northern gateway. Nevertheless, the city was 'well and truly defended' in the king's name. Blood was shed on both sides during the assault, and though Devon was reported to have taken an arrow to the forearm, he did brag that for every one of his men hurt, at least twenty of Warbeck's were wounded in return.

Having lost around two hundred men according to one chronicler's source, at eleven o'clock in the morning Warbeck reluctantly gave the order for his men to withdraw and instead continue the march to the next town of note, Taunton, about thirty miles to the north-east. By midday, Devon claimed he had lost sight of the rebels in the distance, before preparing his weary troops to give chase as per the king's orders to herd the unwitting prey into a trap. When Henry VII received word that the gates of Exeter had held firm, his reaction was to exclaim in relief, 'Blessed bee God.'[17] Incidentally, as a backdrop to this attack, Devon was the father-in-law of Catherine of York, a daughter of Edward IV who was therefore, as per Warbeck's claim to be Prince Richard, his younger sister. It is unclear if there was any temptation on Devon's part to defect, but as events unfolded, Henry had been right to place his trust in his earl not to waver.

On 19 September, the dispirited pretender and his men reached Taunton, Somerset's county seat, where they hoped to find similar enthusiasm for rebellion as had greeted Joseph and Flamank when they passed through earlier in the summer. According to the Milanese ambassador Raimondi, shortly after arrival in the town, Warbeck issued several orders, one of which was to publish 'certain apostolic bulls affirming that he was the son of King Edward'. In populist rhetoric designed to engender support if his claim to be a son of York didn't work, he also pledged to coin money that he claimed would be freely given 'to all'.[18] The most circumspect of kings, Henry VII had prudently ensured papal support for his reign was well publicised throughout England in recent months, so it is uncertain how productive this ruse by Warbeck was, even in an age when many may have accepted what they were told at face value.

Unlike Exeter, the town of Taunton was unwalled with a modest castle undergoing an extensive renovation project. It was not a place which could offer protection from the royal armies headed Warbeck's way, and he must have suspected his position was precarious. The pretender's intention upon landing in Cornwall had been to secure a fortress within which he could establish a foothold from which to challenge Henry's authority – Taunton was far from the ideal spot for this.

The day after his arrival, Warbeck and his captains mustered their forces in the fields around the town for assessment, and the conclusion was not positive. According to Vergil, their leader 'did not put much trust in his army, the majority of his soldiers being armed only with swords, the rest of their bodies being unprotected'. As he and his trusted advisors wandered through the ranks, inspecting the troops in whom they placed their lives, the bitter truth was that these men the pretender counted upon to win him a crown 'were completely unused to warfare' and could not be relied upon to deliver him the prize he desperately sought.[19] The demoralised ranks themselves must also have acknowledged their inadequacies – concerned that 'noo men of honour nor yit of honeste' had flocked to their cause throughout their march, they had slowly started to desert for 'theyr aune savegard'.[20] If Warbeck didn't trust his men, it is likely by Taunton they didn't have faith in him either.

In the meantime, Henry VII's strategy to trap the pretender gathered pace. Aside from ordering the earl of Devon to shadow Warbeck after he left Exeter and obstruct any attempt of flight back into Cornwall, as planned the king had recruited two commanders he trusted completely, Lord Chamberlain Giles Daubeney and Steward of the Household Robert Willoughby, 1st Baron Willougby de Broke, to advance on the rebels from two different directions.

Daubeney's formidable force, described by the boastful monarch as 'an armee royall of peuple soo furnisshed with artilleryes and ordenaunces for the felde as shalbe hable to defende any prince Christien',[21] marched from Oxfordshire into Somerset, reaching Glastonbury on 19 September, the same date Warbeck entered Taunton just twenty miles away. De Broke, meanwhile, who had recently returned to the south coast from the north with the royal fleet, secured the ports before assembling his troops and also heading towards the rebels. It was an aggressive, three-pronged approach, supported by a host of noblemen drawn from across South Wales, Gloucestershire, Hampshire, Somerset and Dorset. His trap set, Henry defiantly declared, 'Wee with our hoast royall shall not be farre, with the mercy of our Lord, for the finall conclusion of the matter.'[22]

If Warbeck had any scouts probing the area for royal activity, he must surely have been alarmed by reports of such a heavy response from the king, particularly as he realised the men under his command were inferior in every aspect. Even if he remained blissfully unaware, true to form Warbeck lost his nerve as he had done in the past. On 20 September, 'in the dede of the nygth', he absconded from his army for the final time, accompanied on horseback by only sixty of his closest companions.[23] For Bernard André, it was yet more proof of the pretender's 'feeble heart'.[24] The perceptive Milanese ambassador Raimondi summed matters up in his report to the duke of Milan four days before Warbeck's flight:

> Everything favours the king, especially an immense treasure, and because all the nobles of the realm know the royal wisdom and either fear him or bear him an extraordinary affection and not a man of any consideration joins the Duke of York.[25]

Hours before the pretender and his small band of intimates furtively abandoned their army, Henry had written from Woodstock to Oliver King, Bishop of Bath and Wells, outlining his aforementioned military strategy for ensnaring the pretender, confidently concluding his letter with the statement, 'Wee trust soone to heare good tydings of the said Perkin.' The king would not need to wait long.[26]

*

During the early hours of 21 September, Perkin Warbeck galloped through the Somerset darkness with his most trusted cohorts scattered around him, all desperately bolting from Taunton in search of somewhere they could evade capture by the royal forces they knew were in the vicinity. Every minute counted – Warbeck, or those in his company, may have known how Henry VII himself had escaped arrest and certain death by a matter of miles during his exile in Brittany in 1484, crossing the border into France just ahead of his pursuers. Had Henry delayed for any reason on that fateful day, there would have been no Tudor dynasty; and now, thirteen years later, the latest pretender to the English crown likewise sought to preserve his liberty just a little longer. Warbeck left any pretence of Richard IV behind, and once more reverted to the miserable and desperate life of an outlaw on the run.

From Taunton, he went east, mindful to remain in sparsely populated rural areas like Cranborne Chase and avoiding any major towns where he may be spotted by those faithful to the incumbent king. Keeping rest to a minimum, the small party eventually crossed the River Avon and dashed into the New Forest, navigating their way through the vast woodland and with each mile came closer the coast, and freedom.

That Warbeck did not seize the opportunity to complete his escape by fleeing abroad at this juncture suggests one of two things; either he made it to the sea, whether at Southampton or elsewhere along the Solent, and found the ports protected by de Broke's men and therefore doubled back, or he was struggling to shake off his pursuers and sought a safe haven at the first chance. The former certainly tallies with the report Henry VII later sent to the mayor of Waterford in which he boasted how he had 'well provided beforehand for the sea coasts', so that there was little prospect of a successful flight. Whatever the reason, on 22 September Warbeck arrived at the Cistercian abbey at Beaulieu and, one could surmise, desperately hammered on the wooden doors of the gatehouse, screaming for sanctuary before he was captured. It was in this bucolic setting, less than five miles from the Solent with the Channel beyond it, the pretender was destined to make his last stand as a claimant to the English throne.

Beaulieu Abbey had been founded during the reign of King John and its French name translated as 'the beautiful place', an indication of the stunning location.[27] Known as the white monks for the colour of their cassock, often partially covered with a black scapular which concealed the shoulders, the Cistercians were an order dedicated to an austere lifestyle with heavy focus on manual labour in order to maintain their self-sufficient existence. With core vows centred around poverty, chastity and obedience, life within the monastery was uncompromising and highly disciplined.[28]

Unlike many other consecrated churches, priories or abbeys, however, Beaulieu was considered an 'exempt abbey', with rights of sanctuary that far exceeded the standard rules other religious sites traditionally possessed. Whereas most holy sites could offer sanctuary to felons for up to forty days, a handful of locations were permitted to shelter offenders until the end of their lives. Beaulieu, along with Beverley, Durham, Westminster, and St Martin's le Grand in London, was one such example with this rare privilege.

As recently as December 1483 the sanctuary status of Beaulieu had been scrutinised when, 'for certain great and urgent causes', Richard III summoned the abbot to Westminster with only six days' notice to present 'all and every such muniments and writings by which ye claim to have a Sanctuary', a demand duly respected. Richard's request occurred just a few months after Henry Tudor had attempted to land on the south coast to press his unlikely claim to the throne, and now, fourteen years later, it was Henry's turn as king to deal with a pretender at Beaulieu Abbey.

Traditional sanctuary law dictated that the person seeking protection had to reach the church and place his hand on the door's knocker before he was captured, though often just entering the grounds of the church was considered enough. The abbey estate at Beaulieu was extensive, and it is unclear if Warbeck claimed sanctuary by merely reaching land owned by the order, or whether he approached the door on the outer gatehouse and grasped the knocker in relief. By whatever manner he besought the abbey's protection, before sanctuary could be granted, the pretender was forced to enter his name on a register, along with his most recent residence and the crime of which he had been accused. It would be fascinating to discover the name he entered, and by which name he was referred to during his visit.

Upon entering the outer gatehouse, Warbeck would have been shown into the grounds proper, passing the water mill and through the great gatehouse which controlled access to the innermost courtyard, at the centre of which was the abbey church with its simple square tower. As reflected in the modest manner in which they lived, Cistercian architecture was utilitarian and devoid of elaborate designs. Whilst walking along the nave inside the church, Warbeck's eyes may even have been drawn to some of the tilework bearing fleurs-de-lys, the French royal symbol English kings had long adopted. The serene environment may even have offered him the opportunity for some reflection on his recent travails. Warbeck's quarters were probably in the Hospitium, detached lodgings reserved for distinguished visitors. The innovative winepress and plentiful fishponds provided sustenance.

Writing in 1533, shortly before the abbey was dissolved, John Tuchet, 8th Baron Audley and the restored son of the Cornish rebel leader killed after Blackheath, described Beaulieu as 'a great sanctuary', and this was what greeted its visitor at the end of September 1497. Stood alone in his thoughts wandering around the abbey grounds, conscious the game was up, it is unlikely Warbeck was able to conjure much enthusiasm for his surroundings, however impressive.

When Giles Daubeney entered Taunton on 22 September and found a disordered army abandoned by its leadership, he promptly ordered a detachment of five hundred men to hunt down Warbeck,[29] which a seventeenth-century family history suggested was under the command of the competent and experienced Welshman Sir Rhys ap Thomas, who may very well have been one of the men Henry summoned from South Wales.[30]

Despite his head start, Warbeck was tracked down by the hunting party, though they were only successful in capturing a handful of his supporters who had fallen behind for one reason or another – perhaps they had sacrificed their freedom to slow their pursuers' progress to let the pretender slip further away, or had unwisely chosen to stand and fight against a more organised foe. By the time the royal force arrived at Beaulieu, Warbeck had already made his way into the abbey, having claimed and been granted sanctuary.[31]

The law, however, did not prevent the soldiers from surrounding the abbey so that escape was not a feasible option for the rebels nervously dwelling within. Richard III had ordered a similar manoeuvre at Westminster in 1483 when attempting to persuade Elizabeth Wydeville to hand over her son, Richard of York, who, somewhat ironically, Warbeck now claimed to be. Supplies, messengers and movement were all restricted in what was, in truth, a siege. Fifteenth-century kings respected sanctuary, but as Edward IV had proved in 1471 when he breached Tewkesbury Abbey to apprehend a handful of Lancastrians including Henry VII's own kinsman Edmund Beaufort, only to a point.

Despite the attempts of later Tudor chroniclers to portray Warbeck as a naïve fool, the pretender was not deluded enough to ignore the desperate situation in which he found himself – there was to be no escape, and no rescue. If he wished to live, submission to a king he hoped would show mercy was the only option available. Henry VII, for his part, had been keen all along to secure Warbeck alive, chiefly to expose the tentacles of the conspiracy against him using the pretender himself as the vehicle to do so, carefully avoiding the creation of a Yorkist martyr in the process.

By chance, Henry had some servants residing within the abbey boundaries when his chief rebel arrived, and it was these men who now acted as mediators between Warbeck and the royal soldiers stationed outside the walls. Warbeck was advised not to bargain, which might arouse Henry's anger, but rather throw himself on the king's mercy. The latter had, after all, proven merciful with Lambert Simnel a decade earlier, and although as an adult Warbeck had to accept a degree of personal culpability for his present situation, there was hope a similar outcome was possible.

As evidenced in the subsequent letter Henry VII wrote to the mayor of Waterford, the king reported that after some deliberation the pretender sent word from the abbey that he promised to 'come unto us to shew what he is and over that, do unto us such service as should content us'. Furthermore, he and his supporters wished to 'put themselves in our grace and pity' and would 'come unto us of their free wills, in trust of our grace and pardon'.[32] Edward Hall later speculated that by this stage Warbeck had grown 'destitute of all hope', and 'lacking comforte, aide and refuge' indeed 'frely departed out of sanctuary and committed hym selfe to the kynges pleasure'.[33]

Richmond Herald, Roger Machado, who was present for Warbeck's humbled emergence from Beaulieu, reported that prior to leaving the pretender shed the plain habit he had been wearing in exchange for costly golden garments, presumably wishing to leave behind the harsh restrictions of sanctuary as a prince rather than a pauper.[34] This submission was likely arranged just before the end of the month, for on 1 October the mayor of London received tidings that Warbeck had indeed surrendered, going at once with his aldermen to St Paul's to give thanks at the altar in the name of the king.[35]

With Warbeck cornered in Beaulieu and his capture imminent, Henry knew the risk of widespread rebellion in the south-west had eased and on 24 September departed his Woodstock base, travelling through Cirencester, Malmesbury, Bath, Wells, and Glastonbury before reaching Taunton on 4 October, by which time he knew the pretender had surrendered.[36] In a concession to the seriousness of the matter, the king had ridden upon a warhorse in full armour, positioned at the head of a 'great compaignie of noble men, knightes and esquyers, prepared and redy with all things necessary for the felde and battayle'.[37]

It is unlikely Henry expected trouble now that Warbeck was neutralised, but nevertheless an armed king in the field was an effective deterrent to any rebels still minded to launch an attack on royal authority. The king was also keen to portray himself to the people as an unconquerable general, able to muster a vast army and call on the support of men of great rank like Edward Stafford, Duke of Buckingham, a far cry from some fretful imposter who repeatedly fled from destiny in the face of danger.

The contrast Henry was keen to express between himself and Warbeck could not have been more apparent, and all along the route scores of commoners lining the streets would have been influenced by this formidable sight passing them by. As the king's armour shone in the autumn sun, he must have appeared an irresistible sight, almost divine to eyes that had never witnessed such a thing. This was what a king was supposed to look like, not Warbeck. Families would have talked about it for generations, perhaps the first and last time they had ever observed a king in all his glory, marching past their simple homes and humble businesses. Incidentally, on his first night in Taunton Henry lost the considerable sum of £9 playing cards, suggesting he was in a somewhat celebratory mood, enjoying some stress-free downtime with his closest friends. The king was evidently not as competent at gambling as he was fighting off pretenders.[38]

The day after his arrival in Taunton on 5 October 1497, Henry VII finally came face-to-face with the man he knew as Perkin Warbeck.[39] This was a momentous occasion for all present in the town's castle, with the king able to stare deep into the eyes of the man who had dared to plot his downfall for the last six years. This self-styled son of York had repeatedly sought, and indeed occasionally secured, support from the king's foreign enemies, had been the focus of betrayal within Henry's own household, and had launched three separate invasions of England with varying success but at great expense to the royal exchequer. Now they met, they talked, and they listened. No one else present surely dared to interrupt any moments of awkward silence between the pair.

The most detailed account of this fascinating summit comes from Richmond Herald Roger Machado, as told to Ambassador Raimondi, who considered his source 'a man of wit and discretion'. Having been led sheepishly into the king's presence, Warbeck 'kneeled down and asked for mercy'. The seconds that passed must have felt an eternity before Henry gestured for him to rise. Eyeing up the blonde-haired figure before him, the king then announced, 'We have heard that you call yourself Richard, son of King Edward.' If there was any reply, it wasn't recorded. Now, the king probed further: 'In this place are some who were companions of that lord, look and see if you recognise them.' Warbeck scanned the faces looking upon him, former Yorkists who now served the Tudor regime, before replying that he knew none of them, for in truth he was not truly Richard.[40]

Bernard André suggested in his incomplete biography of Henry VII that Warbeck had been 'led in trembling', as 'the royal servants themselves had mockingly beaten him black and blue and hissed at his laughable appearance', though there is no mention of this in the ambassador's report, drafted just a fortnight later for a foreign audience outside the English king's control.[41] Henry was not foolish enough to permit his men to inflict physical violence on Warbeck, aware it would have raised questions about the credibility of the pretender's testimony if he appeared in public bearing the signs of a vicious beating. He had been very clear hitherto that Warbeck should be taken alive for this purpose, and to allow his prized capture to be assaulted at this juncture would have proven counterproductive. As with much concerning the pretender, however, the facts remain unclear.

Henry's chief concern at this moment in early October 1497 was not physical retribution but extracting a full and frank confession from Warbeck that could be used to show this thorn in his side for the previous six years was merely a well-spoken imposter, a fraudulent 'prince' who was anything but a Yorkist heir. This was accomplished in comprehensive fashion:

ffirst it is to be knowen that I was born in the Towne of Turney, and my ffaders name is called John Osbek; which said John Osbek was controller of the Towne of Turney. And my moders name is Kateryn de ffaro. And one of my Grauntsires upon my ffaders side was called Deryk Osbek, which died, after whos deth my grauntmother was maried unto the within named Petir flamme; and that other of my grauntsires was called Petir flam, which was Receyvour of the forsaid Towne of Turney and Deane of the Botemen that be upon the watir or Ryver of Leystave. And my Grauntsire upon my moders side was called Petir ffaro, the which had in his kepyng the keys of the Gate of Seynt Johns, within the abouenamed Towne of Turney.

Also I had an Uncle named Maister John Stalyn dwellyng in the parisshe of Saynt Pyas within the same Towne, which had maried my ffaders Sister, whose name was Johane or Jane, with whom I dwelled a certeyn season; and afterward I was led by my moder to Andwarp for to lerne flemmysshe in an house of a Cosyn of myne, officer of the said Towne, called John Stienbek, with whome I was the Space of half a yere. And after that I retourned agayn unto Turney by reason of the warres that wer in fflaunders. And within a yere folowyng I was sent with a Merchaunt of the said Towne of Turney named Berlo, and his Maister's name Alex., to the Marte of Andwarp, where as I fill syke, which sykenesse contynued upon me v. monethes; and the said Berlo set me to boorde in a Skynners hous, that dwelled beside the hous of the Englessh nacion. And by hym I was brought from thens to the Barowe Marte, and loged at the Signe of thold man, where I abode the space of ij monethes.

And after this the said Berlo set me with a merchaunt in Middelborough to seruice for to lerne the language, whose name was John Strewe, with whome I dwelled from Cristmas unto Easter; and than I went into Portyngale in the Cumpany of Sir Edward Bramptons wif in a Ship which was called the Ouenes Ship. And whan I was comen thider I was put in service to a knyght that dwelled in Lusshebourne, which was called Petir Vacz de Cogna, with whome I dwelled an hole yere, which said knyght had but one lye; and than because I desired to se other Cuntrees I toke licence of hym.

And than I put my silf in seruice with a Breton, called Pregent Meno, the which brought me with hym into Ireland. And whan we wer there aryved in the Towne of Corke, they of the Towne, because I was arayed with some clothes of silk of my said Maisters, came unto me and threped upon me that I shuld be the Duke of Clarence sone, that was before tyme at Develyn. And for as moch as I denyed it there was brought unto me the holy Euaungelist and the Crosse by the Mayre of the Towne, which was called John Lewelyn; and there in the presence of hym and other I toke myn Othe as trouth was that I was not the forsaid Dukes Son, nother of none of his blood. And after this came unto me an Englissh man, whose name was Steffe Poytron, with one John Water, and said to me in sweryng grete Othis, that they knew wele I was kyng Richardes Bastarde Son; to whome I answerd with hie Othis that I were not.

And than they advised me not to be afferd but that I shuld take it upon me Boldly, and iff I wold so do they wold ayde and assiste me with all theyr powr agayn the kyng of Englond; And not only they, but they were well assured that therles of Desmond and Kildare shuld do the same, ffor they forsid not what party so that they myght be revenged upon the kyng of Englond; and so agaynst my will made me to lerne Inglisshe, and taught me what I shuld doo and say. And after this they called me Duke of York, the Second Son of kyng Edward the ffourth, because kyng Richardes Bastarde Son was in the handes of the kyng of Englond. And upon this the said John Water, Steffe Poytron, John Tiler, Huberd Bourgh, with many other, as the forsaid Erles, entred into this fals Quarell.

And within short tyme after this the ffrensshe kyng sent unto me an Embasset into Irelond, whose names was Ioyte Lucas and Maister Steffes ffrion, to aduertise me to come into ffraunce; and thens I went into ffraunce, and from thens into fflaunders, and from fflaunders into Ireland, And from Ireland into Scotland, and so into Englond.[42]

There was also a brief addendum added to a French copy of the above confession, a list of names Warbeck claimed to have known during his youth, which added further weight to the authenticity of the declaration:

> Here follow the names of my neighbours living in the Parish of St. Jean, and also my schoolmasters.
>
> First Jehan Pernet, Pierart Pernet, Nicholas du Bos, Jehan Carlier, Michel de Grandmont, Jehan Capelier, Jehan de Genet, Guillem Rucq, Thieri Micquelet, Jerome Capelier, and Michael de la Chapelle.
>
> The first of my teachers: Master Jehan Badoul. And Afterward Master Baulde Muguet, cantor of Notre Dame de Tournai, who taught me to play the manicordium. Also I had another master who taught me my grammar and he was called Master Guilhem. And he lived in a house called Les Bons Enfansts.[43]

This was convincing information, and Henry wasted little time in broadcasting news of the confession far and wide; in his letter to the mayor of Waterford a few weeks later, the king smugly described how Warbeck

> ... immediately after his first coming, humbly submitting himself to us, hath of his free will openly shewed, in the presence of all the lords here with us, and of all nobles, his name to be Pierce Osbeck, whence he hath been named Perkin Warbeck, and to be no Englishman born, but born of Tournay, and son to John.[44]

Henry concluded, 'And so now the great abuse which hath long continued is now openly known by his own confession.' Copies were also printed and sent across England and elsewhere so 'that the trowth of such covyred malice and ffalshode abhomynable mygth be knowyn, to the grete rejoysyng of all the kyngis ffreendis and trewe subgectis'.[45] To ensure the confession reached Italy, the Milanese ambassador was also shown the confession, which he believed to be authentic.[46]

Satisfied, the day after the confession the king and his host departed Taunton and headed towards Exeter, the city which had stood firm throughout the summer in support of his crown. Somewhere amongst the thousands of soldiers, churchmen, and household officials who trudged south-west was Warbeck, no longer at the head of his own forces but his rival's discomfited prisoner. By his own admission, after all, he was merely a common imposter who was the son of a foreign boatman, and his place in the procession likely reflected this status.

The royal convoy entered Exeter on 7 October,[47] exactly a month after the pretender had landed at Whitesand Bay, with the king provided comfortable accommodation in the treasurer's house next to the Church of St Peter. There is little information about where Warbeck was quartered, but satisfactory if secure lodging in Rougemont Castle would have been appropriate. Though Henry was 'right glad and pleased' with his subjects of Exeter[48] and 'thanked them for remaining loyal to him',[49] during his stay in the city he was focused on quelling the air of civil disobedience which had permeated through the communities of the south-west over previous months. He wanted no repeat in the coming years.

The gentry were reproached for not preventing both uprisings from occurring, whilst some of the leading malcontents were identified, rounded up, and executed. Many others were reprimanded severely, with crushing fines imposed on those not deemed quite deserving of death, though of course given no future chance of reprieve should they waver again.[50] Peace would be forcibly restored to Cornwall and Devon, in person by the king and either through the gallows or the purse strings. The policy appeared to work; Henry's letter to Waterford from Exeter described how

the commons of this shire of Devon come dayly before us, in great multitudes, in their shirts, the foremost of them having halters about their necks, and full humble, with lamentable cries for our grace and remission, submit themselves unto us.[51]

It was during this stay in Exeter that Warbeck was briefly reunited with his wife, Katherine Gordon. Henry had sent a detachment to retrieve her from St Buryan's, though it is speculated she had since sought protection in St Michael's Mount, a tidal island just off the coast near Penzance, where she received word the campaign had not gone according to plan.[52] Either way, there was no escaping capture.

When brought to Exeter, Katherine was shown into a chamber where the king and her husband awaited her presence. According to Bernard André, the Scotswoman, 'who had a modest and lovely countenance, surpassing beauty, and the freshness of youth', was presented to Henry VII, 'ashamed and tearful'.[53] Vergil suggests the king was somewhat moved by her appearance: 'When the king saw the woman's beauty he promptly judged her worthy to be among the captive hostages of a general rather than a common soldier.' That is, she should be afforded a more honourable status than had initially been the plan.[54] Of course, more pragmatically, this enhanced status also meant she was separated from Perkin's presence, which may have been the king's actual intention, using her beauty as the justification.

Henry now commanded Warbeck to publicly admit his deception before his wife, which the chastised pretender duly did before yearning for her pardon. It is not unreasonable to suggest that Katherine was shocked to hear these unpalatable words tumble from her husband's trembling lips, recounting how he had invented his royal pedigree, had hoodwinked the Scottish king, and scandalously entered their marriage living a mighty lie. She may have heard courtly gossip that Perkin was an imposter from Tournai, but his assurances in private and the enthusiastic support of her kinsman James IV must have allayed her concerns. Now, in this quiet chamber in Exeter, her husband stood before her declaring their marriage was effectively void as he had entered the union as Richard, not Perkin, and so their future as man and wife was non-existent. André suggests the tragic Katherine was overcome with grief and anger, loudly bewailing her abduction and pleading to be returned to Scotland,[55] though unfortunately, as with many women of the past, Katherine's own voice in her story has been lost to history.

If Katherine did desire to return to her homeland, she would not be granted her wish. Henry instead sent her to London to serve his queen 'as a true and undoubted token of hys triumphe and victory'.[56] For her journey, the king purchased horses, saddles and other supplies[57] and on 16 October wrote to Thomas Stokes personally charging him to obtain some food for the lady.[58] Katherine was also presented with new clothes, including a black satin gown garnished with velvet ribbons and tawny satin, and a black velvet bonnet, and reached

Sheen on 21 October where she was presented to the woman Warbeck had once claimed to have been his elder sister, Elizabeth of York, the queen of England.[59] No record of their initial meeting, or indeed future conversations, is known to have survived, but a position in the queen's household was more than suitable for Katherine, not as Warbeck's wife, but as a noblewoman of Scotland in her own right, as she was forthwith regarded. That she made the best of her situation seems to be case.

Whilst in Exeter, an extraordinary letter signed in the name of Pierrequin Werbecque was addressed to Catherine, the woman identified by the author as 'ma mère', my mother.[60] These, it was claimed, were the words of a fallen son to the mother he had long since abandoned for adventure, the mask of deception well and truly ripped away. This authenticity of this document, dated 13 October, has been questioned by some historians as there are some discrepancies which conflict with other sources; according to one nineteenth-century record, Warbeck's mother's name was in fact Nicaise, though this particular letter is consistent with the pretender's confession in referring to her as Catherine. Her son's name, meanwhile, is given as Pierrequin Werbecque rather than Osbek, as in the confession. Are these inconsistencies that prove the document was a false creation, or can they be explained away as errors, perhaps the wilful editing on the part of a clerk? Catherine would not be the first migrant in history to have two names, one original and one local, after all, and with Tournai a border town often split on French-Flemish lines, it is not inconceivable Warbeck himself would use variations of his name dependent on the audience; this still occurs today. He was Werbecque in French and Osbek in Flemish.

The sheer detail of the letter's contents, however, strongly supports the assertion it was a genuine communication, and if not written personally by the pretender, then certainly produced on his behalf and with his input. The original letter is no longer in existence to be examined further, but two copies have been found in Flemish collections in Tournai and Courtrai, indicating at the very least that they were sent to the region where it was claimed Warbeck originated.

This, therefore, was not intended as a solely English exercise in domestic propaganda, though the fact they survived suggests it wasn't necessarily anticipated it would be a private conversation either, but rather publicly consumed so that any doubt of Warbeck's background could be assuaged. This was not a letter that needed to be produced, the confession already serving Henry's purpose, and to send a contrived document to Tournai where it could be exposed as counterfeit does not tally with the pragmatic and cautious character of the English king.

The letter opens, 'Mother, as humbly as I may, I commend myself unto you,' before the presumed author, Warbeck, explains how 'certain Englishmen made me take upon myself that I was the son of the King Edward of England, called his second son, Richard Duke of York'. He continues anxiously:

> I now find myself in such trouble that if you are not in this hour my good mother, I am compelled to be in great danger and inconvenience, because of the name which, at their instance, I have taken upon myself and the enterprise which I have carried out.

The next paragraph was a conscious effort to convince Catherine, or whoever happened to cast their eyes upon a letter that was no doubt broadcast widely, that Warbeck was indeed her son by discussing intimate family details and referencing mundane memories that evoked a past now long gone:

> And so that you may understand and know clearly that I am your son and none other, may it please you to remember how, when I parted from you with Berlo to go Antwerp, you wept as you said 'God be with you,' and how my father went with me as far as the Porte de Marvis. And also the last letter you wrote to me at Middelburg by your hand, saying that you had been delivered of a daughter, and also that my brother Thiroyan and my sister Jehanne had died of the plague at the time of the procession of Tournai. And how my father, you and I were going to live at Lannoy outside the town; and you remember the beautiful pig-place.

Berlo was mentioned in the confession, as was the claim Warbeck went to Middelburg. It certainly seems plausible a mother would cry as she was separated from her young son, as does a father imparting some final wisdom whilst walking his son towards a new chapter in his life. These are precisely the type of personal and emotional recollections a son would remember for the rest of his life, regardless of where fortune happened to take him. That he recalled the distressing news of his siblings' deaths is certainly to be expected. The following paragraph discusses Henry VII's present attitude towards him, and does not quite seem complimentary, which is reason to again suggest the letter is genuine and written without the king's input:

> The King of England now holds me in his power, to whom I have declared the truth of the affair, very humbly imploring him that his pleasure may be to pardon me of the offence which I have done to him, since I am not his native subject at all, and what I did was at the instigation and wishes of his own subjects. But I have as yet received no good reply from him, nor have I hope of one, at which my heart is very sad. However, Mother, I beg and pray you to have pity upon me and purchase my deliverance.

Thereafter follows a roll call of names, some previously identified as Warbeck's relatives, not only from his confession but also previous investigations into his background: 'Commend me to my godfather Pierart Flan, to Master Jean Stalin my uncle, to my comrade Guillaume Rucq, and to Jehan Bordeau. I hear that my father has departed this life, God keep his soul, which is heavy news to me.'

Signing the letter Pierrequin Werbecque, there is a final, almost pitiful, plea for some funds to improve his surroundings: 'Mother, I pray you to send me a little money so that my guards may be kinder to me for my giving them something. Commend me to my Aunt Stalins, and to all my good neighbours.'

There are undoubted similarities between the letter and the confession, suggesting at the very least they were drafted from the same source of information, though whether that was Warbeck remains a matter of debate. Both have the mother named as Catherine, and both mention an uncle called Jean Stalin. The Tournai merchant Berlo also merits mention in both documents, charged with having taken young Perkin to Antwerp, with his removal on to Middelburg also included. Both documents agree that Warbeck assumed the mantle of a prince only at the behest of Englishmen, rather than through his own guileful initiative. The discretions are minor, though worthy of note: Peter Flamme in the confession is his step-grandfather, whilst the Pierrart Flan of the letter is his godfather, whereas Rucq and Bordeau are new names. In the confession, Warbeck mentions his father in the present tense, whilst in the letter he acknowledges his death. Again, it isn't implausible he learnt of the death in between the writing of both documents, or even spoke in the present tense in the manner of someone who had been away from home for many years and had yet been able to reconcile his mind to current events.

When considering the available evidence together, that is Warbeck's confession, the letter to his mother, and the inquiries made by the Spanish authorities of the Portuguese merchants, there are solid grounds to believe the man the English called Perkin Warbeck was indeed a son of Tournai and not a reborn prince of York. There are certainly discrepancies in each account and the motivations of those behind their publication can be questioned, but enough corroborates to give the story more than a degree of plausibility. To wilfully disregard this evidence as the invention of cunning Tudor officials to suppress Warbeck's true identity both domestically and internationally, whilst giving credence to the pretender's initial story he was simply allowed to leave captivity in the Tower of London because of a compassionate jailor, requires considerable faith, and in truth a rejection of logic.

With no conclusive proof as to the fate of the Princes in the Tower, it cannot be definitively denied that Warbeck was indeed Richard of York, 'raised from the dead' in the scornful words of Vergil, but assessing all currently known information, it is difficult not to accept that the pretender was a very capable imposter with determined backers driven by hatred of the Tudor king.

With Warbeck in captivity, his reputation in tatters, and the West Country suitably punished after several months of disobedience, Henry VII prepared for his return to London, though not before a colossal feast was enjoyed on 2 November, the king's last night in Exeter. Before he left, Henry also presented the city with a hefty ten-kilogram sword embellished with the royal arms, a lasting sign of his appreciation for their defence of his crown. That the king's granddaughter Elizabeth I later bestowed upon the city the motto *Semper Fidelis*, Always Faithful, was in part due to its fidelity during the tense tribulations of 1497.

Travelling back to London through towns such as Bridport, Dorchester, Blandford, Salisbury, Andover, Basingstoke and Windsor, along the route Vergil wrote, with some embellishment no doubt, that the king was greeted 'with the profoundest respect and affection, because with so rapid and fortunate a campaign he had disposed of a dangerous conspiracy and because he had brought back with him as a captive the leader of it'. Huge crowds congregated at the roadsides to catch a fleeting glimpse of Warbeck, 'for most accounted it miraculous that a man of such humble origins should have been bold enough to seek to acquire by guile so great a kingdom'.[61] This certainly sounds plausible; the people of England had heard many rumours about this man in previous years, whether positive or negative, and now they had a rare opportunity to see this so-called prince for themselves. He was a celebrity.

In 'triumphal style'[62] the royal household arrived in Sheen on 18 November, where the king rested for three days before moving on towards Cardinal Morton's episcopal palace at Lambeth. On 23 November, he made the short crossing of the Thames by barge to Westminster, where all the London guilds were assembled for his arrival in their liveries. Whilst Henry was roundly praised for his recent success, a chastened Warbeck was paraded around the Great Hall and openly mocked by those present. Some even swore at him, their faces contorted with rage, and there was little he could do.[63] It was abject humiliation. Four days later, Milanese ambassador Raimondi remarked that Warbeck was pointed out to him in one of Westminster's chambers, though 'he did not seem to care for us to speak to him'.[64] It appears there was little left for the fallen pretender to say, and, with no one coming forward to assume his cause, he was resigned to his fate.

The following day, 28 November, the pretender was forced to ride on horseback through the heart of London, along the tightly packed streets of Cheapside and Cornhill until he reached the Tower, the grand and imposing fortress which had formed the cornerstone of his alleged survival story. Following closely behind, dressed in a hermit's habit with his hands and feet bound, was the king's former sergeant furrier, who several years earlier had fled England to join Warbeck's side, a rash decision he no doubt lamented with every step he now took though the city. Upon reaching the Tower, the furrier was handed over to the guards, whilst his erstwhile master was herded back to Westminster, 'with many a curse' levelled at him from the maddened locals; it was a humiliating spectacle designed to further tarnish his reputation, though Ambassador Raimondi nevertheless respected the fact that Warbeck 'bears his fortune bravely'.[65] The furrier was hanged, drawn and quartered at Tyburn a week later, the price for supporting the pretender.

All things considered, however, it was the view of the Venetian ambassador Trevisano at the end of November 1497 that, in reference to Warbeck and Katherine Gordon, 'the King treats them well', even permitting them to live in his own palace, though prohibited from sleeping together.[66] It was a matter of routine that the pretender had to be publicly shamed to tarnish what credibility he had left amongst the English, but otherwise Henry proved magnanimous in victory. Warbeck was certainly not facing execution as perhaps expected, though whether that was by virtue of his foreign birth or to honour a pledge made on the king's behalf at Beaulieu is unclear.

This is perhaps the clearest indication of Henry VII's certainty that Warbeck was not Richard of York, for if there was any doubt in the king's mind that a legitimate rival to his throne yet lived, his death would have been arranged in some manner, underhanded or otherwise. For the same reason that Richard III is widely suspected of disposing of his nephews in 1483, the same principle applied to Henry in 1497 – to let a rival prince live was a dangerous decision that could backfire, if not in the short term then perhaps many years down the line. The Wars of the Roses themselves had, after all, occurred owing to latent claims to the throne coming to the fore. It should not be forgotten that by overturning *Titulus Regius*, the act Richard III passed which de-legitimised Elizabeth of York, in the event they had survived, Henry had also re-legitimised her brothers, Edward V and Richard of York. That Henry instead permitted Warbeck to exist around the royal court, though carefully monitored lest he show fresh signs of conspiracy, must be interpreted as the king's confidence he was naught but a calculating imposter.

Warbeck's arrest naturally drew reaction from abroad. From Brussels on 16 October, Philip, Duke of Burgundy, sent word to his father Maximilian I that 'monsieur d'York' had been captured by the English king, news which prompted the King of the Romans to urgently send a representative to London in November to negotiate the pretender's handover. It is unclear why Maximilian ever thought Henry would entertain the notion of returning Warbeck into the possession of the very man who was culpable for much of the turmoil in previous years, though as a backup he hoped someone in the English king's household could be convinced, for a generous sum of 10,000 gold florins, to facilitate an escape in some manner. Maximilian no doubt anticipated that if the case was put forward to return Perkin, now acknowledged to be a native of Tournai, there may have been a valid claim for repatriation. By referring to the pretender as 'of York', however, the mission proved unsurprisingly unproductive.[67] Henry was never going to give up his prize capture. Margaret of York, meanwhile, who had known Warbeck in a personal capacity regardless of whether she truly believed him to be her nephew Richard, 'wepte and lamented' the news from England of his capture.[68]

A rebellious summer having given way to a peaceable winter, in December Henry, his family and the royal household retired to Sheen for the Christmas period. It is uncertain if Warbeck was amongst those who travelled. On 18 December, Ambassador Raimondi updated the duke of Milan in a lengthy report about the English king's perpetual issues with the Scottish and French, before concluding more promisingly on domestic matters: 'There is nothing fresh in this kingdom and I do not believe that there will be while this sovereign lives.' It was his observation that Henry's court 'speak of nothing here but of making good cheer'.[69]

Perhaps the good cheer was excessively celebrated, for just five days later, around nine o'clock on the night of 23 December 1497, a fire which started in the royal chambers ravaged the royal palace, reducing Henry's favourite residence to little more than glowing embers, save for two large towers. Costly tapestries, beds, clothes and plate were lost in the flames, with the royal family barely fleeing the disaster alive. It was a shocking episode for all concerned, though not one that appears to have warranted any suspicion, with the well-informed Milanese ambassador asserting it was caused 'by accident and not by malice'.[70] With Henry's wife, mother and children present, if the cause of the fire was indeed arson, it would have been the most despicable of acts, one of the boldest in English royal history.

Whether through chance or choice, Henry VII was a survivor. He had faced repeated invasions from abroad, domestic conspiracies which tested the resolve of his household officers, and violent uprisings amongst his subjects. Even fire had tried to take the king's life, and yet he stubbornly endured. At Sheen, Henry intended to rebuild his palace 'much finer than before', and to rechristen it Richmond after the earldom he inherited from his father, Edmund Tudor. The new palace, conspicuously Tudor rather than Plantagenet, would serve as a pronounced symbol of his dynasty's insurmountable greatness – Henry was making a very visible point, one he hoped would last forever. The Tudors were here to stay.

16

Fresh Revolution

As a result of his capitulation at Beaulieu, Perkin Warbeck's 'reign' as Richard IV had been brought to a muted and bloodless conclusion before he had ever truly threatened to topple the Tudor regime from its gilded perch. Since first surfacing in the south of Ireland towards the end of 1491 and accepting the charge that he was a prince of York reborn, the pretender had promised much in subsequent years, at times securing the backing of some of the principal figures in European politics to embolden his mercurial cause. Six years later, however, and in the custody of the rival he once derided as 'our extreme and mortal enemy',[1] Warbeck's cause had ultimately proved a resounding disappointment.

Lauded as the legitimate Yorkist heir by a determined band of adherents in Cork, against his will according to his confession, Warbeck failed to convince the wider Irish nobility to rally to his banners, and though invited to France by a mischievous Charles VIII in the summer of 1492, had soon been forced to depart when the French king sought peace rather than war with his English counterpart so that he could focus on his Italian ambitions. Crossing the border into the Burgundian Netherlands, Warbeck did find his most steadfast support under the sponsorship and guidance of his alleged aunt Margaret of York, who readily provided shelter, connections and men, before political and economic realities compelled Philip of Burgundy and his father Maximilian I to intervene and restrict their patronage.

After his bold invasion of Kent was ferociously repelled by the locals whose defection he had counted on, Warbeck thereafter failed again to make headway in Ireland before seeking the aid of the war-hungry young Scottish king James IV, though when called upon to embark on another incursion into England, his courage failed him. With a third landing on Irish soil proving fruitless, Warbeck's last stand involved a sanguine expedition to Cornwall that witnessed him flee confrontation once more as the enemy approached, this time into sanctuary before shortly afterwards succumbing to Henry VII's authority. The pretender had boldly pledged for several years he would resurrect the House of York and return it to its rightful place upon the English throne, but as he was marched dejectedly out through the gatehouse of Beaulieu flanked by the royal guards of his adversary, knew he had failed to deliver on that promise.

His new reality as a captive of the English king was a demoralising readjustment for Warbeck, though in many ways it must have proved more bearable than anticipated for a broken rebel of the crown. Rather than being kept out of sight, Henry in fact permitted Warbeck to move freely around the royal court, 'at lyberte wyth many othir benefetis' as one London chronicler described,[2] with access to decent accommodation, an abundance of food and drink, and companionship or fresh air should it be sought. It is reasonable to suggest that the king used his own experience as a youth in Brittany as the blueprint for how a pretender should be treated – not quite allowed full freedom of movement around the city or beyond, but afforded far less restriction on everyday life than one might expect in the circumstances. The royal court was the political and cultural centre of the kingdom wherever it was based, and there would have been enough activity to keep Warbeck occupied, whether it was games, conversation, or feasting. Of course, he himself may have been the attraction to many.

Though presumably observed at all times by any number of guards assigned to him, Warbeck was certainly not kept under lock and key in some dreary chamber to be forgotten about as the months and years passed by. That was a disheartening existence reserved for Edward, Earl of Warwick, arguably the true living Yorkist heir, who remained concealed from public view nearly thirteen years into Tudor rule. If there is any one indication that Henry VII believed Warbeck and Simnel to be the imposters he claimed they were, then it is the stark difference between his treatment of them and his treatment of the unfortunate Warwick – confined deep in the Tower, out of sight and, some determined malcontents aside, out of mind.

It was not dissimilar to what Richard III had attempted with his two other royal nephews back in 1483, though Henry made sure that Warwick could be presented should the situation arise that his presence was required. Warwick, still aged just twenty-three in 1498, had been 'born to misery', Polydore Vergil rued years later, a blameless victim of the bitter turmoil that had engulfed England and torn the House of York apart when he had been little more than a blameless child, his enduring presence now an uncomfortable reality for Henry VII.[3]

During this period of his life, there is no surviving evidence that any meeting occurred between Warbeck and the woman he had claimed through his imposture to be his sister, the queen, Elizabeth of York, despite their existence in close proximity over several months at the end of 1497 and into 1498. Though many, then and now, credited Henry VII's claim to the throne to be through his wife's Yorkist lineage rather than his own modest pedigree, Elizabeth played little to no part in the governance of the dynasty she co-founded, being 'powerless' in the words of one ambassador.[4] It is unclear whether she was purposefully kept away from Warbeck or whether she herself exhibited little interest in him and did not pursue the matter. Their paths must have crossed at court, however briefly, but no comment from any observer exists to shed further light.

It must be considered that if Elizabeth was widely known to have met privately with the pretender, such an encounter would have raised questions within and without the royal household that there was some possibility she gave the rumours credence, for there was no reason for a queen to entertain the son of a Tournai boatman; conversely, she may just have accepted the unspoken assertion that her younger brothers had died in 1483 and focused her energies towards her future, one which centred around her children, Arthur, Margaret, Henry and Mary. From around May 1498, less than seven months after Warbeck's capture, the queen was also pregnant once more, which suggests relations between the royal couple had not been breached by the tribulations of the past year. As one half of what appears to have been a faithful and fruitful marriage, there is little reason to doubt Elizabeth simply accepted her husband's interpretation of events, as since their marriage his enemies were now also hers.

In April 1498, six months after his surrender, Warbeck left London to accompany Henry on a progress into Kent, the king keeping his prize prisoner close to the royal household for the journey. Henry's privy purse records even show a handful of payments relating to Warbeck were authorised during this period, with Robert Jones receiving £1 17s 1d to fund the pretender's horsemeat from the start of February to the end of April, and another of 13s 4d for his riding gown.[5]

The royal tour of Kent coincided with Easter, and on 20 April in Christ Church, Canterbury, near the shrine of Thomas Becket and the burial location of his own great-grandfather John Beaufort, 1st Earl of Somerset, through whom his claim to the throne originated, the king dedicated Warbeck's battle standard at the altar. The banner in question is likely one captured after the pretender's failed attempt to land at nearby Deal in July 1495, as suggested by the reward of £1 made that day to John Bowes of Hythe for bringing the item to the king.[6] This act may explain the true purpose of Warbeck's presence on the progress, and may have been intended as a somewhat sardonic act, for Henry had similarly presented his own standards at the altar after his triumphs at Bosworth and Stoke Field. Warbeck's failure prevented him from his own proud dedication, so now Henry did it on his behalf – with a smirk, one imagines.

It is likely Warbeck returned to London with the king in the first week of May to continue his low-key existence, but just over a month later, around midnight on 9 June 1498, he without warning accomplished as an adult of around twenty-four what he once claimed to have done as a child – he escaped the king of England's custody. In 'fforgetyng the goodnes and gracious dyspocicion of the kyng' by bolting from his chamber at Westminster Palace, possibly out of a window according to the intelligence of a Milanese agent in the city at the time, Warbeck triggered the final descent to his demise, and with it the end of his near-decade-long campaign to win a crown.[7]

Why Warbeck elected to abscond at this particular juncture, without any hope of success and for no discernible reason, remains shrouded by the mists of time. Vergil speculated it was because he either 'found it hard to endure confinement' or 'was instigated to a fresh revolution' by Margaret of York, hoping 'an occasion would present itself for furthering his affairs' once out of English hands.[8] Another suggestion is that the escape was facilitated by royal agents so that he could incriminate himself and provide the authorities with a valid reason to rid the king of his presence permanently.

The Margaret angle seems improbable as it is difficult to believe the dowager duchess was able to freely communicate with the pretender to the extent they could arrange an elaborate escape plan, whilst his confinement in general doesn't appear to have been that challenging, when one takes into consideration the reason he was in captivity in the first place. It is more likely that an opportunity presented itself that evening, and Warbeck, almost preconditioned since a child to the nomadic lifestyle, simply took advantage of the lapse in concentration by his guards.

Still in his early twenties, Perkin had walked upon French, Flemish, Portuguese, Irish and Scottish soil in the guise of a prince, as well as embarking on a celebrated excursion to Vienna a few years earlier to meet Maximilian I at the funeral of a Holy Roman Emperor. The prospect of a comfortable life in London, albeit under intense scrutiny, for the rest of his days likely frustrated the seasoned traveller within him, and as subsequent events show, he had no viable plan in mind when he fled Westminster Palace under the cover of darkness. As Vergil suggested, Warbeck 'could not but be aware that nearly everything he did, planned or thought, not only came to Henry's ears but was openly known to the king' – the idea his flight was anything but spontaneous doesn't stand to reason.[9]

When Warbeck's escape was known there 'was made grete serch',[10] with the king's sea captain Steven Bull and someone named Barnesdeld urgently charged with 'seking for Perkyn'. Another figure by the name of Bradshaw was paid 13*s* 4*d* 'riding for Perkyn', with further payments authorised to four yeomen to keep watch along the Thames by boat.[11] Henry's reaction suggests he had not been expecting the escape, with directives immediately sent to the great ports of Boston, Grimsby, King's Lynn, Ipswich, Southampton, Dover, Hastings and Bristol to be alert for any sign of Warbeck's presence in coming days. The abbot of Beaulieu was also notified should this pretender return,[12] with a letter sent to the earl of Oxford the following day, 10 June, criticising his royal guards for their negligence. The king was hopeful for his recapture, so he could be punished:

> Thorow the folly and simpleness of such as we put in truste to keepe Perkin Warbecke, he is escaped from them, and albeit it is no great force where he be come, yet to the intent he might be punished after his deserte, we would gladlie have him againe. Wherefore cousyn we will and desyre you to cause good and sure serche to be made for him with all diligence all alonge our ports, creeks, and passages in those partes about you, that he in noe wyse passe those waies.[13]

To facilitate his recapture, Henry also pledged a reward of one hundred pounds to the man who apprehended Warbeck, which, despite the gravity of the situation, was noticeably less than the thousand which had been offered a year earlier. If the escape was abetted by royal double agents, as some Venetian merchants speculated,[14] it seems an unnecessary gamble by Henry to permit Warbeck's flight and then put trust in his men to recapture him before he slipped out of the kingdom.

If they were to fail in this duty, then 'Richard IV' would surely have simply resumed his campaign anew rather than disappear into obscurity. Aside from cards and dice, Henry was not a man inclined to gamble when the stakes were so high.

Despite his energetic response, the king had little cause for concern. With the roads teeming with royal guards, houses frantically searched, and boats patrolling the river for any sign of life in the water, a 'terror-stricken' Warbeck barely made it seven miles from his chamber at Westminster Palace, only venturing as far as the grandly named House of Jesus of Bethlehem, a Carthusian priory in Sheen that had been founded by Henry V in 1414.[15]

The priory was home to a small community of around thirty hermits who lived together yet in solitude, each occupying a compact cell arranged around a central cloister. These private servants of God were hardly expecting a royal prisoner to disturb their tranquil and contemplative existence in the early hours of a June morning, and as with much regarding Warbeck, it is uncertain why he ended up at Sheen. He may, for example, have been aware that Edward IV, the man he had once claimed to have been his father, had confirmed the priory's charter in 1461 with the condition they pray for the souls of the Yorkist king and his ancestors and hoped to count on some sympathetic support.[16] Perhaps more likely is the fact that Sheen may simply have been as far as he could get without being caught. He had no plan, no connections, and no chance of evading recapture.

Warbeck could not have failed to realise the priory was less than half a mile from Henry VII's favourite palace, currently in the process of being rebuilt after the recent fire, and he may have known the prior was on friendly terms with the king. There is a suggestion he may even have regretted his rash flight, for according to Vergil when he arrived at Sheen, Warbeck 'threw himself on the mercy of the prior of the house demanding with prayers that the prior should go to the king and intercede to preserve his life'. This 'worthy priest' was moved by Warbeck's piteous appeal and travelled personally to Westminster to seek an audience with Henry, 'in whoos ffavour he stood gretly', during which he 'prayed humbly' on the pretender's behalf that he be spared once more.[17]

For the second time in seven months, Henry decreed that Warbeck would not be killed if he peacefully surrendered, though the understanding by all parties was that his days of liberal movement around court were unsurprisingly at an end. When Spanish ambassador de Puebla updated Ferdinand and Isabella of the latest turmoil in

England, he was of the opinion that Warbeck had escaped 'without any reason', and though he had yet to determine what would become of the pretender, he speculated that 'he will either be executed, or kept, with great vigilance, in prison'.[18]

It was prison rather than execution that awaited Warbeck for his escape, but first, as Henry had expressed in his letter to the earl of Oxford, the absconder was to be publicly punished for abusing the king's leniency and having the audacity to flee. Within the courtyard of Westminster Palace on the morning of 15 June, just six days after his flight, Warbeck was placed into a set of wooden stocks which had been positioned atop a scaffold hastily constructed from empty wine barrels. Unable to move for several hours under the midsummer sun, and 'now despised more by everyone for this treacherous flight', he had to quietly endure the acerbic taunts of the crowds which assembled below him.[19]

A few days after this embarrassment, Warbeck was taken to Cheapside in London, and again placed in the stocks from ten o'clock in the morning until three in the afternoon, prompting a local chronicler to remark how 'he was excedyngly wondred upon'.[20] Henry may have pledged to spare Warbeck's life, but he would not spare him a public shaming in front of first the royal court and then the commoners of London. Once released, the weary pretender was led to the Tower in disgrace 'and there lafft as prysoner'.[21]

Left as a prisoner he certainly was. On 17 July, Ambassador de Puebla wrote to Spain advising that Warbeck was 'now secured in such a manner, and in such a prison, that, with the help of God, he will never be able to play such a trick again'.[22] He would be temporarily removed at the start of August, when Henri de Berghes, Bishop of Cambrai, arrived in England as part of a four-man Burgundian delegation to meet with the king to discuss commercial matters. After Warbeck's recapture, the king had embarked on another extensive progress, this time around East Anglia, and he met with Bishop Berghes during a five-day stay at Hedingham Castle, the family seat of the earl of Oxford that was particularly noted for its imposing seventy-foot stone keep.

It wasn't a straightforward conference between the two parties. Though England and Burgundy had ratified a wide-ranging treaty more than two years earlier, the so-called *Intercursus Magnus*, there were still some difficulties in implementing some of the articles agreed, and the bishop struggled to make headway with the English representatives. Unsure how to break the deadlock, Berghes sought the intervention of de Puebla, but when the Spaniard approached the king, Henry grew agitated, 'and the things he said were by no means sweet'. The king, it would appear, was losing patience with the world around him.

Berghes, however, whom de Puebla praised on account of his 'very respectable and noble personage' and 'most truthful' nature, had other things on his mind than just economic issues, important though they may have been. He requested, and was granted, a meeting with Warbeck, whom he knew from the pretender's time at the court of Margaret of York. Perkin was roused from his chamber in the Tower of London and brought into the presence of the king and the bishop, with events once more keenly observed by the attentive Spanish ambassador, who as usual filed an extensive report to his masters.[23]

The bishop confronted Warbeck and demanded to know why he had imprudently deceived the Burgundian duke and his subjects, to which the pretender solemnly swore to God that Margaret of York 'knew as well as himself that he was not the son of King Edward'. At this moment Henry VII interceded to add that Perkin 'had deceived the Pope, the King of France, the Archduke, the King of the Romans, the King of Scotland, and almost all Princes of Christendom', save for those of Spain, whom the English king credited for remaining wary of the plot from the outset.

De Puebla, who had encountered Warbeck on several occasions during his tenure around the English court, did note 'how much altered Perkin was' during this particular summit. There was no elaboration on the comment, and it is difficult to judge whether this alteration was because of a loss of weight, physical abuse, or perhaps an understandable change in disposition, though de Puebla did believe Warbeck was 'so much changed that I, and all other persons here, believe his life will be very short'. The Spaniard nonetheless added unsympathetically, 'He must pay for what he has done.'

In the days prior to 7 September, when de Puebla updated his Spanish masters with the latest developments,[24] a remarkable letter from Margaret of York arrived at the English court addressed to the king. Though the dowager duchess had waged a relentless campaign against the Tudor monarch since the moment he had wrested the crown from her brother Richard III at Bosworth, earning a rebuke from Henry on account of the 'great malice' she had shown towards him,[25] Margaret now sought a pardon for her behaviour whilst pledging in future her obedience to his rule.

No matter how reluctantly this request must have been made, Margaret's volte-face, like all those other rulers before her who had gradually turned away from Warbeck, was politically and personally expedient; she must have received word of his pitiful state and broken spirit from Bishop Berghes, whilst Henry was exerting intense pressure on Duke Philip to deprive her of her dower lands as per the terms of the Anglo-Burgundian treaty, which she hoped to avoid by showing contrition. The letter not only served as a tacit acceptance of Tudor kingship from this defiant daughter of York, but also indicated that Perkin Warbeck's campaign was, in truth, over.

*

'For once,' mused Polydore Vergil after the events of the 1498 summer, 'the condition of the kingdom was more peaceable,'[26] and this may have prompted Henry to prolong his tour around East Anglia and on to Northamptonshire and Oxfordshire in the months that followed. According to one Milanese agent in England at the time, Agostino de Spinula, it was an expedition full of 'hunting and pleasure', during the which the king 'seems in great peace of mind'.[27] This remark is likely to have had some level of truth. The imprisonment of Warbeck, with no prospect of escape, and news his queen was pregnant once more must have been a colossal weight off Henry's shoulders after recent pressures, and during his time in the fresh air, surrounded by miles of lush green countryside and with his closest companions in tow, he is certain to have rejoiced in the rare serenity.

From Hedingham Castle in the middle of August the royal household continued on to Norwich and afterwards Blickling, where the king stayed overnight in the company of the Boleyn family. Unbeknownst to all present that evening, the Boleyns would within a generation become irretrievably linked with the Tudors for the next five hundred years, though such a prosperous future of course must have seemed inconceivable to the king's young host, Sir Thomas Boleyn, during that evening's festivities. From Blickling, Henry travelled to Walsingham where on 23 August he made his devotions at the Shrine of Our Lady, and from there passed through King's Lynn and Peterborough.

On 7 September, the king paid a brief visit to the Collyweston home of his 'enterely wilbeloved' and 'most lovyng moder', Lady Margaret, which gave him the rare opportunity to unload his innermost thoughts to someone whose loyalty could never be doubted.[28] Huntingdon, Harrowden, Northampton and Banbury were also treated to his royal presence before Henry reached Woodstock on 20 September, the first time he had returned since leaving a year earlier at the head of an army to confront Warbeck. The king did not arrive back in Westminster until the end of November 1498.[29]

Great peace of mind and a pleasant peregrination around part of his kingdom notwithstanding, that recent years had started to take their toll on the forty-one-year-old Henry is evident from Pedro de Ayala's comment that summer that 'the king looks old for his years, but young for the sorrowful life he has led'.[30] As the fifteenth century drew to its close, the pressures of wearing the English crown were proving relentless.

Even whilst on progress, matters of state and family, often entwined and rarely separate for a king, demanded Henry's attention. Though full-scale war with Scotland had been averted due to the Treaty of Ayton, lasting friendship had been difficult to achieve because, as de Ayala observed, 'the old enmity is so great' between the two kingdoms. To try and counteract this ancient rivalry, during the summer the Spanish monarchs had counselled the English king to seek a marital union with his Scottish counterpart, 'necessary for the preservation of peace'.[31] Henry's initial reaction was hesitant, partly on account of the objections of his wife and mother:

> I am really sorry that I have not a daughter or a sister for him; for I have loved him most sincerely since the conclusion of the peace; not to mention that he is my relative. He has behaved very well towards me. I wish to see him as prosperous as myself. But I have already told you, more than once, that a marriage between him and my daughter has many inconveniences. She has not yet completed the ninth year of her age, and is so delicate and weak that she must be married much later than other young ladies. Thus it would be necessary to wait at least another nine years. Besides my own doubts, the Queen and my mother are very much against this marriage. They say if the marriage were concluded we should be obliged to send the Princess directly to Scotland, in which case they fear the King of Scots would not wait, but injure her, and endanger her health.[32]

Though Ayala agreed Princess Margaret was 'very young, and very small for her years', political reality often guided the mind of the medieval king, and by September Henry VII sent his trusty representative Bishop Foxe back north of the border to commence negotiations. The king did so despite protests not just from the leading females of his family, but also some of his subjects who, Ayala noted, jealously begrudged their princess being wed to a Scottish king, for such an honour was supposedly beneath an Englishwoman. The last daughter of an English monarch who travelled north for marriage had been Joan, daughter of Edward II, nearly 170 years earlier, and that union had proven a failure, dynastically and personally. The Welsh-born and Breton-raised Henry VII, however, waved away such criticism, as, 'being more intelligent, and not a pure Englishman' he did not 'share this jealousy'. By November, Milanese ambassador Raimondi confirmed 'that some negotiation is on foot' for the wedding, though it would take five more years to come to fruition, somewhat appeasing the doubters.[33]

Henry spent the final days of 1498 and the first fortnight of 1499 in the London townhouse of Oliver King, the elderly bishop of Bath and Wells, rather than at one of his own residences nearby such as Westminster or Greenwich.[34] King was a sage veteran of the fifteenth-century political scene, starting his rise in the church early in the reign of Edward IV before fulfilling several roles in the Yorkist administration, including as clerk of the signet, French secretary, and in 1480 as the king's secretary, in effect overseeing the monarch's personal correspondence for the final three years of the reign. When Richard III ascended the throne in the summer of 1483, King was replaced and like many former adherents of Edward IV transferred his allegiance to the Tudor faction, for which he was amply rewarded post-Bosworth, reclaiming his post as king's secretary and rising higher in the Church, first as bishop of Exeter and then of Bath and Wells.[35]

There are no reasons given in the records why Henry stayed with King, nor what discussion passed between the men during these winter weeks, but just a year later the bishop commenced an extensive restoration programme at Bath Abbey, which would later be adorned with a statue of the Tudor monarch above the Great West Door. Perhaps an indication of royal patronage is the fact that two master masons involved in the project, William and Robert Vertue, were the king's own sculptors, who would later work on his mausoleum in Westminster. In a letter Bishop King sent to Reginald Bray, Henry's chancellor of the Duchy of Lancaster and highly regarded confidant, the churchman even claimed that the Vertues promised him that once they had completed their work 'ther shal be noone so goodely neither in England nor in France'.[36]

Though a well-known tale would later assert King conceived the project in a dream, there seems no reason to doubt that it was Henry himself who persuaded his bishop during his extended visit to the latter's London townhouse. The finished article would, after all, serve as a dramatic visual indication of Tudor prosperity in a region which had so recently proven hostile to his rule. The people of the south-west would not need to travel to the distant capital to behold Henry's magnificence; he brought it to them.

The final year of the fifteenth century marked the end of a turbulent era in English history, and it would not have gone unnoticed it was exactly one hundred years since the House of Lancaster first ascended the throne under Henry IV, a contentious usurpation with far-reaching consequences that had violently divided the kingdom for several generations afterwards. Henry VII was still wrestling with what he hoped were the last vestiges of the bitter fallout from that usurpation, and when word reached him that yet another pretender had emerged from the shadows to lay claim to the throne, the king's exasperated sigh must have been heard throughout the court.

To Henry's relief, on this occasion there would no hard-won battles on blood-soaked English soil, or a protracted saga played out across the European stage to contend with. The third pretender to rise against the Tudor king was suppressed with such swiftness that his name, unlike that of Lambert Simnel or Perkin Warbeck, was quickly forgotten, not even meriting mention in several chronicles of the period, and only revealed as Rauf, or Ralph, Wilford by Edward Hall half a century later.[37] Polydore Vergil merely referred to him as 'some lad', whereas in other sources he is simply the 'maumet', or puppet.[38]

According to the contemporary *Great Chronicle*,[39] it was in early February 1499 this nineteen- or twenty-year-old son of a London cordwainer first started claiming that he was Edward, Earl of Warwick, spreading the word along the Norfolk–Suffolk border. It is uncertain how Wilford explained away his apparent freedom to anyone who happened to listen, with Warwick widely known to be imprisoned in the Tower, but it is clear that unlike Simnel and Warbeck before him this third pretender to surface in a dozen years failed to cultivate any significant following. Vergil suggested Wilford tried in vain to rouse the people of Kent with his 'absurd fabrication'[40] and for once the meddling of Margaret of York was noticeably absent from this episode – she may very well have known nothing about the plot until it was over.

Vergil instead understood that the impetus behind this latest conspiracy was a bold Augustinian friar named Patrick, who, the Italian reported, was able to persuade Wilford to impersonate Warwick with the promise that 'many of the nobles would support him and make him king', an alluring prospect for a gullible shoemaker's son.[41] The *Great Chronicle*, on the other hand, suggests the youth himself was sorely to blame, for when he was taken and brought before John de Vere, Earl of Oxford, to answer for his crime, Wilford readily confessed that whilst he had been at school in Cambridge, he was stirred in his sleep to assume the captive earl's identity so that he could 'in processe opteyn such powar that he shuld be kyng'.[42] His father, Wilford admitted to Oxford, was not the duke of Clarence, but rather just a tradesman who dwelt in the Black Bull Inn on Bishopsgate Street. That the black bull was a badge once borne by Clarence may or may not have been a coincidence.

Back in 1487, Henry had dealt magnanimously with Lambert Simnel when he was captured, which, though a concession to the boy's tender age, also suggested a good-humoured king still relaxed with the world around him. Even a decade later, when the king got his hands on the adult Perkin Warbeck, there is little evidence the king acted in the vindictive manner that would become a characteristic of his son Henry VIII. Whilst Warbeck had been paraded through London and mocked around court, Henry VII nevertheless granted the fallen pretender his life and permitted him to live in relative comfort until his brief escape. Even then, Warbeck was not sent to the block.

Wilford in 1499 was a different matter, and his unanticipated emergence may have proved the final straw for Henry's patience, weary of fending off rivals for a crown he had now worn for fourteen years. After a brief audience with the king, unrecorded by commentators unlike Warbeck's interview, the youth was sentenced to execution. On 12 February, perhaps not uncoincidentally Shrove Tuesday, a day of absolution, Wilford was hanged wearing just his shirt at St Thomas-a-Watering, south of the city. The body was left in situ for the next four days, visible to anyone using the principal route between London and Canterbury, before it was cut down and buried hurriedly in an unknown location. Wilford's crusade, if it can even be called such, lasted barely a fortnight. He accomplished little personally other than the reward of a brutal death in front of few witnesses, but his foolishness would trigger the bloodshed that was to follow later in the year.[43]

Henry's stress during this latest tiresome affair was hardly eased by the fact his thirty-three-year-old wife Elizabeth was approaching the final days of her sixth pregnancy, three years since the couple's last child, Princess Mary, had been born. The chosen location for what was anticipated to be a risky birth on account of the queen's age was

Greenwich, with the king basing himself at the palace from the first week of February, Elizabeth having been stationed there for several weeks in preparation.[44]

The birth proved difficult, as expected, with 'much fear that the life of the Queen would be in danger', although a healthy prince was born around 22 February with little harm to the mother. The christening took place two days later as Elizabeth recovered, and was considered a 'very splendid' affair that involved a font specially transported from Canterbury at the king's request. Named Edmund in honour of his paternal Tudor grandfather, the Spanish ambassador noted that the festivities were of such grandness it was 'as though an heir to the Crown had been born' – not for the first or last time in his reign, Henry was using his wealth to send a message to his detractors.[45]

The suppression of another pretender and the birth of a sixth child likely motivated the king to seek some reassurance about what the future entailed for himself and his growing dynasty, and this anxiety may account for his enlisting the services of a seer just weeks later. Henry had form in this area; during his march through Wales to challenge Richard III for the crown, he allegedly canvassed a Welsh soothsayer named Dafydd Llwyd about his prospects in battle, gaining confidence for the task ahead when a victory was foretold.[46]

This particular seer, however, who according to de Puebla had prophesied the early deaths of Edward IV and Richard III, told the present king that his life would be in great danger for the remainder of the year because of a hostile faction which operated in the shadows, one which refused to be reconciled to his rule. This was hardly a revelation to a king who had been beset by plots throughout his reign, but nevertheless the words were hardly the comfort he had sought. It is little surprise the Spanish ambassador remarked that same month that Henry 'has aged so much during the last two weeks that he seems to be twenty years older'.[47]

The most significant event that took place in the first half of 1499, however, and which would also play an integral role in triggering the aforementioned bloodshed before the year was out, was that which occurred at Tickenhall Manor in Worcestershire on the morning of 19 May. The king's eldest son, Arthur, the Prince of Wales in whom he placed all his hopes, was married by proxy to Katherine of Aragon, securing the highly sought-after union of the House of Tudor with that of Trastámara. This Spanish alliance had long been crucial to Henry's ambitious vision for the prosperity of his dynasty, and he anticipated it would help sustain his bloodline upon the English throne for generations to come – there was no greater endorsement of Tudor kingship than such an intimate match with Spain.

Standing proxy for Katherine was de Puebla, who at nine o'clock on the designated morning joined Arthur and the senior members of the prince's household in Tickenhall's chapel. Once everyone had assumed their places, John Arundel, Bishop of Coventry and Lichfield, announced in a clear voice to the prince that it was well known his father Henry greatly desired this marriage between Arthur and Katherine to take place, and that de Puebla had been personally authorised by the Spanish princess to perform the necessary rituals in her name. Arthur responded keenly that he 'very much rejoiced' in pressing ahead with the union, not only out of obedience to the pope or his father, but also 'from his deep and sincere love' for his wife-to-be, whom he had nevertheless yet to meet in person.

With his right hand, the prince took the right hand of de Puebla and with his left joined hands with his chamberlain Richard Peel. He declared to all the witnesses present that he accepted the ambassador in place of Katherine, whom he would now forthwith consider his lawful and undoubted wife. The same ritual was repeated in reverse, with de Puebla accepting Arthur as the husband of Katherine, as she had empowered him to do on her behalf.[48]

That Henry was pleased with the marriage is evident from a comment he made to de Puebla when their paths later crossed, saying both he and his queen were 'more satisfied with this marriage than they would have been with any great dominions they might have gained with the daughter of another Prince'. The union had always been a matter of prestige for Henry, rather than one of material gain, an opportunity to raise his dynasty to heights no English king had accomplished through marriage since Henry V had wed Katherine de Valois nearly eighty years earlier. Ferdinand of Aragon, for his part, wrote that he too was glad of the match, for the English king was 'so valiant and virtuous', with Arthur showing promise that he would prove 'so worthy a son'.[49] Everyone, it seems, was happy.

Though de Puebla speculated that 'many of the intrigues which have hitherto been carried on [would] now cease',[50] the assurance of their ambassador was not enough of a guarantee for Ferdinand and Isabella to hand over their precious daughter to the English just yet. It was their desire, or rather demand, that nothing and indeed nobody could bring harm to their beloved daughter once she arrived in England to assume her new life as princess of Wales. It had been stipulated during the negotiations that the *infanta* would only sail for her new home once Arthur reached the age of fourteen in September 1500, but for this to occur, Henry was tasked with safeguarding her position by terminating any and all potential threats which could disrupt the Tudor–Trastámara union. The Spanish intended for Katherine to one day sit next to the English throne as Arthur's queen, and wished for nothing to obstruct this aspiration.

Henry's choice was not a palatable one, but his hand was forced not just by the Wilford affair, but fresh plotting in London; for the preservation of the Spanish alliance through which it was anticipated the Tudor dynasty's supremacy would become unassailable, two young men in the Tower, not for the first time in living memory, had to die.

17

A Stranger Born

Prior to their brief encounters with one another in what would prove the final few months of their lives, Perkin Warbeck and Edward, Earl of Warwick, were not known to each other in any personal capacity before the summer of 1499. When Warbeck was thrown into the Tower after his recapture and left to be forgotten, a miserable existence that had been Warwick's lot from the outset of Henry VII's reign, the pair were essentially strangers who nevertheless retained, and indeed shared in some cases, support from a hardcore affinity of Yorkist loyalists who defiantly refused to submit to Tudor authority. Now incarcerated within the same fortress with little prospect of future release, the lives of the two young men slowly became entwined. It would have devastating consequences.

Henry's fourteen-year reign thus far had been peppered with plots of varying severity, and despite having Warbeck and Warwick, the two most salient threats to his crown, in his custody, the summer of 1499 witnessed one final conspiracy centred around the two, for which detailed court records survive, having been suppressed for several centuries within a leather pouch known as *Baga de Secretis*.[1] According to those documents, the driving force behind this latest scheme was Thomas Astwood, a veteran of the William Stanley intrigue four years earlier and who had only escaped execution on that occasion owing to his youth. As Henry was shortly to discover, his leniency in sparing Astwood a traitor's death had been misguided.

Despite his last-minute reprieve from execution, Astwood failed to reconcile himself to the Tudor monarchy, and may have grown further alienated thereafter due to the financial woes incurred as a result of his costly pardon. By February 1498, Astwood was once more conspiring against the king when he was one of three men, the others being a haberdasher named John Finch and a gentleman servant of Warwick's, Robert Cleymond, who met in Finch's Honey Lane house. During their rendezvous, the host revealed to his guests that he knew of a prophecy which foretold that a bear would one day shake his chains in the streets of London. That the bear was a well-known symbol associated with successive earls of Warwick required little interpretation by those present.

Finch advised Cleymond to let the present earl know as soon as was convenient that the battle cry 'A Warwick! A Warwick!' would soon ring out once more in the streets around the Tower. In the meantime, to raise the prisoner's spirits, he also handed over two pairs of gloves and a pot of spice that should be conveyed to Warwick to use until his freedom could be arranged. With this shadowy meeting in an obscure London lane concluded, the seeds of one more conspiracy against Henry VII, in the name of Warwick, were sown. It was a fresh plot that would also draw into its heart Perkin Warbeck.

Astwood bided his time for several months until, on 10 July 1498, through the agency of a yeoman named John Williams, he was brought into the presence of the earl of Warwick for the first time. According to the indictment later formed against him, Astwood was introduced to the earl by Williams as someone who 'loves you well' and who had 'lately escaped a great danger, for he was to have lost his head', a none-too-subtle reference to past intrigue. Williams assured Warwick that 'you may be sure of me and of Thomas Astwode at all times', to which the naïve earl responded, 'Now, I have a special friend.'

As someone whose dealings with the world outside the Tower had been limited throughout his life, it may be suggested Warwick had developed a gullible nature during his years in captivity, devoid of critical thought, and was perhaps impressionable and susceptible to the blandishments of guests bearing kind words and friendly smiles. Before leaving, Astwood approached the earl and declared passionately, 'My Lord, I love you, and I will place myself in as great peril as I ever was in before to do you good help to put you in your right.'

With Warbeck's recent flight from Westminster heightening tension around the royal court in the summer of 1498, Astwood maintained a low profile over the next year whilst things quietened down before moving forward with the conspiracy. The plan was simply to 'deprive the King of his royal power and set up Edward Earl of Warwick as king' whilst endeavouring to 'destroy the King, his Lords, and his great men'.

Astwood resurfaced on 2 June 1499 when he approached a yeoman named Thomas Pounte seeking a couple of 'good fellows of gentle condition' to aid him for a purpose he wasn't willing to divulge at that moment. On 20 June, he met with an Essex chaplain called William Walker who advised him that 'a certain gentlemen' had found out that preparations for the king's latest summer progress were underway, with plans to visit Winchester and the south coast. Due to the magnitude of a royal peregrination, the itinerary and each of the proposed stops had to be known in advance to ensure accommodation, food and entertainment were catered for, and that sensitive information now found its way to Astwood's ear through Walker. The chaplain also declared confidently the king 'would never return to London alive', a prediction which proved 'a great comfort and joy' to Astwood and his accomplices.

On 12 July, a draper named Edward Dixon entered the conspiracy when he met with a broker called Edmund Carre near St Mary Woolnoth's church on London's Lombard Street, claiming he and a handful of others were preparing to snatch Warwick and Warbeck out of the Tower 'and set them at large'. It was a mission for which Dixon claimed 'divers servants' working inside the fortress were prepared to help. Carre was persuaded by the proposal, and pledged his support to the cause, swearing upon a book to be 'true and secret'.

The plot accelerated at the start of August when Astwood probably discovered from his contact Walker that the king had reached as far as Southampton and Beaulieu on his progress, with plans to shortly leave the English mainland for an extended visit to the Isle of Wight.[2] Any news to or from London would be delayed not just by the distance from the city by land, around eighty miles, but also the crossing of the Solent. It was the opportunity Astwood and his fellow conspirators had patiently awaited for more than a year.

2 August proved a crucial day for the conspirators. On that day figures such as William Lounde, Perkin Warbeck's erstwhile chancellor and chaplain, Thomas Strangeways, Thomas Longford, William Basset, Thomas Ody, and a haberdasher named William Proud were drawn into the plot, as it seems was Warbeck himself. Lounde informed Strangeways that the last time he had seen Warbeck before his capture he had cut some aglets from the end of his hood laces and given them to the pretender. He now repeated the act, imploring Strangeways to pass the aglets, small metallic tubes, on to Longford, who was in personal contact with the prisoner. He also handed Astwood that same afternoon a golden coin he had bent with his teeth, and by these two

tokens from a source Warbeck trusted, he would know to put his faith in the conspiracy.

Basset meanwhile approached Pounte to ask if he would help Warbeck and Warwick escape the Tower, to which Pounte responded, for reasons not expanded upon, that he was only prepared to help the earl. When Pounte probed what they would do in the event the pair were successfully freed from the Tower, Basset explained, 'I will provide for them a ship, which William Proude and Edward Dyxson will help to get filled with woollen cloths and the Earl will cross the sea in that ship.' Such an act would take him outside Henry VII's control, and hope was that a force could be assembled to return one day. Thomas Ody also proved eager to pledge his support, desperately confessing to Astwood, 'By the mass, I am in want of money and I care not what to do, either to fight or to rob in order to have money.' He hoped they would achieve success for 'then money would be current, and it is not now'. It seems financial reward, not dynastic revolution, was the motivation for at least one of the rebels.

The conspiracy continued to develop quickly. A clerk named John Walsh also approached Astwood to ask about Warbeck's wellbeing in yet another clandestine meeting, speculating that if they had been in Ireland he would have resumed rumours of Warbeck's Yorkist pedigree, for he was personally certain the pretender was 'the second son of King Edward IV'. It was a disparate crew, some seeming to favour Warwick over Warbeck and vice versa, but all agreed that either was a preferential option upon the English throne considering the person who now occupied that position.

The indictment passed against Warwick suggests he was kept informed of proceedings by Cleymond, who stayed with him each night in his chamber. It is likely through Cleymond's influence that the earl was reported to have knocked on the floor of his room to encourage Warbeck, who was stationed below, to 'be of good cheer and comfort'. This is the first known contact between the two. A shadowy Flemish clerk known only as Jacques also entered the intrigue at this stage, pressing a letter into Warbeck's hands with Cleymond's help, the contents of which are frustratingly unknown. The temptation is to suggest some connection between Margaret of York and the plot, but this would be pure speculation based on little more than the clerk's nationality, which may or may not have been a coincidence.

Though a servant of Warwick's, Cleymond was permitted some degree of movement around the Tower for he was able to meet with Warbeck in the latter's chamber, revealing further details of the plan and how he would escape his prison. After listening to the particulars, Warbeck's advice was that Cleymond and his accomplices should seize control of the Tower by 'subtlety or craft', perhaps using the stocks of gunpowder to create a series of fires that would serve as a distraction to allow them to slaughter the constable's men. When Cleymond relayed this to Warwick later that night, the innocent earl did not comprehend for what reason they would commit such an act, with his servant having to explain, perhaps not for the first time, that his friends intended to break him out of the Tower. They would stop only to loot Henry's treasury and seize as much money, plate and jewels as they could carry before fleeing overseas in Basset's boat. Cleymond encouraged the earl:

> My Lord you are well minded in what danger, sadness, and duress you here remain; but if you will help yourself according to the form and effect of the communication and discourse between us, you shall come out of this prison with me, I will take you out of danger, and leave you in surety.

Warwick gave his assent for the plan to go ahead, and in doing so committed treason without perhaps fully understanding the consequences of what he was agreeing to. Cleymond even provided the earl with a hanger, or short sword, with which to defend himself if called upon to do so; despite the House of York's proud military record, it is unlikely this particular scion had ever received martial training of any kind.

Two days later, 4 August, was another day of frenzied activity. Though the details are vague, according to the indictment Warwick bored a hole through the floor of his chamber, opening a direct line of communication with Warbeck in the room below. The earl reportedly greeted his fellow prisoner, 'How goes it with you?' before once more instructing him to 'be of good cheer', advice that was repeated in another letter from the Flemish clerk Jacques. That Warbeck required repeated motivation to keep his spirits up suggests the pretender had grown increasingly despondent, depression perhaps taking hold after a year in captivity and which now prompted him to break free, despite the risk of capture and execution. One wonders what other unreported conversation passed between the pair, Warbeck and Warwick, during their long hours locked in their chambers.

Yet another conspirator, Walter Bluet, entered Warbeck's chamber on this day to hand him a file to cut through the iron bars on his window, and a hammer to break the chains that bound him. Longford also arrived to provide some white thread that could be used to receive letters through the window, with Astwood delivering a book of prognostication to further raise his morale. Astwood also took precautions to arrange for a fake shackle to be fashioned for Warbeck to wear so that any guards checking in would not be aware of anything untoward. John Audley, brother of the lord executed for his part in the Cornish uprising two years earlier, was another who came forward to offer assistance, receiving from Warbeck a coded book, whilst Finch arranged for a 'certain roll of prophecy' to be handed to Warwick for him to read, one which no doubt was intended to encourage him to lay claim to the throne. Astwood, Carre, Proude, and Dixon, meanwhile, met with Thomas Masborough, a former bowyer of Edward IV, near St Mary Woolnoth church to discuss the conspiracy further, with all taking the opportunity to swear they would be 'true and secret to their fellowship'.

True and secret though the principal plotters pledged to be, and despite his integral role in the conspiracy thus far, Cleymond lost faith later that same day and abruptly advised Warwick that their plans had been revealed to the king's council. He suspected Warbeck was the source of betrayal. Fearing arrest, Cleymond anxiously left the earl's side and started making his way towards sanctuary in Colchester, though en route he encountered fellow conspirator Thomas Warde, who persuaded him to head for Westminster instead, where he could at least remain in close contact with the plot as it unfolded. It is unknown just what had spooked Cleymond.

Further intrigue took place three weeks later on 24 August when John Finch hosted another meeting at his Honey Lane house to discuss prophecies, for which Warde was present along with a Dr Alcock. Cleymond also must have been present at some stage, despite his earlier panic, for he passed to Finch a token from the earl – a piece of linen cloth on which was painted the image of St Mary. Finch reiterated his prediction that they would all shortly see Warwick crowned king of England. Astwood was also involved in the exchange of tokens that day, passing to Cleymond a picture of a cross painted on parchment to be taken to Warbeck 'for his relief and aid'.

Cleymond had been right to be wary, however, despite his continued involvement; the king's council did know about the plot, and once they had accrued enough information to corner and then destroy the conspirators they pounced from the shadows. There is little information about how or when the arrests occurred, or if there was any fierce resistance, but the royal guards did not have to travel far to round up the rebels, for the conspiracy had been centred around, and indeed within, the Tower of London.

In the meantime, Henry's enduring peace with France proved fruitful that summer when the new French king Louis XII authorised the handover of John Taylor, one of Warbeck's earliest champions, who had fled across the Channel after the debacle at Taunton two years earlier. That this was a significant moment for Henry is evident from a dispatch the Milanese ambassador Raimondi wrote in July, who noted that whilst the English envoys were returning from France carrying the colossal figure of 100,000 crowns, the king's French pension, even for someone driven by money and the security it brought, the king attached 'more importance' to getting his hands on Taylor than the cash.

Joining Taylor in captivity was the former mayor of Cork John Atwater, who had been seized in Ireland by the earl of Kildare the previous year on account of his lengthy record of treachery against the English king. He, too, was now transferred across the sea ready to stand trial alongside those he had collaborated with for nearly a decade. With the Tower of London conspirators arrested without incident, Henry VII was relieved to have two of Warbeck's original and most fervent supporters finally in his custody. The Warbeck campaign was hurtling towards its conclusion after nine years, and it was an ending that would not feature this most enigmatic of pretenders seated anywhere near the English throne.[3]

As with much regarding the life and times of Perkin Warbeck, this entire episode has proved controversial, with the suggestion amongst some historians that the plot was fabricated by Henry VII's royal agents, facilitated by Cleymond's involvement as an inside man to secure valid grounds for the lawful execution of the earl of Warwick. The king was certainly capable of exploiting existing plots to deploy his investigators into the field strategically to identify, then expose, as many rebels as possible, as witnessed with the William Stanley affair in 1495, but there is little evidence such schemes were invented to achieve his aims. Quite simply, throughout the 1490s, Henry didn't need to – his reign was one filled with those who resented his place upon the throne, and once he had been made aware that pockets of treachery were occurring in the shadows of his realm, he merely had to bide his time and let the plotters condemn themselves with their own careless actions.

This was the strategy Henry adopted in 1499; the evidence is convincing that there was a plot involving Thomas Astwood and a handful of others, one that did briefly enter the chambers of Warwick and Warbeck in the Tower, and the authorities allowed it to play out until enough ammunition was gathered to justify the destruction of those involved. Henry was a shrewd and streetwise monarch, possibly the wisest ever to sit upon the English throne, and just as he had throughout his reign he exploited the situation to his benefit rather than devising it. Few kings reacted as decisively to threats as Henry VII.

As for Warbeck – did he reveal details of the plot to Henry's officials, as per Cleymond's accusation, perhaps to alleviate his miserable existence by earning the king's gratitude? There is not enough evidence to make a solid assertion, but whilst it is true he did have contact with all the principal parties involved and possessed an abundance of inside information that would have been of value to the authorities, the pretender made no mention of any arrangement upon arrest as a bargaining tool to avoid execution. Considering his penchant for flight and how desperate he may have grown in captivity after a fascinating life of adventure that had taken in all the major European courts, it is difficult to dismiss Warbeck's sincerity in abetting Astwood and Cleymond with their plan. If they had successfully seized the Tower and breached the defences from within, he would surely have fled with them and assumed the identity of Richard IV once more.

In the end, whether Warbeck gave up the plotters or the intrigue was revealed through some other manner, perhaps even Cleymond himself, the episode only served to hasten both his demise and Warwick's. If the indictments are correct, and there is little reason to doubt that some dubious conversations had taken place between the accused, treason had been committed by word alone.

On 12 November 1499, the king's council assembled in Westminster, attended by the foremost figures in the realm.[4] All the bishops were present, as were members of Henry's nobility such as the duke of Buckingham, the earls of Northumberland, Oxford, Surrey, Essex and Ormond, and a host of barons and household officials. Also in attendance were the realm's leading justices, led by Chief Justice Fineux, whose duty it was to show the councillors evidence 'of certaine treasons conspired of Edward namyng himself of Warwick and Perkin and other within the Tower'. Fineux believed that it was shown 'by the confessions of the said Edward and other' that they had indeed intended to have 'deposed and destroied the Kinges person and his blode'.

The results of his investigation led Fineux to claim decisively before the council that 'Edward intended to have bin King', though was apparently willing to step aside for Warbeck if the latter 'had bin Kinge Edward sonne'. It was the opinion of all the judges, Fineux concluded, 'that thei have done Treason and deserved death'. When the matter was thus passed to the king and his councillors to enquire whether they should proceed or not, each and every councillor recommended that not only should due process of the law be followed, but Warbeck and Warwick should be executed in the event of a guilty verdict. It was a unanimous decision taken by the leading figures in the realm. Warbeck, referred to in the indictment as 'Peter Warbeck of Tourney, born under the obedience of the Archduke of Austria and Burgundy', was the first to be tried.

Removed from his chamber in the Tower on Saturday 16 November, Warbeck was brought through the city to the White Hall in Westminster for his arraignment. There is little record of the proceedings, but it is known that standing beside Warbeck for judgement on account of their 'certeyn treasons' were his long-serving companions John Taylor and John Atwater,[5] perhaps those most responsible for his present predicament as the men who had so enthusiastically lauded him as a Yorkist prince shortly after his arrival in Cork eight years earlier. The trio had dared to dream, but here they now stood, still side-by-side, nervously awaiting the verdict that they would be put to death. Had it all been worth it?

The trial appears to have consisted of little more than all three defendants hearing the respective charges they were accused of before a guilty verdict was passed. Each would be sentenced to a full traitor's death for their crimes. Edward Hall placed blame for the conspiracy on the shoulders of Warbeck, who 'by false persuasions and liberall promises' had corrupted those around him, and though others were implicated in the indictment as the driving force behind the plot, there was little doubt from the chronicler that the pretender had earned his death.[6] Writing from London to his Yorkshire-based master Sir Robert Plumpton, eyewitness John Pullen reported that the judgement passed ruled that

> they shold be drawn on hirdills from the Tower, throwout London, to the Tyburne, and ther to be hanged, and cutt down quicke, and ther bowells to be taken out and burned; ther heads to be stricke of, and quartered, ther heads and quarters to be disposed at the Kyngs pleasure.[7]

The record is silent on Warbeck's reaction to what must have been the devastating realisation that all his plotting and schemes had brought him to this dreadful moment. Assuming the identity of a Yorkist prince may have, at times, provided the young man with an exhilarating lifestyle that saw him acclaimed in some of the richest royal courts of the period, but in the end he had simply wandered too close to the flame that was now set to burn him too many times. Did he bewail the judgement, shed a tear, or even chastise the councillors? Did he meekly accept the verdict as his mind raced through a thousand thoughts at once?

Whilst the condemned trio, Warbeck, Taylor and Atwater, were returned to the Tower to await their final days, on 18 November in the Guildhall it was the turn of the other leading conspirators to be tried, including Astwood, Masborough, Strangeways, Finch, Proude, Bluet, and Ray. Like Warbeck, all were swiftly found guilty of intending to 'set at libertie therle of Werwyk and Perkyn', with all likewise sentenced to the horror of a traitor's death, save for Masborough and Proude who were instead returned indefinitely to prison.[8]

The following day, 19 November, in his capacity as great chamberlain and high admiral of England, John de Vere, 13th Earl of Oxford, was formally appointed by the king to fulfil the office of high steward so that he could preside over the trial of Warwick. Unlike the other defendants, Warwick would have his case heard by a jury of his peers in concession to his rank – Warbeck, by contrast, had not been afforded this right as he was not considered to be a prince of the blood.

After receiving the indictment personally from Chief Justice Fineux and Mayor Alwyn, the ageing Oxford issued summons that Warwick's presence was requested in Westminster's Great Hall two days later for his trial. The lords, Oxford declared, would then hear the case and 'give judgement according to the laws and customs of England'.

Though given the outward appearance of a fair hearing, *The Great Chronicle* suggests the outcome had been predetermined and the trial was conducted 'withouth any processe of the lawe',[9] a scathing reproach to the king and his lords. When consideration is given to the wider political and dynastic climate of 1499, the event does appear to have been little more than a show trial. Regardless of his father's attainder over two decades earlier, which theoretically removed him from the line of succession, Edward of Warwick nevertheless had the misfortune that an abundance of royal blood coursed through his veins. Though the wary Henry VII had been careful to keep the Yorkist prince in seclusion for most of his life, a network of supporters had persistently sought to press his claim throughout the reign. Men like John Taylor and Thomas Astwood refused to abandon the earl's claim, and indeed the entire Lambert Simnel affair, which Henry had been forced to defeat in battle, had been predicated upon the Warwick name.

With the internal threat of Warwick enduring fourteen years into the reign, through little fault of the earl himself, and external pressures from the Spanish to rid the kingdom of all and any pretenders, real or imagined, it should be little surprise if the king had advised Oxford and his fellow judges what their verdict would be. These men, who formed the core of Henry's aristocracy and largely owed their wealth and status to him, were hardly politically imprudent – they would have known without prodding from their sovereign that Warwick's death would decisively eradicate a lingering problem that affected them all, securing their own as well as the king's future in the process. The most successful medieval noblemen knew how to survive. It was a ruthless world, and one in which only those willing to commit unpalatable deeds from time to time could hope to prosper. This had been an unfortunate feature of English political life for centuries, and indeed continues to some extent in the modern day.

On 21 November, with Oxford seated gravely beneath a cloth of estate, surrounded by twenty-three other magnates, including the duke of Buckingham and the earls of Northumberland, Kent, Surrey, and Essex, the defendant was brought into the court by Thomas Lovell, Lieutenant of the Constable of the Tower. The charges were read out for Warwick's benefit, principal amongst them that he treasonously colluded with a conspiracy to flee the Tower with the king's great rebel Perkin Warbeck, intending thereafter to usurp the throne. Rather than contest the charges, Warwick made the judges' task simple when he freely confessed his guilt to all he had been accused of, before submitting to the king's grace and pleading for mercy.[10]

The earl's motivation for pleading guilty in this manner is unclear, and it is often speculated he did not understand the proceedings and possibly confessed in ignorance. He may, of course, have felt intimidated by a situation that was alien to him, having spent so many years in the Tower, and yielded far easier than someone else in his position would have. Edward Hall suggested half a century later that 'many men' doubted he submitted of his own free will because of 'hys innocency', and that he may have been enticed to plead in such a manner, which is plausible. Warwick certainly doesn't appear to have put up any resistance to the charges or attempted to explain his alleged actions. With guilt therefore assured by his own admission, it fell upon Oxford, Warwick's great-uncle by marriage, to pass judgement against his fellow earl, declaring to all present: 'That the said Earl of Warwick should be taken to the Tower of London, and from thence drawn through the middle of London to the gallows at Tyburn, and there hanged, cut down, disembowelled, and quartered in the usual manner.'

Whilst Warwick was returned to his chamber in the Tower to wait out the final days of what had proven a miserable life, attention shifted back once more to Perkin Warbeck. The day of his execution soon arrived. There is no information about how he spent the days between his trial and execution, alone with his thoughts. Perhaps he prayed for divine intervention, or let his mind wander to happier memories in the company of his wife Katherine, his time at the various European courts where he was treated as an honoured guest, even further back to his carefree childhood, wherever that had truly occurred. Did he regret his actions of the past decade which had brought him to this moment, or was the adventure itself worth an early death? Did he tremble in fear, or had he found peace in his faith? We cannot know.

On the morning of 23 November 1499, the royal guards roused Warbeck and Atwater and prepared the pair for their final journey from the Tower to Tyburn. It was a four-mile trek that took the condemned pair through the centre of London and past the jeering mob that thronged the streets for one last glimpse of the figure who had boldly claimed to have been their rightful Yorkist king.

With a halter around his neck, even now, at the moment of his greatest despair, Warbeck remained a curiosity to the commoners, for whom he was something akin to a celebrity. This broken spectacle before them had just a few years earlier been at the forefront of a number of attempted invasions, having gained acceptance as a prince reborn across Europe and even marrying a beautiful Scottish noblewoman. For the locals, a sight of this blonde-haired figure in his early twenties on his way to the gallows was worth emerging from their homes and taverns in the brisk late autumn. It was an occasion which likely remained a talking point within families for years to come – the day the fake prince walked to his death.

When he arrived at Tyburn, Warbeck was met by even larger crowds, a 'greate multitude' according to one impressed London chronicler,[11] who had flocked to witness his final moments. In the centre of the horde was a small scaffold which had been erected for the occasion, a makeshift gallows atop which stood the gibbet with a noose from which Warbeck would hang. The king, in his final act concerning the pretender, had commuted Warbeck's sentence to one reserved for common thieves. A life which had started, by his own eventual admission, about a quarter-century earlier in Tournai, was now to end in front of hundreds of strangers a few miles to the west of London.

Granted the courtesy of some last words, Warbeck chose to address the people before him rather than maintain his silence as was his right, and confessed for a final time that he was not Richard, Duke of York. It was reported by one chronicler that he

> ... took It there uppon his deth that he nevyr was the persoon which he was namyd nor any thyng of that blood, But a stranger born lyke wyse as beforn he hadd shewid, and that he namyd hym sylf to be the secund sone of kyng Edward was by the meane of the said John a watyr there present.[12]

As their respective nooses swayed in front of them, one can only wonder what Warbeck's companion on the scaffold, John Atwater, felt about being so publicly blamed for their current predicament. Even if it was true, and there is reason to believe that Atwater and Taylor were instrumental in encouraging him to declare his supposed royal lineage, even at this desperate moment Warbeck exhibited a cowardly trait in refusing to acknowledge his own culpability, preferring to blame someone else.

It is, however, difficult to give credence to the fact that with his soul's salvation at the forefront of his mind, he would have lied about his identity at this juncture. There was no reason to; his wife Katherine had been integrated into the queen's household, and there is scanty evidence of a living child to be concerned for, let alone any land or estates to pass on. Stood in front of a sizeable crowd with a noose about to replace the halter around his neck, Warbeck's sole concern with his final breaths was not with the life he was soon to depart, but the one he believed he was about to enter.

We have no real indication as to the extent of his religious devotion, but there is little reason to believe it would not have been other than conventional for the period, an entrenched belief in God and the afterlife. As with all persons during the fifteenth century, he would have deeply feared the forthcoming judgement he faced. This was a final opportunity to make reparation for his misdemeanors, and it is likely he was earnest with his words. This moment, perhaps above all else, is the single most important indicator of Perkin's identity.

Composing himself once he had reached the end of his declaration, Warbeck finally asked for the forgiveness of the king and all those he had offended, and 'there upon the Galowis took his deth paciently'.[13]

Later Tudor commentators such as Polydore Vergil and Edward Hall were not complimentary in their assessment of his life. For Hall, 'with false persuasions and untrew surmises', Warbeck had shamefully 'broughte many noble personages to deth and utter perdicion',[14] whereas Vergil's verdict was more poetical, if no less damning:

> This was the end of Peter Warbeck, who despised his humble origin, and by twisting falsehood into truth, truth into falsehood, deceived many, including men of considerable standing, until at last he fell upon the scaffold, victim of his own deceit.[15]

Once Warbeck's body had fallen limp and death was verified, he was cut down from the noose and posthumously beheaded. The bloodied head that once hoped to don a crown was instead taken to London Bridge, spiked upon a pole and placed high on display overlooking the Thames, a grisly fate shared with many traitors before him. His mutilated body was taken to the Augustinian Friary and buried in a location of which no known trace remains.[16]

Five days later, on 28 November, it was the turn of the twenty-four-year-old earl of Warwick. In deference to his title and undisputed royal blood, he was spared the humiliating journey from London to Tyburn. According to the *Great Chronicle*, Warwick was instead brought out of his chamber in the Tower by two servants and at the outer gate delivered into the custody of the city sheriffs, who were responsible for escorting him to nearby Tower Hill. It was here between two and three o'clock in the afternoon, and in the shadow of the fortress he had called home for most of his life, that Edward of Warwick was beheaded. As his blood stained the temporary wooden scaffold, Warwick's death represented the end of the legitimate male line of the mighty House of Plantagenet, brought to a brutal and tragic conclusion.[17]

Unlike with Warbeck's death, the same Tudor commentators were noticeably more despondent at Warwick's demise, with Hall in particular lamenting that it was 'by the dryft and offence of another man' that the naïve earl 'was brought to his end and confusion', having been kept so long in the Tower 'out of al company of men and sights of beastes' that he 'coulde not descerne a Goose from a Capon'. Hall also suggested that it was the earl's title, Warwick, rather than his conduct, that was the reason for his death, for

Ferdinand of Aragon feared that 'as longe as any erle of Warwicke lyved, that England should never be clensed or purged of Cyvyle warre and prevy sedicion, so much was the name of Warwyke in other regions had in feare and gealousy'.[18] The enduring continent-wide legacy of Edward's famous grandfather Richard Neville, popularly remembered as Warwick the Kingmaker, had done his cause little good in the end.

Vergil, meanwhile, reported that 'the entire population mourned the death of the handsome youth', an 'unhappy boy' who had been 'committed to prison not for any fault of his own but because of his family's offences'. Because of his Yorkist blood, and if Hall was correct his Neville descent, Warwick 'had to perish in this fashion in order that there should be no surviving male heir to his family'. Vergil also placed blame for the earl's death on Warbeck's shoulders, claiming the imposter directed the conspiracy whereas Warwick merely 'took part in the scheme quite innocently'.[19] That one London chronicler made the point of pleading to Jesus to take mercy upon Warwick's soul further suggests there was widespread sorrow about his unfortunate demise.[20]

Henry VII's own reaction to the execution suggests the king was regretful such action had to be taken, necessary though it had been to secure his own family's future. Warwick's head was not spiked upon London Bridge as Warbeck's had been and left to rot in the winter cold, but rather taken by boat along with his body to Bisham Abbey for burial. At the king's own considerable expense of £12 18s 2d, the earl was interred near his kingmaking grandfather and other relations.[21]

There was one final round of executions the following day to bring the 1499 episode to its gory conclusion. As Warwick's body was being conveyed upstream to Bisham, the rest of the conspirators were handed their sentences; Astwood, Bluet, Ray, Strangeways and Finch were to be hanged, drawn and quartered, though the latter two did ultimately escape the gallows. There are no trial proceedings for Audley, Cleymond, Lounde or Warde, though the latter is known to have died in the Tower years later, perhaps a fate shared by some of the others. Audley, it is known, was pardoned after six years of imprisonment. Of those sentenced to die, only two were executed – Bluet, and the ringleader who had been reprieved once before, Thomas Astwood. Hanged until nearly dead, disembowelled, and finally beheaded, what constituted their remains joined Warbeck's body at Austin Friars.[22]

The original driving force behind Warbeck's crusade for the throne, meanwhile, John Taylor, a figure bitterly opposed to Tudor rule from the outset of the reign, also curiously escaped execution, though he did remain imprisoned for the remainder of Henry's lifetime. He was also one of a handful of men specifically excluded from a general pardon at the outset of the following reign of Henry VIII – perhaps perpetual captivity rather than a traitor's death was the deal the French had sought in exchange for Taylor's handover.[23] Of course, Taylor was someone who could attest to the fact that Warbeck's claim had likely been a creation of his own back in 1491, and though we have no evidence about the particulars of his life in prison, Henry conceivably kept the rebel alive to serve as a credible source of information if needed. For someone as implacable as Taylor, perhaps life without freedom was worse than death.

Within the space of a week, Henry VII had, within the parameters of the judicial process and with the backing of his senior lords, destroyed a pretender who had been a persistent nuisance for nearly a decade, keeping the name Richard of York alive with his every movement in direct defiance of the Tudor crown. Moreover, he had rid himself of a genuine Yorkist prince that had long been the focus of seditious activity, even if, as most sources concur, one not involved in any significant personal capacity.

Just as Edward IV had done in 1471 after overwhelming his Lancastrian rivals in battle, it was now the first Tudor king who crushed the seed of his enemies. With particular reference to Warbeck, though just as fitting when applied to other challenges, Francis Bacon wrote in the early seventeenth century:

> It was one of the longest plays of that kind that hath been in memory, and might perhaps have had another end, if he had not met with a King both wise, stout, and fortunate.[24]

After fourteen years upon the throne, Henry VII was ready to move beyond these troubling plays, and forward with his reign. The time was nigh, albeit far later than he had intended, to finally consign the internecine strife of the fifteenth century to the past. He had won.

18

The Most Savage Harshness

As well as heralding the turn of a new century, 1500 marked the fifteenth of Henry VII's reign, the longest unbroken spell upon the throne of a king since Henry VI was deposed in 1461. The king, who was to turn forty-three at the end of January, anticipated the new year would finally signal the dawning of a new era for the dynasty he had founded, one freed from the complex shackles of the past which he had thus far struggled to shake off.

There was ample reason to be optimistic. First and foremost, Henry VII had a thriving family; there is little reason not to believe he was contentedly married, with his wife Elizabeth of York having provided six children by 1500, aged between one and thirteen – Arthur, Margaret, Henry, Elizabeth, Mary, and Edmund – of whom only one, the youngest daughter named for her mother, had passed away in infancy.

The union between Henry and Elizabeth had been pivotal in giving the king, hitherto a comparatively unknown Lancastrian earl with an average claim to the throne, an acceptable mandate to rule England in spite of other options, though he cautiously ensured he was crowned and endorsed by parliament so that he was constitutionally king with or without his bride's involvement. If she died, for example, he and his line, whether of Elizabeth's blood or not, remained on the throne. Nevertheless, the tacit understanding when he became king was that Henry owed much of his acceptance amongst Edward IV's influential former affinity to the fact he had pledged to marry the Yorkist king's eldest daughter. Though he could not admit as much officially so as not to undermine his claim, it is highly unlikely this

Tudor pretender would ever have made it as far as Bosworth Field without this promise.

Henry, so far as the evidence shows, did not appear to resent his wife because of her dynastic importance, proving to be a decent husband and father. There is no known record of him taking mistresses, let alone fathering illegitimate children as previous kings had. The contrast with his son, Henry VIII, could not be more marked. The king's privy purse expenses, meanwhile, show regular payments were authorised for the benefit of his wife and children, at odds with the unfair label of miser which has attached itself to a man who proved rather liberal with his coin for much of the reign. Bows and books were bought for his sons, and musical instruments for his daughters.

As for Prince Arthur, it is known he regularly played dice and cards, even losing money in the process, whilst the sums the king stumped up for the Scottish wedding of his daughter Margaret, political benefits notwithstanding, were astronomical – one payment records £16,000 spent on jewels and plate alone, with another made to James IV for £2,333 6s 8d. The messenger who brought tidings of Margaret's safe arrival in Scotland, Thomas Shurley, was treated to the generous sum of £6 13s 4d for his efforts, whilst in 1508, proving he had not forgotten about his eldest daughter, Henry sent her the gift of a frontlet, a decorative band worn on the forehead. Although it is true Queen Elizabeth's dower was less than that of her predecessors and her Yorkist inheritance carefully managed by the king, she was also regularly treated to gowns, jewels, and furs.[1] Henry VII undoubtedly went to extraordinary lengths to accumulate treasure, and his increasing avarice as time wore on is clear, but as money came into his hands, it often passed out just as quickly.

We can glean some further insight into Henry's relations with his loved ones through family correspondence early in the new century. In late 1503, his 'humble douter' Margaret wrote to her father from her new home in Scotland, miserably confessing she wished she was still with him, whilst in a Book of Hours Henry handed her before the journey north he had touchingly written, 'Remember yr kynde and lovyng fader in yor good prayers.'[2] The king's mother, Margaret Beaufort, meanwhile, lovingly referred to her son as 'all my worldly joy' in one letter, praying the Lord would grant him 'as longe good lyfe, helthe, and joy, as your moste nobyll herte can dessyre'.[3] In 1504, visiting Spanish ambassador Hernan Duque de Estrada also observed the close dynamic between Henry and his family, when he reported favourably upon the king's skills as a father:

> It is quite wonderful how much the King likes the Prince of Wales. He has good reason to do so, for the Prince deserves all love. But it is not only from love that the King takes the Prince with him; he wishes to improve him. Certainly there could be no better school in the world than the society of such a father as Henry VII. He is so wise and so attentive to everything; nothing escapes his attention. There is no doubt the Prince has an excellent governor and steward in his father. If he lives ten years longer he will leave the Prince furnished with good habits, and with immense riches, and in as happy circumstances as man can be.[4]

There are no known instances where relations within the Tudor family were significantly breached, and even when Queen Elizabeth declared her unhappiness about the prospect of Princess Margaret departing for Scotland before she was old enough, the king's reaction was to compromise rather than overrule. The queen was certainly excluded from holding any position of overt authority, but in a reign designed to bring several decades of conflict to an end, this was hardly the time for novelties such as joint rule. Elizabeth assumed a role seen as traditional for English queens, raising her children, accompanying her husband in an official capacity when required, and supervising her household, rather than actively participating in matters of policy. It may be suspected that Henry consciously excluded her from assuming a leading role, and whilst this may be partly true, there exists no reason to suggest Elizabeth herself ever forced the issue. Her motto, after all, was 'humble and reverent', and this may have reflected her nature.

The queen was certainly widely respected, at home and abroad; to an attentive London chronicler, Elizabeth was 'noble and vertuous',[5] whilst one Venetian ambassador praised her 'great ability' and another noted approvingly she was 'in conduct very able'.[6] Polydore Vergil judged her to be 'a woman of such a character that it would be hard to judge whether she displayed more of majesty and dignity in her life than wisdom and moderation'.[7] In one contemporary description of her funeral, she was even lauded as 'one of the most gracious and best beloved Princesses in the world'.[8]

Elizabeth was a woman Henry must have been proud to have married, and as shown by his distressed reaction to her death in 1503, that he loved her must not be solely attributed to her lineage, which would be a deeply cynical interpretation of the union. The queen, in turn, was nothing if not devoted to her family throughout the tribulations of her husband's reign. They were a solid unit.

Much has been made of the queen's relationship with her mother-in-law Margaret Beaufort, with the suggestion that some degree of animosity existed between the two foremost women in the king's life. Any evidence of ill feeling, however, does not stand up to scrutiny. The suggestion there were issues between the pair largely stems from two separate reports made in July 1498 by Spanish visitors to England.

Firstly, Johannes de Matienzo, sub-prior of Santa Cruz and who had only arrived in London two weeks earlier, wrote that Elizabeth, a 'very noble woman' who was 'much beloved' by the people, was noticeably 'kept in subjection by the mother of the King', though he doesn't expand on the matter. That same month, Pedro de Ayala, the Spanish ambassador to Scotland temporarily assigned to London, added that Henry was 'much influenced by his mother and his followers in affairs of personal interest', before adding speculatively, 'The Queen, as is generally the case, does not like it.'[9]

If both statements are accurate, it need not automatically follow that the long-standing relationship between the two women was one replete with animosity. Then, just as now, family tensions could periodically turn into small disputes that were soon forgotten, and which had no long-term bearing on an otherwise healthy relationship. In this scenario, it seems highly likely that two observant newcomers to England merely witnessed a temporary falling-out between Margaret and Elizabeth and recorded this otherwise unremarkable disagreement for all posterity.[10]

Margaret Beaufort had been around Elizabeth since the latter had been a mere child, and had watched her grow from a beautiful Yorkist princess under Edward IV into a woman worthy, by blood and character, of mothering the fledgling Tudor dynasty. They had been a part of each other's lives for nearly two decades, and it must be expected during that time there had been the odd moment of tension, just as there would have been periods of contentment and happiness. All things considered, the likelihood is that the pair got along well enough not to cause the man they both loved any additional headaches whilst he fended off the various assaults on the crown that kept them all in their positions of privilege. There is no other evidence to suggest with certainty anything to the contrary.

Away from family matters, by the turn of the century Henry VII had succeeded in retaining the loyalty of most of his nobility, including those who had served with distinction under the Yorkist kings Edward IV and Richard III. Their men had now, in effect, become his men. The only notable figures to have openly turned on their Tudor king within the first fifteen years of the reign had been John de la Pole, Earl of Lincoln; John Tuchet, Lord Audley; and Sir William Stanley; all other rebels were drawn from the gentry and below, men of little national standing who had failed thus far to coordinate a sustained attack on their target.

Henry may not have provoked a natural outpouring of love from all his nobility, but he was certainly respected enough to have retained control of his crown whilst minimising insurgency within the ranks, surpassing other deposed kings before him who, for various reasons, alienated those who were supposed to serve the throne. He had also evaded conflict with the Church, though did perhaps exert undue influence over bishopric appointments to ensure his leading prelates were willing to advance his interests if called upon.

As well as rebuilding royal control, Henry was a builder in the traditional sense, another effective if expensive tactic to enhance his prestige in the minds of his impressed subjects and awestruck visitors. Completed in 1501 and named for the hereditary title he held prior to acceding to the throne, Richmond Palace was certainly state-of-the-art and designed to be a very explicit indication of Tudor magnificence, rather than a remnant of Plantagenet rule as Sheen Palace had been before it.[11] To one captivated observer, Richmond was an 'erthly and secunde paradise', an ornate red-brick wonder with several turrets of varying height rising towards the heavens, each topped with bulbous, eye-catching cupolas. It was, this particular visitor wrote in wonder after he had beheld the palace before him, the 'bewtyouse examplere of all propir lodgynes'.[12]

The interior was no less impressive, indeed 'most glorious and joyefulle to consider and beholde'; the timber-roofed Great Hall was liberally covered with rich Arras tapestries, many depicting famous battles from history, an allusion no doubt to Henry's own victories on the battlefield. Images of earlier English kings, including mythical rulers like Arthur and Brutus, were also painted on the walls, with a prominent spot high on the left-hand side reserved for the incumbent, who, the observer thought, was 'as worthy that rumme and place with thoes glorious princes as eny king that ever reigned in this lond'. Large glassed bay windows allowed an abundance of natural light to illuminate every corner of the hall, a feature repeated in the galleries throughout the palace.

The chapel, meanwhile, was well paved and heavily decorated with more cloth of Arras and gold, with the altars bedecked with relics, jewels and rich plate. The roof was painted azure and littered with the king's personal emblems such as red roses and portcullises, with depictions of two sainted English kings, Edward the Confessor and Edmund the Martyr, and the Welsh king Cadwaladr, on the walls. Elsewhere were an array of similarly decorated passages and galleries as well as dedicated dancing chambers and secret closets reserved for the royal family. Outside, the gardens, 'moost faire and pleasaunt', featured a diverse collection of trees that produced exotic fruits for visitors to enjoy, and 'housis of pleasure' in which guests could play chess, dice, cards, bowls and tennis. Richmond had been conceived as a modern palace fit for the greatest of kings, just as Henry had intended.[13]

The two most palpable threats to Henry's crown, meanwhile, Warbeck and Warwick, had been permanently dealt with, and with their deaths the danger of domestic insurrection supported by foreign reinforcements had abated significantly. In January 1500, Ambassador de Puebla felt confident enough to write that with their executions, 'England has never before been so tranquil and obedient as at present', and that with their demise 'there does not remain a drop of Royal blood' in the kingdom, 'the only Royal blood being the true blood of the King, the Queen, and, above all, the Prince of Wales'.[14] This wasn't strictly accurate, but did highlight the perceived strength of Henry's grip on the crown after 1499.

The king's foreign policy, an intricate web of treaties negotiated with some of the shrewdest potentates of the period, was also integral in strengthening this grasp, and by the advent of the sixteenth century he was on favourable terms with most of the continent's leading rulers. The key objective, as always for Henry when dealing with his rivals, was the pragmatic preservation of his crown, and for him the grandiose if popular ambitions of previous English kings to conquer France were mostly suppressed, the 1492 campaign notwithstanding. Henry found joy gambling with friends over small amounts of money, but he certainly was not someone to gamble away resources chasing glory when the odds were stacked against a favourable outcome. He had put his life on the line in dramatic circumstances when he won the crown at Bosworth; once in the hot seat himself, he played it safe.

Anglo-Scottish relations had thawed considerably since the border war of 1497, which cleared the path for an extensive triumvirate of treaties to be signed in Richmond on 24 January 1502, which pledged to end any conflict between the nations in perpetuity, as well as pressing forward with the marriage between the English princess Margaret and the Scottish king, James IV. That the treaty was the first of its kind agreed between England and Scotland since 1328 underscores the achievement of all involved, and though war would be resumed after Henry VII's death, the marriage had long-term consequences that would ultimately unite the two crowns, and indeed the island.[15]

Despite continued involvement in the Holy League, Henry remained on amiable terms with the French and resisted pressure to wage war against them, whilst after several years of tension with the two Hapsburgs, Maximilian I, King of the Romans, and his son Philip, Duke of Burgundy, relations had also softened, with the ageing Margaret of York's influence not nearly as noticeable as it had once been. The dowager duchess would die at the end of 1503, having failed to witness the toppling of the Tudor monarchy she so detested.

Friendship with Burgundy in particular was a crucial development for the English king, as it was in the Netherlands that both Simnel and Warbeck had been able to cultivate a formidable degree of support, which in the political fallout had proven detrimental to the lucrative Anglo-Burgundian economic relationship crucial to both countries' prosperity. Following up on the treaty of 1497, Henry VII and Philip of Burgundy met for the first time during the summer of 1500 at a summit in Calais, during which it was observed 'they treated one another like father and son'. The duke even freely declared 'he loved Henry, and regarded him as his protector'.[16] A series of royal marriages between the two Houses were also proposed, a sign of a promising relationship for many years to come that only recently would have been unthinkable.[17] In 1503, the English king even funded an elaborate stained-glass window in Antwerp's towering cathedral, replete with Tudor imagery with a crowned Lancastrian Red Rose the most prominent badge between the arms of Henry and Elizabeth. That he was able to accomplish this in an area which had long provided refuge to Yorkist dissidents must have brought great satisfaction to the Tudor king. Across the rest of the decade, meanwhile, Henry would hand over the enormous sum of £120,000 to Philip's father Maximilian I, including one cash payment of £30,000, ostensibly for the latter's Turkish crusade and to secure his election as Holy Roman Emperor, but in all likelihood intended to discourage any future support for Yorkist rebels.

The Tudor king continued to benefit from the support of Pope Alexander VI in the new century, the latter having recently bestowed upon Henry a sword and cap of maintenance in recognition of his role in the Holy League. Though there would always be progress to be made due to the fast-changing winds of European diplomacy, Henry had certainly proven himself the equal of his fellow rulers, and, through sheer will and a sharp mind that drew admiration from afar, had raised England to a status it had scarcely experienced since the final days of Henry V's reign. When one considers the position of weakness from which he acceded to the throne, a little-known Welshman raised in Brittany and propelled towards the throne on the whims of the French government, his achievements by the early 1500s were unquestionably impressive.

It was the Spanish alliance, however, above all others, that had been a fixation of Henry's from early in his reign, keen as he was to unite his young dynasty with one of the most esteemed families on the continent. With the marriage, by proxy, between his heir Arthur and the *infanta* Katherine of Aragon taking place in May 1499, Henry's decision to execute Warbeck and Warwick in the following November after the conspiracy in their name had been exposed had likely been heavily influenced by the demands of the Spanish monarchs. It does not seem coincidental that the treaty between the two parties was formally and conclusively ratified by Ferdinand and Isabella on 20 January 1500, just two months after the two pretenders were put to death.[18] However unpalatable the act may have seemed in private, it was something Henry had to do in order to seal the Spanish deal. Preparations were hastened for the princess to embark for her new life in England, though illness and bad weather delayed her journey, much to an impatient Henry's frustration. He could not relax until Katherine was in England.

Just fifteen years old, with blue eyes and striking auburn hair, Katherine left her parents behind at Alhambra in the Granada region and travelled through the heart of her parents' kingdoms to Laredo on the northern coast, sailing from her homeland for the last time towards the end of September 1501. The voyage was not without its difficulties owing to inclement weather, and when the fleet drifted into Plymouth harbour about three o'clock on the afternoon of 2 October, it was 160 miles south-west of its anticipated destination in Portsmouth. The reception, however, was no less grand; the Spanish ambassador boasted to Katherine's parents that she was welcomed ashore as though 'she had been the Saviour of the world', and in some ways, to the English who now beheld her, she was. This marriage represented a core part of Henry VII's strategy to ensure civil war did not return to England again, and this was likely widely understood amongst his people.[19]

There was certainly something poetic in Katherine arriving unheralded on the Cornwall–Devon border, where just four years earlier a popular uprising threatened to topple the family whose line her blood was now expected to bolster. This was further evidenced when the Spanish princess's convoy advanced from Plymouth to Exeter, the city in which Perkin Warbeck had formally confessed for the first time that he was an imposter, and whose demise cleared one of the key obstacles that had stopped her assuming her new life as the English queen-in-waiting. If Warbeck had represented the Yorkist past, Katherine, a figure of hope with distant Lancastrian blood in her veins and now the bride of a Yorkist-Lancastrian husband, undoubtedly represented the Tudor future, one forthwith galvanised on account of its Spanish connection.

Shortly after her arrival, Henry VII wrote to Katherine and was effusive in his praise, barely concealing his happiness that she was finally on English soil, declaring, 'We cannot well say or express the great pleasure, joy, and consolation which we have from it.' The king assured Katherine that he looked forward to 'seeing your noble presence, which we have often desired, both for the great graces and virtues which we hear it has pleased God to give your person, as also for the mutual amity, confederation, and good alliance between our good cousins the king and queen of Spain your parents and us'. He hoped she would henceforth regard him as her 'good and loving father'. In return, Henry pledged to 'treat, receive, and favour you like our own daughter'.[20] He would, in time, fail to keep this promise.

Katherine's journey took her out of the south-west and steadily towards London, with Henry dispatching his trusty steward Robert Willoughby de Broke to meet her. Thomas Howard, Earl of Surrey, was likewise handed urgent orders to muster some men and attend upon her at once – it was imperative she reached the capital safely, and in comfort.

The king, however, grew exasperated by the delay and was eager to see the young woman he had spent more than a decade pursuing for his son, and so on 4 November he left Richmond having decided he would meet her on the way. Word was sent to Prince Arthur that he was to meet his father en route, and the pair were reunited in Easthampstead where a royal hunting lodge occupied part of the southern reaches of the Windsor Forest.[21]

From the lodge, father and son continued their journey together on to nearby Dogmersfield to meet the Spanish entourage. The trip gave Henry some valuable time with his son, time to perhaps impart some final snippets of fatherly wisdom or direction about the upcoming nuptials, an increasingly rare moment to enjoy one another's company, particularly as the teenage heir had recently departed to the Welsh Marches to further his princely education. Henry had never known his father, and though he had been protected more than capably by his uncle Jasper, such moments may have weighed on the king's mind with regard to his own personal loss. It may even have influenced his own behaviour as a parent, a role in which he appears to have been more than adequate.

The manor at Dogmersfield was held by the bishop of Bath and Wells, and therefore currently in the possession of the king's secretary and friend, Oliver King, making it an ideal location for such a momentous if unscheduled meeting to take place. Much of what is known about this initial meeting on 6 November, and the celebrations that followed, was recorded in vivid detail by an anonymous member of the king's household.

When near, Henry sent word to the princess's camp that he intended to speak with her, but to his surprise was met with robust resistance from the Spanish protonotary who declared he had received strict instructions from his sovereign lord, Ferdinand of Aragon, that Katherine should not 'have eny meting, ne use eny maner of communycacion' with Henry or Arthur until the blessed day of marriage. In the fields outside the town, the English king sought the advice of his council about this unforeseen obstacle, with all concluding that as the wedding treaty had been ratified by both parties and the princess had already travelled considerably into his dominions, he was surely within his rights to press the matter and force a meeting, regardless of Ferdinand's wishes.[22]

At around two or three o'clock in the afternoon, Henry entered Dogmersfield where Katherine's retinue protested his presence, claiming the princess was resting after an exhausting journey and should not be disturbed. The impasse was only ended when Katherine astutely intervened and invited her new father-in-law into her chamber for 'an honorable metyng'. Many 'goodly wordes' were exchanged during this first encounter before Henry briefly departed so he could change out of his riding garments. He returned a little while later with the prince in tow, marking the first time Arthur and Katherine laid eyes upon each other. It must have been an intense, if possibly awkward, moment between two teenagers who carried the hopes of their respective nations upon their shoulders.

Whatever words passed between the pair were spoken in Latin, helped along by some of the bishops who were also present. That evening, a group of minstrels was summoned to the manor for entertainment, with dancing enjoyed by all before Henry and Arthur departed for Windsor early the following morning. Katherine, meanwhile, her private introduction to the Tudors complete, continued her separate journey to Lambeth in preparation for her official reception.[23]

That Henry was satisfied with the personable young figure that had greeted him at Dogmersfield is clear from a subsequent letter he wrote to Ferdinand and Isabella regarding their daughter, describing how he 'much admired her beauty, as well as her agreeable and dignified manners'.[24] When reunited with his queen at Richmond and quizzed about their daughter-in-law, Henry confirmed that 'he likyd hir person and behaviour'.[25]

Katherine's formal entry into London took place on 12 November 1501, and despite Isabella's request that Henry ensure 'expenses were moderate', over a year earlier a Spanish ambassador had reported that preparations were underway for 'festivities such as never before were witnessed in England', noting a request had been made from the king for the City of London to help fund the spectacle.[26] Henry unashamedly strove to exploit the marriage for all it was worth – he had, after all, sought the Spanish match with the intention to raise the profile of his dynasty at home and abroad, and no opportunity was wasted to send a message to the watching world, starting with the princess's arrival in his capital. In a clear indication of the new confidence Henry felt after overcoming the various threats to his crown, in just a few weeks he had dismissed the desires of both Ferdinand and Isabella. He was going to do things his way.

Riding a mule richly trapped in the Spanish manner, Katherine was led from Lambeth to London by an array of England's foremost nobles, including the duke of Buckingham and the earls of Northumberland, Surrey, Essex and Kent. The most visible presence at her side throughout, however, was the ten-year-old Prince Henry, Duke of York, embarking on his first significant royal engagement. Both Henry and Katherine were of course unaware they would one day be married themselves, albeit in altogether different circumstances.[27] Upon reaching London Bridge, crammed with houses and shops either side of the street and with spiked heads of the condemned often left on show as a deterrent, Katherine was confronted by the first of six extravagant pageants that were performed for her benefit as she made her way through the city to St Paul's Cathedral.

Each of the elaborate scenes was a costly exercise designed not only to extol the virtues of Katherine and Arthur through a series of poems, speeches and songs of allegory and mythology, but to draw attention to the supremacy of Henry VII and his dynasty. At every conceivable opportunity, royal symbols associated with the king, such as the Lancastrian red rose, the Richmond greyhound, the Welsh red dragon, and the Beaufort portcullis, were displayed, with the entire spectacle offering dynastic propaganda on an impressive scale, precisely as intended.[28] Henry was shrewd enough to ensure his presence was not a distraction, however, keenly observing matters from the house of a haberdasher named William Geoffrey, who must have been beyond honoured to host his king. With the king were his son Arthur, stepfather Thomas Stanley, Earl of Derby, and the earls of Oxford and Shrewsbury. In the chamber next door were Queen Elizabeth and Margaret Beaufort, their gaze no doubt focused intently upon the young girl who would represent the third generation to marry into the Tudors.[29]

The following day, Henry VII held court at Baynard's Castle, so recently one of the leading residences of his wife's Yorkist ancestors and which he had renovated so that it was considered 'far more beautiful and commodious for the entertainment of any prince'.[30] Here, overlooking the Thames, the king met with the Spanish ambassadors in a chamber opulently decorated with cloth of Arras, seated the entire time beneath a rich cloth of estate. Beside him upon cushions fashioned from cloth of gold were his two 'dere and wilbeloved' sons, Arthur and Henry, observing and learning as their father, arguably at the peak of his powers, played the part of gracious host. Elsewhere in the palace, Katherine met privately with Queen Elizabeth, perhaps discussing their shared roles as the women who had been tasked, through no choice of their own, with strengthening the House of Tudor. Late in the evening, after all conversation had been exhausted, the principal figures retired for the night, ready for the main spectacle the following morning, the highly anticipated royal wedding.[31]

Whereas his own wedding fifteen years earlier had taken place in Westminster Abbey, Henry ordered his son's nuptials to take place in St Paul's, right in the heart of the city, which naturally ensured maximum exposure. The Londoners were not people to turn away from a celebration on their doorsteps, and true to form crowded the streets in astonishing numbers, many perhaps having occupied the same spot two years earlier to observe Warbeck's final journey to the gallows in vastly different circumstances. Though their voices have long been lost to time, each man, woman and child present was a witness to history, each soul expected to pass down through the generations their memories of the golden moment the House of Tudor was united with the esteemed Trastámaran rulers of Spain.

Prince Arthur entered the church from his nearby lodgings between nine and ten o'clock in the morning, whilst Katherine was led in afterwards through the West Door, accompanied once more by the young duke of York with her train borne by the queen's sister, Cecily of York. Both bride and groom were resplendent in white satin, with Katherine's head concealed by a white silk coif that was bordered with gold, pearls, and other precious stones. Her hair hung loose over the shoulders, with her dress given extra volume using hoops, an unknown concept in England at the time.[32] Wandering eyes inside the church meanwhile would have noticed the expensive tapestries on the walls depicting various noble and valiant acts. An abundance of shimmering gold, plate, and religious relics were placed on display. In the middle of the nave a seven-hundred-foot-long bridge of timber covered in red cloth had been constructed, an elevated walkway which ensured as many as possible of those fortunate to have crammed into the church could catch a glimpse of the bride and groom.[33]

Once the lengthy religious observances and marriage rites had been completed, presided over by Henry Deane, archbishop of Canterbury, Katherine and Arthur turned hand-in-hand and curtseyed to the crowd, prompting some observers to shout out joyfully, 'King Henry!' and 'Prince Arthur!' The king, watching from a concealed closet in the company of his queen, must have been delighted with how proceedings had unfolded, capped with hearing his name reverberating throughout the church. His popularity on this most celebrated of days would not have been harmed, of course, by the elaborate wine fountain positioned outside the West Door, which resembled a green mountain upon which Tudor and Trastámara badges were displayed and had a small gate through which the masses could enter during the day to fill their cups.[34] With so many drunken toasts raised to the generosity of the king, Henry would have considered the money well spent.

The wedding celebrations of November 1501 truly represented the single moment when, after several draining years of diplomatic wrangling whilst anxiously fending off various challenges for his crown, all Henry's dynastic and political ambitions were realised in one fell swoop. As he wrote to Ferdinand and Isabella once the gluttonous feasting and hotly contested tournaments had drawn to their close, 'Although the friendship between the houses of England and Spain has been most sincere and intimate before this time, it will henceforth be much more intimate and indissoluble.'[35] That an agreement of perpetual peace was signed with the Scottish three months later, on 24 January 1502, confirming his daughter Margaret's marriage to James IV, merely added to Henry's optimism that his reign was about to belatedly enter the golden age he had promised back in 1485.[36]

However, for all this hope of a glorious conclusion to his tenure upon the throne, Henry's kingship, indeed his life, was destined to end darkly. From 1502 onwards, there was a marked decline into a paranoid and rapacious autocracy engendered by a series of personal tragedies and ill health that left the fretful king imbued with a sense of vulnerability perhaps greater than ever before – certainly since his youthful years of exile in the wilderness evading Yorkist plots.

The perturbing difference between the present and the past for Henry was that he now had a young family, and his responsibility as a father, if not a king, was to ensure their preservation even if it cost him his reputation as the just ruler, the saviour of England he once claimed to be. Survival became paramount, and survival alone.

*

Death had visited Henry VII's inner circle prior to the triumphant wedding festivities of November 1501, though those celebrations may have assuaged the king's grief for the time being. In 1499, John Welles, 1st Viscount Welles and as Margaret Beaufort's half-brother an uncle of the king, passed away, as did John Cheyne, Baron Cheyne, two men who had befriended Henry when he himself was a mere pretender in exile. Both had also been present on the victorious Bosworth campaign, where fleeting acquaintances had developed into a lifelong brotherhood. Henry owed a colossal debt of gratitude to Cheyne in particular, who had gallantly taken a direct hit from Richard III on the battlefield that may have been just enough to divert the rampaging Yorkist king from reaching his vulnerable Tudor target.

In mid-June 1500, meanwhile, during their return from what had been a productive visit to Calais to meet with Duke Philip of Burgundy, Henry and Elizabeth had received the dreadful news at Canterbury that their youngest child, Prince Edmund, had died at Hatfield Palace.

There can be little doubt the death would have affected the parents, as the sixteen-month-old toddler's personality would have just begun to develop as he grew into an integral part of the expanding Tudor nursery. The funeral took place on 22 June, with the cortège brought through London by an 'honorable Company' of men led by the duke of Buckingham before the prince was interred near the shrine of St Edward in Westminster Abbey.[37]

Another crippling bereavement occurred on 15 September that year when Henry's longstanding chancellor Cardinal John Morton, 'a man worthy for his many and grete actis, and specially for his grete wysdam', passed away at his manor in Knole, Kent. Morton's death deprived the king of one of his most valued and experienced advisors, his mentor even, and certainly had a deleterious effect on the final nine years of his reign.[38] Other significant prelates who died around this period included the long-serving archbishop of York, Thomas Rotherham, in May 1500, John Alcock, Bishop of Ely, in October 1500, and Thomas Langton, Morton's chosen replacement as archbishop of Canterbury, in January 1501. Henry's treasurer of fifteen years, John Dynham, 1st Baron Dynham, also passed away in the first month of 1501.

These losses, however troubling personally and politically, paled into insignificance with the devastation Henry felt at the start of April 1502 when a solemn messenger rode into the courtyard at Greenwich carrying news that the king's eldest son, Arthur, the teenager whose joyful wedding had been celebrated so exuberantly by the royal family just a few months earlier, had also died.[39]

The future had appeared so promising for those concerned when the festivities gradually wound down following the wedding. Arthur wrote to his new in-laws on 30 November 1501, a fortnight later, that he had 'never felt so much joy in his life as when he beheld the sweet face of his bride', adding that 'no woman in the world could be more agreeable to him' before pledging to 'make a good husband'.[40] The couple left London for Ludlow a month after their marriage, Arthur presiding over the region's estates in his capacity as prince of Wales and gradually learning the art of kingship. The much-celebrated union lasted barely four months.

According to the same contemporary observer so informed about the wedding, on 2 April 1502 in his private chamber, a 'petifull disease and sikenes' with 'great violens' fatally overpowered the unfortunate Arthur, to the 'dolour, sorow and great discomfort' of the realm, not to mention his family and intimate companions. The details are vague and positive diagnosis is not possible, but the illness does appear to have taken the prince, his household, and his parents by surprise. The messenger conveying the news hurried from Ludlow to Greenwich in just two days, carrying the 'moost sorowfull and hevy tydynges' for the attention of the king's counsellors. After absorbing the dreadful information, they summoned Henry's personal confessor, an Observant friar, who the next morning was handed the delicate task of entering the king's chamber earlier than customary to break the news. After ordering everyone out of the room, the friar addressed his king sombrely in Latin: 'If we have received good things by the hand of God, why should we not receive evil?'[41]

Henry immediately grasped the gravity of the situation and sent at once for his wife to join them so they could 'take the peynfull sorowes' together. When told what had transpired, the king took the news hard, for Queen Elizabeth was forced to attend upon him with 'full, great, and constant confortable wordes', reminding her distraught husband that as an only child himself, he had yet been preserved by God to reach the heights he did, and that this same God had provided them 'a faire, goodly, and a towardly yong Prince and two faire Princessis' that yet lived, Henry, Margaret and Mary. Whilst the king was forty-five in 1502, Elizabeth had just turned thirty-six, and the hope was she may yet conceive more children, though that naturally did not diminish the loss of a second son, and third child overall. Memories of the last time they had all been together, laughing and jesting at the wedding, no doubt plagued the thoughts of both.

Henry thanked Elizabeth for her soothing companionship, but when the queen returned to her chamber, 'naturall and modirly remembraunce of that great losse smote hir so sorrowfull to the hert', and it was the king's turn, in 'true, gentill, and feithfull love', to hurry through the palace corridors to her aid, tenderly comforting her in the manner she had earlier consoled him.[42] This tragic incident is a rare glimpse into the private marriage, one initially conceived through political necessity and opportunism but which had developed into a union of trust, fidelity, and even love. Now, they found comfort in each other's doleful embrace.

Henry had built his entire future upon the projected greatness of Arthur, the glimmering symbol of hope that would drag England away from dynastic conflict and towards the promise of a new Arthurian golden era. Though it is uncertain if the prince could ever live up to the expectations foisted upon him since his birth, his death was nevertheless devastating personally and politically, and marked the fourth successive prince of Wales to pass whilst still a youth, following the heirs of Henry VI, Edward IV and Richard III, an ominous portent for the present sovereign. The prince was buried quickly, albeit with considerable honour as befitting his status, in Worcester, though not before the death was marked with a solemn dirge in every London church, including St Paul's.[43] Each time the bells tolled for his dead son it must have sent a shiver down Henry's spine.

Katherine of Aragon, meanwhile, widowed before she could even make her mark as princess of Wales, had also fallen ill, though she recovered. Arthur's death, however, may have made her later question whether this marriage, sealed in blood by the execution of Edward of Warwick, was cursed. Exactly fifty years after the earl's death, Cardinal Reginald Pole, Warwick's nephew and himself possessing Yorkist blood, recalled how Katherine suffered 'grievous trouble and remorse' over the matter, and that 'Divine justice thus punished the sin of her father King Ferdinand', who had declared 'he would not give her to one who was not secure in his own kingdom', a decision which led to the death 'of that innocent Earl'. One wonders if Henry felt the same way after his son's untimely demise, perhaps still plagued by Warwick long after he had been put to death. Cardinal Pole would, after all, further suggest that ordering the earl's execution had been the one deed of which the king 'so greatly repented on his death-bed'.[44]

Back in London, Henry attempted to pick up the pieces of his shattered plans. Queen Elizabeth did indeed fall pregnant soon after Arthur's death, within a month in fact, and despite planning to give birth at Richmond was forced to enter confinement in the Tower of London early in the new year, 1503. On 2 February, another Tudor princess was born and quickly baptised Katherine, though her life would be tragically short-lived. Elizabeth herself developed a fever soon after the birth, and died on 11 February, just a few days after her baby daughter. It was the queen's thirty-seventh birthday.[45]

The Tower had played a significant role in the troubles that had plagued the Tudor crown in recent years, whether as the location where William Stanley and Edward of Warwick met their end, or the fortress from which Perkin Warbeck briefly escaped and was imprisoned until the day he was hanged. It was also exactly twenty years since Elizabeth's two younger brothers had disappeared from public view beyond the Tower's walls, the mystery of their whereabouts the catalyst not only for Henry's rise, but also the strife that followed.

The queen's funeral was as spectacular as one might imagine for such a popular, not to mention a dynastically crucial, figure.[46] Henry delegated the planning to his treasurer, Thomas Howard, Earl of Surrey, and the comptroller of the household, Richard Guildford, with orders not to stint in honouring the woman lauded by a sorrowful herald as 'one of the most gracious and best beloved princesses in the world in her tyme beinge'.

As Elizabeth died in the Tower, the route the funeral cortège took towards Westminster Abbey was the very same as that she took in 1487 for her coronation. Some in the crowd may have been at both events, perhaps privately reminiscing about the joy of the earlier celebration as they paid their final respects to the revered queen, whilst many hundreds, perhaps even thousands, jostled for position so close to the roadside they could feel the heat of the torches borne by those in the procession.

Led by two hundred poor men clad from head to toe in black, the parade progressed through the city with Elizabeth's household staff, the mayor, and an array of noblewomen on horseback accompanying the queen for her final journey. Present amongst the hushed masses were representatives from France, Spain, Portugal and Venice, each solemnly bearing torches in a show of pan-European respect that through his all-encompassing fog of grief may have proven something of a comfort to Henry.

Elizabeth's casket was pulled along in a carriage filled with black velvet and blue cloth of gold cushions, alongside which walked several knights holding banners that featured various royal emblems associated with the king and queen. Most observers would have been transfixed by the lifelike effigy of the queen affixed to the top of the coffin, which depicted Elizabeth crowned in a robe of estate clutching a sceptre in her right hand garnished with gold and jewels. This was the queen in all her earthly glory, how Henry and his council intended people to remember her.

Once the procession reached Westminster Abbey, the coffin was placed on to a wooden hearse covered with more black cloth of gold, embroidered with Elizabeth's submissive motto 'humble and reverent' and the queen's arms, impaled with those of her king. The queen's body lay in state overnight and was attended to by the leading women of her household, one of whom happened to be Lady Katherine Gordon, the wife of Perkin Warbeck who had entered the queen's service after the pretender's arrest nearly six years earlier.

There is little record of Katherine's life during the period after Warbeck's capture, other than her continuing presence in the court of Henry VII, or her feelings regarding the fate of her husband. The queen's death, however, seems to have opened the door for her to belatedly move forward with her own life. Though she would not remarry during Henry's reign, for reasons that can only be speculated upon, once his son acceded to the throne, Katherine ultimately remarried three times, in turn becoming the wife of James Strangways, Matthew Craddock, and Christopher Ashton, all regionally rather than nationally significant figures. When she died in 1537, forty years after her first husband was apprehended, Warbeck was the only person she married who did not merit a mention in her will, unsurprising considering his status as an executed Tudor rebel. A Scottish noblewoman connected to royalty, this would-be Yorkist queen of England was buried quietly in Fyfield, Oxfordshire, a manor she had been granted by Henry VII from the attainted estates of another Tudor outlaw, John de la Pole, Earl of Lincoln.[47]

There is no known record of surviving children born of Katherine and Warbeck, with the only indication there were any coming from the pen of the Venetian ambassador Adrian Trevisano in September 1497, when he reported from London that the pretender had arrived in Cornwall, 'leaving his wife and children' behind in Penryn. It is not beyond the realms of possibility that any children born to the pair were later hidden from public knowledge by the Tudor administration, but it seems unlikely Henry VII could have suppressed such dynastically sensitive information completely; if children did exist, enough people in Scotland, Ireland and Cornwall would have known of their existence to let it slip. Henry unquestionably possessed great influence, but could not control idle gossip beyond his reach, as shown by the entire Warbeck enterprise.

That a child was born in the first year of their marriage but died during its parents' voyage between Scotland and Cornwall cannot be dismissed, and may account for Katherine's safekeeping in sanctuary shortly after her arrival in the south-west. There is no mention, however, of any child in her will, and when Trevisano personally encountered the couple in London two months after he wrote of these children, he made no further mention of their existence.[48] It remains, therefore, wholly unproven any child of Warbeck's blood was born, let alone living in the years after his demise.

In 1503, however, Katherine Gordon's immediate preoccupation was placing one of the palls on the coffin of Elizabeth of York. The burial ceremony was presided over by the bishop of London, William Warham, and after the queen's lead coffin was lowered into the ground within Westminster Abbey, her weeping chamberlain and household staff stepped forward to break their ceremonial staves of office in the customary manner, casting them into the grave to signal symbolically the end of their service to her. To aid Elizabeth's passage to the afterlife, her husband Henry ordered 636 masses to be sung for her soul. In total, the devastated king spent nearly £3,000 on the proceedings, a figure which dwarfed the otherwise considerable sum of just under £600 he contributed to Arthur's funeral.[49]

If Henry had been shaken by Arthur's death, then Elizabeth's sudden demise completely incapacitated the king, who for the first time in his reign physically and mentally collapsed. According to an informed herald, news of his wife's death was 'as heveye and dolorous to the kings heighness as hath been sene or heard of', and after empowering Surrey and Guildford to take care of matters, he 'tooke with him certain of his secretest and prevely departed to a solitary place to passe his sorrows and would no man should resort to him'.[50]

The mask of a strong king, resolute beyond measure and in absolute control of his faculties even during moments of intense pressure, had finally slipped. The double blow of Arthur's death followed by Elizabeth's over ten months had broken Henry. He sought solace in private, away from those bearing well-meaning but irrelevant words of comfort or advice. What could anyone say to him that would ease the pain he felt deep in his soul, an aching that could never be relieved? It is telling that the king forthwith abandoned the Tower as one of his royal residences, and aside from a brief visit in 1507 never returned to the fortress in which his wife died hoping to bolster the family with another heir. Henry was, in a word, disconsolate.

The king wasn't the only Tudor grief-stricken by Elizabeth's sudden demise, of course. The presentation page of an elaborately decorated early sixteenth-century manuscript depicts the crowned king seated upon a throne receiving a copy of the work in his robes of estate, but it is the scene around him that is particularly poignant.[51] To his right are seated the young princesses Margaret and Mary, both clad in black mourning hoods, whilst in the background weeping upon the empty bed of his mother is Prince Henry, the future King Henry VIII, aged just eleven at the time. Four years later, in a revealing letter to Erasmus, the bereaved boy would describe learning of his mother's passing as 'hateful intelligence' and a 'wound to which time had brought insensibility'.[52] One can only wonder what impact this loss had on his future marital dramas.

When Henry VII did finally abandon his chamber, it was an altogether colder and more isolated man who emerged, one who 'began to treat his people with more harshness and severity than had been his custom', mused a disapproving Polydore Vergil.[53] Aside from the deaths of his wife, two sons, and Cardinal Morton since the turn of the century, another series of losses in the king's most intimate circle deprived Henry of a support network when he needed it most. His steward of the household, and the commander who had helped secure royal victories over Perkin Warbeck and the Cornish in 1497, Robert Willoughby de Broke, had died in August 1502, followed by another close confidant, his chancellor of the Duchy of Lancaster, Reginald Bray, in June 1503. The king's stepbrother George Stanley, Baron Strange, meanwhile, passed away in December 1503, followed in turn by his father, and Henry's stepfather, Thomas Stanley, 1st Earl of Derby, in the subsequent summer. Henry could only watch helplessly as those he had always relied upon continued to slip away.

The king's eldest daughter, Princess Margaret, meanwhile, departed for Scotland in June 1503, just a handful of months after her mother's death, with Henry solemnly accompanying her as far as his mother Margaret Beaufort's home at Collyweston. Within the space of three years, he had lost two sons, Edmund and Arthur, his wife Elizabeth, and now bid a permanent farewell to young Margaret, whom he would never lay eyes upon again. There can be little doubt Henry had grown disillusioned with and demoralised by the world around him on account of these losses. What man wouldn't? In the final years of the reign, he simply had fewer people he could trust to turn to for guidance, or to temper the extremities of his character. He was increasingly alone.

On top of this devastating personal grief, Henry also had to contend with worsening ill health as he got older, apologising to his mother in a July 1501 letter for not writing more on account of his declining sight.[54] In September 1503, there was even concern for the king's survival when Hugh Conway, Treasurer of Calais and one of his earliest supporters in exile, was reported as saying, 'The kyngis grace is but a weke man and syklow, not lykly to be no longe lyvis man.' That Henry was not expected to be a long-lived man worried Conway when he considered the 'world that shouldbe after hym', a reference to the succession. Some men, he speculated, spoke of the duke of Buckingham as a contender to be king, whereas others preferred Edmund de la Pole, the earl of Suffolk and younger brother of John de la Pole, Earl of Lincoln, who had been the driving force behind the Lambert Simnel affair in 1487. None of these men that Conway had encountered in Calais, however, 'spake of my lord prynce', the young Henry Tudor.

When the king was informed that such discussions were taking place, it represented his greatest fear, that he would follow Henry VI, Edward IV and Richard III in failing to secure his dynasty's survival after his death.[55]

Suffolk's errant behaviour around the turn of the century 'greatly disturbed' Henry, who in the words of Vergil soon 'began to fear fresh upheavals'.[56] With Yorkist blood in his veins and as the younger sibling of a notorious rebel killed in battle attempting to unseat Henry, Suffolk had been kept under close watch by the Tudor king throughout the reign, and though he had briefly succeeded to his father's dukedom in 1492, was soon demoted by the king to the rank of earl as he couldn't afford the upkeep. Whilst this may understandably have been the source of some bitterness, Suffolk nevertheless rallied for the king against the Cornish in 1497 and exhibited no outward signs of treason until he was indicted for murder in September 1498.

Though pardoned of the crime, Suffolk raised Henry's suspicions when he fled overseas in July 1499, the same summer that the plot to break Warbeck and Warwick out of the Tower of London was exposed to royal officials. The earl did return to England a few months later and resumed his duties as if nothing was untoward, but in August 1501 abruptly absconded for the second time, this time taking with him his younger brother Richard and seeking the protection of Maximilian I, a tactic similar to Warbeck's eight years earlier. Once more, a potential Yorkist alternative, two in fact, were loitering ominously abroad, and in possession of a king who had already sponsored a couple of previous pretenders in Simnel and Warbeck. It was a case of history threatening to repeat itself for Henry, who could only respond by issuing a series of sizeable payments to Maximilian and imprisoning a third de la Pole brother, William, who had remained in England.

Though recognised in some continental reports as 'the White Rose', Suffolk's undisputed Yorkist lineage proved insufficient for him to emulate Simnel and Warbeck during his five years abroad. When Philip of Burgundy was shipwrecked in England in 1506, Henry VII leapt upon this good fortune to persuade his stranded guest to hand over the earl, and as the duke was desperate to continue his journey onwards to Castile, he readily agreed. Suffolk was surrendered into English hands and sent straight to the Tower where he would languish for the remainder of the reign until eventually executed under Henry VIII in 1513.[57] He may have been the right man to challenge Henry VII, but his campaign came at the wrong time. The younger de la Pole, Richard, remained at large until he was killed at the Battle of Pavia in 1525, the final Yorkist claimant to openly lay claim to the English throne, forty years after Bosworth.

Suffolk's capture represented another pretender that Henry had overcome with little incident, but that is not to diminish the nervousness the king felt about the earl's movements between 1501 and 1506, particularly as by 1502 two of his three sons were dead, with no guarantee the third would survive to adulthood. The political settlement between York and Lancaster that his marriage embodied was now weakened as a result of Elizabeth's death, and if he remarried and fathered further sons, there was no guarantee he could retain traditional Yorkist support. Just a handful of years into the new century, the prospect of a healthy Tudor succession suddenly appeared slender. Henry was on the rocks.

This emotional and political turmoil explains in part why Henry's reign declined into one characterised by repression and suspicion in his final years. Without the administrative prowess of Bray – 'when Henry fell into error he was bold enough moderately to admonish and reprove him' – the political guidance of Morton, who likewise 'also did not fear to act in like manner',[58] or even the calming and supportive influence in private of Queen Elizabeth, the worst excesses of the king's character rose bitterly to the fore. His dogged focus in these final years was more than ever on enriching the crown whilst suppressing his subjects, whether friend or foe, a policy he had come to consider the shrewdest method to secure the Tudor succession.

The two men the king tasked with maximising his feudal prerogatives were Richard Empson and Edmund Dudley, very capable and vigorous administrators who set to work exploring how to fill the royal treasury. Dudley in particular pored over the parchment rolls and accounts with utmost efficiency, scouring for old or forgotten debts to the crown and following them up with an assiduity that proved extremely profitable for Henry. Wholly committed to crown service, they were also responsible for the increased prosecution of bonds and recognisances, that is financial penalties or suspended fines, from 1504 onwards. Their purpose was to enforce good behaviour and law and order through the fear of economic ruin for those who failed to toe the line. Payments, meanwhile, were demanded in exchange for royal pardons, and as a consequence the gulf in wealth between the crown and those beneath grew wider as the reign wore on, exactly as Henry envisioned. He was making himself insuperable.[59]

Much of what Empson and Dudley accomplished was strictly within the bounds of the law, but the excessive nature of their sustained campaign was hardly customary in recent memory and served to fuel a climate of suspicion and fear throughout the kingdom. Vergil believed the astute pair had 'been given the job by the king not so much to administer justice as to strip the population of its wealth, without respite and by every means fair or foul vied with each other in extorting money', in particular targeting the rich rather than the poor. Henry even supposedly admitted that he 'wished to keep all Englishmen obedient through fear', and with financial penalties 'so rapidly applied that all people, in terror of losing their wealth, at once began to behave themselves'. It was a tough policy that appeared to work. Nonetheless, the Italian rued, it was 'the most savage harshness', and whilst the king may not have initially been greedy, he 'gradually laid aside all moderation and sank into a state of avarice'.[60]

Ensuring no opportunity was lost to boost his coffers whilst emptying those of his subjects, Henry often closely scrutinised the account books himself. Such deeply unpopular rapacity had two effects: firstly, it destroyed his reputation for several hundred years, obscuring much of his accomplishments in recovering England's position on the continental stage after decades of internal strife, and secondly, it helped impose widespread compliance that saved the remnants of his dynasty from destruction.

By the end of the reign, the English crown was not merely solvent, but overflowing in riches, and undoubtedly all the safer for it. Though written several years after his death, Henry may have identified with a concept the Italian political theorist Niccolò Machiavelli wrote about in *Discourses on Livy*, wherein he speculated that provided the outcome is ultimately positive for the kingdom and its people, most actions, however 'extraordinary and irregular', can be excused, 'for although the act condemns the doer, the end may justify him'.[61]

That Henry was not imposing such punishing measures on his subjects out of innate spite, but rather as a concerted policy to safeguard the Tudor succession, is suggested by Vergil. The Italian wrote that the king 'was not unaware that, as a result of this ruthless extortion, there were many who rather feared than loved him', but nevertheless, 'his sole interest was to ensure his safety' and guarantee his subjects 'remained more thoroughly and entirely in obedience to him'. He was, in effect, policing his people. In that respect, the chosen course of action makes some degree of sense if one places oneself in Henry's shoes during the first decade of the fifteenth century, though this did not prevent his burdened populace denouncing bitterly what they interpreted to be 'the greed of their monarch'.[62]

That Henry regretted such systematic exploitation in the final weeks of his life is possible; in his will, the king left instructions that 'if any persone of what degree soevir he bee, shewe by way of complainte to our Executours, any wrong to have been doon to hym, by us [or] any man can for any cause reasonable, clayme any debt of us, or shewe that we have wronged hym', the matter was to be investigated by committee and restitution made.[63] Bishop John Fisher, tasked with reading the eulogy at the king's funeral, also made reference to the fact that just two months before his passing Henry had expressed a desire for 'a true reformacyon' of his ways and to pardon all those he had hurt with his unjust laws, something duly carried out a few days prior to his death.[64]

Dudley, meanwhile, knew boundaries had been crossed, and confessed as much shortly after his master's death when he and Empson were arrested on trumped-up charges of treason, a widely popular move by the new administration. Whilst languishing in prison awaiting his fate, Dudley cited eighty-four cases in which he felt people had been unjustly wronged and deserving of restitution, though such belated remorse could not save him or Empson; both were executed in August 1510.[65]

Henry VII, a boy raised in penniless exile dependent on the goodwill of his protectors and vulnerable for most of his youth to changing political winds outside his control, equated financial prosperity with dynastic security as a middle-aged king, and there is no reason to suggest he was mistaken in this judgement. Despite his intentions to found a dynasty accepted by all Englishmen, the reign had shown across its two decades that there would always be some Yorkist pretender waiting in the shadows, genuine or fake, not to mention the abundance of other nobles descended from royal stock who were no less unlikely candidates for the crown than he himself had been prior to Bosworth. The de la Pole, Stafford, Talbot and Percy houses, for example, could claim some degree of descent from Edward III, not to mention the York claim that existed in Edward IV's daughters, as could a host of foreign royal families including the Stewarts of Scotland, the Aviz of Portugal, the Hapsburgs of Burgundy and Germany, and the Trastámarans of Spain. A decent army, favourable weather, an ambivalent nobility and – to the medieval mind – the judgement of God made it possible to topple a king. Henry decided that his route to safety was to restore solvency to the crown so that he could simply outspend any rivals if needed, whilst limiting the opportunities for any overmighty subjects to rise. It was deeply unpopular, but it worked.

Widowed in his mid-forties with just one living son, the twelve-year-old Prince Henry, the Tudor dynasty's future essentially rested upon the king surviving long enough to ensure the throne was peaceably passed on to an adult heir, something not accomplished since Henry IV's death in 1413. The dark fate of the Princes in the Tower – their presumed fate at least – had not been forgotten, and it was one Henry VII sought to avoid for his own son at all costs. He was growing richer than ever; he just had to live that bit longer to secure the greatest and most important triumph of his reign.

19

Epilogue – One Rose

The final years of Henry VII's reign were tough, both for those subjects fearful of falling foul of a strategically avaricious king, and for the monarch himself, persistently ill and plagued by anxiety over the future of his dynasty. Polydore Vergil's eyewitness account of the reign's dark climax reported that the king was 'greatly incapacitated' with sickness for each of the final three springtimes of his life,[1] which is corroborated by a series of observations by the attentive Spanish and Venetian ambassadors.

In April 1507, the Spaniard Roderigo de Puebla noted that the king had been severely ill throughout Holy Week, confined to his chamber in Richmond and unable to eat or drink for six days straight, to the point 'his life was despaired of'. By October, however, the same ambassador was able to write in wonder that Henry had recovered sufficiently over the summer to be considered in 'perfect health', even taking part in hunting and hawking sessions. The king's recuperation proved short-lived. In August 1508, it was the Venetian's turn to report that Henry was once more 'very ill, and in extremis', though it was not until early 1509, when he again fell sick whilst at Hanworth Manor, that it finally became clear the tenacious Tudor monarch was 'utterly without hope of recovery'. His strapping son, at over six feet already dwarfing most men around court and with enormous limbs that impressed de Puebla, was just a few months shy of eighteen years old when the king's body at last gave up the struggle.[2]

A vivid insight into Henry's final moments is found in the eulogy given at his funeral by Bishop John Fisher, later printed at the request of the king's bereft mother, Margaret Beaufort.[3] Around the beginning of Lent, Fisher recalled that the increasingly fragile king summoned his confessor to his chamber, to whom Henry 'with all dylygence and great repentaunce' declared that he intended to change his ways, promising a true reformation of his laws so that justice might be executed better in future. He was also heard to pledge 'many tymes with grete sorowe' within earshot of his servants 'that yf it pleased God to sende hym lyfe they sholde se hym a new chaunged man'. His despairing wish would not be granted.

By mid-April 1509, the king was bedridden in Richmond for what would prove the final time, and was unable to take his meat or drink for several days, however well it had been prepared by his cooks. In excruciating pain and tormented by the mental anguish of preparing to face divine judgement, two days before his death Henry desperately asked for his monstrance, a religious vessel likely crafted from gold, which he kissed and fiercely beat against his chest. It was a pitiful sight that reduced those waiting upon him to tears. According to Fisher, Henry's final suffering before death lasted for twenty-seven hours, a dreadful period during which the king constantly wailed on account of the pain, often crying out for 'helpe and socoure' against the 'cruell assautes of deth' which were 'fyers and sharpe ayenst him'. Wanting release, in his suffering he appealed to Jesus:

> O my blessyd Jhesu, o my moost mercyfull Jhesu, o my lorde and creatour Jhesu. O my lord delyver my soule, delyver my soule from the myseryes of this worlde, delyver my soule from these deedly paynes, delyver my soule from this corruptyble body, delyver my soule from the bondes of synne, delyver my soule from my mortall enemyes, delyver my soule from the daungers of everlastyne deth.

The grave scene at the king's bedside was captured in an evocative sketch by the herald Thomas Wriothesley[4] showing fourteen figures gathered around Henry at the end: three doctors clutching flasks, two clerics, and nine others identifiable by their coats of arms, namely Richard Foxe, Bishop of Winchester; George Hastings, Baron Hastings; esquires Richard Weston, Richard Clement, Matthew Baker, Hugh Denys; and gentlemen ushers John Sharpe, William Tyler and William Fitzwilliam. Not portrayed in the drawing was the prince, who, it is known from Fisher's eulogy, had been summoned at some point for some final words of advice from his father before 'commyttynge unto hym the laborous governaunce of this realm'. On the evening of 21 April 1509, Henry VII passed away aged fifty-two. The turbulent reign of the first Tudor king was over.

The death was kept quiet for two days whilst his loyal servants worked tirelessly to ensure the succession was safeguarded from any unexpected challenges. Once the news of the king's death was released, everything was already in place for the young prince, now Henry VIII, to be widely recognised as the new king. As England came to terms with the first change in governance for a quarter of a century, the dead king's body was washed and embalmed before lying in state in various chambers around Richmond Palace, the opulent home that he had erected. It wasn't until 9 May, two and a half weeks after his death, that Henry's funeral cortège left his palace for burial, following the well-trodden route through Southwark to London Bridge, across the Thames and into St Paul's.

The coffin and carriage was drawn by seven sturdy coursers, each draped in black velvet bearing the royal arms. Atop was a realistic effigy of the king, its weary face crafted from Henry's death mask. To the left marched his nobility, whilst to the right were assembled the bishops and clergy, walking with their king for the final time. Household staff, city officials, and foreign emissaries led from the front, with Sir Edward Darrell tasked with holding aloft the king's standard. Just behind the carriage walked Henry's Welsh uncle Sir David Owen bearing a steel helmet capped with a crown of gold, followed by Edward Howard, a younger son of the earl of Surrey, who was wearing the king's armour and brandishing his battle-axe. If the effigy on top of the coffin depicted the worn-down and aged Henry at his death, then Howard's charge was to evoke memories of how the king had appeared in his younger days at the battles of Bosworth and Stoke Field – glorious moments of Tudor triumph. When the convoy reached St Paul's West Door, due to its weight the coffin was carried into the church by twelve members of the king's guard, where it was reverently placed upon a wooden hearse before the altar.[5]

Henry lay in state overnight, and the following morning before a packed congregation Bishop Fisher delivered his lengthy eulogy from the pulpit, a rambling stream of consciousness that was, as one may expect from Margaret Beaufort's confessor, an adulatory account. It did not tell the full story of Henry's reign, or provide an unbiased account of his character, but by dying in his own bed and surrounded by his own men, and not, for example, on the battlefield like Richard III or in prison like Henry VI, the way was clear for such exaltation. To Fisher, Henry's

... politic wisdom in governance was singular, his wit always quick and ready, his reason pithy and substantial, his memory fresh and holding, his experience notable, his counsel fortunate and taken by wise deliberation, his speech gracious in diverse languages, his person goodly and amiable, his natural complexion of the purest mixture, his issue fayre and in good number; leagues and confederacies he had with all Christian princes, his mighty power was dread everywhere, not only within his realm but without also, his people were to him in as humble subjection as ever they were to king, his land many a day in peace and tranquillity, his prosperity in battle against his enemies was marvellous, his dealing in time of perils and dangers was cold and sober with great hardiness.[6]

With Henry's greatness extolled before the masses in St Paul's, the procession thereafter continued to Westminster Abbey where the king had left explicit instructions in his will that he was to be buried next to his wife. For Henry, relying on champions such as Fisher to establish his legacy as one of England's greatest sovereigns, whether true or otherwise, had not been enough. No sooner had he overseen the completion of his grand palace in Richmond than he embarked on another ambitious building programme, this time for the intended site of his eventual interment.

Throughout his reign, Henry had persistently sought the canonisation of his half-uncle 'of blissed memorie' Henry VI, around whom a cult had developed in the years following his suspected murder in 1471. The Tudor king intended to house the would-be saint's shrine in Westminster, with his own tomb placed nearby, and in October 1502 the existing thirteenth-century Lady Chapel was pulled down so a new, extravagant replacement could be erected upon the rubble. The foundation stone of this new chapel, intended to serve as a perpetual memorial to two King Henrys for as long as the world endured, was laid on 24 January 1503.[7]

The vast building project was only completed in 1519, a decade after Henry VII's death, and proved to be a chapel of such magnificence the antiquarian John Leland would regard it nothing less than 'the wonder of the entire world'. In particular, the fan-vaulted roof that was embellished with multiple hanging pendants provided a visual spectacle unlike anything seen in England at the time, rivalled perhaps only by that of King's College, Cambridge, another project Henry was involved in. With the drive for Henry VI's canonisation and translation losing steam owing to the financial demands of the papacy, the king whose tomb came to be the sole focal point of the chapel was the benefactor responsible for the chapel's conception in the first place, Henry VII.

Westminster had not been an accidental choice as the final resting place for Henry's earthly remains. He knew the abbey, the 'commen sepulture' as he referred to it in his will, was regarded as one of the most prestigious in the kingdom, long associated with English royalty as the customary site where scores of kings had been crowned, most recently himself, and later buried. Instructions were even left for a gold three-foot statue of himself, clad in armour and prominently holding the crown won on the battlefield at Bosworth, to be placed in a position of honour before the tomb of St Edward the Confessor.[8]

By electing to be buried in Westminster, rather than Windsor, for example, where the bodies of Edward IV and Henry VI lay, Henry VII was placing himself firmly in the pantheon of venerated Plantagenet, Norman and even Anglo-Saxon monarchs who ruled before him, perhaps even above when one considers the stunning chapel he had built to house his body. In death, Henry continued a policy he had vigorously followed throughout his reign – he was making a bold, dynastic statement to reinforce the legitimacy of the Tudors.

The sculptor tasked with producing the bronze and marble masterpiece that would rest upon the king's vault was Pietro Torrigiano, a Florentine banished from his homeland for a string of violent incidents, including breaking the nose of his colleague, one Michelangelo Buonarroti. Torrigiano's work captured a remarkable likeness of the king and queen, lying side-by-side with their hands clasped in prayer. In each corner were positioned four gilt bronze angels, those on the east end holding aloft the royal arms with a pair of cherubs supporting the arms of the queen below.

The double tomb was encircled by an iron grate which created a private, chapel-like enclosure in the heart of the chapel that was topped with royal arms. Upon the grate was provision for one hundred tapers to be placed, which in accordance with the king's instructions were to be lit on appropriate anniversaries, during the principal feasts, and whenever any reigning king or queen set foot into the abbey. Four more protruding brackets to hold tapers were also placed on each side of the grate, each containing an eye-catching crown-shaped drip pan. Within the enclosure was a small altar upon which were a couple of golden reliquaries containing an alleged piece of the holy cross and a leg of St George.[9]

Designed in the Italian manner, the structure was far more ornate than anything of its kind seen in England before, surpassing all previous royal examples. If a tomb told the story of the man buried beneath, then Henry VII was surely the greatest king England had ever known, and no doubt this was the reaction it was designed to stir in all who beheld the wonder in person. When one factors in the Lady Chapel in which the tomb stood as the central attraction, Henry's resting place was the finest of any English monarch.

By contrast, Richard III's remains were lost to history after the Dissolution until their recent rediscovery beneath a Leicester car park, whereas Henry VIII, alone of his fellow Tudor monarchs, rests under a modest marble slab in St George's Chapel, Windsor. The bodies of Lambert Simnel, Perkin Warbeck, and Edward of Warwick have long since vanished; Warbeck is somewhere beneath the former Augustinian complex in the heart of the much-changed City of London, Warwick is underneath the ruins of Bisham Abbey, and Simnel's location is presently unknown.

It has been claimed the remains of two other royal figures of interest to this period are interred near Henry VII in his Lady Chapel. On 17 July 1674, workmen in the Tower of London uncovered a wooden box ten feet beneath a stone staircase that contained two skeletons. As Thomas More had speculated early in the reign of Henry VIII that the princes were initially buried at the foot of a staircase, the later assumption was that these remains must in fact be the missing princes, and four years later they were interred in Henry VII's Lady Chapel by orders of the current king, Charles II. In concession to their supposed royal status, the skeletons were placed inside a fine marble monument designed by Christopher Wren, with an inscription that partially read 'Here lie the relics of Edward V, King of England, and Richard, Duke of York', before the speculative and baseless addition, 'These brothers being confined in the Tower of London, and there stifled with pillows, were privately and meanly buried, by the order of their perfidious uncle Richard the Usurper.'

Despite the initial identification of the bones as the princes, and the flawed confirmation of this fact when they were further analysed in 1933, it remains to be seen whether these remains are truly those of the two Yorkist boys, or even if they are boys at all. If it could be proved in future the skeletons are the princes, it may not answer who killed the tragic pair, but will at least end speculation about Perkin Warbeck's imposture – he could not possibly have been one of the princes if they had been buried in the Tower.

On the morning of 11 May 1509, however, such matters lay in the future. Around six o'clock, before the city emerged from its slumber, the foremost nobles and clergy of the realm had gathered in the chapel. Together they heard three masses sung before observing the lowering of Henry's coffin, covered with black velvet embroidered with a white cross of satin, 'with Reverence' into the vault that already contained that of his queen. Once the coffin came to rest, all the assembled bishops and abbots stepped forward to place their own crosses on top, before Archbishop of Canterbury William Warham dropped in a handful of soil. The earls of Surrey and Shrewsbury, the king's treasurer and steward respectively, made their way to the grave where they snapped their staves of office and cast them into the darkness. The vault was closed, with a rich cloth of gold placed over the spot beneath which the king now rested alongside his wife.[10]

The silence was only broken when the heralds stepped forward to remove their heraldic tabards, crying out in one loud voice that reverberated around the ancient abbey, 'The noble King Henry the Seventh is dead.' Once the echoes faded, they put back on their tabards, and bellowed with considerable enthusiasm in French, 'God send the noble King Henry the Eighth long life!'[11] With these few words, the focus shifted from Tudor father to son, and from king to king. This transferral of allegiance, of power, and of the crown had been Henry VII's sole objective in his later years; it was his final triumph.

Six weeks later, in the very same abbey, the glorious figure of Henry VIII was crowned King of England, with those assembled crying, '*Vivat, vivat Rex*!' four times when the traditional coronation rituals had been completed. 'Long Live the King!' And what a king he appeared to be. According to Vergil, the youth was distinguished

> ... by his handsome bearing, his comely and manly features (in which one could discern as much authority as good will), his outstanding physical strength, remarkable memory, aptness at all the arts of both war and peace, skill at arms and on horseback, scholarship of no mean order, thorough knowledge of music, and his humanity, benevolence, and self-control.[12]

Everybody, the Italian assured his readers, 'loved him', for he represented hope. As Londoners rejoiced with feasting, bonfires and games to mark the dawning of a new reign, likely replicated throughout the kingdom, Henry VII had accomplished what no previous English king had managed for eighty-seven years, and that was to oversee the peaceful bequeathing of his crown to his son. Henry VI, Edward IV and Richard III failed where Henry VII succeeded.

This had not been an inevitable outcome, and in fact just five years earlier had seemed improbable when rumours of the king's apparently imminent demise were known to be discussed in Calais, and possibly in other homes and taverns throughout the land. If Henry had died as early 1504 or 1505, it would not be exaggeration to suggest there was a significant chance the Tudor dynasty would not have existed, perhaps displaced by the House of Buckingham or Suffolk. Henry VII's reign would have become a mere footnote in the tumultuous annals of English history.

Henry VII did, however, cling on long enough to pass on in peaceful fashion the crown he had fought hard to win, and even harder to keep, to a seventeen-year-old heir just about old enough to assume personal command. It was a crown that would be worn in turn by three of his grandchildren, Edward VI, Mary I, and Elizabeth I, before passing into the Scottish Stewart line of his daughter Margaret. Henry's descendants, in fact, still occupy the throne over five hundred years later, and every single monarch that ruled after him can trace his or her descent from the first Tudor.

In light of the issues he had with pretenders, his hard-hitting financial policies and restrictive laws designed to curb noble power, it is often overlooked Henry assumed the throne with a serious handicap, having arrived in England a little-known, Welsh-born and Breton-raised protégé of the French regime possessing an inconsequential blood claim to the throne. No king of England was less suited to rule the country upon their coronation than Henry, a penniless stranger to noble and commoner alike who had no experience of overseeing even a modest estate, let alone a vast and fractured kingdom. That he was able to reach the end of his reign twenty-four years later in an insuperable position, not only the first English king to avoid overthrow since 1422, but also able to re-establish the strength, wealth, and stability of the crown in the process, was remarkable. This was not accomplished through luck, but rather sheer hard work, meticulous attention to detail, and an iron-willed determination to outlast any and all rivals before him.

Of the Perkin Warbeck affair in particular, but which could be extended to all other plots against the Tudor king, the cartographer and antiquarian John Speed wrote admiringly in 1611, 'The push it gave to his sovereignty did thoroughly try his sitting, being of force enough to have cast an ordinarie rider out of sadle.'[13] The implication, of course, was that Henry had been no ordinary sitter.

This improbable rise from exile to king was truly a rags-to-royal-riches story, and without the benefit of hindsight, there is little reason to suppose that in the summer of 1485, a Lancastrian-descended pretender named Henry Tudor should have founded a new dynasty whose name, and legacy, endures to the present day. Henry himself would have recognised the weakness of his position from the moment the battle-worn crown was handed to him at Bosworth Field, which accounts for the extraordinary lengths he went to in order to brand his dynasty with heraldic propaganda that sought to sell his story to the people. If he spotted an opportunity to draw attention to his various badges, such as the Red Dragon of Cadwaladr, the White Greyhound of Richmond, or the Beaufort Portcullis, then the king did so without limitation. His Lady Chapel in Westminster Abbey was but one example where the badges were copiously displayed, on the stone walls, in the windows, and even as part of the woodwork.

Another badge that Henry adopted upon coming to the throne was the Red Rose, a little-known symbol of the House of Lancaster. Together with the more visible White Rose of his wife's Yorkist ancestors, in a remarkable piece of dynastic self-promotion, the king combined both roses to create one combined double rose, an alluring visual image of reconciliation, peace, and harmony. It was sewn onto the livery of household staff, moulded onto buildings, painted into manuscripts, and in 1489 formed part of the design for the new sovereign gold coin. Whereas some violently rejected the political indoctrination emanating from the Tudor administration, as shown by the various rebellions during the reign, others came to accept, perhaps even believe in, this relentlessly bruited concept of unity, certainly enough to consign contentious dynastic fidelities to the past in submission to the new order.

Sometime around the coronation of Henry VIII, the new king's former tutor, the poet John Skelton, celebrated his one-time pupil in a work known as *A Laud and Praise Made for Our Sovereign Lord the King*, which opened:

> The Rose both white and red,
> In one rose doth now grow[14]

Henry VII's concerted strategy to create a simplistic and visual narrative of dynastic unity had, therefore, been picked up after his death by men like Skelton, and would lead to later sixteenth-century writers setting down in the historical record how the first Tudor king had brought the bitter wars to a close with relative ease. William Shakespeare perhaps captured such sentiment perfectly when he wrote that Henry had been responsible for returning to England 'smooth-faced peace' that brought 'smiling aplenty and fair prosperous days'. It was an appealing, and enduring, concept that was embodied in 1509 in the magnificent figure of Henry VIII, the towering rose both red and white.

As the twenty-four-year reign had shown, however, in truth the journey from Bosworth Field through to the springtime of 1509 could hardly be termed peaceful. Polydore Vergil had certainly been perceptive when he noted Henry VII 'evaded peril not without effort'.[15] Though there were undeniably moments of spectacular pageantry excessively celebrated by the masses, Bosworth had not marked the end of pitched battles on English soil, nor foreign-backed invasions fronted by rival claimants for the throne that threatened to reopen the bitter wounds of civil war. The blood of many rebels stained the block, and the spiked heads of those who had unsuccessfully challenged the crown were a common sight along London Bridge. Henry never comfortably occupied his throne.

History, however, as the saying goes, is often written by and on behalf of the victors, and Henry VII's reputation as the king who returned peace to England after three decades of conflict has long been assured in the public consciousness, accurate or otherwise. Notwithstanding Henry's triumph and the effective propaganda campaign before and after his death, which sought to enhance his glory and diminish his rivals, the names and deeds of Simnel, Warbeck, and Warwick, that triumvirate of pretenders who threatened to derail the House of Tudor long before dynastic immortality was obtained during the reigns of Henry VIII and Elizabeth I, live on five hundred years later. The remarkable story of Henry VII's struggles with the pretenders that blighted his turbulent reign remains one of the most fascinating periods in English history, about which, frustratingly, many questions remain tantalisingly unanswerable.

Notes

Abbreviations
AH – Polydore Vergil *Anglica Historia*
Andre – The Life of Henry VII
Chron. Lon. – Chronicles of London
Collectanea – John Leland's
  Brittannicis Collectanea
Contemporary – The Reign of
  Henry VII from contemporary
  sources
CPR – Calendar of Patent Rolls
CPReg – Calendar of Papal Register
Croyland – Ingulph's Chronicle of the
  Abbey of Croyland
CSPM – Calendar of State Papers,
  Milan
CSPS – Calendar of State Papers, Spain
CSPV – Calendar of State Papers,
  Venice

EH – *Excerpta Historica*
Great – Great Chronicle of London
Letters – Letters and Papers Illustrative
  of the Reigns of Richard III and
  Henry VII
Mancini – Dominic Mancini's The
  Usurpation of Richard III
Materials – Materials for a History of
  the Reign of Henry VII
OL – Original Letters, Illustrative of
  English History
PL – The Paston Letters
Plumpton – Plumpton Correspondence
RotParl – *Rotuli Parliamentorum*
YHB – York House Books

1 The Year of Three Kings

1. Croyland pp. 481-483
2. Mancini p. 67
3. ibid pp. 67-69
4. ibid p. 73
5. Ross, C., *Edward IV* (1974) pp. 425-426
6. Croyland p. 485
7. Vergil p. 173
8. Croyland p. 486
9. Vergil p. 173
10. Croyland p. 487
11. Mancini p. 77
12. ibid p. 79
13. Chron. Lon. p. 190; Croyland p. 487
14. Croyland pp. 487-488
15. Mancini p. 91
16. RotParl VI pp. 124-125
17. Croyland p. 488
18. Raine, A., '*York Civic Records Vol. 1*' in Yorkshire *Archaeological Society, Record Series Vol. XCVIII* (1939) pp. 73-74
19. PL Vol III p. 306

20. Croyland pp. 488-489
21. Bentley, S., *Excerpta Historica; or Illustrations of English History* (1831) pp. 16-16
22. Croyland p. 489
23. ibid p. 489
24. Fabyan, R., *The New Chronicles of England and France* (ed. H. Ellis, 1811) p. 668
25. Chron. Lon. p. 190
26. Great p. 234
27. Croyland pp. 490-491
28. Ricard, R., *The Maire of Bristowe Is Kalendar by Robert Ricart* (ed. L. T. Smith, London, 1872) p. 42
29. Mancini p. 93
30. Wroe, A., *Perkin, A Story of Deception* (London, 2004) p. 526
31. Great p. 237
32. Arthurson, I.; Kingwell, N., 'The Proclamation of Henry Tudor as King of England' in *Historical Research Vol. 63* (1990) pp. 100-104
33. Great pp. 236-237

2 The Triumphing General
1. Croyland p. 503
2. Vergil p. 244; Croyland p. 504
3. Croyland p. 504
4. Commines, P., *The Memoirs of Philip de Commines, Lord of Agenton Vol II* (ed. A. R. Scoble, London, 1877) p. 64
5. Croyland p. 505
6. Vergil p. 226; Great p. 238
7. Croyland p. 504
8. Vergil p. 227
9. Fabyan p. 673
10. Vergil p. 227
11. *Letters of the Kings of England Vol. I* (ed. J. O. Halliwell, London, 1848) pp. 169-170
12. AH p. 3
13. Croyland p. 504
14. AH p. 3
15. Fabyan p. 673
16. For following account, Wickham Legg, L., *English Coronation Records* (London, 1901) pp. 219-239
17. Andre p. 33
18. Fisher, J., *The Funeral Sermon of Margaret Countess of Richmond and Derby, Mother to King Henry VII and Foundress of Christ's and St John's College in Cambridge, Preached by Bishop John Fisher in 1509* (ed. J. Hyers, Cambridge, 1840) p. 126
19. For following account, RotParl VI pp. 267-384
20. 'Vatican Regesta: 685' in CPReg 1484-1492
21. Andre p. 35
22. AH p. 11
23. CPR 1485-1494 pp. 39-40
24. Materials Vol. 1 p. 419
25. Cavell, E., 'Henry VII, the North of England, and the First Provincial Progress of 1486' in *Northern History XXXIX* (2002) p. 189
26. See next chapter
27. For following account, *A Volume of English Miscellanies Illustrating the History and Language of the Northern Counties of England* (ed. J. Raine, London, 1890) pp. 53-57
28. Croyland pp. 513-514
29. Cavell p. 191
30. Materials Vol. 1 p. 462
31. Malory, T., *Le Morte D'Arthur, Sir Thomas Malory's Book of King Arthur and of his Noble Knights of the Round Table* (ed. E. Strachey, London, 1897) p. 63
32. Cunningham, S., *Prince Arthur, the Tudor King Who Never Was* (Stroud, 2016) p. 20

33. ibid p. 24
34. AH p. 9

3 *Rebels and Traitors*
1. Kirke, H., 'Sir Henry Vernon of Haddon' in *Journal of the Derbyshire Archaeological and Natural History Society Vol. 42* (1920) p. 12
2. Materials Vol. 1 p. 282, 358
3. Plumpton p. 50
4. AH pp. 7-9
5. Croyland p. 495
6. CPR 1467-1477 p. 51
7. CPR 1476-1485 p. 62, 213, 343, 365
8. Fabyan p. 672
9. RotParl VI p. 276
10. CPR 1485-1494 p. 64, 101-102
11. Letters Vol. 1 p. 235
12. AH p. 11
13. ibid p. 11
14. CPR 1485-1494 p. 133
15. Williams, C.H., 'The Rebellion of Humphrey Stafford' in *English Historical Review XLIII* (1928) pp. 182-184, 188
16. CPR 1485-1494 pp. 106-107
17. Williams pp. 186-187
18. Hall pp. 427-428
19. AH p. 11

4 *Insatiable Hatred*
1. PL Vol. III p. 329
2. Weightman, C., *Margaret of York, The Diabolical Duchess* (Stroud, 2012) p. 18
3. ibid pp. 55-56
4. ibid pp. 18-20
5. Kirk, J. F., *History of Charles the Bold, Duke of Burgundy Vol III* (Philadelphia, 1868) p. 547
6. Croyland p. 478
7. ibid p. 478
8. Commines Vol. II p. 17

9. AH p. 17
10. Weightman pp. 78-79
11. Croyland p. 464
12. CPR 1467-1477 p. 307, CPR 1476-1485 p. 236
13. Croyland pp. 461-465; *Historie of the Arrivall of Edward IV in England and the Finall Recoverye of his Kingdomes from Henry VI* (ed. J. Bruce, London, 1838) pp. 1-12
14. Croyland pp. 469-470
15. PL Vol. III p. 38, 98, 102
16. RotParl VI p. 172
17. CPR 1467-1477 p. 438
18. CPR 1476-1485 pp. 72-73
19. Croyland pp. 478-480
20. RotParl VI pp. 193-195
21. Croyland p. 480
22. Fabyan p. 666
23. RotParl VI p. 194
24. CPR 1476-1485 p. 61, 68-69, 88-92, 94-103, 115, 117-119, 121, 123-124, 126, 128-132, 134-139, 155-159, 161, 163-165, 167, 173-174, 176, 180-181, 190-192, 200, 202-204, 206, 211, 217, 247, 288, 311, 316, 318, 328
25. ibid p. 67
26. ibid p. 212
27. ibid p. 319
28. Mancini p. 69
29. Wickham Legg pp. 193-197
30. Ross, C., *Richard III*, p. 148
31. CPR 1476-1485 p. 365
32. AH p. 3
33. Williams p. 183
34. Weightman p. 153
35. Plumpton IV pp. 53-54
36. Bennett, M., *Lambert Simnel and the Battle of Stoke* (Gloucester, 1987) p. 50
37. AH p. 17
38. ibid p. 17
39. ibid p. 19

5 A Joiner's Son

1. *Concilia Magnae Britanniae et Hiberniae Ab Anno MCCCL Ad Annum MDXLV* Vol. 3 (ed. D. Wilkins, London, 1737) p. 618
2. *The Register of John Morton, Archbishop of Canterbury 1486-1500 Vol. 1* (ed. C. Harper-Bill, Leeds, 1987) p. 25
3. AH p. 17
4. Materials Vol. 2 p. 148; Higginbotham pp. 162-165
5. AH p. 19
6. Vergil p. 214
7. Materials Vol. 2 p. 58
8. Materials Vol. 1 pp. 172-173
9. *Epistolae Academicae Oxon, Registrum F Vol. II* (ed. H. Anstey, Oxford, 1898) pp. 513-523
10. AH p. 17
11. CPR 1467-1477 p. 96
12. Ross, C., *Richard III* p. 159
13. CPR 1476-1485 p. 477
14. RotParl VI pp. 397-400
15. ibid pp. 436-437
16. ibid p. 397
17. Bennett pp. 45-47
18. *RotParl* VI p. 397
19. Croker, T.C., *Popular Songs of Ireland* (London, 1886) p. 309
20. Andre pp. 44-47
21. AH p. 21
22. Croyland p. 494
23. CPR 1436-1441 p. 109, 327, 335; CPR 1446-1452 p. 101; CPR 1461-1468 p. 246
24. CPR 1485-1494 p. 41
25. CPR 1405-1408 p. 235; CPR 1416-1422 p. 98
26. MS. Wood F.10 folio 197r
27. BL, MS. Cotton Julius B.XII, f. 29
28. AH p. 13-15
29. CPR 1476-1485; CPR 1485-1494; CPR 1494-1509
30. *Fasti Ecclesiae Anglicanae 1300-1541* (ed. J. M. Horn, London, 1967)
31. AH p. 25

6 A Mad Dance

1. For following section, Lydon, J., *The Making of Ireland, From Ancient Times to the Present* (Abingdon, 1998) pp. 84-119; Connolly, S. J., *Contested Island: Ireland 1460-1630* (Oxford, 2007) pp. 58-63
2. Lydon p. 103
3. Bryan, D., *Gerald Fitzgerald, The Great Earl of Kildare 1456-1513* (Dublin, 1933) pp. 1-25
4. Connolly p. 61
5. Bryan pp. 8-9
6. ibid pp. 34-42
7. ibid p. 104
8. Weightman p. 153
9. Bennett p. 63
10. Richards, J., *Landsknecht Soldier 1486-1560* (Oxford, 2002) p. 14, pp. 30-42
11. YHB pp. 557-558
12. *Letters to the Kings of England Vol. 1* (ed. J. O. Halliwell, London, 1846) p. 171
13. AH p. 21
14. Materials Vol. II p. 106, 128, 135
15. AH p. 21
16. For itinerary, Materials Vol. II pp. 136-138; CPR 1485-1494 pp. 169-172, 179
17. AH p. 21
18. PL Vol. III p. 355
19. Materials Vol. II pp. 152-153
20. *The Register of Thomas Rotherham, Archbishop of York 1480-1500 Vol. I* (ed. E. E. Barker, Torquay, 1976) p. 220
21. *Register* pp. 222-223

22. YHB pp. 557-558
23. CPR 1467-1477 p. 362, 491;
    CPR 1476-1485 p. 180; Baldwin
    pp. 25-26
24. RotParl VI p. 397
25. Bryan pp. 106-113
26. *The Book of Howth, Calendar of
    the Carew Manuscripts Preserved
    in the Archiepiscopal Library at
    Lambeth* (ed. J. S. Brewer & W.
    Bullen, London, 1871) p. 189
27. Howth p. 189
28. Croker pp. 294-296
29. ibid pp. 296-298
30. Bryan p. 108; Baldwin p. 131

7 *The Fortunes of War*
 1. RotParl VI p. 397
 2. Andre p. 45
 3. AH p. 21
 4. YHB p. 569
 5. Emery, A., *Greater Medieval
    Houses of England and Wales,
    Vol. 1 Northern England*
    (Cambridge, 1996) pp. 240-241
 6. CPR 1485-1494 p. 133
 7. AH p. 21
 8. RotParl VI p. 397; CPR
    1485-1494 p. 119
 9. RotParl VI p. 397
10. AH p. 20; Ekwall, E., *The
    Place-Names of Lancashire*
    (Manchester, 1922) p. 212
11. Bennett pp. 73-74; Baldwin p. 40
12. Cunningham, S., 'Henry VII
    and Rebellion in North-
    Eastern England 1485-1492,
    Bonds of Allegiance and
    the Establishment of Tudor
    Authority' in *Northern History
    Vol. 32* (Leeds, 1996) p. 63
13. AH pp. 21-23
14. CPR 1485-1494 p. 191
15. Cunningham, *Henry VII and
    Rebellion* pp. 64-65

16. Leland, J., *The Itinerary of John
    Leland in or about the Years
    1535-1543 Vol. 1* (ed. L. T.
    Smith, London, 1910) p. 80
17. YHB p. 570
18. Bietenholz, P. G. & Deutscher, T.
    B., *Contemporaries of Erasmus;
    A Biographical Register of the
    Renaissance and Reformation Vol.
    3* (London, 1995) p. 358; Trapp,
    J. B., 'Urswick, Christopher (1448-
    1522)' in Oxford Dictionary of
    National Biography (Oxford,
    2004); AH p. 23
19. YHB p. 544, pp. 550-551
20. ibid p. 549
21. ibid pp. 555-556
22. ibid pp. 557-558
23. ibid p. 569
24. ibid pp. 570-571
25. ibid pp. 571-572
26. ibid pp. 571-572
27. AH pp. 23-25
28. ibid p. 23
29. Collectanea Vol. 4 p. 210
30. ibid pp. 210-212
31. ibid p. 212
32. ibid p. 213
33. ibid p. 213

8 *The Noble Triumph*
 1. Collectanea Vol. 4 pp. 213-214
 2. Hall p. 434
 3. André p. 46
 4. Collectanea Vol. 4 p. 210
 5. ibid p. 214
 6. CPR 1485-1494 p. 111
 7. Vergil p. 224
 8. *The Stonor Letters and Papers
    1290-1483 Vol. II* (ed. C. L.
    Kingsford, London, 1919) p.
    163
 9. RotParl VI pp. 397-400
10. AH p. 25; André p. 47; Hall p.
    434

11. AH p. 25
12. AH p. 25; Hall p. 434
13. Great p. 241
14. AH pp. 25-27
15. Hall p. 434
16. Collectanea Vol. 4 p. 214
17. André p. 47
18. AH p. 27
19. André p. 47
20. AH p. 27
21. Vergil p. 25; Hall p. 434; YHB p. 573; Collectanea Vol. 4 p. 214
22. Bacon, F., *History of the Reign of King Henry VII* (ed. J. R. Lumby, London, 1881) p. 37
23. Collectanea Vol. 4 p. 214
24. YHB p. 573
25. AH p. 25
26. André p. 47
27. AH p. 25
28. '1497' in CSPM pp. 310-341
29. Berners, J., *The Boke of Saint Albans by Dame Juliana Berners, containing Treatises on Hawking, Hunting and Cote Armour* (ed. W. Blades, London, 1901) pp. 35-87
30. Oggins, R.S., *The Kings and their Hawks; Falconry in Medieval England* (London, 2004) p. 18
31. Howth p. 190
32. Gunn, S., *Henry VII's New Men & The making of Tudor England* (Oxford, 2016) p. 25
33. 'Henry VIII: May 1524, 21-25' in *Letters and Papers, Foreign and Domestic, Henry VIII Vol. 4 1524-1530* (ed. J. S. Brewer, London, 1875) pp. 142-156
34. Baldwin, D., *Stoke Field, the Last Battle of the Wars of the Roses* (Barnsley, 2006) p. 82
35. CPR 1560-1563 p. 91
36. CPR 1416-1422 p. 98
37. *Calendar of the Manuscripts of the Most Hon Marquis of Salisbury Part IX* (London, 1902) p. 163
38. Hall p. 435
39. YHB p. 573
40. Collectanea Vol. 4 p. 214
41. Materials Vol. II p. 158
42. YHB p. 577
43. AH p. 27
44. ibid p. 27
45. Hall p. 435
46. YHB pp. 587-588
47. ibid p. 588
48. Temperley, G., *Henry VII* (London, 1917) p. 412
49. Collectanea Vol. 4 pp. 216-218
50. Materials Vol. II p. 189
51. RotParl VI pp. 397-400
52. Materials Vol. II p. 410, 458
53. Baldwin, *Stoke Field* pp. 123-124
54. Contemporary Vol. III (ed. A. F. Pollard, London, 1914) pp. 156-157
55. Materials Vol. II pp. 315-317
56. André p. 47
57. Hall p. 438
58. Collectanea Vol. 4 p. 218
59. ibid p. 218
60. ibid pp. 218-219
61. ibid pp. 219-222
62. ibid pp. 223-225, 228
63. '1489' in CSPS pp. 20-26
64. AH p. 57

9 Werbecque of Tournai

1. Campbell, L., 'The Authorship of the Recuiel d'Arras' in *Journal of the Warburg and Courtauld Institutes Vol. 40* (1977) pp. 301-313
2. Chron. Lon. pp. 219-221
3. AH p. 63
4. Commines Vol. I p. 357; Lowell, F. C., *Joan of Arc* (Cambridge, 1896) p. 143

5. Roth, C., *'Perkin Warbeck and his Jewish Master'* in *Transactions of Jewish Historical Society of England Vol. 9* (1920) pp. 143-162; Chron. Lon. pp. 219-221
6. CPR 1467-1477 p. 340, 357, 481
7. Wroe, A., *Perkin, A Story of Deception* (London, 2004) pp. 525-528
8. Chron. Lon. pp. 220-221
9. Gairdner, J., *History of the Life and Reign of Richard the Third to Which is Added the Story of Perkin Warbeck from Original Documents* (Cambridge, 1898) p. 334
10. Chastel de la Howarderie, Comte P. A. du, *'Notes sur la Famille de l'aventurier Perkin Warbeck'* in *Bulletins de la Société Historique & Littéraire de Tournai Vol. 25* (1893) pp. 410-414
11. Letters Vol. II p. 375; CPR 1494-1509 p. 14, 44
12. '1489' in CSPS pp. 43-51; Madden, F., *Documents Relating to Perkin Warbeck with Remarks on his History* (London, 1837) pp. 4-5
13. Contemporary Vol. I pp. 82-84; RotParl VI pp. 454-455
14. Materials Vol. 1 p. 201
15. '1491-1495' in CSPV pp. 203-226
16. André p. 60; Vergil p. 63; Hall p. 462
17. '1497' in CSPM pp. 310-341
18. Mancini p. 93
19. AH p. 57
20. Chrimes p. 155; Cunningham *Henry VII* pp. 157-158; Tanner, J. R., *Tudor Constitutional Documents A.D. 1485-1603* (Cambridge, 1930) pp. 249-262; RotParl VI pp. 385-408
21. Contemporary Vol. I pp. 69-72
22. ibid pp. 69-71; AH p. 39; Chron. Lon. pp. 194-95
23. Cunningham, *Henry VII and Rebellion* pp. 68-71; Chrimes p. 80
24. AH p. 29
25. ibid pp. 29-37
26. Weightman pp. 158-59; Mackie pp. 94-97
27. *'Henry VIII: July 1529, 22-31'* in *Letters and Papers, Foreign and Domestic, Henry VIII, Volume 4, 1524-1530* (ed. J. S. Brewer, London, 1875) p. 2587
28. Collectanea Vol. 4 pp. 179-180
29. AH p. 63
30. '1493' in CSPS pp. 43-51
31. Letters Vol. II p. 55
32. Quinn, D. B., *'Guide to English Financial Records for Irish History 1461-1558, with Illustrated Extracts, 1461-1509'* in *Analecta Hibernica No 10* (1941) p. 54
33. CPR 1485-1494 p. 367
34. Quinn p. 55
35. CPR 1485-1494 p. 368; Quinn pp. 55-56
36. Bryan p. 156; Ware, J., *The Annals of Ireland During the Reign of King Henry the Seventh* in *The Antiquities and History of Ireland* (Dublin, 1705) p. 21
37. *Accounts of the Lord High Treasurer of Scotland Vol. 1 AD 1473-1498* (ed. T. Dickson, Edinburgh, 1877) p. 199
38. Chron. Lon. p. 221
39. CPR 1477-1485 p. 221, 413; CPR 1485-1494 p. 17

10 War of Necessity

1. Vale, M., *The Ancient Enemy; England, France and Europe*

from the Angevins to the Tudors 1154-1558 (London, 2007) p. 1
2. 'July-December 1485' in *Rymer's Foedera Volume 12* (ed. T. Rymer, London, 1739-1745) pp. 271-280
3. CPR 1485-1494 p. 351, 352, 356, 393
4. RotParl VI p. 440, 442-444
5. CPR 1485-1494 p. 366
6. '1491-1495' in CSPV pp. 203-226
7. AH p. 147
8. Cunningham, *Henry VII* p. 69
9. Contemporary Vol. I pp. 89-90
10. 'January-June 1492' in *Rymer's Foedera Volume 12* pp. 465-482
11. Mackie, J. D., *The Earlier Tudors 1485-1558* (Oxford 1952) p. 109
12. Cunningham, *Henry VII* p. 71
13. 'July-September 1492' in *Rymer's Foedera Volume 12* pp. 482-487
14. Letters Vol. II p. 373; Mackie p. 108
15. EH pp. 91-92
16. Cunningham, *Henry VII* pp. 71-73
17. AH p. 59
18. 'November 1492' in *Rymer's Foedera Volume 12* pp. 494-505
19. AH p. 55, 57
20. Contemporary Vol. III pp. 6-25; AH p. 59
21. '1489' in CSPS pp. 43-51
22. Chron. Lon. p. 221
23. Arthurson, I., *The Perkin Warbeck Conspiracy 1491-1499* (Stroud, 1994) p. 51
24. AH p. 65
25. CPR 1476-1485 p. 491, 549-550
26. '1489' in CSPS pp. 43-51
27. AH p. 65
28. Cunningham, *Henry VII* pp. 73

11 My Only Son
1. AH p. 17
2. Madden pp. 4-6

3. Chron. Lon. p. 221
4. AH p. 65
5. Hall p. 463
6. Weightman pp. 125-127
7. AH p. 65
8. Madden pp. 8-9
9. *Tudor Royal Proclamations Vol. 1, The Early Tudors 1485-1553* (ed. P. L. Hughes and J. F. Larkin (London, 1964) p. 25
10. Madden pp. 4-6
11. 'July 1495' in CSPS pp. 57-66; Morel-Fatio, A., *Marguerite d'York et Perkin Warbeck in Mélanges d'Histoire offerts a M. Charles Bémont* (Paris, 1913) pp. 411-416; Wroe pp. 126-129; Arthurson pp. 56, 69
12. Nichols, J., *A Collection of all the Wills Now Known to be Extant, of the Kings and Queens of England, Princes and Princesses of Wales, and Every Branch of the Blood Royal* (1780) pp. 350-351
13. Hall p. 464
14. CPR 1485-1494 pp. 441-442
15. Arthurson p. 66
16. Great p. 248
17. Letters Vol. II p. 375
18. Gairdner pp. 276-277; *Letters of the Kings of England Vol. 1* (ed. J. O. Halliwell, London, 1848) pp. 172-173
19. AH p. 67
20. Hall pp. 465-466
21. ibid p. 466
22. AH p. 71
23. Hall p. 466
24. AH p. 69
25. *Tudor Royal Proclamations Vol. 1* p. 35
26. Great pp. 248-249
27. Arthurson p. 70
28. Gairdner pp. 281-282
29. ibid p. 283

30. ibid p. 283
31. Mackie p. 122
32. Arthurson p. 80
33. Gairdner p. 282
34. Madden pp. 12-14; Letters Vol. II pp. 292-297; Gairdner p. 284
35. CPR 1485-1494 p. 419, 423-424; Bryan pp. 180-181
36. CPR 1494-1509 p. 12, 15
37. Gunn p. 12
38. Hall p. 471
39. AH p. 81
40. Bryan pp. 185-196; Conway, A., *Henry VII's Relations with Scotland and Ireland 1485-1498* (Cambridge, 1972) pp. 118-130, 210
41. Letters Vol. 1 pp. 388-404

12 *The Devilish Enterprise*
1. Hall p. 467
2. CPR 1485-1494 p. 49, 59, 101, 142, 196
3. Arthurson p. 62; PRO KB9/934/5
4. EII p. 100; Temperley p. 415; Chron. Lon. p. 203
5. Great p. 258
6. CPR 1476-1485 p. 368; CPR 1485-1494 p. 11, 354
7. Hall p. 469
8. Arthurson pp. 93-95; Jones, M. K., 'Sir William Stanley of Holt: Politics and Family Allegiance in the Late Fifteenth Century' in *Welsh History Review* Vol. 14 (1988) pp. 1-22
9. Great p. 238
10. AH p. 75; CPR 1476-1485 p. 47, 274
11. CPR 1485-1494 p. 85, 353; Letters Vol. II p. 291
12. AH p. 69
13. Hall pp. 464-465
14. Letters Vol. I p. 235
15. Hall pp. 467-468
16. AH pp. 73-75
17. CPR 1494-1509 p. 13
18. EH pp. 100-101
19. Great p. 256
20. Madden p. 15
21. AH p. 75
22. Hall p. 469
23. AH p. 75
24. Hall p. 469; AH p. 75
25. CPR 1494-1509 pp. 29-32
26. Chron. Lon. p. 204; Great pp. 256-257
27. Hall p. 469
28. Great p. 258; Chron. Lon. p. 204; Archibold, W. A. J., 'Sir William Stanley and Perkin Warbeck' in *English Historical Review* Vol. XIV (ed. S. R. Gardiner & B. L. Poole, London, 1899) pp. 529-534
29. EH p. 101
30. Arthurson p. 97
31. Gairdner pp. 291-292
32. Kleyn pp. 193-195; Gairdner p. 289
33. Gairdner p. 295; Weightman p. 167; Mallet, M. & Shaw, S., *The Italian Wars 1494-1559: War, State and Society in Early Modern Europe* (Abingdon, 2014) pp. 27-34; Vernon, H. M., *Italy from 1494 to 1790* (Cambridge, 1909) p. 18-20; Currin, J. M., 'Henry VII, France and the Holy League of Venice: the Diplomacy of Balance' in *Historical Research* Vol. LXXXII no. 217 (Oxford, 2009) pp. 529-530; 'March 1495' in CSPS pp. 55-56
34. Letters Vol. I pp. 264-265
35. Arthurson pp. 107-108
36. Weightman p. 167
37. AH p. 81
38. Hall p. 472

39. *Historie of the Arrivall of Edward IV in England* p. 2
40. AH p. 83; RotParl VI pp. 504-505
41. Hall p. 472
42. 'July 1495' in CSPS pp. 57-66; Gairdner pp. 295-296
43. PL Vol. III p. 386; Chron. Lon. pp. 205-206
44. 'July 1495' in CSPS pp. 57-66
45. Arthurson p. 118
46. Hall p. 472; Chron. Lon. p. 205; Arthurson p. 120; 220-221
47. Great p. 260
48. 'July 1495' in CSPS pp. 57-66; Hall pp. 472-473
49. Letters Vol. II p. 375; CPR 1494-1509 p. 42; Gairdner p. 298; Great p. 259
50. Bryan p. 181; 197
51. Smith, C, *The Ancient and Present State of the County and City of Waterford, Containing a Natural, Civil, Ecclesiastical, Historical and Topograhphical Description Therefore* (Dublin, 1774) pp. 123-124; *MS 632, f. 255b* in *Calendar of the Carew Manuscripts Preserved in the Archiepiscopal Library at Lambeth Vol. VI* (ed. J. S. Brewer & W. Bullen, London, 1871) p. 472; Ryland, R. H., *History, Topography and Antiquities of the County and City of Waterford* (London, 1824) pp. 30-32; Gairdner pp. 321-323
52. Hall p. 471
53. Temperley p. 415
54. CPR 1494-1509 p. 14
55. EH p. 105; Baldwin, D., *'King Richard's Grave in Leicester'* in *Transactions of the Leicestershire Archaeological and Historical Society* 60 (1986) pp. 21-24;

56. Holinshed, R., *Chronicles of England, Scotland and Ireland Vol/ III* (London, 1808) p. 477
56. Letters Vol. II p. 375; EH p. 101, 102
57. EH pp. 103-104
58. Arthurson p. 110
59. Chron. Lon. p. 207
60. Contemporary Vol. I pp. 112-115, 128-129; 'July 1496' in CSPS pp. 107-114; '1496' in CSPV pp. 226-252; 'July 1495' in CSPM pp. 293-310; Gairdner, *Henry the Seventh* pp. 137-145; Currin pp. 526-546
61. Bacon pp. 146-147; Mackie p. 139; Rymer Vol. 12 pp. 578-591; Madden pp. 18-19; Contemporary Vol. II pp. 286-309

13 Shame and Derision

1. 'July 1498' in CSPS pp. 167-180
2. '1481-1485' in CSPV pp. 141-159
3. McDougall pp. 2-11; Ross, *Richard III* pp. 45-47
4. McDougall pp. 12-51; Conway pp. 1-23
5. 'July 1498' in CSPS pp. 167-180
6. '1491-1495' in CSPV pp. 203-226
7. 'April 1496' in CSPS pp. 89-99; Arthurson p. 117; McDougall pp. 120-121
8. McDougall pp. 118-120
9. Conway p. 31
10. McDougall p. 121
11. 'November 1495' in CSPS p. 72
12. McDougall p. 122; *Accounts of the Lord High Treasurer of Scotland Vol. 1* p. 267
13. Hall p. 474
14. AH p. 87
15. Hall p. 474
16. McDougall p. 122; '1498' in CSPM pp. 341-364

17. Great p. 262
18. AH p. 87
19. 'December 1495' in CSPM pp. 72-79
20. McDougall pp. 122-123; *Accounts of the Lord High Treasurer* pp. 263-264
21. 'April 1496' in CSPS pp. 89-99
22. *Accounts of the Lord High Treasurer* p. 268; Arthurson p. 124, 140; McDougall p. 123
23. Letters Vol. I p. 26; Contemporary Vol. I pp. 138-139; Arthurson p. 142
24. Contemporary Vol. I p. 140
25. TNA E101/414/6 f.2r
26. CPR 1494-1509 p. 52
27. TNA E101/414/6 f.10r
28. Vergil p. 190; AH p. 6
29. Arthurson p. 132; TNA E101/414/6 f.22r
30. CPR 1494-1509 pp. 67-68
31. Arthurson p. 148
32. Great p. 260
33. Conway pp. 223-225
34. Bryan p. 203
35. Conway pp. 226-232; Bryan pp. 204-207
36. Conway p. 231
37. CPR 1494-1509 p. 76; Bryan pp. 211-212; Contemporary Vol III p. 285
38. Contemporary Vol. I p. 136
39. Contemporary Vol. I pp. 136-137; McDougall p. 126; Conway pp. 236-239
40. Contemporary Vol. I pp. 138-139, 142
41. ibid pp. 141-142
42. EH p. 108
43. *Accounts of the Lord High Treasurer* p. 296
44. Chron. Lon. p. 210
45. Henry, R., *The History of Great Britain, From the Invasion of it by The Romans under Julius Caesar* Vol. XII (London, 1814) pp. 387-392
46. AH p. 87
47. Wroe pp. 525-528
48. Great p. 262
49. Lewis, K., *Kingship and Masculinity in Late Medieval England* (Abingdon, 2013) p. 253
50. AH p. 89
51. 'July 1498' in CSPS pp. 167-180
52. AH pp. 87-89
53. McDougall p. 132; Chron. Lon. p. 210
54. AH p. 89
55. Chron. Lon. p. 210
56. Madden pp. 30-32
57. '1496' in CSPV pp. 262-252; 'October 1496' in CSPS pp. 129-130
58. AH p. 145
59. Great p. 274
60. EH pp. 110-111

14 Mortal War

1. AH p. 89
2. Tudor Royal Proclamations p. 38
3. Chron. Lon. p. 211; Great p. 275
4. Hall p. 482
5. McDougall p. 99, 127; Mackie p. 137
6. Hall p. 476
7. AH p. 91
8. Chron. Lon. pp. 212-213
9. Hall p. 476; RotParl VI pp. 513-515
10. EH pp. 110-111
11. Arthurson pp. 221-222
12. CPR 1494-1509 pp. 86-88; McDougall p. 134
13. CPR 1494-1509 p. 88, 89, 91, 93
14. Arthurson p. 156
15. CPR 1494-1509 p. 93
16. Arthurson, I., 'The King's Voyage into Scotland: The War that Never Was' in England in the

Henry VII and the Tudor Pretenders

Fifteenth Century Proceedings of the 1986 Harlaxton Symposium (ed. D. Williams, Bury St Edmunds, 1987) pp. 8-9
17. McDougall pp. 134-135; Arthurson p. 155
18. '1497' in CSPS pp. 131-146
19. AH p. 91
20. 'November 1531' in CSPV Vol. 4, 1527-1533 pp. 291-307
21. Contemporary Vol II p. 249, 252
22. AH pp. 91-93; Hall p. 47
23. AH p. 91; Chron. Lon. p. 216
24. Hall p. 477
25. AH p. 93
26. RotParl VI p. 544
27. Great pp. 276-277
28. EH p. 112; Temperley p. 416
29. Great pp. 275-276
30. TNA E101/414/6 f.75v, 76r
31. Chron. Lon. p. 214
32. Great pp. 276-277
33. RotParl VI p. 544
34. Great pp. 276-277; AH p. 97
35. Chron. Lon. pp. 215-217
36. Tudor Royal Proclamations pp. 39-40
37. Chron. Lon. p. 217
38. Letters Vol. I pp. 104-110
39. Chrimes p. 90; Gairdner pp. 318-319; McDougall p. 138
40. TA p. 301, 342-345; Arthurson p. 170; Mackie p. 144
41. Contemporary Vol. I p. 156
42. Temperley p. 156; 'August 1498' in CSPS pp. 180-195
43. Hall p. 481
44. Great p. 280
45. McDougall pp. 138-140; Temperley pp. 153-154
46. Mackie p. 148
47. Contemporary Vol. I p. 158; Vol II pp. 323-333; EH p. 113
48. '1497' in CSPV pp. 252-266; '1497' in CSPM pp. 310-341

49. AH p. 145
50. Cavill, P.R., *The English Parliaments of Henry VII 1485-1504* (Oxford, 2009) p. 43

15 Endgame
1. Chron. Lon. p. 217; OL Vol. I pp. 32-33
2. Gairdner pp. 318-319
3. Great p. 281; Hall pp. 483-484
4. Cox, J.C., *The Sanctuaries and Sanctuary Seekers of Mediaeval England* (1911, London) pp. 214-220
5. Andre p. 66
6. RotParl VI pp. 544-545
7. AH p. 105
8. '1497' in CSPM pp. 310-341
9. Chron. Lon. p. 217
10. Great p. 281
11. Arthurson, I.; Kingwell, N., 'The Proclamation of Henry Tudor as King of England' in *Historical Research Vol. 63* (1990) pp. 100-104
12. Hall p. 483
13. AH p. 105
14. TNA E101/414/6 f.87r
15. Attreed, L.C., 'A New Source for Perkin Warbeck's Invasion of 1497' in *Mediaeval Studies Vol. 48* (1986) pp. 519-521
16. AH p. 105
17. Chron. Lon. p. 217; OL pp. 34-37
18. '1497' in CSPM pp. 310-341
19. AH p. 107
20. Great p. 282
21. Attreed p. 520
22. OL pp. 32-35
23. Great p. 282
24. Andre p. 66
25. '1497' in CSPM pp. 310-341
26. OL p. 35
27. Ryland p. 34

356

28. For following paragraphs see Fowler, J. K., *A History of Beaulieu Abbey A.D. 1204-1539* (London, 1911) p. 16, 35-36, 61-75, 93-98, 156-162
29. Great p. 282
30. Griffiths, R. A., *Sir Rhys ap Thomas and his Family; A Study in the Wars of the Roses and Early Tudor Politics* (Cardiff, 2014) pp. 241-245
31. AH pp. 107-109
32. Ryland pp. 34-35
33. Hall p. 486
34. '1497' in CSPM pp. 310-341
35. Chron. Lon. p. 218
36. Temperley p. 416
37. Hall pp. 484-485
38. EH p. 114
39. ibid p. 114
40. '1497' in CSPM pp. 310-341
41. Andre p. 67
42. Chron. Lon. pp. 219-221
43. Wroe pp. 383-384
44. Ryland p. 35
45. Great p. 286
46. '1497' in CSPM pp. 310-341
47. Temperley p. 419
48. Arthurson '*Western Rising*' p. 2
49. AH p. 109
50. Arthurson '*Western Rising*' p. 2; Mackie p. 146
51. Ryland p. 36
52. Hall p. 485
53. Andre p. 68
54. AH p. 109
55. Andre p. 69
56. Hall p. 486
57. EH p. 115
58. Letters Vol. II p. 73
59. Arthurson p. 192
60. Wroe pp. 412-413; Gairdner pp. 329-331
61. EH p. 115; AH p. 111
62. AH p. 111

63. Chron. Lon. p. 219
64. '1497' in CSPM pp. 310-341
65. 1497' in CSPM pp. 310-341; Chron. Lon. pp. 221-222; Great pp. 283-284
66. '1497' in CSPV pp. 252-266
67. Philpot, R., *Maximilian I and England 1477-1509* (London, 1975) pp. 170-171
68. Hall p. 486
69. '1497' in CSPM pp. 310-341
70. '1498' in CSPM pp. 341-364

16 Fresh Revolution

1. Henry, R., *The History of Great Britain, From the Invasion of it by The Romans under Julius Caesar* Vol. XII (London, 1814) pp. 387-392
2. Great p. 287
3. AH p. 3
4. 'July 1498' in CSPS pp. 167-180
5. EH p. 117
6. ibid p. 117
7. Chron. Lon. p. 223; Great p. 287; '1498' in CSPM pp. 341-365
8. AH p. 115
9. ibid p. 115
10. Chron. Lon. p. 223
11. EH p. 118
12. E101/414/16 f.30r
13. *The Manuscripts of the Marquess of Abergavenny, Lord Braye, G.F. Luttrell Esq, Etc; Historical Manuscripts Commission Tenth Report, Appendix, Part VI* (London, 1887) p. 2
14. '1498' in CSPV pp. 267-276
15. AH p. 115
16. CPR 1461-1467 pp. 160-161
17. Chron. Lon. p. 223; AH p. 115; Great p. 287
18. 'June 1498' in CSPS pp. 150-153
19. Chron. Lon. p. 223; AH p. 115

20. Chron. Lon. p. 223
21. Great p. 287
22. 'July 1498' in CSPS pp. 153-167
23. 'August 1498' in CSPS pp. 180-195
24. 'September 1498' in CSPS pp. 195-199
25. *Letters of the Kings of England* Vol. 1 (ed. J. O. Halliwell, London, 1848) pp. 172-173
26. AH p. 117
27. '1498' in CSPM pp. 341-364
28. OL Vol. I pp. 43-46
29. Temperley p. 416
30. 'July 1498' in CSPS pp. 153-167
31. 'July 1498' in CSPS pp. 167-180
32. ibid pp. 167-180
33. '1498' in CSPV pp. 267-276
34. Temperley p. 416
35. Chrimes p. 117
36. *Proceedings of the Somersetshire Archaeological and Natural History Society*, Vol. 60 Part II (Taunton, 1914) pp. 1-4
37. Hall p. 490
38. AH p. 117; Great p. 290
39. Great p. 290
40. AH p. 117
41. ibid p. 117
42. Great p. 289
43. ibid p. 289
44. Temperley p. 416
45. '1499' in CSPS pp. 199-213; EH p. 120; Great p. 289
46. Griffiths, R.A. & Thomas, R.S., *The Making of the Tudor Dynasty* (Sparkford, 2005) pp. 158-159
47. '1499' in CSPS pp. 199-213
48. ibid pp. 199-213
49. 'August 1498' in CSPS pp. 180-195; '1499' in CSPS pp. 199-213
50. 'August 1498' in CSPS pp. 180-195

17 A Stranger Born

1. For following indictments see *Fifty-Third Annual Report of the Deputy Keeper of the Public Records* (London, 1892) pp. 31-36; *Third Report of the Deputy Keeper of the Public Records* (London, 1842) pp. 216-218; Arthurson pp. 196-218
2. Temperley p. 417
3. '1499' CSPM pp. 364-381; Arthurson pp. 210-212
4. *Select Cases in the Council of Henry VII* (ed. C. G. Bayne & W. H. Dunham, London, 1958) p. 32
5. Chron. Lon. p. 227
6. Hall p. 490
7. Plumpton Vol. 4 p. 142
8. Chron. Lon. p. 227
9. Great p. 291
10. ibid p. 291
11. Chron. Lon. p. 227
12. Great p. 291
13. ibid p. 291
14. Hall p. 490
15. AH p. 117
16. Great p. 291
17. Chron. Lon. p. 227; Great p. 291
18. Hall p. 490
19. AH pp. 117-119
20. Chron. Lon. p. 228
21. Chron. Lon. p.227; EH p. 123
22. Arthurson p. 215; Great p. 292
23. *Letters and Papers, Foreign and Domestic, Henry VIII Vol. 1* (ed. J. S. Brewer, London, 1862) p. 5
24. Bacon p. 178

18 The Most Savage Harshness

1. EH p. 88, 105, 112, 124, 125, 129, 133; BL Add MS 59899 f.27r; BL Add MS 59899 f.31r; E36/214 f.71v; E36/214v, *The*

Chamber Books of Henry VII and Henry VIII, 1485-1521 (ed. M. M. Condon, S. P. Harper, L. Liddy, S. Cunningham and J. Ross)

2. Jewitt, L., *Chatsworth* (Buxton, 1872) pp. 38-39
3. OL pp. 42-48
4. 'August 1504' in CSPS pp. 328-331
5. Chron. Lon. p. 258
6. '1497' in CSPV pp. 252-266; '1503' in CSPV pp. 295-298
7. AH p. 133
8. *Privy purse expenses of Elizabeth of York: Wardrobe Accounts of Edward the Fourth* (ed. N. H. Nicolas, London 1830) p. xcvii
9. 'July 1498' in CSPS pp. 153-180
10. Laynesmith, J., *The Last Medieval Queens; English Queenship 1445-1503* (Oxford, 2004) p. 208
11. Great p. 295
12. *The Receyt of the Ladie Kateryne* (ed. G. Kipling, Oxford, 1990) p. 71
13. *Receyt* pp. 71-74, 77
14. 'January 1500' in CSPS pp. 213-216
15. Mackie p. 158
16. 'June 1500' in CSPS pp. 220-238
17. Great pp. 293-294
18. 'January 1500' in CSPS pp. 213-216
19. '1501' in CSPS pp. 253-265
20. Letters Vol. 1 pp. 126-128
21. *Receyt* pp. 5-6
22. ibid pp. 6-7
23. ibid pp. 7-8
24. '1501' in CSPS pp. 253-265
25. *Receyt* pp. 8-9
26. '1501' in CSPS pp. 253-265; 'June 1500' in CSPS pp. 220-238; Great p. 292

27. *Receyt* pp. 8-9, 12
28. ibid pp. 12-31
29. *Receyt* pp. 30-31; Great p. 306
30. Stow, J., *A Survey of London Written in the Year 1598* (ed. W. J. Thomas, London, 1842) p. 26
31. *Receyt* pp. 36-37
32. ibid pp. 41-44
33. ibid pp. 39-40
34. ibid pp. 41-45
35. '1501' in CSPS pp. 253-265
36. Chron. Lon. p. 255
37. Great p. 294
38. ibid pp. 294-295
39. *Receyt* p. 79
40. '1501' in CSPS pp. 253-265
41. *Receyt* p. 79
42. ibid pp. 80-81
43. Chron. Lon. p. 255
44. September 1549, 1-15' in CSPV Vol. 5 pp. 239-267
45. Chron. Lon. p. 255
46. Laynesmith pp. 122-127; Chron. Lon. p. 255; *The Antiquarian Repertory: A Miscellaneous Assemblage of Topography, History, Biography, Customs, and Manners Vol IV* (ed. F. Grose & T. Astle, London, 1809) p.652-665
47. Busch, W., *England Under the Tudors, Henry VII* (London, 1895) pp. 440-441
48. '1497' in CSPV pp. 252-266
49. EH p. 128, 130
50. *The Antiquarian Repertory* p. 655
51. Peniarth MS 482d f. 9r
52. *The Letters of King Henry VIII* (ed. M. St Clare Byrne, Newcastle, 1936) pp. 4-5
53. AH p. 127
54. OL p. 46
55. Letters Vol. 1 pp. 231-240
56. AH p. 125
57. '1506' in CSPV pp. 310-327; AH pp. 136-138
58. AH p. 135

59. Cunningham pp. 218-219;
    Elton, G. R., 'Henry VII:
    Rapacity and Remorse' in
    The Historical Journal Vol. 1
    (1958) pp. 21-39; Elton, G. R.,
    'Henry VII: A Restatement'
    in *The Historical Journal* Vol.
    4 No 1 (1961) pp. 1-29; Cooper,
    J. P., 'Henry VII's Last Years
    Reconsidered' in *The Historical
    Journal* Vol. 2 No 2 (1959) pp.
    103-129
60. AH pp. 127-131
61. Machiavelli, N., *Discourses on
    the First Decade of Titus Livius*
    (ed. N. H. Thomson, London,
    1883) p. 42
62. AH p. 127-131
63. *The Will of King Henry VII*
    (ed. T. Astle, London, 1775) pp.
    11-13
64. Elton, 'Rapacity' p. 35
65. Harrison, C.J., 'The Petition of
    Edmund Dudley' in *The English
    Historical Review* Vol. 87
    (London, 1972) pp. 82-99

19 Epilogue
 1. AH p. 143
 2. 'April 1507' in CSPS pp.
    406-414; 'October 1507' in
    CSPS pp. 433-441; '1508' in
    CSPV pp. 329-332; '1509' in
    CSPV pp. 332-347; 'October
    1507' in CSPS pp. 433-441
 3. *The English Works of John
    Fisher, Bishop of Rochester Part
    I* (ed. J. E. B. Mayor, London,
    1876) pp. 268-288
 4. BL Add.MS.45131 f.54
 5. Collectanea p. 303-304
 6. Fisher, *The English Works Part
    I* p. 269

 7. Condon, M., 'God Save The
    King! Piety, Propaganda
    and the Perpetual Memorial'
    in *Westminster Abbey: The
    Lady Chapel of Henry VII*
    (ed. T. Tatton-Brown & R.
    Mortimer, Woodbridge, 2003) p.
    59
 8. Condon, M., 'The Last Will of
    Henry VII: Document and Text'
    in *Westminster Abbey: The Lady
    Chapel of Henry VII* (ed. T.
    Tatton-Brown & R. Mortimer,
    Woodbridge, 2003) p. 133
 9. Wilson, C., 'The Functional
    Design of Henry VII's
    Chapel: A Reconstruction' in
    *Westminster Abbey: The Lady
    Chapel of Henry VII* (ed. T.
    Tatton-Brown & R. Mortimer,
    Woodbridge, 2003) pp. 175-176
10. Collectanea pp. 306-309
11. Collectanea p. 309
12. AH p. 151
13. Speed., *The History of Great
    Britain Under the Conquests of
    the Romans, Saxons, Danes and
    Normans* (London, 1614) p. 738
14. *The Complete Poems of
    John Skelton Laureate* (ed. P.
    Henderson, London, 1931) p.
    25
15. AH p. 9

Bibliography

Published Primary Sources

A Volume of English Miscellanies Illustrating the History and Language of the Northern Counties of England (ed. J. Raine, London, 1890)

Accounts of the Lord High Treasurer of Scotland Vol. 1 AD 1473-1498 (ed. T. Dickson, Edinburgh, 1877)

Andre, B., *The Life of Henry VII* (ed. D. Hobbins, New York, 2011)

The Antiquarian Repertory: A Miscellaneous Assemblage of Topography, History, Biography, Customs, and Manners Vol IV (ed. F. Grose & T. Astle, London, 1809)

Berners, J., *The Boke of Saint Albans by Dame Juliana Berners, containing Treatises on Hawking, Hunting and Cote Armour* (ed. W. Blades, London, 1901) pp. 35-87

The Book of Howth, Calendar of the Carew Manuscripts Preserved in the Archiepiscopal Library at Lambeth (ed. J.S. Brewer & W. Bullen, London, 1871)

Calendar of the Manuscripts of the Most Hon Marquis of Salisbury Part IX (London, 1902)

Calendar of Papal Registers Relating to Great Britain and Ireland (ed. J.A. Twemlow, London, 1960)

Calendars of Patent Rolls (54 vols. HMSO, London, 1893-1916)

Calendar of State Papers and Manuscripts in the Archives and Collections of Milan 1385-1618 (ed. Allen B. Hinds, London, 1912)

Calendar of State Papers Relating to English Affairs in the Archives of Venice 1202-1509 (ed. R. Brown, London, 1864)

Calendar of State Papers, Spain 1485-1509 (ed. G.A. Bergenroth, London, 1862)

The Chamber Books of Henry VII and Henry VIII, 1485-1521 (ed. M. M. Condon, S. P. Harper, L. Liddy, S. Cunningham and J. Ross)

The Chronicles of London (ed. C. L. Kingsford, London, 1905)

Commines, P., *The Memoirs of Philip de Commines, Lord of Agenton* (ed. A. R. Scroble, London, 1877)

The Complete Poems of John Skelton Laureate (ed. P. Henderson, London, 1931)

Concilia Magnae Britanniae et Hiberniae Ab Anno MCCCL Ad Annum MDXLV Vol. 3 (ed. D. Wilkins, London, 1737)

Epistolae Academicae Oxon, Registrum F Vol II (ed. H. Anstey, Oxford, 1898)

Fabyan, R., *The New Chronicles of England and France* (ed. H. Ellis, London, 1811)

Fifty-Third Annual Report of the Deputy Keeper of the Public Records (London, 1892)

Fisher, J., *The English Works of John Fisher, Bishop of Rochester Part I* (ed. J. E. B. Mayor, London, 1876)

Fisher, J., *The Funeral Sermon of Margaret Countess of Richmond and Derby, Mother to King Henry VII and Foundress of Christ's and St John's College in Cambridge, Preached by Bishop John Fisher in 1509* (ed. J. Hyers, Cambridge, 1840)

The Great Chronicle of London (ed. A. H. Thomas & I. D. Thornley, London, 1938)

Historie of the Arrivall of Edward IV in England and the Finall Recoverye of his Kingdomes from Henry VI (ed. J. Bruce, London, 1838)

Holinshed, R., *Chronicles of England, Scotland and Ireland* Vol III (London, 1808)

Ingulph's Chronicle of the Abbey of Croyland with the Continuations by Peter of Blois and Anonymous Writers, (ed. H. T. Riley, London 1854)

Leland, J., *Joannis Lelandi antiquarii De rebus Britannicis collectanea* Vol. 4 (ed. T. Hearns, London, 1774)

Leland, J., *The Itinerary of John Leland in or about the Years 1535-1543* Vol. 1 (ed. L. T. Smith, London, 1910)

Letters and Papers, Foreign and Domestic, Henry VIII (ed. J. S. Brewer, London, 1862-1875)

Letters and Papers Illustrative of the Reigns of Richard III and Henry VII (ed. J. Gairdner, London, 1861)

Letters of the Kings of England Vol. 1 (ed. J. O. Halliwell, London, 1848)

The Letters of King Henry VIII (ed. M. St Clare Byrne, Newcastle, 1936)

Machiavelli, N., *Discourses on the First Decade of Titus Livius* (ed. N. H. Thomson, London, 1883)

Mancini, D., *The Usurpation of Richard III,* (ed. C. A. J. Armstrong, 1984)

Materials for a History of the Reign of Henry VII Vol. 1-2 (ed. W. Campbell, London, 1873)

The Paston Letters, 1422-1509 A.D. Vol. 1-6, Henry VI 1422-1509 (ed. J. Gairdner, London, 1872)

The Parliament Rolls of Medieval England 1275-1504 Vol. XVI Henry VII 1489-1504 (ed. R. Horrox, London, 2005)

Original Letters, Illustrative of English History, including Numerous Royal Letters Vol. I (ed. H. Ellis, London, 1825)

Plumpton Correspondence, A Series of Letters, Chiefly Domestick Written in the Reigns of Edward IV, Richard III, Henry VII and Henry VIII (ed. T. Stapleton, London, 1839)

Privy purse expenses of Elizabeth of York: Wardrobe Accounts of Edward the Fourth (ed. N. H. Nicolas, London, 1830)

The Manuscripts of the Marquess of Abergavenny, Lord Braye, G.F. Luttrell Esq, Etc; Historical Manuscripts Commission Tenth Report, Appendix, Part VI (London, 1887)

The Receyt of the Ladie Kateryne (ed. G. Kipling, Oxford, 1990)

The Register of Thomas Rotherham, Archbishop of York 1480-1500 Vol. I (ed. E. E. Barker, Torquay, 1976)

The Reign of Henry VII from Contemporary Sources Vol. I-III (ed. A. F. Pollard, London, 1914)

Ricard, R., *The Maire of Bristowe Is Kalendar by Robert Ricart* (ed. L. T. Smith, London, 1872)

Rotuli Parliamentorum, Vols 1-6 (London, 1767-77)

Select Cases in the Council of Henry VII (ed. C. G. Bayne & W. H. Dunham, London, 1958)

The Stonor Letters and Papers 1290-1483 Vol. II (ed. C. L. Kingsford, London, 1919)

Stow, J., *A Survey of London Written in the Year 1598* (ed. W. J. Thomas, London, 1842)

Third Report of the Deputy Keeper of the Public Records (London, 1842)

Tudor Royal Proclamations Vol. 1, The Early Tudors 1485-1553 (ed. P. L. Hughes and J. F. Larkin, London, 1964)

Vergil, Polydore, *Three Books of Polydore Vergil's English History, Comprising the Reigns of Henry VI, Edward IV, and Richard III* (ed. H. Ellis, London 1844)

Vergil, Polydore, *The Anglica Historia of Polydore Vergil A.D. 1485-1537* (ed. D. Hay, London, 1950)

The Will of King Henry VII (ed. T. Astle, London, 1775)

York House Books 1461-1490 (ed. L. C. Attreed, Stroud, 1991)

Published Secondary Sources

Archibold, W. A. J., 'Sir William Stanley and Perkin Warbeck' in English Historical Review Vol. XIV (ed. S. R. Gardiner & B. L. Poole, London, 1899)

Arthurson, I., *The Perkin Warbeck Conspiracy 1491-1499* (Stroud, 1994)

Arthurson, I., 'The King's Voyage into Scotland: The War that Never Was' in *England in the Fifteenth Century Proceedings of the 1986 Harlaxton Symposium* (ed. D. Williams, Bury St Edmunds, 1987)

Arthurson, I., 'The Rising of 1497: A Peasant of the Peasantry?' in *People, Politics and Community in the Later Middle Ages* (ed. J. Rosenthal & C. Richmond, Gloucester, 1987)

Arthurson, I.; Kingwell, N., 'The Proclamation of Henry Tudor as King of England' in *Historical Research Vol. 63* (1990)

Attreed, L. C., 'A New Source for Perkin Warbeck's Invasion of 1497' in *Mediaeval Studies Vol. 48* (1986)

Bacon, F., *History of the Reign of King Henry VII* (ed. J.R. Lumby, London, 1881)

Baldwin, D., 'King Richard's Grave in Leicester' in *Transactions of the Leicestershire Archaeological and Historical Society 60* (1986)

Baldwin, D., *Richard III* (Stroud, 2012)

Baldwin, D., *Stoke Field, the Last Battle of the Wars of the Roses* (Barnsley, 2006)

Bennett, M., *Lambert Simnel and the Battle of Stoke* (Gloucester, 1987)

Bentley, S., *Excerpta Historica; or Illustrations of English History* (London, 1831)

Bietenholz, P. G. & Deutscher, T. B., *Contemporaries of Erasmus; A Biographical Register of the Renaissance and Reformation Vol. 3* (London, 1995)

Bryan, D., *Gerald Fitzgerald, The Great Earl of Kildare 1456-1513* (Dublin, 1933)

Busch, W., *England Under the Tudors, Henry VII* (London, 1895)

Campbell, L., 'The Authorship of the Recuiel d'Arras' in *Journal of the Warburg and Courtauld Institutes Vol. 40* (1977)

Cavell, E., 'Henry VII, the North of England, and the First Provincial Progress of 1486' in *Northern History XXXIX* (2002)

Cavill, P. R., *The English Parliaments of Henry VII 1485-1504* (Oxford, 2009)

Chastel de la Howarderie, Comte P.A. du, 'Notes sur la Famille de l'aventurier Perkin Warbeck' in *Bulletins de la Société Historique & Littéraire de Tournai Vol. 25* (1893)

Condon, M., 'God Save The King! Piety, Propaganda and the Perpetual Memorial' in *Westminster Abbey: The Lady Chapel of Henry VII* (ed. T. Tatton-Brown & R. Mortimer, Woodbridge, 2003)

Condon, M., 'The Last Will of Henry VII: Document and Text' in *Westminster Abbey: The Lady Chapel of Henry VII* (ed. T. Tatton-Brown & R. Mortimer, Woodbridge, 2003)

Connolly, S. J., *Contested Island: Ireland 1460-1630* (Oxford, 2007)

Conway, A., *Henry VII's Relations with Scotland and Ireland 1485-1498* (Cambridge, 1932)

Cooper, J. P., 'Henry VII's Last Years Reconsidered' in *The Historical Journal Vol. 2 No. 2* (1959)

Cox, J. C., *The Sanctuaries and Sanctuary Seekers of Mediaeval England* (1911, London)

Croker, T. C., *Popular Songs of Ireland* (London, 1886)

Cunningham, S., 'Henry VII' (London, 2007)

Cunningham, S., 'Henry VII and Rebellion in North-Eastern England 1485-1492, Bonds of Allegiance and the Establishment of Tudor Authority' in *Northern History Vol. 32* (Leeds, 1996)

Cunningham, S., *Prince Arthur, The Tudor King Who Never Was* (Stroud, 2016)

Currin, J. M., 'Henry VII, France and the Holy League of Venice: the Diplomacy of Balance' in *Historical Research Vol. LXXXII No. 217* (Oxford, 2009)

Ekwall, E., *The Place-Names of Lancashire* (Manchester, 1922)

Elton, G. R., 'Henry VII: A Restatement' in *The Historical Journal Vol. 4 No. 1* (1961)

Elton, G. R., 'Henry VII: Rapacity and Remorse' in *The Historical Journal Vol. 1* (1958)

Emery, A., *Greater Medieval Houses of England and Wales, Vol. 1 Northern England* (Cambridge, 1996)

Fasti Ecclesiae Anglicanae 1300-1541 (ed. J. M. Horn, London, 1967)

Fowler, J. K., *A History of Beaulieu Abbey A.D. 1204-1539* (London, 1911)

Gairdner, J., *Henry the Seventh* (London, 1889)

Gairdner, J., *History of the Life and Reign of Richard the Third to Which is added the Story of Perkin Warbeck from Original Documents* (Cambridge, 1898)

Griffiths, R. A., *Sir Rhys ap Thomas and his Family; A Study in the Wars of the Roses and Early Tudor Politics* (Cardiff, 2014)

Griffiths, R. A. & Thomas, R.S., *The Making of the Tudor Dynasty* (Sparkford, 2005)

Gunn, S., *Henry VII's New Men & The Making of Tudor England* (Oxford, 2016)

Harrison, C. J., 'The Petition of Edmund Dudley' in *The English Historical Review Vol. 87* (London, 1972)

Henry, R., *The History of Great Britain, From the Invasion of it by The Romans under Julius Caesar Vol. XII* (London, 1814)

Higginbotham, S., *The Woodvilles; The Wars of the Roses and England's Most Famous Family* (Stroud, 2013)

Jewitt, L., *Chatsworth* (Buxton, 1872)

Johnson, L., *So Great a Prince; England and the Accession of Henry VIII* (London, 2016)

Jones, M. K., 'Sir William Stanley of Holt: Politics and Family Allegiance in the Late Fifteenth Century' in Welsh History Review 14 (1988)

Kirk, J. F., *History of Charles the Bold, Duke of Burgundy* (Philadelphia, 1868)

Kirke, H., 'Sir Henry Vernon of Haddon' in *Journal of the Derbyshire Archaeological and Natural History Society Vol. 42* (1920)

Laynesmith, J., *The Last Medieval Queens; English Queenship 1445-1503* (Oxford, 2004) p. 208

Lewis, K., *Kingship and Masculinity in Late Medieval England* (Abingdon, 2013)

Lewis, M., *Wars of the Roses; The Key Players in the Struggle for Supremacy* (Stroud, 2015)

Lowell, F. C., *Joan of Arc* (Cambridge, 1896)

Lydon, J., *The Making of Ireland, From Ancient Times to the Present* (Abingdon, 1998)

Mackie, J. D., *The Earlier Tudors 1485-1558* (Oxford, 1952)

Madden, F., *Documents Relating to Perkin Warbeck with Remarks on his History* (London, 1837)

Mallet, M. & Shaw, S., *The Italian Wars 1494-1559: War, State and Society in Early Modern Europe* (Abingdon, 2014)

Malory, T., *Le Morte D'Arthur, Sir Thomas Malory's Book of King Arthur and of his Noble Knights of the Round Table* (ed. E. Strachey, London, 1897)

Martin, F. X., 'The Crowning of a King at Dublin, 24 May 1487' in *Hermathena Number 144* (Dublin, 1988)

Morel-Fatio, A., *Marguerite d'York et Perkin Warbeck in Mélanges d'Histoire offerts a M. Charles Bémont* (Paris, 1913)

Nicholas, D., *Medieval Flanders* (London, 1992)

Nichols, J., *A Collection of all the Wills Now Known to be Extant, of the Kings and Queens of England, Princes and Princesses of Wales, and Every Branch of the Blood Royal* (1780)

Oggins, R. S., *The Kings and their Hawks; Falconry in Medieval England* (London, 2004)

Philpot, R., *Maximilian I and England 1477-1509* (London, 1975)

Proceedings of the Somersetshire Archaeological and Natural History Society, Vol 60 Part II (Taunton, 1914)

Quinn, D. B., 'Guide to English Financial Records for Irish History 1461-1558, with Illustrated Extracts, 1461-1509' in *Analecta Hibernica* No 10 (1941)

Raine, A., 'York Civic Records Vol. 1' in *Yorkshire Archaeological Society, Record Series Vol. XCVIII* (1939) pp. 73-74

Richards, J., *Landsknecht Soldier 1486-1560* (Oxford, 2002)

Ross, C., *Edward IV* (Los Angeles, 1974)

Ross, C., *Richard III* (London, 1981)

Ross, J., *The Foremost Man of the Kingdom; John de Vere, Thirteenth Earl of Oxford (1442-1513)* (Oxford, 2011)

Roth, C., 'Perkin Warbeck and his Jewish Master' in *Transcations of Jewish Historical Society of England Vol. 9* (1920)

Ryland, R. H., *History, Topography and Antiquities of the County and City of Waterford* (London, 1824)

Smith, C, *The Ancient and Present State of the County and City of Waterford, Containing a Natural, Civil, Ecclesiastical, Historical and Topograhphical Description Therefore* (Dublin, 1774)

Smith, G., 'Lambert Simnel and the King from Dublin' in *The Ricardian Vol. 10, No 135* (1996)

Speed., *The History of Great Britain Under the Conquests of the Romans, Saxons, Danes and Normans* (London, 1614)

Tanner, J. R., *Tudor Constitutional Documents A.D. 1485-1603* (Cambridge, 1930)

Temperley, G., *Henry VII* (London, 1917)

Trapp, J. B., 'Urswick, Christopher (1448-1522)' in *Oxford Dictionary of National Biography* (Oxford, 2004)

Vale, M., *The Ancient Enemy; England, France and Europe from the Angevins to the Tudors 1154-1558* (London, 2007)

Vernon, H.M., *Italy from 1494 to 1790* (Cambridge, 1909)

Ware, J., *The Annals of Ireland During the Reign of King Henry the Seventh* in *The Antiquities and History of Ireland* (Dublin, 1705)

Weightman, C., *Margaret of York, The Diabolical Duchess* (Stroud, 2012)

Wickham Legg, L., *English Coronation Records* (London, 1901)

Wilkins, C., *The Last Knight Errant: Sir Edward Woodville and the Age of Chivalry* (London, 2010)

Wilkinson, J., *The Princes in the Tower* (Stroud, 2013)

Wilkinson, J., *Henry VII's Lady Chapel* (London, 2007)

Williams, C. H., 'The Rebellion of Humphrey Stafford' in *English Historical Review XLIII* (1928)

Wilson, C., 'The Functional Design of Henry VII's Chapel: A Reconstruction' in *Westminster Abbey: The Lady Chapel of Henry VII* (ed. T. Tatton-Brown & R. Mortimer, Woodbridge, 2003)

Wroe, A., *Perkin, A Story of Deception* (London, 2004)

Acknowledgements

Writing a book can be a lonely experience, such is the nature of the beast, but the finished product is never something accomplished alone. Support during the writing process comes in many guises, each instance of which is vital to crossing the finishing line.

For assistance, feedback and expertise in their respective fields, I'd like to thank in no particular order Matthew Lewis, Dr Sean Cunningham, Ian Brandt, Allan Harley and the Beaufort Companye, Michèle Schindler, Ian Coulson, Dr Jonathan Foyle, Julian Humphrys, Edward Meeks, Susan Abernethy, Dr Áine Foley, Vincenzo De Meulenaere, Lauren Johnson, Leo Canham, Helen and Andy Stewart of Albion Historical Falconry, Beaulieu Abbey Enterprises for permission to photograph the ruins, Naomi Woodburn of the University of Cambridge Reference Department and Zoe Stansell of the British Library Manuscripts Reference Service, and the vast community of historians on various social media platforms ever ready to chip in when called upon. I'd also like to express gratitude to my editor Alex Bennett, Shaun Barrington and the team behind the scenes at Amberley for their patience, and all those elsewhere who give up their precious time to provide an outlet for history to be consumed and enjoyed by us all. In particular, the support of Dr Helen Castor has been and continues to be inspiring, and the research assistance and guidance of Dr Samantha Harper. As ever, this work is built upon the astonishing sweat, tears and determination of those historians who have come before me. My gratitude to each and every one of you.

On a private note, I must acknowledge the considerable personal support and goodwill offered by family, friends and strangers throughout the writing period, with special mention to my parents Michelle and Mohammed, sisters Nadia and Yasmin, the Bradshaw family, and of course Vera the ever-present cat. I have learnt that the kind nature of people knows no bounds when called upon during testing times, and that community does still exist. Finally, I'd like to pay tribute to tireless NHS staff throughout the country, charity volunteers everywhere, and in particular the compassionate team at St Leonard's Hospice, York, all of whom have and continue to go above and beyond to improve the lives of others. As ever, this book is for my wife, Katherine, and has only been completed in her memory.

Index

Keyley, James 208
King, Oliver, Bishop of Exeter 192, 240, 259, 287, 318
King's Lynn 281, 285
Klinkhamer, Ludwig 185
Knaresborough, Richard 108
Knole, Kent 323
Knyfton, Nicholas 164

Lake, Richard 163
Lalaing, Roderigue de 203, 221, 227
Lambeth Palace 74, 243, 274
Langton, Thomas, Archbishop of Canterbury 323
Langtree, Lambert 82
Lathom 207
Launceston 255
Layton, Roger 133
Lee, Lambert 82
Leicester 32, 33, 50, 118, 208, 340
Leland, John 338
Lewelyn, John 145, 266
Limerick 89, 206
Lincoln 42, 53, 132
Linlithgow 217, 218
Lisbon 143, 144, 145, 266
Llwyd, Dafydd 290
London 50, 55, 69, 92, 97, 116, 169, 187, 198, 233, 239, 240, 244, 254, 261, 269, 273, 279, 281, 283, 289, 306, 319
Longford, Thomas 295, 298
Loredo, Spain 316
Loughborough 118
Louis VII, King of France 161
Louis VIII, King of France 161
Louis X, King of France 161
Louis XI, King of France 60, 162, 163
Louis XII, King of France 299
Lounde, William 295, 307
Lovell, Francis, 1st Viscount Lovell 51, 52, 54, 57, 58, 59, 61, 63, 74, 78, 79, 81, 87, 93, 95, 96,

100, 103, 104, 105, 107, 108, 113, 114, 115, 123, 124, 126, 127, 136, 181
Lovell, John, 8th Baron Lovell 51
Lovell, Thomas 39, 129, 130, 240, 244, 303
Lucas, Loyte 158
Ludlow 19, 20, 22, 90, 243, 324

Machado, Roger 188, 263, 264
Malines 59, 60, 80, 81, 174, 175, 177, 185, 187, 188, 201
Malmesbury 263
Malory, Thomas 46
Mancini, Dominic 22, 23, 24, 28, 150
Manuel I, King of Portugal 144
Margaret of Anjou, Queen of England 65, 98, 163
Margaret of Austria 184
Margaret of York, Duchess of Burgundy 52, 54, 60, 61, 62, 63, 65, 77, 80, 81, 87, 95, 96, 100, 142, 149, 172, 173, 174, 175, 176, 177, 178, 181, 184, 185, 187, 190, 197, 201, 202, 203, 205, 209, 210, 216, 227, 275, 277, 280, 284, 285, 288, 296, 315
Marie of Anjou, Queen of France 167
Mary, Duchess of Burgundy 61, 62, 63, 64, 66, 95
Mary I, Queen of England 342
Masborough, Thomas 298, 302
Masham 108, 109, 111, 112, 113
Matienzo, Johannes de 312
Maximilian I, King of the Romans 61, 62, 95, 154, 155, 158, 164, 165, 171, 173, 174, 176, 183, 185, 186, 187, 188, 190, 201, 202, 207, 209, 210, 211, 215, 221, 275, 277, 281, 315, 330
May, Lambert 82
Mayne, John 80
Maynooth 91

About the Author

Nathen Amin is an author from Carmarthenshire, West Wales, who focuses on the fifteenth century and the reign of Henry VII. He wrote the first full-length biography of the Beaufort family, *The House of Beaufort*, an Amazon #1 bestseller. He is currently writing *The Son of Prophecy*, charting Henry Tudor's rise to power.